Cleopatra

to

Christ

Cleopatra

to

Christ

Jesus was the great grandson of Cleopatra VII.

by
Ralph Ellis

Edfu Books

Adventures Unlimited

Cleopatra to **Christ**

First published in 2006 by Edfu Books

Published in the U.K. by:
Edfu Books
PO Box 165
Cheshire
CW8 4WF
info@edfu-books.com
U.K.

Published in the U.S.A. by:
Adventures Unlimited
PO Box 74
Kempton, Illinois
60946
auphq@frontier.net
U.S.A.

First edition July 2006

U.K. paperback edition
ISBN 0-9531913-3-8 (978-0-9531913-3-8)

U.S.A. paperback edition
ISBN 1-931882-64-9

Printed in the United Kingdom by T.J. International, Padstow.

The moon herself grew dark, rising at sunset,
Covering her suffering in the night,
Because she saw her beautiful namesake, Selene,
Breathless, descending to Hades,
With her she had had the beauty of her light in common,
And mingled her own darkness with her death.

Eulogy to Cleopatra Selene.

Ourania, o'er her star-bespangled lyre,
With touch of majesty diffused her soul;
A thousand tones, that in the breast inspire,
Exalted feelings, o 'er the wires 'gan roll—
She sang of night that clothed the infant world,
In strains as solemn as its dark profound—
How at the call of Jove the mist unfurled,
And o'er the swelling vault—the glowing sky,
The newborn stars hung out their lamps on high,
And rolled their mighty orbs to music's sweetest sound.

Ode to Muse Ourania,
James Percival.

Acknowledgments

First and foremost I would like to dedicate this book to Mr A J Bethell, who researched and ruminated on this same topic nearly 100 years ago and deposited his resulting manuscript in the British Library. It is my belief that Mr Bethell missed much of the available evidence and arrived at the wrong conclusions; however, the manuscript he created was certainly the inspiration upon which this book was founded.

Secondly, I would like to thank Mike Dash, who wrote a letter to the Daily Mail listing the many bizarre book titles he had found. Among these titles was the manuscript by Mr Bethell, which is how I discovered it. In Mike Dash's defence, it has to be admitted that Mr Bethell's argument, that Jesus was the son of Queen Cleopatra, stretched both chronology and biology to its very limits. However, Mr Bethell had also highlighted a number of key points that allowed me to discover the real truth about the ancestry of Jesus. My thanks to both of you.

Finally I would like to thank Margaret, my travelling companion on my tour of Jordan, whose knowledge of history and the classics was inspirational and made the trip memorable. If I can be as youthful at the age of 83, I will consider myself very lucky.

Ralph Ellis
November 2006
Cheshire.

www.edfu-books.com

Contents

Royal Family

In my previous works, I have demonstrated that Jesus was a prince, related in some manner to the Egyptian royal line. But the finer details of exactly who Jesus was related to, and how far back into Egyptian history one needed to go in order to find these family links, were unclear. The problem being, of course, that any potential researcher of the New Testament story has very little to go on. The biblical and historical accounts that detail Jesus' birth and ancestry can be summarised in a single paragraph, and that is simply not enough information to place him into the historical record – or is it?

This children's story of the life of Jesus, as it is presented to us in the New Testament accounts, is well known. He was supposedly a poor carpenter born in a stable, a disadvantaged child who rose to become a great leader and teacher. However, as I demonstrated in the book *Jesus*, this fairy-tale bears no resemblance to the truth whatsoever. There is more than enough evidence within the biblical texts themselves to conclusively prove that Jesus' family were actually wealthy, educated and influential characters within Judaean society.

Jesus himself was not a carpenter but a *tekton* or an 'architect'; although this term probably refers more to the speculative side of the masonic Craft than the construction profession. He received a good education in Egypt, at a time when the majority of the population were illiterate. His friends, Zacharias and Nicodemus, were very rich; while another supporter, Joanna, was the wife of Herod's vizier or prime minister. It was also demonstrated in the book *Jesus,* by carefully scrutinising the accounts of Josephus Flavius, that Jesus was governor of Tiberias, owned a castle in that region and controlled a private militia some 600 strong. More importantly, Jesus' birth was deemed by Herod to be a threat to his royal lineage, forcing him to apparently kill all the male infants in the region in order to eradicate this pretender to the throne – an act or rumour which clearly demonstrates that Jesus was a prince of some influence within Judaean society. In fact, the mocking claim of Jesus to be the 'King of the Jews' was no mockery at all, for he was indeed a legitimate pretender to many of the thrones of the Middle East. Undoubtedly, Jesus' parents' ultimate goal was to see him seated upon one of those thrones, which is why the king and tetrarchs of Judaea feared his presence in that region.

I have also previously demonstrated the strong links between Jesus and Egypt, which is why my first book on this topic was entitled *Jesus, Last of the Pharaohs*. However, at that point in time I was unable to discover in what way Jesus could have been related to the Egyptian royal line. Unfortunately, the texts of the Bible and Talmud are incomplete and both show obvious signs of heavy editing. If Jesus was truly a pretender to the thrones of the Near East, a legitimate royal pretender of Egyptian heritage, it was in nobody's interest to further his claims by recording his true ancestry. So the biblical texts have left us with vague commentaries on his parents and siblings, and two biblical genealogies in the New Testament that completely contradict each other.

The additional paragraphs that refer to Jesus in the works of Josephus Flavius, which I have highlighted in previous works, add a great deal more information about the former's life. They again demonstrate Jesus' wealth and status, but they add precious little to his family background and ancestry. One paragraph in each of Josephus' *Antiquities* and *The Jewish War* calls Jesus the 'Egyptian False Prophet', which again demonstrates the possible links with the pharaonic dynasties, but does little to explain his parentage.

However, if my assertion is true and Jesus was descended from the Egyptian royal line, then a number of problems arise which some of my more vociferous detractors have described as being 'insurmountable'. Firstly, if Jesus was of the royal line of Egypt, what was he doing in Judaea? Secondly, if Jesus was of the royal line of Egypt, why was his birth visited by Magi from Persia, instead of *sem*-priests from Egypt? Thirdly, if Jesus was of the royal line of Egypt, his presence in Judaea implied that he had been exiled from his former homeland. For what reason and at what time was such an illustrious family exiled to Judaea?

Egyptian or Persian?

The problem is this. The various texts that detail the circumstances of Jesus' birth and education would seem to be incompatible. According to these, we would appear to be looking into the historical record for an exiled prince who was of both Egyptian and Persian descent. In addition, we need to discover a prince who was influential enough to make his mark on the history of Judaea, but obscure enough to be easily lost to most of real recorded history. The question is, therefore, whether any prince within the historical record would fit all of these widely differing requirements.

Strange as it may seem, there is such a royal family. They were indeed influential kings and queens, and yet it is known that they were exiled from their homeland and settled in an area called Bethanya [Bethany], near Judaea, in about AD 4. They brought with them into exile 500 cavalry and 100 relations and retinue; an account which tallies with Josephus' accounts of the biblical family maintaining their own military forces. In Syrio-Judaea, this exiled royal family raised a new generation and founded a new society that competed strongly with the traditional Judaean authorities in Jerusalem.

Moreover, members of this exiled royal family were not only directly related to Queen Cleopatra VII of Egypt, but also to Emperor Julius Caesar of Rome and to King Phraates IV of Parthia (or Persia). In other words, this family was hugely influential, relatively unknown, suddenly impoverished and, in addition, uniquely related to all three of the major empires of this era. With its enfeebled exiled circumstances this family was essentially powerless, but never without influence. They were also impoverished, for a royal family with such an illustrious pedigree, but never without wealthy, well-placed backers and supporters.

Here, we have a previously influential royal family living in obscure exile in biblical Bethany, and yet this is a family that appears to meet all of our diverse requirements. This was indeed a family that would have been visited by the Parthian Magi, yet is likely to have educated its sons in Egypt. This was indeed a family that could have made Herod (the tetrarch) fear for his position, sufficient for him to want to eliminate all the male children of Judaea.

The sparse historical facts that detail the life of this royal family seem to fit our list of requirements rather well, but the unanswered question is: was this really the family of the biblical Jesus and his brothers and sisters? As this story unfolds, readers will find a wealth of compelling circumstantial evidence that leads us towards an earth-shattering conclusion – that Jesus was directly descended from Julius Caesar of Rome, Queen Cleopatra VII of Egypt and King Phraates IV of Parthia. But in the end, despite all of the evidence, only the reader can decide if the case has been proven.

Notes to the reader

a.   Because of the radical nature of this book, it has been necessary to highlight the difference between standard orthodox assumptions and those generated by my lateral view of theology. Throughout this book, therefore, I have used curved brackets ( ) to denote orthodox assumptions and square brackets [ ] to denote my radical new assumptions. I hope that this serves to clarify the text.

b.   The references in the text are numerous. To ease the problem of continuously referring to the reference section at the back of the book, some references have been prefixed. Prefixes are as follows:

B = Bible, K = Koran, J = Josephus, T = Talmud, S = Strabo
M = Manetho, N = Nag Hammadi, KN = Kebra Nagast.

It may also be advantageous to explain in modern terms some of the locations that are being discussed.

Armenia	=	Kurdish region in eastern Turkey and western Iraq.
Auranitis	=	region to the east of the river Jordan.
Aurania	=	see Auranitis above.
Babylon	=	southern and eastern Iraq.
Bactria	=	east of the Caspian Sea. Afghanistan and Turkmenistan.
Bithynia	=	northeastern Turkey.
Bethanya	=	region to the east of the river Jordan.
Cappadocia	=	southeastern Turkey.
Hadramaut	=	Yemen.
Gaulanitis	=	the Golan Heights northeast of the Sea of Galilee.
Israel	=	region to the west of the Sea of Galilee.
Judaea	=	region around Jerusalem.
Lydia	=	western Turkey, near the Maeander river.
Mauretania	=	central and western North Africa.
Media	=	northwestern Iran.
Najd	=	Saudi Arabia.
Parthia	=	originally Bactria, but the empire spread to Iran, Iraq and eastern Turkey.
Persia	=	an earlier empire occupying roughly the same region as Parthia.
Samaria	=	region to the west of the river Jordan.
Scythia	=	Ukraine. Sometimes given as Bactria.
Syria	=	Modern Syria, but sometimes a term for all of the Levantine coast including Judaea, Israel and Tyre.

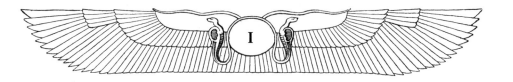

Chess Game

The entire foundation for this new history of the New Testament lies upon the historical fact that a powerful, but relatively obscure, royal family was exiled from Parthia (Persia) in about AD 4. They travelled with their courtiers, relatives and a small army to Syria, which at that time came under the control of the Herod tetrarchs (three of the sons of Herod the Great). There, they built a new city state that declared its independence from Jerusalem and Damascus, and it is entirely possible that one of their sons eventually declared himself as 'king' of the region. The argument I shall be pursuing, which is admittedly speculative at this moment in time, is that this governor of an insignificant city state in Syrio-Judaea was the biblical Jesus.

But if this character was so insignificant, then why did he and his family cause such ripples in the geopolitics of the Near East during the first century AD? The answer lies in his ancestry because, as I have already suggested, he was related to all of the key players in that era's royal and political chess game. The evidence for this will grow as the chapters progress, but perhaps we should digress for a while to look at the chess board itself, and the various pieces that were upon it in this era.

Egypt

Egypt had been under the control of the Persians twice between 525 and 332 BC, but after Alexander the Great's defeat of Darius III at Issus in southeastern Turkey, Egypt came under the control of the Macedonian Greeks. Alexander died in 323 BC and, after a few power struggles, Egypt

1

came under the control of the Ptolemaic dynasty, who were descendants of Alexander's general Ptolemy, son of Lagus. Egypt remained powerful under the Ptolemaic pharaohs, with many of the fine temples we see today in Upper Egypt being completed during this era. She was also a key player in the politics of the wider regions, but the nation's undoing was the constant sibling rivalry for the throne.

Time after time the Ptolemaic kings and queens of Egypt were ruthlessly deposed, and this instability drained the nation's resources. This problem became a crisis when Ptolemy Aulets XII, the flute player, was exiled to Rome during a general uprising. In Rome, Ptolemy XII plotted his return to Egypt and was eventually successful in 55 BC, but crucially this was achieved with Roman assistance and might. This backing of Rome signalled the end of Egypt as an independent nation and thus we find that Ptolemy XII's famous daughter, Cleopatra VII, essentially became a vassal of Rome. Cleopatra did attempt, as we shall see, to turn the political and strategic tables on the Romans, but all her plotting and scheming eventually came to nothing and Egypt was to remain a conquered nation.

Rome

One of many legends has it that Rome was founded by Prince Aeneas, who fled from the ruins of the sacked city of Troy. This mythology is interesting, given the alternative location for the city of Troy that I suggested in the book *Eden*. However, the Roman Republic was not founded until much later, in 509 BC according to Livy. Having grown steadily in power, the Romans flexed their might against Greece in the early third century BC and the Phoenicians of Carthage in the late third century BC. The republic then grew in size and influence to become masters of the Mediterranean and beyond. This potted history takes us up to the era of Julius Caesar and his close association with Cleopatra VII of Egypt; a topic which will be addressed in more detail later.

Parthia

The Parthians originated in the Iranian highlands, to the west of the Caspian Sea. They were consummate horsemen, and their mounted archers played a key role in establishing the resulting Arsacid dynasty. This association with mounted archers is an important element in this story, as this elite force became a prime symbol on Parthian coinage and it therefore identifies a key biblical player as being of Parthian origin.

Around 250 BC King Arsaces, after whom the dynasty is named, took his forces out of modern Turkmenistan and rode deep into Seleucid (Persian) territory. Having taken the city of Herat, a prime city on the major trade route known as the Silk Road, the Hellenistic Seleucid empire of Persia that had been founded by Alexander the Great collapsed, and the Arsacid empire of the Parthians took control. The borders of this new empire were pushed out westwards until they impinged upon the eastern borders of the expanding Roman Empire, and the boundary between the two lay in or around the eastern borders of modern Syria.

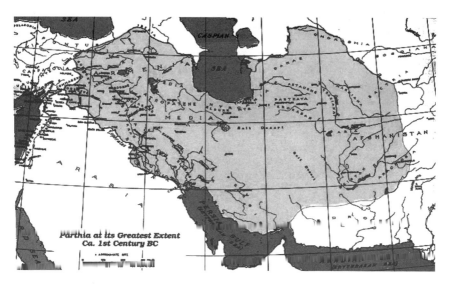

Fig 1.   The Parthian Empire in the first century BC.

Judaea

Sandwiched between these three key players, who were each vying for the territories of the Near East, was the insignificant but key nation of Judaeo-Israel. The population of Judaeo-Israel was a fusion of many (often related) nationalities, including Jews, Canaanites, Phoenicians, Judaeo-Persians, and Syrians. However, Strabo says that the majority of the citizens of Judaea were Egyptians, and this observation equates well with my proposals that the Jews not only came from Egypt (upon the biblical exodus) but were actually Egyptians themselves.

Judaeo-Israel was essentially a Roman vassal state, which was

Fig 2. The Treasury, one of the Nabatean 'tombs' at Petra.

governed by King Herod the Great from 37 to 4 BC. Although Herod was a vassal of Rome and was required to do their bidding, Cleopatra VII was becoming very influential in Roman politics and so Herod had to contend with Cleopatra's fickle whims and policies too.

Cleopatra's primary desire was to enlarge her kingdom and influence, and she was quite happy to manipulate her 'husband' Mark Antony to achieve her ends. Cleopatra had already persuaded Antony to give her Phoenicia, some of the Arabias and the southern portion of Judaea around Jericho, after his successful campaigns in the region in 34 BC, but there was still the troublesome semi-independent province of Judaeo-Israel that lay at the outer reaches of her growing empire.

Accordingly, Cleopatra encouraged Antony to get Herod to attack King Malchus of Nabataea (Petra), indicating that this was to punish Nabataea for late payment of its tribute to Egypt. However, this demand came at a highly inopportune moment for Herod, as Mark Antony had just entered into a civil war with Octavian-Augustus Caesar and could have benefited from the support that Herod had promised him. Herod dutifully attacked Nabataea, but then Cleopatra undermined the whole campaign by supporting the Nabataeans! There was a logic in this madness, even if the logic was highly skewed with duplicity, treachery and avarice. As Josephus recalls:

> And now Cleopatra persuaded Antony to entrust Herod (the Great) with the war against the Arabs – if he won she would become mistress of Arabia, if he lost, the mistress of Judaea. She would be using one ruler to get rid of the other. [J1]

In other words, Cleopatra was manipulating all and sundry, including her 'husband' Mark Antony, in order to further her goal of Egyptian world domination. King Herod the Great was thus placed in a very awkward and dangerous position, and there was a great danger that he would eventually be deposed by his stronger Egyptian 'ally'. However, fortune was smiling on Herod in his moment of adversity, as it had so many times before.

Herod was a loyal supporter of Mark Antony, but at Cleopatra's insistence he had been in Arabia during the great sea-battle of Actium. Mark Antony was comprehensively defeated by Octavian-Augustus in this sea-battle so Herod had lost his powerful Roman mentor and ally, and now Augustus Caesar ruled all of the Roman empire. Crucially, however, Herod's absence from the battle of Actium meant that he had not actually fought against Augustus, and so he was able to beg the forgiveness of the new emperor and retain his Judaean kingship.

That Herod managed to juggle these many competing rivalries in the international political arena, plus his many internal problems, shows that he was in many ways a consummate diplomat and an astute ruler – before age and jealousy befuddled his senses. Herod died in 4 BC and since he could not decide on a successor, the kingdom was bequeathed to three of his sons; Herod Archelous gained control of Judaea, Herod Antipas of Israel and Herod Philip of Syria. It is Herod Philip who becomes central to the unfolding story, as it is in the Syrian provinces that the exiled royal family from Parthia settled.

To the east of Judaea and to the south of Syria lay the relatively insignificant nation of Nabataea, which Herod had been preoccupied with, whose capital city was the famed yet concealed city of Petra. The Nabataeans were a Semitic people who may have been related to the Sabeans of Yemen, and spoke an Aramaic (Hebrew) dialect. The Nabataeans were not major players in this epic drama, but they were said to have assisted the exiled Parthian royalty in the construction of their new city in southern Syria.

Biblical Judaea

In addition to this secular history of Judaea, we also have the accounts of the New Testament. Here we discover another problem, for when dealing with the biblical accounts we enter a completely new world; and this is not one bedeviled by the usual historical uncertainty, but instead it is bedeviled by the scourge of deliberate deception. Saul (St Paul), the creator of Christianity, and the Christian clergy who followed him, never needed a historical foundation for their iconic hero, Jesus. In fact, many details of his true ancestry are likely to have clashed spectacularly with the new ideology that the Church leaders were trying to peddle. By necessity, therefore, all mention of Jesus' family history was censored from the outset. Saul only needed an icon to sell to the plebeians, and this was an icon that was fully divorced from its historical reality. In fact, the reputation of the early Church was such that the letters of Peter had to plead with congregations that there had been no fabrications or adulterations of the text:

> For we have not followed cunningly devised fables, when we made known unto you the power and coming of our Lord Jesus Christ, but were eyewitnesses of his majesty. [B2]

But the truth was that much of the New Testament had been altered and amended during the first few centuries of Christian history. While Saul may well have initiated these distortions to true history, one of the prime suspects for the later amendments to the original text has to be Bishop Eusebius, who has been described as:

> ...the first thoroughly dishonest and unfair historian of ancient times. [3]

One of the first casualties of this editing and censorship was Jesus' marriage to Mary Magdalene. The fact that Jesus was married has received a major boost recently with the publication of *The Da Vinci Code*; however, many books have previously championed this otherwise unmentionable fact, including my own *Jesus, Last of the Pharaohs*. The Church has softened its stance in recent years and the abject denials of Jesus' marriage have now evolved into the occasional response of 'there is no evidence' or even 'it is always possible'. However, the truth is that the Bible itself describes the marriage of Jesus and Mary Magdalene in the verses that discuss the marriage at Cana, as I pointed out in the book *Jesus*. The Book of Revelations makes this even clearer when it says:

> Let us be glad and rejoice, and give honour to him: for the marriage of the Lamb is come, and his wife hath made herself ready. And to her was granted that she should be arrayed in fine linen, clean and white: for the fine linen is the righteousness of saints. And he saith unto me, Write, Blessed are they which are called unto the marriage supper of the Lamb. [B4]

> And there came unto me one of the seven angels which had the seven vials full of the seven last plagues, and talked with me, saying, Come hither, I will show thee the bride, the Lamb's wife. [B5]

The Lamb is, of course a reference to Jesus himself. The Catholic Church tries vainly to persuade us that the 'wife' in these verses actually pertains to the Church itself – that Jesus was being accepted into a 'marriage' to the Church. But it is obvious to anyone who is in full command of their faculties that the 'wife' was the true physical wife of Jesus – Mary Magdalene.

Not only has this marriage of Jesus been divorced (*sic*) from its true historical reality, but so too has the wider biblical narrative. We have all heard the stories from the New Testament in which Jesus did this, the disciples did that, and the Romans were doing something in the background. But what these stories never attempt to do is place these biblical events into the wider perspective of the geopolitics of first millennium Judaeo-Israel. As we have already seen, contrary to the biblical perception of history, Judaea was not the main focus of attention in this era; instead, it was simply a minute element within a much larger political picture, a minnow in a pool of giant predators that swarmed around it. Judaea only came through many of these political upheavals relatively unscathed because it was a convenient buffer region to the wider strategic manoeuvres and battles that were going on all around it. Mark Antony had already received a bloody nose in his clashes with the Parthian army, so as long as Judaea maintained good relations with Rome it could happily act as a mercenary army for the Empire. Had Judaeo-Israel been a little more diplomatic in its later internal struggles and its dispute with Rome, it would doubtless have escaped its eventual destruction in AD 70.

The New Testament and the Christian clergy try their utmost to convince us that Jesus was a political and social nobody in this political maelstrom between Parthia and Rome, and so they attempt to convince their followers that Jesus was a humble carpenter, who happened to change the theology of an entire region. So is it possible that the Church authorities are correct, and Jesus was simply the political nonentity of popular mythology? Is this the reason that he does not seem to appear in any of the historical accounts of the Near East?

The fairy stories that emanate from the Church would like us to think so, but if Jesus and the actions that he took were in any way important to the wider world in this era, it is much more likely that this was because he belonged to or was related to that larger political picture in some manner. The way in which he was a part of that wider perspective is the primary subject of this book, for as I have already stated, it is highly likely that he was a direct descendant of Queen Cleopatra VII of Egypt and King Phraates IV of Parthia. It was only because his royal ancestry was known to the authorities in this era that anyone took any notice of him in the first place, and it was again this royal heritage that allowed him to speak his mind without getting into too much trouble. For Jesus had friends in high places, as the Bible readily admits. The Babylonian Talmud, the Jewish commentary on the Old Testament, says exactly the same thing when it relates:

> Rabbi Papa said 'This is (Mary Magdalene) of which they say, "She was the descendant of princes and rulers, she played the harlot with carpenters." ' [T6]

In other words, the Judaic priesthood understood that Mary Magdalene was a royal princess; so is this what the authors of the New Testament were trying so valiantly to hide from us? But why would the Christian Church prefer its heroes to be paupers, rather than influential royals? What was the political situation in the years leading up to the birth of Jesus, and why was this royal heritage so contentious that the Catholic Church initiated a cover-up that has lasted for over two millennia?

As is usual in any era, there was a web of allegiances and disputes between the leading players in world politics at this time. As we have seen, the three leading contenders for power in the Western and Eastern Empires in the first century before the birth of Jesus were: Egypt, under the rule of Cleopatra VII; Rome, which was just stabilising itself under the autocratic rule of Julius Caesar; and Parthia (Persia), which was ruled by Phraates IV of the Arsacid dynasty. Between them, these rulers held sway over most of Europe, the Middle East and North Africa. There were some disputes and wars between these empires, but there was cooperation too. The following is a potted history of the primary players in this international chess game.

Julius Caesar

Julius, who was born in 100 BC, had conquered Gaul (France) in the 50s BC and wanted to return to Rome in triumph. The Senate, ever fearful of the might of the Roman army, ordered Julius to disband his army and return alone. Julius ignored the Senate and crossed the Rubicon, the frontier of Rome, with one of his legions in 49 BC. By law, Roman armies were not allowed into Rome and so this deliberate act of insubordination ignited a civil war. The Senate rallied around Julius Caesar's former partner in the First Triumvirate, Pompeius Magnus, who is more commonly called Pompey. But Julius Caesar proved the more able army commander, and having pursued Pompey's armies around Spain and Italy, Julius Caesar finally defeated Pompey at the battle of Pharsalus in Greece in 48 BC. Pompey escaped the battle scene and fled to Egypt, but was killed on his arrival there. It was in Egypt that Julius Caesar, having pursued Pompey to these shores, was to meet Cleopatra VII.

Cleopatra

The history and legends of Cleopatra VII, the most famous of all the
Cleopatra queens of Egypt, intertwine and mingle so that the one cannot be
separated from the other. Here was a glamorous, intelligent and successful
queen, a woman who was not shy of using her womanly charms to fulfil her
personal advancement and Egypt's political strategy. The spectacle and
pomp of her reign were truly awe-inspiring, with the queen boasting that
she could spend ten million *sesterces* on a single meal.* In a similar fashion,
Shakespeare says of Cleopatra's mighty flagship at the start of the famous
battle of Actium:

> The barge she sat in, like a burnished throne,
> Burned on the water; the poop was beaten gold,
> Purple the sails, and so perfumed, that
> The winds were love-sick with them,
> the oars were silver. [7]

Purple was, of course, the inordinately expensive dye controlled by the
Phoenicians in Tyre. So expensive was it, and so vivid the hue, that it became
the colour of kings and emperors. It is said that the imagery of Cecil B de
Mille's or Joseph Mankiewicz's epic films about Cleopatra adversely colour
our perceptions, but perhaps they were not so far wide of the mark in their
lavish portrayals. This was truly an age when royal spectacle confirmed
royal authority and cowed the rebellious masses. As long as the workers had
their bread and beer, who would be so bold as to deny that Cleopatra was a
daughter of the gods?

Cleopatra VII was born in 69 BC, the daughter of the Greco-Egyptian
Pharaoh Ptolemy XII. After a short co-regency with her father, who died in
51 BC, Cleopatra married her younger brother Ptolemy XIII. Relations
between brother and sister were obviously strained, as an armed dispute
ensued during which Cleopatra was forced to flee to Judaea or Syria in the
spring of 48 BC. Ever resourceful, however, Cleopatra gathered an army
together and re-invaded Egypt from the east, but the battle was
inconclusive.

It was at this very moment that Pompey turned up in Egypt, hotly
pursued by Julius Caesar. Ptolemy XIII, Cleopatra's brother, thought he

---

* Since a slave could cost 6,000 *sesterces*, one might speculate that one *sesterce* had the
equivalent value of a modern Euro. Cleopatra is reputed to have achieved her claim by
dissolving a large pearl earring in vinegar and drinking it.

would ingratiate himself with Julius by murdering Pompey and presenting the new Roman emperor with his enemy's severed head. However, the cunning plan spectacularly backfired, as Julius Caesar was still an admirer of Pompey, despite their mutual hostilities. In addition, Ptolemy had actually been a supporter of Pompey before his defeat, and so Ptolemy's cowardly treachery earned himself the displeasure of Julius Caesar and a place in Dante's *Inferno* as an arch-traitor.

The previous pharaoh of Egypt, Ptolemy XII, had decreed that Rome should arbitrate if there was a dispute between his children, and so Julius Caesar proceeded to do so. Ptolemy XIII tried to prevent this mediation by blocking Cleopatra's attempts to visit Julius, and this is why legends say that she was delivered to him in a carpet roll (in a pile of bedclothes according to Plutarch). [8]

Whether or not Julius was infatuated with Cleopatra at this point in time, he did try to arbitrate fairly. But a civil war broke out in Alexandria and Julius Caesar had to temporarily flee for his life. However, in the ensuing melee, Ptolemy XIII drowned in the Nile and his other sister Arsinoe was arrested. When all the dust settled in the spring of 47 BC, Cleopatra VII was sole ruler of Egypt and was enjoying a Nile cruise as the lover of Julius Caesar. Egypt was not short of wealth or resources, but it desperately lacked a formidable army. However, a union, both political and personal, between Egypt and Rome would surely produce the empire to end all empires. Cleopatra's strategic aims and dreams were all approaching fruition in the ecstasy of sexual union.

It would be nice to leave the story at this blissful moment, with the great Sun-god Ra setting on the western horizon and the two imperial lovers entwined in each others' arms, enjoying a vintage red from crystal glasses. But, unfortunately for them, the politics of this era were not that stable. Julius Caesar was assassinated in 44 BC and Cleopatra, who had been in Rome at the time, fled back to Egypt with her son Caesarion. The Roman empire

Fig 3. Bust of Cleopatra VII.

was then split up into the Second Triumvirate, with Mark Antony in the Near East, Octavian (Augustus) in Rome and Lepidus in Spain.

Marcus Antonius, or Mark Antony, had been a leading supporter of Julius Caesar and after his assassination, Antony was given control over Rome's eastern regions. Part of Antony's plan for control of the Near East was a strategic alliance with Cleopatra of Egypt. Likewise, Cleopatra saw in Antony another potential leader of all the Roman empire, and so she consummated a strategic and personal alliance with Mark Antony in 41 BC. This dual union was to bear fruit with twins, Alexander Helios and Cleopatra Selene in 40 BC. Despite his youthful age, the boy twin, Alexander, was given nominal rule over all of Parthia and the east, even though these kingdoms had not yet been conquered by this new Romo-Egyptian alliance. One cannot help seeing Cleopatra's influence here – it was not necessarily Antony who wanted to conquer and rule Parthia (Persia), but Cleopatra. Parthia was the old mortal enemy of Egypt, not Rome, and the newly crowned prince Alexander Helios bore the dynastic titles of Egypt, not of Rome.

Phraates

Parthia (Persia) does not really enter this tangled tale until a few years after Julius Caesar's death. It is thought that King Phraates IV was born in about 60 BC, and he came to the throne in 37 BC. But there is a problem with Parthian history, and that is that there is very little of it, for some reason:

> They left few records, indeed, we really know very little of the internal history of the Parthians, and would have known still less but for the frequent wars between them and the Greeks and Romans. [9]

This dearth of information makes us overly reliant not only on Roman records, as the quote indicates, but also on the Judaean historian Josephus Flavius. King Herod of Judaea tried not to tangle with the powerful Parthians, but the two nations were close neighbours and so the politics of Parthia were mentioned in the works of Josephus on more than one occasion.

As has already been mentioned, the triumvir of Rome in this region was Mark Antony, who had concluded a strategic and personal alliance with Cleopatra VII of Egypt. With Egyptian support and funding, Antony attacked Phraates IV in Parthia almost immediately after he had come to the throne. But Antony's war against Parthia went badly, and he was forced to withdraw with heavy losses. Even worse, the Roman Triumvirate alliance fell apart and Antony found himself at war with Octavian (Augustus) in Rome. Antony was forced to cede much of his territory in the far east in order to shore up his position on his western borders with Octavian.

This western pressure on Antony's forces should have made Phraates' kingdom relatively safe, but an internal dispute threw up a pretender to the throne called Tiridates, who managed to depose Phraates IV in about 32 BC. But Phraates counter attacked a few years later, and Tiridates fled to the Romans.

Rome was not faring much better, as far as internal stability was concerned, and Mark Antony was eventually defeated at the great sea-battle of Actium in 31 BC. Antony returned to Egypt, defeated and despairing. The dreams of both Antony and Cleopatra had evaporated, and both were reputed to have died at their own hands in 30 BC. With Octavian (Augustus) being the sole remaining triumvir, the senate crowned him as Caesar Augustus Princeps, and emperor of Rome in 27 BC.

One of the first things that Augustus (Octavian) had to deal with was the stability of his eastern boarders. With Mark Antony having been a common enemy of both Augustus and Phraates IV, the two new leaders – in both Rome and Parthia – shared some common ground, around which a deal could be negotiated. Augustus decided that diplomacy was the order of the day, and so a deputation set out from Rome on the long journey to Parthia, bearing some precious tributes and tasked with seeking an alliance with King Phraates. One of the presents given to Phraates IV was a mysterious but very special lady, and she is central to this story.

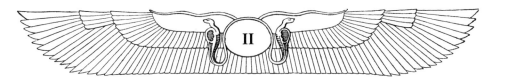

Thea Muse Ourania

The year is 30 BC. Following the great naval battle of Actium, Antony and Cleopatra were dead and Octavian Augustus now presided over a unified Roman Empire that stretched from northern France to Upper Egypt, and from western Spain to the borders of Parthia (Persia). He was sole master of all he surveyed, with only one possible rival to his throne – the young son born of Julius Caesar and Cleopatra, Caesarion, who was already being hailed as the rightful pharaoh of Egypt. As a matter of political expediency, Augustus had him murdered. In the autumn of 30 BC Augustus left Egypt for Syria, to 'settle the affairs of the east'. En route he bestowed Cleopatra's personal bodyguard of Galatians upon a grateful King Herod the Great, who had skilfully (or luckily) dodged the shifting political allegiances in the region and remained in power as a client king of Rome.

The reason for Augustus' prolonged stay in Syria was most probably due to this being his most troublesome border. King Artaxes of Armenia had attacked King Artavasdes of Media. Phraates IV of Parthia had been deposed by an upstart prince called Tiridates. But Phraates IV was restored to the throne with the aid of the Scythians, and Tiridates fled to the Romans. Tiridates was most probably a Parthian prince, as the name Tiridates means 'Great Archer' in Persian, and the reverse of most Parthian coins portray an archer.

In short, there was a general sense of turmoil in the region, and all the parties in these diverse disputes looked towards Rome for military assistance. In fact, it is not difficult to see Augustus' hand behind the uprising in Parthia by Tiridates. It suited Augustus to have Parthia under his control, but Parthia had already proven itself an intractable nation to take by sheer military force, since it had already inflicted two great defeats upon the supposedly invincible Roman army. What better method than to take control of Parthia through a puppet prince, who would thereafter always be grateful to Rome for their assistance and support. However, whatever the cause of the insurrection, Phraates was only exiled from Parthia until 26 BC, when he made a successful return to power with the assistance of his Scythian allies.

Following this protracted stay in Syria, Augustus may then have briefly visited Greece before finally returning to Rome in August 29 BC to celebrate his various triumphs. There he had Cleopatra's other children by Mark Antony – twins Alexander Helios and Cleopatra Selene, and Ptolemy Philadelphus – paraded through the streets of Rome. The children were just ten and four years old respectively, and it is said that the golden chains they had to wear were so heavy they could hardly lift them. But, following this ritual humiliation, Augustus was magnanimous to the young children and they were all raised with Livia and Octavia, Augustus' wife and his sister respectively, in a household full of various imperial orphans.

Jubba II

Although we know that Cleopatra's children were looked after by Augustus and Octavia, we don't know what happened to them all, as nothing more is heard of the male children. It is unlikely that they were murdered, like Caesarion was, as Augustus had already spared their lives and raised them in his household. However, it is also unlikely that they survived into adulthood, as they would surely have been mentioned in one historical account or another. The only child of Cleopatra we do know about is Cleopatra Selene, who was given as a diplomatic bride to King Jubba II of Mauretania.

In fact, King Jubba (Iuba) had a lot in common with Selene, as he was also lucky to have survived the turmoil of the previous decades. His father had backed the wrong horse during the Roman civil war between Julius Caesar and Pompey, and so the captured king and his son were paraded through Rome as captives of Julius Caesar. King Jubba I had to endure five years of a Roman jail before being publicly beheaded; but his son was spared and became a friend of the young Octavian-Augustus. When Octavian became emperor, he reinstated his old playmate as King Jubba II of Mauretania (Numidia) in 25 BC, and to complete this royal appointment he gave Jubba the young princess Cleopatra Selene of Egypt as his bride.

Now this bridal match was quite a coup for the 25-year-old Jubba. Cleopatra Selene was an attractive teenager, she was the daughter of one of the most famous monarchs in that era, and she was also regarded as a manifestation of the goddess Isis. Selene must have brought great prestige to his small North African nation, and she certainly seems to have remained independent of her husband in many respects. Coins of Selene are always inscribed in her native Greek, as opposed to Jubba's coins which are marked in his adopted Latin. Their son was called Ptolemy, which demonstrates that Selene regarded her bloodline as being the superior. It is also suspected that their daughter was called Cleopatra.

Whatever the domestic politics of the Mauretanian royalty, the small nation seemed to remain stable and prosperous until Jubba's death in AD 23. After a long and successful reign, the couple were buried in a magnificent circular mausoleum known as the Kubr-er-Rumia (the Grave of the Roman Lady) by the Muslims and as the Tombeau de la Chrétienne (the Tomb of the Christian) by the French. [1] Note here that the tomb

Fig 4. Cleopatra Selene.

of Cleopatra Selene is being linked with Christianity, as this may be important in later chapters. The tomb is situated in modern Kolea, Algeria and unfortunately, due to the recent rise in Islamic fundamentalism, it is not possible to visit the area. However, the French did a number of surveys of the tomb back in the nineteenth century and these provide us with some interesting results.

Firstly, there is the overall design of the tomb. The tomb has a square base which supports a large, squat cylinder surrounded by sixty Ionic columns. Perched on the top of this is a conic pyramid, which has not been smoothed out but rather forms a series of small steps to the very top of the cone. This arrangement may look unusual and even unique, but this is not so. Further eastwards in Algeria at Batna, there is the Medracen Mausoleum, a monument whose history is unknown but whose design is strikingly familiar.

Likewise, if one travels eastwards across to the original hub of the Parthian empire, which is located to the east of the Caspian Sea in modern Turkmenistan, we find the Sultan Tekesh Mausoleum in Kunya Urgench. The history of this tomb is highly uncertain, as it predates the Mongolian invasions of this region in the thirteenth and fourteenth centuries, which destroyed the records and history of the kingdom. The tomb is thought to date from the eighth century Muslim period, but that is only a guestimation as the true ownership of this tomb is unknown and so an earlier date is entirely possible. Though smaller than the tomb of Cleopatra Selene, this mausoleum exhibits all of its attributes, including the square base, the cylindrical drum surrounded by columns and the conic roof structure. See the colour section for a comparison.

While we might speculate that this similarity was a coincidence, based upon the desire to create a monument out of three mathematical structures in order to honour the Great Geometrician of the Universe, it is also possible that there were cultural links between Selene's North African

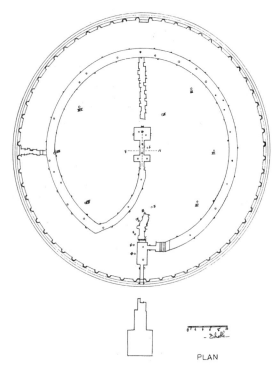

Fig 5. *Plan view of the tomb of Jubba II and Cleopatra Selene.*

Kingdom and Parthia, through which the mathematical understanding and technology for this type of design flowed. As we shall see shortly, those links may well have included a lost sister of Cleopatra Selene, who became queen of Parthia.

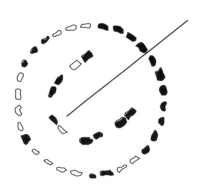

Fig 6. *Outline of Stonehenge.*

Whatever the method of transmission was for this design, its roots lie back in the very ancient past, in an era during which the properties of mathematics and astronomy were considered to be sacred in themselves. Indeed, if one would like to speculate freely, it is entirely possible that the design for Jubba and Selene's tomb was originally based upon the overall design of the Minorcan *talayots* and the geometry of Stonehenge.*

While this suggestion may sound a little bizarre, the form and design of these two monuments are somewhat similar. Selene's mausoleum exhibits sixty columns around its cylindrical base, instead of Stonehenge's thirty, but the general outline and the alignment to astronomical features is strikingly similar. It has already been proposed, by the puzzle designer and historical researcher Bruce Bedlam, that Stonehenge also once sported a conical roof structure; but since this would have been made of wood it has long since disappeared.

In addition, both of these monuments were purposely designed to include mathematical functions within their structure. The Stonehenge monument contains two prominent Pythagorean triangles within its layout, as I have explained in a previous work. Jubba and Selene's mausoleum is similar, in that the diameter of the lower cylinder is 60.85 m. This may not mean much, as we are using the wrong units, but since the drums of the columns that surround the tomb's lower cylinder each measure about 52 cm in height, I think we can safely say that this mausoleum was laid out in units of the Egyptian Thoth cubit (tc). (This is the Royal or Sacred cubit of Egypt, measuring 52.35 cm.) Bearing this in mind, the diameter of the lower cylinder of the mausoleum becomes 116.22 tc. While this length may not seem very illuminating either, if we multiply it by Pi (22 : 7) to get the circumference of the lower cylinder, the result is 365.25 tc – or the number of days in a year.

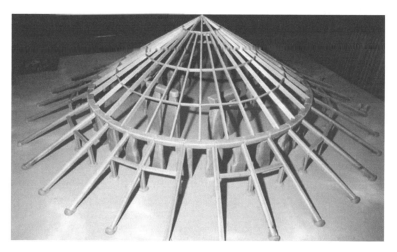

Fig 7. Stonehenge with conical roof structure (with thanks to Bruce Bedlam).

---

* See the colour section in the accompanying book *Scota* for a picture of the Minorcan *talayots*.

The reason for placing 60 columns around the lower cylinder of Jubba and Selene's tomb now becomes apparent. If we divide the circumference of the monument by 12, the result is 30.44 tc, or the number of days in a Solar month. Thus every five columns around the circumference of the tomb represents one month of the year. This identification with the Solar year means that Jubba II may have triumphed over his wife in the design of their last resting place. For Cleopatra Selene, whose name clearly identifies her with the Moon goddess, would no doubt have preferred 52 columns around the perimeter of her tomb – to represent the number of Lunar weeks in the year. (Four Lunar weeks equal a Lunar month, and so there are 13 Lunar months in the year.) Jubba II would have been represented by the male aspect of Helios, the Sun, as indeed was Selene's brother, Alexander Helios; while Selene herself would have been represented by the changeable female aspect of the Moon. Thus it would initially appear that the mausoleum was built to honour the Sun-god (Helios, Mithras, Ra, Aton, Amen), whom Jubba II no doubt revered.

However, this fine mausoleum is a deliberate blend of geometrical forms, and we have not yet looked at the cone-shaped pyramid upon its summit. Unfortunately, as with the Giza pyramids, this aspect of the monument was the first to be pillaged for its stones during the Islamic era, and most of the references to the height of the cone are taken from its present height. Since I have not yet found an accurate inclination for the cone, its original height is difficult to ascertain. However, from an analysis of pictures, and from estimating the number of missing layers to the cone, my best guess is that the inclination was originally 41 degrees and the original number of steps was originally 47. The height of each step is said to be 0.58 m, or 1.1 tc, and this would make the original cone 52 tc high, a number representing the Lunar weeks in the year.

It would be interesting to see if this is correct; for if it is, then it would seem that the female Lunar aspect of Selene was also honoured within the same monument. Within the design of the mausoleum, the two geometric figures of cylinder and cone honour the Great Geometrician of the Universe (god), while their measurements honour the Sun and Moon. Thus the diktats of traditional Egyptian dualism are preserved and honoured, and the royal couple of Mauretania become conjoined in death as Sun and Moon together.

Phraates

The marriage of Cleopatra Selene and Jubba II was celebrated in about 25 BC, and it was at about this time that Phraates IV unexpectedly regained the throne of Parthia, with the assistance of the Scythians; while the upstart Prince (King) Tiridates fled to Rome. Augustus, who had probably backed Tiridates in the first place, was not in a position to do much about this and must have decided to offer a hand of friendship to the Parthians instead of meddling further in their politics. However, this olive branch was hampered by Augustus' refusal to return the rebel prince/king (Tiridates) to Parthia, so that he could be dealt with by King Phraates. This Roman loyalty to the rebel prince (and king) again suggests that Augustus had backed his bid for the Parthian throne.

Faced with possible Parthian anger over his harbouring a renegade prince, Augustus had to do something to placate Phraates IV. There was also the small matter of the captured Roman standards to deal with. In the battles with Parthia that preceded his reign, Rome had lost two of its military standards, one by Crassus in 53 BC and the other by Mark Antony in 36 BC. These standards were powerful totems to the people of Rome in general and to the military establishment in particular, and Augustus knew that he would achieve a small symbolic victory just for having these all-important standards returned.

Augustus therefore had two problems to deal with in regard to Parthia and, with a military campaign out of the question, the only other option was diplomacy. It was for these reasons that Augustus sent various gifts to Phraates IV, to ease the tensions between the two great powers. Strangely enough, these gifts included the presentation of an 'Italian concubine' by the name of Thermusa, who was given as a personal chattel to Phraates IV. However, there is a great mystery here, for all of the contemporary historians, bar one, are totally silent on the subject of this mysterious lady. Yet, this lady was no common whore, who was being passed around the various rulers of the empire, for this lady rapidly became queen of Parthia and Phraates' chief wife.

The only historian who does venture to mention this lady is our old friend Josephus Flavius, the Jewish historian. But such was the deafening silence from all the other commentators and historians of this era, that Josephus' ribald tale about Thermusa and her son became another example of his 'unreliability' as a historian. That was, of course, until Parthian coins with Thermusa's image and name on them started turning up in the east; causing a minor flurry of historical embarrassment. It is my belief that many modern authorities like to champion Josephus Flavius' supposed 'unreliability' as a historian because his accounts clash strongly at times with the biblical narrative. However, more often than not it is Josephus' accounts that are correct, and it is the biblical accounts that are wrong. Josephus says of this mysterious and curiously unmentionable lady:

> Phraates ... had a love affair with an Italian concubine whose name was
> Thermusa, who had been formally sent to him amongst other presents by
> Julius Caesar. He first made her his concubine, but he being a great admirer
> of her beauty, and in the process having a son by her whose name was
> Phraataces, he made her his legitimate wife. [J2]

Thermusa did not simply become King Phraates' wife, she actually became
his chief wife, and so her son became next in line for the throne. But how
was this achieved? How did a common 'concubine' supersede the legitimate
bloodline wives of Parthia? The answer is probably to be found in the
example of King David, who similarly made a common soldier's wife,
Bathsheba, his chief wife. In a similar fashion to Thermusa, it was through
this 'commoner' that the great King Solomon was born. With the bloodline
of the royals being of paramount importance, I did not believe this biblical
tale at all, and thus I comprehensively demonstrated in the book *Solomon*
that Bathsheba was no commoner at all. The lady was called Bath-Sheba
בת-שבע, which means the Daughter of Sheba, and when she married the
king (her father) she became the Queen of Sheba.

The tale is more complex than this, but it is as certain as anything
can be in the Torah (or Tanakh) that Bathsheba was of royal blood, and the
daughter of the king she married. Given her rapid rise to power and
influence, it is likely that Thermusa was royal too, and in order to discover
the necessary evidence we need to look more closely at her brief history.

Firstly, Josephus is wrong about the sender of this gift, for it was
Augustus Caesar and not Julius Caesar who sent her. We know this because
Julius was dead before Phraates IV came to the throne. It is often said that
this mistake was due to Augustus being called Gaius Octavian Caesar before
he became emperor, while Julius was called Gaius Julius Caesar. While this
is possible, it is also possible that Julius Caesar did 'send' Thermusa in some
fashion – because she may well have been his daughter

Secondly, this lady could not have been a simple 'Italian concubine'.
This was a diplomatic gift from one of the most powerful leaders in the
world at that time to another. Would Augustus Caesar have chosen a low-
born concubine as a gift for King Phraates IV? Of course not. When
Augustus sent a gift to Jubba II, the king of Mauretania, he gave him
Cleopatra Selene, the daughter of Queen Cleopatra VII of Egypt (by Mark
Antony). But Jubba II was another of the minnows of Roman geopolitics
at that time, so why in this case did Jubba get an Egyptian princess while
Phraates IV, king of all Parthia (Persia), was presented with an 'Italian
concubine'?

If Thermusa was a concubine, then this was not a diplomatic gift
and a token of respect by Augustus – but a bold diplomatic snub to the

Parthian king, and the result would have been a declaration of war on Rome. But no, Phraates was so impressed with his lowly 'concubine' that he made her his chief wife and later proceeded to make several risky political manoeuvres in order to make her son first in line for the Parthian throne.

So who was the mysterious Thermusa who so charmed Phraates IV? When looking at this situation from this new perspective, one reason for Thermusa being called a 'concubine' or 'slave' may be that the Parthians considered a hostage to be a 'slave'. This alternative view is apparent when Josephus narrates the return of a son of Phraates IV to Parthia, after being taken hostage by Rome for a number of years:

> Vonones was preferred above the rest and sent to them ... However, they soon changed their minds ... for they could not think of obeying the commands of one who had been a slave (for so they called those who had been hostages). [3]

Thermusa had most definitely been a hostage of Rome, so perhaps this is one reason why she was called a 'concubine'. Nevertheless, considering Thermusa's meteoric rise to the position of chief wife of the king of Parthia (Persia), it is clear that she was a very important lady, but who exactly was she? And if she was indeed so prestigious, then why were all the Roman historians so quiet about her background and ancestry? What was there to hide? And why was it that the only historian to mention her at all was a Jewish historian from Judaea? Is this latter point in any way significant?

Ides of March

Having considered all the possibilities, the early twentieth century researcher A J Bethell deduced that Thermusa must have been Cleopatra VII, the queen of Egypt herself. While it is possible that Cleopatra did not die by the traditional asp bite in 30 BC, it is difficult to see how her presence in Rome was kept quiet for 15 years, or of what use she would be to Rome. Moreover, I do not think that Cleopatra would have been quite the perfect match that King Phraates of Parthia was expecting. Cleopatra was born in 69 BC, which would have made her 44 years old by the time Augustus sent his gifts to Parthia. While Cleopatra VII would still have been a prestigious wife to the king, she may also have been past childbearing age; and in royal dynastic terms, there is little point in having a sacred royal bloodline that cannot reproduce itself. No, there are too many problems involved with this scenario, and so we must look elsewhere for an alternative genealogy for the mysterious Thermusa.

Another possibility for her ancestry is contained in the reports that were given after the death of Julius Caesar. After Julius and Cleopatra's cruise down the Nile, Julius had some urgent campaigning to do in Bithynia, where he defeated Pharnaces II with ease in 47 BC. It wasn't until the summer of 46 BC that Julius and Cleopatra were able to meet up in Rome and for Cleopatra to make her grand entry into the city, as depicted in Joseph Mankiewicz's epic film, starring Elizabeth Taylor. Many historians doubt this extravagant portrayal, but considering the ostentatious and lavish royal court in which Cleopatra lived, I have no doubt that Cleopatra would have enjoyed making as much of a spectacle as was humanly possible.

Cleopatra and the infant Caesarion were then installed in the Trastevere, Julius Caesar's villa on the trans-Tiber. This caused an amount of scandal, because Calpurnia, Julius' wife, was being forced to house her husband's foreign mistress and their child. In fact, so bold was Julius that rumours circulated that he was going to marry Cleopatra, which would have entailed a change in the law because polygamy was not allowed in ancient Rome. Nevertheless, Julius and Cleopatra did live together in Rome as a pseudo 'king and queen' of the Roman Empire. But just as the rumours started to escalate, Julius was off to quell an uprising in Spain and did not return until the autumn of 45 BC, while Cleopatra made herself at home in Julius' Trastevere villa.

The historian Prof Erich Gruen doubts that Cleopatra could have stayed so long in Rome, as Egypt could not have remained stable without her presence. But I think that this view ignores Cleopatra's strategy and the balance of military power in the region. Egypt was rich in resources, especially gold and food, but she was militarily weak. Rome was desperate for resources but conversely had produced the most formidable army ever seen on the European continent. Cleopatra's position as queen of Egypt was safe as long as she was the mistress (or 'queen') of Julius Caesar – for if she were to be deposed, the new pretender to the

Fig 10. Bust of Cleopatra VII.

throne of Egypt would have to answer to Caesar and to Rome. This was a formidable deterrent to any potential uprising in Egypt; as Professor Macurdy says:

> With Arsinoe (Cleopatra's sister) in Rome (as a captive) and Ptolemy XIII (her brother) drowned in the Nile, the young queen (Cleopatra VII) had little to fear so long as she had at her side the greatest Roman of the moment. [4]

Prof Gruen also doubts the story by the historian Appian that Julius Caesar placed a statue of Cleopatra in the Temple of Venus Genetrix, next to the Roman goddess, and that it survived into the reign of Augustus. Why, he asks, should a statue of a deposed foreign queen still receive veneration in a Roman temple dedicated to Venus? Actually, Appian may have been correct in his assertion, because Venus was the Greek Aphrodite, who was Phoenician Astarte, who was in turn the Egyptian Ast 𓏏𓊨 or Isis. Similarly, Cleopatra was also considered to be an incarnation of Isis, as were all of the Ptolemaic queens of Egypt, and so this statue in the Temple of Venus may have been a generic statue dedicated to Isis. Thus the two statues in the Temple may well have been different manifestations of the same goddess, and perhaps in this we see a reason why the people of Rome accepted Cleopatra so easily.

The common people may have wanted to keep the statue because, as I have shown in my previous works, Isis – the archetypal mother goddess – was a very influential deity in the ancient world. So influential was she that she became the template for the Christian Madonna and Child. The Christian feast of Easter was also taken directly from the feast of Isis; indeed the name Easter was taken directly from the Egyptian name for Isis, which was Ast or Est 𓏏𓊨 . Cleopatra was considered by many to be an incarnation of Isis, and so the people may well have seen Cleopatra as Venus in earthly form. Who better to lead the Roman Empire than an exceptional army commander and a goddess.

Cleopatra was not only safe in Rome, she was also quietly plotting an Egyptian takeover of the Roman empire. To

*Fig 11. Isis and Horus,
Madonna and Child.*

Rome, which was a patrilineal society, Caesarion, Caesar's child by Cleopatra, was no particular national threat for the child was obviously Roman. But to Egypt, which was a matrilineal society, Caesarion was quite obviously an Egyptian prince, not a Roman successor. Had Cleopatra been able to manoeuvre Caesarion into being Julius Caesar's legal successor, her Egyptian takeover of Rome from within would have been complete. But, strange as it may seem, Julius never publicly acknowledged Caesarion as his son, and neither did he acknowledge him as his successor in his will. [5]

This omission is rather strange, and has provoked much speculation as to whether the child was actually his. But since Julius and Cleopatra were on their Nile cruise together at the critical time, it would seem difficult for the child to be anyone's but Caesar's, and so it has been speculated that Julius did not want to create a civil war by providing Rome with a highly contentious half-Egyptian successor. The recent epic BBC television series, 'Rome', dealt with this very topic, and the view of the historical producers of this series was that a lowly foot-soldier was responsible for Caesarion – although, in being a popularist series, this may well represent another element of added spice to the story-line. However, this scenario would indeed explain Julius' strange failure to acknowledge Caesarion as his heir.

In the autumn of 45 BC Julius returned from Spain to take up residence once more with Cleopatra, but the politics of the era were conspiring against him. A faction was conspiring to proclaim Julius as king of the Roman Empire, and it is difficult not to see Julius' hand acting quietly behind the scenes to promote this conspiracy. Julius Caesar, as king of the Roman Empire, would have needed a queen of royal blood to consummate the royal union, and who else but Cleopatra would have been his first choice? Accordingly, at the festival of Lupercalia, Mark Antony stepped up onto the rostrum to place a royal diadem (or crown) upon Julius Caesar's head to proclaim him as king. But instead of adulation, the crowds remained silent and, judging the mood of the populous in an instant, Julius pushed the diadem away from his head and proclaimed that only the god Jupiter could be king of Rome. The crowds roared their approval of this. Clearly, now was not the time to be assuming royal pretensions.

However, many in the Senate were now convinced that Julius did indeed want to be king, and that his choice of queen would be Cleopatra of Egypt and not his legal wife, Calpurnia. It was for this reason that, come the fateful day of 15th March 44 BC – the Ides of March – Julius Caesar was assassinated by a group of senators, including Marcus Junius Brutus. In an instant, all of Cleopatra's careful planning and intrigues had been dashed. Her protector had gone, and her child had not been named as Julius Caesar's heir. She was not only now in danger from the Roman squabbles over a new emperor, but the protection she had enjoyed from potential pretenders to the throne in Egypt had also evaporated. There was nothing else she could do but flee back to Egypt as fast as possible, to stabilise her position there. This she did, and that may well have been the end of the story, but as she left Rome a number of curious remarks were penned by Cicero:

> The rumour about the queen (Cleopatra) is losing strength.

> I would like to know the truth about the queen (Cleopatra) and about that Caesar too.

> I would like the story about the queen (Cleopatra) to be true. [6]

Clearly there was a great rumour circulating about Cleopatra before she left Rome for Egypt, but what exactly were these covert whisperings all about? Well, it would seem that there was a strong rumour about 'that Caesar', but the rumour then diminished for some reason. The Caesar in question is unlikely to have been Julius, as he was now dead. Instead, the rumour may have been related to Caesarion's disputed paternity; but since Caesarion was not mentioned in Julius' will, that particular rumour was now largely irrelevant – it was highly unlikely that Caesarion could now become the next emperor. Likewise, the rumour is again unlikely to have been about Caesarion, as Julius Caesar's son was clearly known by the diminutive form of Caesar, which is clearly a different title. So who was this new Caesar? Why the intrigue and why did the rumour diminish with time?

It is entirely possible that the answer to this is to be found in the later comments penned by Cicero. It is said that he opined:

> Writing to Atticus on 10 May 44. After expressing sorrow at hearing of a miscarriage, Cicero says that he hopes or wishes that 'it may be true' about the queen (Cleopatra) and 'that Caesar of hers'. [7]

A direct translation of Cicero's letter reads:

> I am grieved to hear of Tertia's loss of an expected child ... (but) I should be glad of such a loss in the case of the queen (Cleopatra) and that [expected] scion of the breed of Caesar. [8]   (Author's brackets.)

It would seem that the persistent rumour floating around Rome when Julius Caesar was assassinated was that Cleopatra was pregnant. So the import of Cicero's letter is that he is secretly hoping that Cleopatra also has a miscarriage, just like Tertia had had recently. The unknown 'Caesar' who he was alluding to in his earlier letter may therefore have been Cleopatra's unborn second child – a child who would have been most certainly fathered by Julius Caesar. And since Cicero mentions a scion or heir, and Rome was a patrilineal society, Cleopatra must have been desperately hoping for a son.

This pregnancy may sound unlikely, bearing in mind the almost total lack of historical commentary on this matter, but actually it is not such a dubious suggestion. Julius had returned from Spain in the autumn of 45 BC, and he was not assassinated until the spring of 44. Meanwhile, Cleopatra was living openly in his trans-Tiber villa as the emperor's mistress. Even if Julius did have another mistress in Spain, it was always the soldier's solemn duty to re-consummate a relationship upon his return from an expedition, and it is therefore a certainty that Julius and Cleopatra slept together and had conjugal relations once more in the autumn of 45. Julius' seeming lack of virility aside, the possible pregnancy of Cleopatra that Cicero alludes to is therefore more likely than unlikely.

However, following Julius' death, Cleopatra and Caesarion (and the unborn child) were highly vulnerable. In the circumstances, Cleopatra's most potent form of defence against the senators who had murdered Julius Caesar (and against her other enemies in Rome) would be to go to a reputable seer and divine the sex of her unborn child – for if it was a boy it would have a strong claim to become the next emperor, much more so than the unfortunate Caesarion. Caesarion was of unknown parentage – he had arrived in Rome as an infant and Julius had pointedly failed to acknowledge him as his son, for whatever reason. What were the Romans to think? This new pregnancy was, however, conceived in the limited confines of the Trastevere villa, and everyone knew that the only possible father was Julius Caesar himself. Who would dare murder the Queen of Egypt and the unborn true heir to the Roman Empire?

Thus Cleopatra's first move was to go straight to the temple – most probably the Temple of Venus that contained her own statue. The nervous priestess and seer who Cleopatra consulted, being faced with a 50 - 50 chance and a tempting pot of gold, said that her unborn child was most definitely a boy. This was 'that Caesar' that Cicero was alluding to, and this was the reason for his wanting Cleopatra to have a miscarriage. A new contender to the throne of the Empire at this late stage would have upset the entire apple cart, and possibly led to civil unrest, as well as ensuring that an Egyptian prince became emperor.

But the crisis was soon over, and the rumour 'lost strength'. Why? Well, if Cleopatra had conceived this new child in the September or October of 45 BC, then the child would have been born in the May or June of 44. In other words, the baby could have been due very shortly after Cicero's second letter was written. Cleopatra was hoping for a boy, but if the seer guessed wrongly and the child was a girl, then Cicero would have been most happy. This was the story that he wanted to be true, and this is the reason for the rumour about Cleopatra's 'Caesar' losing its strength.

Despite this obviously being a worrying subject for the contemporary historians, which was clouded in much secrecy and intrigue, there is one other allusion to Cleopatra's second pregnancy by Julius Caesar. A coin was discovered with the image of Cleopatra suckling a child, which is usually interpreted as being the infant Caesarion. However, the coin also contains the legend 'Kupr', the name for the island of Cyprus, and so the coin is indicating that Cleopatra was ruling Cyprus at the time. [9]

P J Bicknell and others have argued that Cleopatra did not gain control over Cyprus until 44 or 43 BC. But Caesarion was born in 47 BC, which would have made him too old to be a suckling infant at this time. To explain this strange anomaly away, it has been argued that this image on the coin was therefore representative of Cleopatra's incarnation of the Egyptian goddess Isis, and thus the representation is therefore the standard icon of Isis and her son Horus. However, while that is possible, the image may also be that of Cleopatra and her new daughter by the late Julius Caesar.

So is this phantom child simply my own conjecture, or is there any substance to these rumours and speculations? Well, the translation of Cicero's letter by Prof Macurdy seems to be self-explanatory; Cleopatra was pregnant shortly before the death of Julius Caesar, and I am certainly not alone in this speculation. The following are comments by historians who have been working closely in this field:

> However, it is quite likely, from Cicero, that Cleopatra was pregnant in late 45 or early 44. If this pregnancy was not Caesarion, then it presumably miscarried or resulted in a child who did not long survive birth. [12]

> Moreover, another child was the natural result of the continued union of Caesar and such a fecund woman as Cleopatra, who desired to have heirs for Caesar and the Roman-Egyptian empire. [13]

> Since the question of the paternity of (Cleopatra's) son Caesarion was to be hotly discussed in Rome, it seems not unlikely that Cleopatra would wish to have another child by Caesar at the time when she was living in his house, when there would be no doubt that Caesar was the father. [14]

But there was no further mention of this 'phantom' pregnancy. Was Cleopatra bluffing? Did she miscarry, as Cicero desired? While either of these suggestions are plausible, the most likely reason why the contemporary historians fell silent, on the topic of Cleopatra's second pregnancy through Julius Caesar, is that the pregnancy resulted in an unexpected and unwanted daughter. No accounts were written about this child because she was of no benefit to anyone, and a great disappointment to Queen Cleopatra herself. Cleopatra already had an heir to Egypt – her son Caesarion – what she did not have was an indisputable male heir to Rome, born of Julius Caesar. The new daughter could not be this heir because Rome was a patrilineal society with a patrilineal ruling class. In short, Cleopatra's unwanted and rejected daughter probably became one of many royal children in this era who slipped into obscurity, as did her later sons by Mark Antony. However, that obscurity was not to last forever.

New generation

We now move on a decade or so. After Julius' murder, Cleopatra had allied herself with one of his successors, Marcus Antonius or Mark Antony. Together, the couple controlled the south and east of the Roman Empire, and together they had three children; a twin daughter and son who were named Cleopatra Selene and Alexander Helios, and another son called Ptolemy. But Cleopatra's dreams of taking over the whole of the Roman Empire were again to be shattered, and following the defeat of Mark Antony at the great sea-battle of Actium, Augustus (Octavian) pursued Antony and Cleopatra back to Egypt in late 31 BC.

Egypt effectively capitulated to the Romans at this point in time and lost its independence completely. After it was explained to Cleopatra that she would be a central part of the victory parade in Rome, to be dragged through the streets shackled in golden chains, she chose to kill herself instead. With the Roman empire now controlling all of Egypt, Augustus took all of Cleopatra's children to Rome to celebrate his triumph, in which they were indeed paraded in golden chains. These included Selene, Helios and Ptolemy, but was there an older fourth child too?

Back in Rome, Augustus took his time sorting out the loose ends of his empire. As was mentioned previously, to strengthen his position in North Africa, Augustus decided to give his old friend Jubba II the teenage daughter of Cleopatra VII, Cleopatra Selene, as wife and queen. With his southern border secure in the hands of a loyal client-king, Augustus now looked towards the east, where Phraates IV has just retaken his throne from the upstart Parthian prince, Tiridates. In order to placate King Phraates and cement a lasting alliance with the powerful Parthian empire, he needed to give Phraates something special, something that would demonstrate Rome's respect for Parthia and Augustus' desire for a lasting peace and friendship between these two great empires. Jubba II had already been given the hand of Cleopatra VII's daughter in marriage, and so the mighty King Phraates IV would need something much more prestigious than this. What Augustus does, is to give King Phraates an Italian concubine called Thermusa. Jubba II, the minnow of Mauretania, gets a princess and goddess of Egypt, while King Phraates IV of all Parthia gets a whore!

Thea Muse

As has already been laboured at some length, for this diplomatic offering to make any sense, quite plainly Thermusa could not have been a common concubine and must have been a royal princess of some stature and breeding. In the circumstances, she can only have been the long-forgotten 19-year-old daughter of Cleopatra VII and Julius Caesar, who would have been in her prime for bearing Phraates sons and daughters of royal and sacred Egyptian blood. While this deduction may seem like a leap of faith at this stage, there are many reasons for thinking that this is true.

Firstly, it is an established fact that Egyptian princesses had already been given to the kings of Parthia. During the New Kingdom era such diplomatic marriages were forbidden, as Egyptian princesses were never given to foreign kings. However, the Egyptian Ptolemaic dynasty sent many a princess to Persia, as the two royal families shared a common Greek heritage during this era. It was in this manner that in 150 BC a certain princess called Cleopatra Thea became the wife of three Seleucid kings: Alexander Balas, Demetrius II and Antiochus VII. The Seleucid empire was founded by one of Alexander the Great's generals, Seleucus, and at its height it controlled all of the Persian lands. However, by the reign of Alexander Balas the ruling Seleucid dynasty had become unstable and it was soon to be eclipsed by the growing might of the Parthian Arsacid dynasty. But if the Seleucid dynasty could be blessed with a dynastic alliance with the royal line of Egypt, then why not the Parthian Arsacid dynasty too?

Secondly, there is the interesting matter of the names of Phraates' wives. A document known as the Second Avroman Parchment records the wives of Phraates IV in 20 BC, just five years after the gift of Thermusa to King Phraates IV. It gives their names as being Olenieire, Baseirta, Bistheibanaps and Cleopatra. [15] This last name is odd, because while an Egyptian princess called Cleopatra Thea had married into the Seleucid dynasty, there is no trace of a dynastic alliance between Egypt and the Parthian Arsacid dynasty. So where did this wife called Cleopatra come from? I think the obvious answer is that Thermusa was only a nickname for this princess, and her real name would have been Cleopatra, because in reality she was Cleopatra's daughter. Cleopatra VII's second daughter was called Cleopatra Selene, and so it is likely that any daughter by Julius Caesar would have been named likewise.

Thirdly, even the name Thermusa contains echoes of the Egyptian queen, Cleopatra. The full title of this 'Italian concubine' was Thea Muse Ourania, meaning 'Goddess Muse Ourania' (more accurately pronounced as Thea Mus<u>a</u> Ourania in the Greek). In Greek mythology Ourania was actually the Greek *muse*, or inspirational goddess, of astronomy and since Ourania was in charge of the heavens she was often considered to be the Muse of Heaven, or the Muse of the Stars. In fact, the name Ourania was derived from ouranos ουρανος meaning 'heaven', and so a literal translation of Thea Muse Ourania would be 'Goddess of Heaven' or, by implication, the 'Queen of Heaven'.

But Ourania was not the original Queen of Heaven, for that title must surely go to the Egyptian Isis. In the second century AD, Lucius Apuleius had a vision of Isis, who described herself as:

> I am she that is the natural mother of all things, mistress and governess of all the elements, the initial progeny of worlds, chief of powers divine, <u>Queen of Heaven</u>, the principal of the Gods celestial, the light of the goddesses: at my will the planets of the air, the wholesome winds of the Seas, and the silences of hell be disposed; my name, my divinity is adored throughout all the world in divers manners, in variable customs and in many names ... the Egyptians ... do call me Queen Isis. [16]

Isis was not, of course, the only Queen of Heaven, and so we find that there were a succession of goddesses who were manifestations of Isis. The name of the Phoenician goddess <u>Ast</u>arte, for instance, has been taken directly from the Egyptian Ast or Est 𓊨𓏏𓆇 , which was the original Egyptian name for Isis. So it should not be a surprise that Astarte is then described in the *Encyclopaedia Britannica* as being the Queen of Heaven, for she was indeed the Phoenician Isis. In her turn, the Phoenician Astarte can be seen as an ancestor of the Greek Aphrodite, the goddess of love, and Selene, the goddess of the Moon. This is why Muse Ourania was also sometimes called Venus Ourania, because she was so closely associated with Venus-Aphrodite.

Since all of the Ptolemaic queens of Egypt modelled themselves upon the goddess Isis, many of these names and titles display a great deal of synergy with Queen Cleopatra VII. Likewise, since Isis was known as the Queen of Heaven, Cleopatra VII named her twins (by Mark Antony) Alexander <u>Helios</u> and Cleopatra <u>Selene</u>, or Alexander Sun and Cleopatra Moon. As she was now the mother of the Sun and the Moon, Thea Muse Cleo-Patra (Cleopatra VII) could just as easily have been recognised as being Thea Muse Ourania, the Goddess of the Heavens.

We have no idea what Cleopatra VII's second child (by Julius Caesar) may have been called, but Thea Muse Ourania (Josephus' Thermusa) would have been a distinctly appropriate title, if only as a hypocorism or nickname.

Fourthly, the name of the pharaoh's daughter, who supposedly found the infant biblical Moses and brought up this child in the royal court of Egypt, was called Thermuthis. [17] Several theologians have seen in this name a hint of the pharaonic name Tuthmoses, and have tried to make links accordingly. However, the Egyptian version of this same name was actually known as Renenutet ⟨hieroglyphs⟩, and the link to Josephus' princess called Thermuthis lies in the fact that the Greek name for Renenutet was Thermuthis. Now Renenutet was a fertility goddess in the guise of a serpent, and she was strongly linked to the goddess Isis. In other words, the Egyptian princess who reared Moses in the royal court was either called Renenutet-Isis, or she was being regarded as a personification of Renenutet-Isis. [18]

There is also a desperately awful pun being made here by Josephus' scribes, which certainly works in the English, and since the visual imagery would have been the same in all languages it should also work in the Greek or Hebrew. * The goddess Renenutet ⟨hieroglyphs⟩ was known as 'She who Rears Up', with the visual imagery here being the cobra rearing up ready to strike. But of course Josephus' *Antiquities* says that is was Princess Thermuthis who 'reared' the infant Moses, and so it could be said that she 'reared up' the child. A poor form of wit, I know, but the Egyptian texts are full of this predictable and not always witty repartee.

So what does the biblical Egyptian princess called Thermuthis have to do with Cleopatra and Thea Muse? Well Cleopatra was also doomed to be a personification of the goddess Isis, as were all the Ptolemaic queens, as we have seen. Isis was known as the Queen of Heaven, or perhaps the

---

* In the Hebrew the terms are *omnah* אמנה meaning 'raise' and *quwm* קום meaning 'rise'. Since both terms refer to something standing upright, the pun should also work in the Hebrew.

Queen of the Stars. This was a title held by many of the Egyptian and biblical royalty, including the Queen of Sheba, whose name can be literally translated in the Egyptian as being the 'Queen of the Stars'. In addition, the goddess Renenutet, or Thermuthis, was said to be the image of Isis in the guise of a cobra; while in a similar fashion it was said that Cleopatra was bitten by an asp (although most modern biologists indicate that the Egyptian cobra would have been the preferred reptile). So Princess Thermuthis and Queen Cleopatra were both closely associated with Isis and also with a snake.

It was most probably for this reason that Josephus Flavius managed to turn the name Thea Muse into Thermusa, because the latter name is very similar indeed to the name of Thermuthis, the princess who found and reared Moses. His alteration seems to indicate that the 'Italian concubine' called Thea Muse can be equated both with an Egyptian princess and also with the goddess Isis, and if she were a daughter of Cleopatra VII then we can do just that.

Fifthly, Thea Muse Ourania can also be strongly linked with the Greek Aphrodite, the goddess of love, who was simply a much later incarnation of the Egyptian Isis (Ast or Est 𓊨𓏏𓆇). In a similar fashion, Cleopatra VII's title was derived from the Greek terms *clio* and *patra*.

Neter-t Merites   Cleopatra-t

Fig 12. Cartouches of Cleopatra VII.

The term '*clio*' is said to have been derived from the Greek *muse* Clio, the *muse* of poetry and history, which would result in a name meaning 'Poetical Muse of my Father'. However, the general opinion is that Cleo-Patra's title means 'Glory of my Father'. It is likely that this translation is mirrored in Cleopatra's Egyptian royal title, which was Neter-t Merites 𓊨𓏏𓈝 which means 'Goddess Love of Father' or perhaps even 'She, the Goddess of Love'. By using the Greek term for 'goddess', Cleopatra's Egyptian name might then become 'Thea Aphrodite' or 'Goddess of Love', a fitting title for an incarnation of Isis.

Thus Thea Muse Cleo-Patra (Cleopatra VII) and Thea Muse Ourania seem to have had very similar titles in many respects. Both were named after the Greek muses, and both were named after the goddess Isis; so Thea Muse Ourania would have been a fitting hypocorism for the daughter of the great Egyptian queen.

Sixthly, Phraates IV and Thea Muse Ourania had at least two children that we know of. There was Phraates V, a son who was known as Phraataces (which is a diminutive of the name Phraates) and Julia Ourania. The reason why the latter is significant is to be found in the clan names of Rome. Julius' full name was Gaius Julius Caesar (or Caius Yulius Caesar). The term Julius showed that he was from the Julius family, or clan, and the name Caesar demonstrated that he was of the Caesar branch of that larger family. The term 'Caesar' meaning 'emperor' only came into vogue after Julius' reign.

Clan or family names were rigidly adhered to, much as the clan names in Scotland are, although it has to be said that slaves sometimes took the clanname of their master. However, here we have a princess of Parthia who has been given the name of the Julian family in Rome. So why was this done? If Thea Muse was simply giving her daughter the name of her Roman patron, then she should have been called Octavian (Augustus). The choice of the family name of Julius demonstrates once again that Thea Muse was related to Julius Caesar, as Josephus Flavius suspected – and indeed she *was* related to Julius because she was his daughter by Cleopatra VII

Finally, there is the suggestion by the French historian, Jeulpani, that Julia Ourania married Ptolemy of Mauretania. Now if Thea Muse (Thermusa) was indeed a daughter of Cleopatra VII, then this would have been a strategic alliance between North Africa (Mauretania) and Persia (Parthia) that made every sense. The mother of Ptolemy of Mauretania was Cleopatra Selene, the daughter of Cleopatra VII, and so this possible marriage alliance between Ptolemy of Mauretania and Julia Ourania would have been a marriage of royal Egyptian cousins, both of whom were directly descended from Cleopatra VII. [19] It would seem unlikely that this alliance would have been arranged if Thea Muse were not a daughter of Cleopatra VII. (See the family tree in the appendix.)

The evidence suggests that a branch of the Ptolemaic royal line had been forcibly uprooted from Egypt, by Rome, and deposited in Parthia; where it appears to have taken root and prospered. But this story is not about Parthia, it is supposed to be about Judaea and the biblical accounts of the New

Testament. So how, in this case, does the mighty royal family of Parthia become involved in the events in Judaea that shaped modern Christianity? Well, the New Testament recounts a tale of turbulent times and some of this turbulence was about to strike the Parthian royal family.

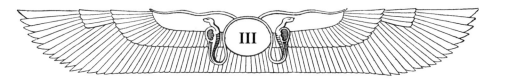

Ourania and Aurania

A few years after the gift of Thea Muse to Phraates IV, in about 20 BC, Augustus journeyed to the east once more and reopened his friendly diplomacy with the Parthian king. The subject on Augustus' mind was the ongoing dispute about the Roman military standards, which had been captured by the Parthians in 53 and 36 BC. While it may seem a little strange to organise a diplomatic mission to retrieve a lost standard, or regimental colour, these standards were actually highly important elements of the Roman fighting machine. Indeed, an entire military campaign was organised in order to retrieve the standards lost by Varus in the Teutoburger Wald of Germany. Likewise, Mark Antony's 36 BC campaign into Parthia was spurred on by the prospect of retrieving a lost standard; but he only succeeded in losing yet another standard to the Parthians. Again, the BBC series 'Rome' dwelt on this very subject, and depicted Caesar's legions retrieving a lost standard in Gaul.

The standards themselves came in many guises, with early examples being an eagle, wolf, horse or boar. Only in later centuries was the design standardised around the *aquila* eagle design with the legend SPQR attached to it. These famous initials stand for *Senatus Populusque Romanus* or 'the Senate and the People of Rome', which was not exactly who the army were fighting for after Julius Caesar took the throne as emperor.

Having mentioned the military standards, it would be remiss not to look at the similar cult of the Roman *fasces*. One of the prime symbols of office for high dignitaries and for the emperor himself was the *fasces*, which comprised an axe secured within a bundle of rods and tied together with red tapes. Unfortunately, the origins and meaning of this design seem to have been completely lost to the Romans, let alone modern historians. However, if the reader will allow me the liberty of continuing my thesis that most of

Western civilisation seems to have sprung from Egypto-Judaic roots, the true meaning of the *fasces* can perhaps be divined. This is not simply a point of academic interest, as the *fasces* is still an important emblem today.

Since the *fasces* was carried by Roman court officials, the axe portion of the *fasces* is said to represent punishment – the ultimate judicial sanction of decapitation. However, it is much more likely that the axe was derived from the Egyptian god-axe ⌐, a symbol that was adopted by the influential Minoan empire, who no doubt transported it all over the Mediterranean during their extensive trading voyages. The Roman *fasces* is said to have originated with the Etruscans, and since the Etruscans were related to the Sea People alliance and to the later Phoenician

Fig 16.   A statue of Cincinnatus holding the Roman Fasces – from which we derive the word fascism.

empire, this would seem entirely reasonable. Instead of symbolising punishment, therefore, the axe would have represented divine power.

The bundle of rods that form the bulk of the *fasces* are again said to represent the sanction of punishment by the courts, with the criminal facing the possibility of being lashed. However, the true origin for the meaning of these rods can perhaps be glimpsed from the number of *fasces* that were carried before the various high officials, which were six, twelve or twenty-four, depending on their rank. This would suggest that the *fasces* pertained in some manner to the zodiac, or perhaps the twelve tribes of Israel. That the latter is the more likely can be clearly seen in a quote from Josephus:

Moses only desired the heads of the tribes to bring their rods, with the names of their tribes inscribed upon them, and that he should receive the priesthood in whose rod god should give a sign. This was agreed to. So the rest brought their rods, as did Aaron also, who had written the tribe of Levi on his rod. These rods Moses laid up in the tabernacle of God. [J1]

Thus each of these rods symbolised, and was inscribed with, the name of a tribe of the Hyksos-Israelites. Thus it is likely that the twelve rods, had Moses tied them together in a *fasces*, would have been a symbol of unity between the often fractious Hyksos-Israelite tribes. Taken together, the axe and the rods would then represent the unity of the Hyksos-Israelite tribes and their being bound to the divine power of the one god, which was represented by the axe symbol. This argument would make sense of the available archaeological and epigraphic information about the *fasces*, but it would make the symbol's later usage rather incongruous.

The *fasces* was prominently used, for instance, by the German and Italian Fascists during the Second World War – indeed the term 'fascist' comes directly from the name of the *fasces* itself. However, it would now appear that the emblem of the Fascists was an Egypto-Judaic symbol – but only the most foolhardy of historians would have mentioned this to the Nazis.

Fig 17. The Lincoln Memorial in Washington. Lincoln's hands rest upon two fasces.

Notwithstanding the *fasces'* modern association with Fascism, it is still a widely used symbol of authority. It is used as an emblem by the Spanish police, for instance, and also for French passports; and it used to appear on the American dime coin. More interestingly, two prominent *fasces* form the armrests of the seat upon which Abraham Lincoln sits in the Lincoln Memorial. In other words, the authority of the American establishment is directly related to the authority of the Roman Senate, and perhaps before that to the authority of the Egyptian state. Finally, bearing in mind the Roman use of the *fasces* within their court system, the use of red tape for binding important court documents also, no doubt, stems from the design of the *fasces*.

Diplomacy

On this particular diplomatic mission to Parthia, Augustus was successful and the long-lost military standards were returned by the Parthians to Rome – on 12th May 20 BC to be precise, according to Gardthausen. [2] But what had caused this change of heart by the Parthians, after all this time? Augustus himself relates on the Ancyra Monument that:

> The Parthians I compelled to restore to me the spoils and standards of three Roman armies, and to seek as suppliants the friendship of the Roman people. These standards I deposited in the inner shrine which is in the Temple of Mars Ultor. [3]

Using a level of political spin worthy of Britain's current Labour Party, Augustus here infers that he forced the Parthians to return the standards by threats of force. However, Augustus was not in a position to threaten the Parthians, and so it is much more likely that this success was the result of Thea Muse's manipulation of her husband, the king. As Josephus says:

> Now (Thea Muse) was able to persuade (Phraates IV) to do anything that she said... [4]

The reason for Thea Muse's assistance to Rome in this matter was that she was plotting a long-term strategy to ensure that her son became the next king of Parthia, and it was likely that she would need Roman assistance in this endeavour. She no doubt wrote to Augustus and promised the return of the standards, as he is highly unlikely to have made such a long journey to the east on the off-chance of a successful negotiation with Phraates IV. As far as Thea Muse was concerned, the *quid pro quo* was that Augustus would accept all of Phraates IV's other sons as hostages, leaving her son free to take the throne of Parthia when her husband died. Queen Thea Muse had been gifted to King Phraates in about 25 BC and so her son, Phraataces, may have been three or so years old by this time.

Whatever the case, Thea Muse's influence over the old king must have been complete, because he agreed to this bizarre proposition; and a few years after the return of the Roman standards, Phraates sent his four sons to Rome as hostages. It is often thought that Phraates may have been persuaded that his sons were plotting to depose him, and this is why he agreed to send them away to Rome. But to have not foreseen the devious designs of Thea Muse, in clearing the way for her son to be king, was a fatal mistake. Of course, Phraates may have wanted his youngest son, Phraataces, to take the throne, but not in the way that events transpired.

Augustus Caesar must have been delighted by this fortuitous outcome. He had not only recovered the lost military standards without firing so much as an arrow, but he could (and did) claim great political credit back in Rome for doing so. Florus and Strabo write of this eventuality:

> The Parthians, as if they repented of their victories, brought back of their own accord, the standards taken from Rome. [5]

> Phraates was so anxious to obtain the friendship of Augustus Caesar that he even sent the trophies. [S6]

Yes indeed. Phraates had been so anxious to placate Rome that he had held onto the military standards for 33 and 16 years respectively! Clearly, Phraates was in no hurry to placate Rome and so it is likely that the only friendship he wished to enhance was that of his domineering Romo-Egyptian wife, Thea Muse Ourania [Cleopatra II of Parthia].

In addition, Augustus must have been even more delighted that he now had the four princess of Parthia as hostages, which he could perhaps use as leverage at some point in the future. Augustus' current working relationship with Thea Muse was obviously cordial and mutually beneficial, but if things turned more sour he could always threaten to install one of his puppet princes on the throne of Parthia.

While the maverick (but reliable) historian Josephus Flavius pointedly states that the princes of Parthia were sent to Rome at the bidding of Thea Muse to allow her son to became king, the cautious Strabo takes the more orthodox line:

> (Phraates) was apprehensive of conspiracy and attempts on his life ... He therefore removed his sons out of the way with a view to annihilating the

hopes of the disaffected ... The sons who live in Rome, are entertained as princes at the public expense. [57]

It is true that the usurper from 29 BC, called Tiridates, had most probably been a Parthian prince; and it is true that many a king has been uncertain about his son's intentions; however, I still prefer Josephus' version of events. For one thing, the sending of these princes to Rome could only be seen as a sign of Parthian weakness, which would not look good on either the domestic or the international front. Conversely, it was also a propaganda coup for Augustus, who milked this 'victory' for all it was worth. Would Phraates really wanted to have an emboldened Rome on his doorstep, and possible rebellion at home, simply to remove a vague threat from his sons? Was there no other way of dealing with this situation?

On the Ancyra Monument Augustus Caesar writes:

> Phraates, son of Orodes, king of the Parthians, sent all his sons and grandsons to me in Italy, not because he had been conquered in war, but rather seeking our friendship by means of his own children as pledges. And a large number of other nations experienced the good faith of the Roman people during my principate who never before had had any interchange of embassies or of friendship with the Roman people. [8]

It is also a fact that King Phraates IV did not 'remove all his sons'. He removed all except Phraataces, the son of Thea Muse, and it was conveniently Phraataces who became the next king of Parthia. As Josephus said in a quote earlier in this chapter, Thea Muse was able to persuade Phraates to do anything. But this decision by King Phraates must once again call into question Thea Muse's supposed humble heritage. The sons who Phraates had sent to Rome were of the Arsacid dynasty, who had ruled Parthia since 250 BC. For Phraates to be sidelining this powerful and illustrious dynasty, in favour of a son through Thea Muse, indicates that her bloodline must have been even more famous and possibly sacred, and what other royal line than the Egyptian's could have achieved this?

King Phraates' bargain with Rome also implies that Rome was happy with Thea Muse's and Phraataces' royal credentials, and that Phraates IV himself trusted Rome not to interfere with Phraataces' succession. For Rome was now the baby-sitter to four of Parthia's most famous princes, and could have easily used these Arsacid princes to foment revolt and insurrection in Parthia. That Rome did not entertain this thought demonstrates a tacit acceptance of Phraataces' claim to the Parthian throne.

The presence of Phraates' four sons in Rome was also a veiled warning to the young Phraataces that he needed to be a wise and just ruler. For King Phraates had deliberately left his Arsacid sons in Rome, instead of ruthlessly disposing of them, so that Phraataces would always risk the introduction of pretenders to the throne, backed by the power of Rome. Thus the actions of King Phraates may not have been quite so bizarre after all, and he may instead have deliberately ensured that Parthia would remain at peace with Rome long after his own death.

Regicide

So, with the four sons of King Phraates IV safely out of the running for the Parthian throne, the only true winner in all respects was Thea Muse – who only had to wait for her husband to die for her and her offspring to inherit the entire Parthian empire. The only minor snag with this plan was that Phraates was proving to be a little uncooperative in this regard, and was intent on living a full and long life. The obvious answer to this problem was for Thea Muse to hasten her husband's departure from this world. Accordingly, it is thought that King Phraates was poisoned by Thea Muse in about AD 2. With her husband out of the way, Thea Muse proceeded to appoint herself as Queen of Parthia in a co-regency with her son. And in a bizarre twist to this plot, in order to seal this co-regency of Parthia, Thea Muse then married her son, Phraataces.

Josephus Flavius is the only historian to relate these facts to us and, as I said before, his lurid accounts of this court intrigue were dismissed out of hand – until coins bearing the name of Thea Muse Ourania started turning up in Iran. But these were not simply coins of Thea Muse, instead, they come complete with the image of her son, Phraataces, on the reverse – with their images being titled 'king' and 'queen'. The full account of this intrigue, as narrated by Josephus Flavius, is as follows:

> Phraates, king of the Parthians died at about this time as a result of a conspiracy led by his son Phraataces, which began for the following reason. Phraates, when he already had legitimate sons, fell in love with an Italian slave girl named Thermusa, who had been sent, along with other gifts, by Julius Caesar. At first he treated her as a concubine, but with the passing of time, he was so taken by her beauty, and after she had a son named Phraataces, he declared her his lawful wife and held her in honor. When she achieved such influence that the king would do whatever she said, she, eager to obtain the kingship of the Parthians for a son to whom she had given birth, realized that she could only obtain her desire by contriving the removal of the legitimate children of the Parthian king,

convinced him to send the legitimate children to Rome as hostages. They were sent to Rome, because it was not easy for Phraates (IV) to refuse the commands of Thermusa.

Phraataces, who was alone being prepared for the throne, considered it a dangerous and tedious thing to take power handed over by his father; so he plotted, with the assistance of his mother, to do away with his father. There is also a story that he had sexual relations with her. He was detested for both reasons, since his subjects considered incest with his mother no less evil than patricide, so he was embroiled in civil war before he had gathered much strength, driven from the throne and died. [19]

Now this marriage between Thea Muse and her son Phraataces is a revealing event, for this incestuous royal relationship was not a Parthian custom, nor was it a Roman custom; the Romans even banned polygamy, let alone incest. However, incest was most definitely an old established Egyptian custom, and one that had been enthusiastically adopted by the Greco-Egyptian Ptolemaic dynasty. Nearly every Ptolemaic king and queen entered into an incestuous marriage of one kind or another, with Cleopatra VII's marriage to two of her younger brothers being a prime example. This evidence again suggests that Thea Muse was of Egyptian royal ancestry, and she was – through her mother Cleopatra VII. Strangely enough, this unpopular marriage between Thea Muse and Phraataces was mentioned by the biblical Jesus, as we shall see later, and this fact pulls this investigation ever closer towards its final conclusion.

Quite obviously, the attempt to force this incestual, Egyptian royal custom upon an unwilling Parthian court and population failed completely. Like Akhenaton before her, Thea Muse was reforming the traditions of the nation too far and too fast, and so the people rose up in revolt. The result was that within a couple of years Queen Thea Muse and her husband-son, King Phraataces, were exiled from Parthia. But where to? The information provided by Josephus is nonspecific, as he merely says that Phraataces was 'driven from the throne and died'. This sentence may initially make it appear that the exile was fatal, and that Phraataces died almost immediately; but that is not necessarily so, for Josephus is merely indicating that the king died in exile. In truth, Phraataces may have lived for many years before dying, while still remaining in exile.

The epitaph of Augustus Caesar inscribed upon the Ancyra Monument is only a little more illuminating when it records that:

Kings of the Parthians, Tiridates, and later Phraates, the son of King Phraates, took refuge with me as suppliants. [12]

It is highly likely that 'Phraates, son of Phraates' was a reference to Phraataces, as that is what the latter name means; and so Augustus appears to be claiming that Phraataces 'took refuge' with him, presumably somewhere within the territories of the vast Roman Empire. The Cambridge History of Iran fleshes out this account with more detail when it indicates that:

> The new king (Phraataces) was driven from the throne in AD 4 and himself fled to Roman Syria, where he did not long survive. [13]

So the general opinion of historians is that Phraataces and Thea Muse ended up in Syria. But, apart from its close proximity to Parthia, why did the exiled royal couple choose Syria for their new residence? The answer to this question can probably be found in Josephus' *Antiquities* once more. Here, Josephus relates a story that Herod the Great's eastern border with Parthia was insecure. Since King Herod and King Phraates did not exactly see eye-to-eye, Herod was keen to settle some of his countrymen in Batanea, towards the east, to make this area more easy to defend.

Several locations are mentioned in the various texts, which lay to the east of Judaea and these are Gamala, Gaulanitis, Batanea and Trachonitis, and some of these locations will become important later in this research. Unfortunately, the precise geographical layout of many of these provinces and towns is unknown, but all of these areas lay to the east of the river Jordan and probably encompassed parts of what is now Jordan and Syria – between Amman and Damascus. Josephus says of this situation:

> Accordingly when (Herod) understood that there was a man that was a Jew was come out of Babylon, with five hundred horsemen, all of whom could shoot their arrows on horseback; and with a hundred of his relations, and had passed over the Euphrates and now abode at Antioch (in the north of the Levant opposite Cyprus). (Herod) sent for this man and promised to give him land in the area of Batanea ... he also promised to let him hold the country ... tax free. [J14]

Here we have a Jew from Babylon (Parthia) who was influential and powerful enough to own his own army, but nevertheless he was still evicted from Parthia and was forced to settle in lands to the east of the river Jordan that had been given to him by Herod. Given the modern political and theological map of Iraq (Babylon), which hardly seems very Jewish, this might sound like a fanciful tale; but in fact it is probably correct. The Jews had been (inadvertently) settled in Babylon by Nebuchadnezzar, who originally took them as captives. However, the Jewish community thrived in

Babylon and after they were set free by Cyrus the Great, many of them stayed on and became influential members of the Babylonian community, so it is not so unlikely that a Jew from across the Euphrates had a private army of 500 mounted archers.

In actual fact, the Jews of Iraq were a prominent feature of that country until the 1940s. However, the entire Arab world launched attacks against modern Israel in 1967 and 1973 (the Six Day and Yom Kippur wars), but were comprehensively beaten on both occasions by the Israelis. The result of these conflicts was the displacement of people throughout the region, with Palestinian exiles heading east and Iraqi Jews heading west. But while Israel accepted the Palestinian exiles back into the West Bank, the Iraqis refused to acknowledge the Jewish refugees; and in effect, the Iraqis had ethnically cleansed the entire Jewish population of Iraq. The Western press makes a great play on the plight of the displaced Palestinians, but for some reason ignores the Jewish refugees from the Arab lands of the Middle East.

It would seem that there were Jewish refugees from Babylon (Iraq) even at the turn of the first century AD, but who exactly was this 'influential Jew' with 500 mounted archers? Josephus says that his name was Zamaris, who had a son called Jachim and a grandson called Philip. Josephus is also saying that Zamaris and his men arrived in eastern Judaeo-Israel during the rule of Herod the Great, which would place this event in the years prior to 4 BC. Indeed the established date for Herod's annex of Trachonitis is about 25 BC.

This chronology would make it highly likely that this character called Zamaris was actually the Parthian prince called Tiridates, who temporarily became king of Parthia between 29 and 25 BC. Tiridates was, of course, thrown out of Parthia by Phraates IV, and so he would have been looking for lands to occupy during his exile. The account of Josephus would seem to be indicating that Tiridates fled to Antioch, but that Herod the Great gave him lands to the east of the Jordan to settle. The clue to Zamaris being one and the same as Tiridates is that Zamaris arrived in Judaeo-Syria with 500 mounted archers, and the name Tiridates means 'Great Archer' in Persian.

The only problem with this assertion is that it is unlikely that Tiridates, who was a Parthian prince, was a Jew. Having said this, the Jews were very influential in Parthia and it is known that a later king, Artabanus III, was crowned as king of Parthia by an influential Jew called Izates. In the circumstances, it is not so improbable that a Parthian prince had converted to Judaism.

It is also possible that Josephus' account has confused the exile of Prince Tiridates with the exile of Queen Thea Muse and King Phraataces.

Thea Muse was, of course, of Egyptian extract, and so she would have closely identified herself with the Judaism that was being practised in this era, as this early form of Judaism was distinctly Egyptian in its form, function and heritage. As the other books in this series have demonstrated, the Israelites were actually the Hyksos-Egyptians from Lower Egypt, and so their theology would have been distinctly Egyptian in nature. The biblical Book of Jeremiah makes this perfectly clear when it says that the Jews of the sixth century BC worshipped the Queen of Heaven, or the Queen of the Stars. [B15]

As we have already seen, the primary Queen of Heaven in Egypt was the goddess Isis, whose name was originally pronounced as Est or Ast 𓊨𓏏𓁐 . In later cultures and lands Isis became Astarte, Ishtar and Aphrodite. However, in the era of the biblical prophet Jeremiah, the Queen of Heaven who was most revered was the Queen of Sheba, whose name means the Queen of the Stars (Queen of Heaven) and who I have already identified as being Maachah Tamar II, the Egyptian daughter-wife of King David.

Even the monotheistic Judaism that we are more familiar with today was based upon the theology of the cult of Pharaoh Akhenaton, the 'heretic' pharaoh of the fourteenth century BC. I have already identified Akhenaton's brother, TuthMoses, as being the biblical Moses, which is why the hidden, singular deity of Akhenaton was called Aton and the hidden, singular Jewish god is sometimes called Adon.

So, in many respects Thea Muse's and Phraataces' Egyptian heritage could have identified them as being 'Jewish'; as many of the Jews of this era were similarly of Egyptian heritage. As the historian Strabo says of the people of Israel around the turn of the first century AD:

> This region lies towards the north; and it is inhabited ... by mixed stocks of people from Egyptian and Arabian and Phoenician tribes ... But though the inhabitants are mixed up thus, the most prevalent of the accredited reports in regard to the Temple at Jerusalem, represents the ancestors of the present Judaeans as Egyptians. [S16]

So the assertion that Zamaris was a Jew who fled from Babylon with 500 mounted archers could have been correct, for the flight of Queen Thea Muse Ourania and King Phraataces to Judaeo-Syria could have been interpreted in exactly this manner. The royal couple were certainly not of pure Parthian extract, and their incestuous marriage clearly marked them out as Egyptians [or Hyksos-Israelites]. More evidence for this will be given in later chapters. However, the fact that the Babylonians who settled in Batanea were most definitely something to do with Thea Muse and Phraataces can also be ascertained via a few pieces of interesting evidence.

Firstly, Thea Muse Ourania and Phraataces were the queen and king of Parthia. Although they had been exiled from that empire, they would undoubtedly have retained the support of some elements within the Parthian army. The primary armed forces in Parthia were the mounted archers, which is why the archer became a symbol of the nation. But the mention of a sizeable private army strongly suggests that this was a royal exile, and not the relocation of a disaffected baron. So if anyone could have left Babylon (Parthia) with 500 mounted archers and 100 relatives and officials – a sizeable retinue that does seem to be well in excess of the aspirations of any private individual – it would have been Queen Thea Muse and King Phraataces.

Secondly, there is the name of this Jewish exile who is supposed to have arrived with an army of mounted archers, which was Zamaris. The word *zamar* means 'bald' in both Hebrew and Persian. The Persian word *zamir* is quite explicit, referring to 'thin-haired', while the Hebrew version, *zamir* זמר, means 'prune', with close links to the concepts of 'woolly' and 'bristles'. In the circumstances, this is highly likely to have been an oblique reference to Julius Caesar, as the name Caesar means 'hair' in Latin and Julius was frequently ribbed about his receding hairline. While Prince Tiridates may have been linked to Augustus Caesar, who gave him sanctuary within the empire, the strongest link between a Caesar and a Parthian prince has to be between Julius Caesar and Phraataces. Given the new ancestry of Thea Muse being forged in these chapters, Phraataces would have been Julius' grandson and so Zamaris (the bald one) would have been an appropriate nickname, even though Phraataces himself was not in any way bald.

Thirdly, the most compelling piece of evidence – to prove that Thea Muse Ourania settled in this province called Batanea, to the east of the river Jordan – is that the alternative name for this region was Auranitis (Hauranitis). Indeed, the area is still known as the Hauran. Modern text books will say that the name Auranitis (Aurania) was derived from the Hebrew word *khavran* חורן meaning 'hollow' or 'cave'; however, this just has to be a convenient error as it does not even sound correct. The proper derivation is from the Hebrew *haran* הרן, which became the Greek *oranos* ορεινος, with both words meaning 'mountain'. However, it was from the sacred 'mountains' of Egypt, the pyramids, that an association between mountains and heavens was derived – an association that gave rise to the age-old adage 'as above, so below'. This argument is reinforced by the interpretation of John Lightfoot, the venerable seventeenth century theologian who said that:

> Mount Hauran (not the region called Hauran) is reckoned up amongst those

hills, at the top of which, by lifting up some flaming torches, the Jews were wont to give notice of the new year. [17] (Author's brackets.)

Although Lightfoot would not be aware of the deeper meaning of this celebration, since the Hyksos-Israelites were descended from Egypt, the original 'mountains' that were used in this ritual were located at Giza. The pyramids were the man-made mountains that reached out to the heavens, and the Great Pyramid [Mt Sinai] with its platform on its summit, may even have been the greatest astronomical observatory of the ancient world; from which torches could indeed be waved. It was through this symbolism that *oranos* ο ρ ε ι ν ο ς, meaning 'mountain', became *ouranos* or *auranos* ο υ ρ α ν ο ς meaning 'heaven'. So the lands to the east of the river Jordan were not named after a boring cave, but after the great, imperishable celestial heavens. In fact, to be more precise, the lands of Aurania (Auranitis) were not named after the heavens themselves, they were actually named after the queen who took up residence in this very location: Queen Thea Muse Aurania (Ourania), whose name could be interpreted as meaning 'the Queen of Heaven'.

Fig 18.   Painting adorning the Gornji Grad cathedral in Slovenia, which demonstrates how pyramid iconography can be covertly introduced into orthodox Christianity. See the book 'Jesus' for further examples.

Josephus' report about an exiled Parthian Jew, who fled to Judaeo-Syria with 500 mounted archers and 100 of his own family and courtiers, may well have been a reference to the exile of Queen Thea Muse Ourania and King Phraataces. That this extract was placed in the chapters in Josephus' *Antiquities* that deal with Herod the Great's reign may have been due to the fact that it was Herod Philip, the son of Herod the Great and the tetrarch of Syria, who subsequently ruled these very same lands to the east of the river Jordan. In other words, the exile of Zamaris probably occurred in AD 4 instead of 25 BC, and it was actually Herod the tetrarch (Herod Philip) who welcomed these exiles into the lands to the east of the river Jordan that became known as Batanea or Aurania (Auranitis). (The flight of a Prince Tiridates from Parthia to Syria in 25 BC may have be mistaken with the flight of another, better-known Prince Tiridates from Parthia to Syria in AD 36.)

If Zamaris' exile was in AD 4, then we now have a good idea of exactly where Thea Muse and Phraataces would have fled to. Herod Philip, being the ruler of the lands of modern Syria and Jordan, required a friendly military force to secure his eastern borders with Parthia, and who better to perform this task than an exiled Parthian prince (or king) who had just strolled into his realm with 500 mounted archers. The offer of lands free of tax to this royal exile would have been a small price to pay, considering the security they could offer to the eastern borders of Herod Philip's realm. The subsequent history of this region will fully support this assertion, as we shall see shortly.

Umm el-Jimal

Where exactly in the province of Batanea or Aurania did Thea Muse locate her new capital city? What we are looking for here is a new city that was founded in the first century AD; and bearing in mind the illustrious Egypto-Parthian ancestry of Thea Muse, perhaps we are also looking for a city that tried to reflect the former royal grandeur that she was used to. There is one such site in the Kingdom of Aurania, modern Hauran, and that is the long abandoned city of Umm el-Jimal, which is situated out on the vast rolling plains that lie to the east of modern Amman:

> Although it was continuously occupied for 800 years from the first century BC to the eighth century AD and again from World War I to the present, Umm el-Jimal shows no evidence of occupation before the first century, and it lay completely abandoned between AD 750 and the 20th century. [18]

The pottery stratigraphy of the site was quite conclusive in this respect.

Although early Roman pottery was found, it was all mixed with middle Roman pottery and so the earliest date for the settlement of this site would appear to be the turn of the first century AD. These dates should place this fine city, once home to some 5,000 or more inhabitants, well within the sphere of influence of the Nabataean kingdom, which resided just to the south of Aurania at Petra, and it is the Nabataeans who are regarded as the prime candidates for the founding of this city. However, the archaeology of the site simply fails to confirm this. Professor De Vries says of this lack of evidence:

> Consider this archaeological puzzle: the distinctive Nabataean pottery, so common at southern sites, is almost totally lacking at otherwise identifiable Nabataean sites such as Umm el-Jimal. [19]

If these people at Umm el-Jimal were not Nabataean, then where did they come from? There are many inscriptions on the site, which are mostly written in Greek, with only a few in Nabataean and one or two in Arabic. This may seem to count against an association with Thea Muse and Phraataces and their Egypto-Parthian exiles; but of course Thea Muse herself was the daughter of Cleopatra IV, who was a Ptolemaic queen whose first language was Greek. Furthermore, the Seleucid dynasties of Persia (Parthia) were also Greek, and no doubt many of the courtiers in Parthia still spoke Greek. This preference can be seen in the coins of Parthia, including those of Thea Muse and Phraataces, which have Greek inscriptions. This preference for the Greek language lasted right through the Arsacid dynasty, but later coins demonstrate that the Greek language was being lost, as the inscriptions are only of garbled Greek letters.

Greek had also become the common language of Israel/Syria, which is why the New Testament accounts were all written in Greek and the lands around Galilee to the west of Aurania were regarded as completely Hellenistic. However, while the predominant language of this area and of Umm el-Jimal in particular was definitely Greek, the names given in these inscriptions demonstrate that many of these people must have had Arabic or Aramaic origins. Despite this hint of a Greek-speaking Arabic (Parthian) heritage, the exact ancestry of this new town in Aurania remains elusive. Again, Professor De Vries says of this conundrum:

> Granted that the inhabitants were indigenous to the general area, we still ask, "Where did they come from?" and "Why did they settle here?" It is probable that they were simply nomads of the region attracted to a more sedentary life by the new stability of Roman order, perhaps even encouraged by the Roman authorities in the same way that modern Bedouin have been by the Jordanian Government. [22]

As we have already seen, the most likely explanation for the settlement of Umm el-Jimal is given in Josephus' *Antiquities*, where he clearly states that a man called Zamaris had fled from Parthia with 500 mounted archers and 100 close relations and courtiers. Herod the tetrarch (probably Herod Philip) had settled these refugees in Batanea, a location which we now know was almost identical to Auranitis (Aurania), in order to secure his eastern borders with Parthia. The archaeologists who have worked at Umm el-Jimal have recognised the strategic importance of the site, and they indicate that el-Jimal:

> ... fits well with the Roman development of a fortified frontier from Aqaba to the Euphrates, the Limes Arabicus, as a defense line against threats of nomadic raiding and Persian invasion. [23]

That Umm el-Jimal was a strategic frontier city is borne out by its extensive fortifications, and no doubt this city did indeed serve as a salient city that supplied the other smaller fortifications in the surrounding region. But this was not strictly speaking a Roman defensive system, it was actually Judaic, with the kings and regional commanders of the region being the Herod tetrarchs (Herod Archelous and Herod Philip). Although it has to be said that both Herod tetrarchs and their father Herod the Great were given control over these lands by Rome, and it was Rome who oversaw and occasionally underpinned the tetrarch's troop movements in the area and the wider political strategy of her eastern borders.

The ruins of Umm el-Jimal that are visible today are actually the remains of the Byzantine town that was built several centuries after the original settlement. In fact, it would appear that the location of the city moved by a few hundred meters, and the ruins of the old town were stripped away and reused in the new. The fact that many tombstones were reused as building material in the new Byzantine city may also point towards these new settlers being of different cultural origins, for they had no respect for the dead of the old town.

The exact nature of the old town is not fully understood as it is much ruined, however this was no mud-brick or wattle-and-daub village for rustics:

> ... the architecture is less elaborate than in the Byzantine town, but the place is extremely rich in high quality pottery, including much imported wares such as *terra siggilata*. The new balloon photographs reveal the intriguing possibility that the settlement may have been planned with a rectangular layout. [24]

The fact that the new inhabitants of this area had the resources to build an entire new city out of stone, while simultaneously importing luxury goods from the Roman empire, would suggest great wealth – the kind of wealth that an exiled royal family might have been able to take with them on their recent flight from Parthia. Also, the fact that these imported goods all appear to be Roman, while Parthia lay on the province's doorstep, would suggest that the town did not have trading relations with Parthia. Indeed, if this town was conceived, constructed and inhabited by Thea Muse and her fellow exiles from Parthia, this would not be so surprising.

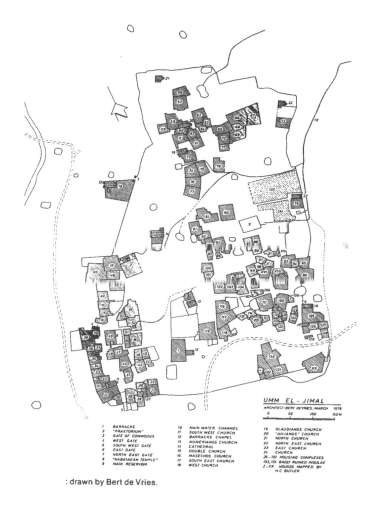

UMM EL - JIMAL

ARCHITECT: BERT DEVRIES, MARCH 1978

1 BARRACKS	10 MAIN WATER CHANNEL	19 KLAUDIANOS CHURCH
2 "PRAETORIUM"	11 SOUTH WEST CHURCH	20 "JULIANOS" CHURCH
3 GATE OF COMMODUS	12 BARRACKS CHAPEL	21 NORTH CHURCH
4 WEST GATE	13 NUMERIANOS CHURCH	22 NORTH EAST CHURCH
5 SOUTH WEST GATE	14 CATHEDRAL	23 EAST CHURCH
6 EAST GATE	15 DOUBLE CHURCH	24 CHURCH
7 NORTH EAST GATE	16 MASECHOS CHURCH	25 - 132 HOUSING COMPLEXES
8 "NABATAEAN TEMPLE"	17 SOUTH EAST CHURCH	133,134 BADLY RUINED INSULAE
9 MAIN RESERVOIR	18 WEST CHURCH	I - XX HOUSES MAPPED BY H.C. BUTLER

: drawn by Bert de Vries.

Fig 19. Map of the city of Umm el-Jimal in Aurania (modern Hauran) – the Mother of Egypt and birthplace of the biblical Jesus.

The ruins that remain at the site today are extensive and while they are not so ornate and decorative as the Roman city in nearby Jerash, the ruins suggest that both the old and the new cities were well constructed and relatively luxurious. There are several enormous water storage cisterns that would have provided generous supplies of water during the long, dry summers, while many of the houses appear to have been three or four storeys high; the latter feature being similar to the high-rise apartments constructed in Saba, in modern Yemen.

The livestock of the Jimalians were also well provided for, with accommodation being constructed for the flocks and herds within each house. This would again indicate that the Jimalians had a siege mentality of the inhabitants of a border-fortress city, for even their livestock had to be corralled within the city walls. The following description of these animal pens and stalls may be of importance in later chapters:

> In most cases, a large portion of the bottom floor (of each building) was used to house animals. There are rooms with well-constructed mangers, often with tethering devices for large animals (donkeys, horses, cows), and bigger rooms for the simple indoor penning of smaller animals (sheep, goats). [25]

The origins of the name of Umm el-Jimal remains a mystery, and Professor Howard Butler, who did much of the early archaeology of this site, says of the name for this town:

> This ancient ruined city has long been called by the Arabs Umm idj-Djimal (Umm el-Jimal), which, being translated, is 'Mother of Camels'.... It is not definitely known what the city was called in Roman or early Christian times; but 'Mother of Camels' it is now, and no name could fit it better, especially in the spring time when the Bedouin, with hundreds of breeding camels, pitch their tents around the walls of the city. [26]

As Professor De Vries points out, the name of a town is an important element, because unless its name is known it cannot be placed within the historical record with any certainty. Was it the town of Surattha from Ptolemy's *Geography?* Or was it perhaps the town of Thainatha from the *Notitia Dignitatum?* The truth is that, despite Umm el-Jimal being quite a substantial settlement, nobody knows what it was originally called, although it is known that the present name goes back at least to the early nineteenth century.

So, Umm el-Jimal currently remains aloof from the historical record because its original name is unknown. Or is it? What if the Arabic name for the town *is* the original? What if it may be linked to the biblical town of

Gamala? This possibility has been largely discounted because the name does not entirely fit the location. 'Mother of Camels' might suggest a Bedouin trading post or a center of some caravan route, which Umm el-Jimal was not (originally). Rather, the town was a strategic frontier post, a local military supply center, and in the later Byzantine era it became a devout Christian city, containing no less than fifteen Christian churches. So why then, apart from the odd nomadic traders on their camels passing by, was the town called Jimal, meaning 'camel'?

The answer probably lies in the Egyptian interpretation of this word, for the Arabic word for camel was probably derived from the Egyptian original, which was *kamar (kamal)* 〰🐦🐍🐦⊤🦅. However, this Egyptian word for a camel had another meaning, and that was Kam 🐦🐍⊗ which referred to the country of Egypt itself. In other words, an alternative rendering for Umm el-Jimal might well be 'Mother of Egypt'. Cleopatra VII was known as the Isis of Egypt, and since Isis was the mother of all living things, then it is likely that Cleopatra was also known as the Mother of Egypt. The possibility exists, therefore, that Cleopatra's daughter, Thea Muse Ourania, inherited this title and used it for the new town she founded in exile. And so the town of Umm el-Jimal in Aurania was actually the town of Umm el-Kam(el) in Ourania – the Mother of Egypt in the Kingdom of Thea Muse Ourania.

Julia

Finally, there is the interesting case of the name for one of the Byzantine churches in Umm el-Jimal. Now these churches were built many centuries after Thea Muse and should have had nothing directly to do with these events, except that one of the inscriptions on a window lintel was rather older than it was first thought to be:

> In 1956 G Corbett did an architectural study of the 'Julianos' Church in order to test Butler's conclusion that this church had been built in AD 344. Corbett concluded that the Julianos Inscription from which the date was derived was actually a funerary inscription reused secondarily in the building.[77]

So an old tombstone had been reused in the construction of a later Byzantine church, and this tombstone was dedicated to someone called Julianos, a Greek rendering of the Latin Julia. It may or may not be coincidental, but the daughter of Thea Muse was called Julia Ourania. Has the tombstone of Thea Muse's daughter been discovered in Umm el-Jimal?

Fig 20. The Julianos inscription at Umm el-Jimal.

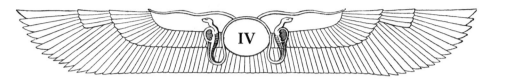

Fourth Sect of Judaism

The next important character of note in this region and era springs, once more, from the lands to the east of the river Jordan. His name is given as Judas the Gaulonite, who came to prominence at about the time of the Jewish taxation under the Roman consul Cyrenius (Quirinius), in about AD 6. This is the taxation event that is mentioned in the biblical account of the birth of Jesus:

> And it came to pass in those days, that there went out a decree from Caesar Augustus, that all the world should be taxed. (And this taxing was first made when Cyrenius was governor of Syria.) And all went to be taxed, every one into his own city. And Joseph also went up from Galilee ... to be taxed with Mary his espoused wife, being great with child. And so it was, that, while they were there, the days were accomplished that she should be delivered. [B1]

Note here that the governor in charge of the taxation was Cyrenius, who was based in Syria, not Judaea. This may be an important point in the arguments to come. So it was during this taxation census that the biblical Jesus was said to have been born, or in other words, Jesus was born in AD 6. This verse does, of course, greatly conflict with the accounts that say that Jesus was threatened by King Herod the Great, and his reported murder of all the infants in Bethlehem; an event which, if it ever occurred, would place the birth of Jesus just prior to 4 BC.

This topic has been widely debated in my and other works and so I don't propose to go into great detail here. Suffice it to say that Herod the Great did murder a number of children because of a dispute over the royal succession, but these were all his own. The fact that Jesus is said to have been threatened by this royal infanticide again demonstrates that he was of royal blood.

Having said this, it is more likely that Jesus was born during the great taxation under Cyrenius, and so we need to account for this error. The differing birth dates being given in the biblical account may be due to many reasons, but one possibility is that, since Jesus had brothers, this may be a record of two sons being born to Mary: one in 4 BC, the other in AD 6. Alternatively, the account in Matthew about Herod killing the children may be referring to Herod Archelous, the son of King Herod the Great, who was Tetrarch (king) of Judaea from 4 BC to AD 6. As this rather short reign-length suggests, Archelous was quickly deposed for being as much of a tyrant as his father was in his later years, so this confusion between the tyrannical Herod Archelous and the equally tyrannical Herod the Great is always possible.

This new character in our saga, Judas, came to power during this great taxation under Cyrenius and he was known as the Gaulonite; that is, someone from the Golan Heights that lay to the east of the Sea of Galilee. In other words, Judas was from almost exactly the same area as the exiled Prince Zamaris from Parthia, who had settled his people to the east of the Jordan in Batanea, or Auranitis (Aurania). That there is a link between these two characters is implied by their common concerns. It was stressed by Josephus Flavius that Prince Zamaris was given the lands of Batanea tax free, in order to protect Herod's eastern borders from attacks by the Parthians. Yet Judas the Gaulonite (or Judas of Gamala) came to power as part of a powerful Jewish faction who were fighting the new Roman taxation by Cyrenius.

> Judas, a Gaulonite of the city of Gamala ... became zealous to draw the people to revolt, who both said that this taxation was no better than an introduction to slavery, and exhorted the nation to assert their liberty. [J2]

In other words, both Zamaris and Judas arose from the same region and both had the same political concerns: taxation and independence, both from Jerusalem and from Rome. In addition, this same Judas was also said to be a Galilean from the city of Gamala, which is interesting as Galilee and Gamala are on opposite banks of the Jordan and are therefore not entirely compatible with each other.

So was Judas simply a nickname for Zamaris? Well, Ioudas (Judas) Ιουδας is simply a Greek rendering of the Hebrew word for a Jew. Since Zamaris was pointedly said to have been a Jew, and an exotic Babylonian Jew no less, then he may well have been called 'the Jew' as a common nickname. So yes, this Judas of Gamala (Judas the Gaulonite) may well have simply been another name for Zamaris – the Babylonian Jew who arrived in Judaeo-Syria with 500 mounted archers and 100 relatives and courtiers, and who may have founded the city in Batanea called Umm el-Jimal. While this is all a little speculative at present, there is another reference to Judas of Gamala in the Acts of the Apostles that sheds some more light on the matter:

> Then stood there up one in the council, a Pharisee, named Gamaliel, a doctor of the law, had in reputation among all the people, and commanded to put the apostles forth a little leniency ... For before these days rose up Theudas, boasting himself to be somebody; to whom a number of men, about four hundred, joined themselves: who was slain; and all, as many as obeyed him, were scattered, and brought to nought. After this man rose up Judas of Galilee (Gamala) in the days of the taxing, and drew away much people after him: he also perished; and all, even as many as obeyed him, were dispersed. [B3]

This indicates that before Judas there was another revolutionary called Theudas Θευδας. But, as the theologian Adam Clarke acknowledges, Theudas is probably a corruption of the name Judas. So here we have two similar characters, possibly a father and son, both of whom were revolutionaries and both were known as being prominent Jews from Gamala. Note that the man defending the disciples was a man called Gamaliel; a name derived from the root *gamal* meaning 'camel', as is the city of Gamala. In the circumstances, this 'name' has to be a reference to an important person from Gamala, for the text is talking about Judas of Gamala. This Pharisee called Gamaliel may have been Zamaris' compatriot, Zadok the Pharisee. The obvious link here between the city of Gamala and the city of Umm el-Jimal (Gamal) will be explored later.

The point of this particular investigation is that this would seem to be the same Judas of Gamala who is mentioned later as being the leader of the 'fourth sect' of Judaism, and who is likely to have been from Babylon (Parthia). If so, it would seem that there were three generations of revolutionaries, who were known as Zamaris, Jacim and Philip (by Josephus Flavius) or Theudas and Judas (according to the author of Acts), who were important religious leaders of a new sect of Judaism, and who were living in Gamala, a city that resided in Batanea (or Aurania). The fact that these people were said by Josephus to be Babylonians, strongly links them with the Parthian exiles of Thea Muse. However, the fact that these religious revolutionaries lived in Batanea also strongly links them with the gospel accounts, as we shall see shortly.

This confusion of locations is not exactly a minor point, to be glossed over as a scribe's transcription error of no importance. Here is a family that may well link the Parthian exiles of Thea Muse with the family of Jesus, and so what we now need is a reference to the biblical Jesus that places him in the same context; one that demonstrates that he too was related in some fashion to the town of Gamala. Strange as it may seem, there was a later character who was given the exact same title as Judas of Gamala, but this character was much better known – for this revolutionary from Gamala was indeed called Jesus. As I have pointed out in the book *Jesus*, there were several Jesuses mentioned in the works of Josephus Flavius, one of whom was called Jesus of Gamala and another who was called Jesus of Sapphias:* the governor of Tiberias who came from Galilee.

However, upon further research, I have already demonstrated that these two Jesuses were actually the same person, and in addition they also seem to be inextricably linked to the biblical Jesus. Thus we have a situation where Judas the Gaulonite was from Gamala and Galilee while the biblical Jesus was also from Gamala and Galilee. But these two characters were not the same individual, as this Judas came to power in about AD 6 and the biblical Jesus was not at his peak of influence until about AD 60. (The book *Jesus* explains this later date, rather than the orthodox AD 30.)

There is the possibility, however, that these two characters – Judas of Gamala and Galilee [Zamaris] and Jesus of Gamala and Galilee [Jesus] were related; perhaps even father and son. Evidence for this can be seen in the name of Zamaris' son, who was called Jacim. The name Jacim is derived from the Greek *jacin* υακιν meaning 'sapphire', and in a similar fashion I have already identified the biblical Jesus with Josephus Flavius' character who was called Jesus of Sapphias. Thus the son of Zamaris appears to have had the same name as Jesus himself, and so Jesus of Sapphias may have referred to 'Jesus whose mother was called Sapphias (Sapphira)'. The reference to a sapphire may well relate to Jesus mother, Mary, who is always identified with the colour blue, as we shall see.

Likewise, the reference to Galilee may not be exactly what it seems either. Just as the biblical authorities like to persuade us that Jesus came from Nazareth, when that town did not exist in that era, they also like to imply that Jesus came from Galilee. But the strange linking of Judas the Galilean, who was nevertheless from across the river Jordan in Gamala, strongly suggests that the term Galilee did not refer to a location; for Gamala

---

* I had previously thought that the term Sapphias was derived from the city of Sepphoris in Galillee. However, Sapphira Σαπφειρη was the wife of Ananias and this couple were mentioned directly before the character called Judas of Gamala in Acts 5:37. Since Ananias was simply a priestly title, Judas and Ananias may have been one and the same, and thus this Jesus was probably the son of Sapphira (the blue lady) and Ananias.

and Galilee were miles apart. But if Galilee was not a reference to the Sea of Galilee, then what did it mean? Well, in actual fact, the name Galilee is actually taken from the Greek *galilaia* γαλιλαια, which means 'circle'.

Therefore, there are two alternatives for the true meaning of *galilee* in this context. Firstly, it may simply refer to a revolutionary or a fanatic. Note that exactly the same term is given today to a person or society that upsets the social apple-cart. A revolution tends to turn a society completely around, and so the proletariat become the leaders and the leaders become the proletariat. In other words, a revolution makes society revolve in a circle, or in a *galilee*. Thus the title 'Jesus the Galilean' may simply refer to 'Jesus the Revolutionary', the Che Guevara of first century Judaeo-Israel.

Alternatively, having written so much about the circling rituals of the Hyksos-Israelite people, it is also possible that this term refers to this circling ritual. This ritual is still performed today, of course, but it is now to be found in the Al-Haram mosque at Mecca rather than in Israel or Egypt. That both Judas of Gamala and Jesus of Gamala may have been involved in these same circling rituals further strengthens the links between the two characters. Also, the fact that these circling rituals survived more openly in the lands of Parthia, rather than in the Judaeo-Christian West, likewise strengthens their links to Parthia.

However, the circling rituals did not die out completely in the West, for circling is also a central part of masonic ritual, where it is known as the 'first point' or the god principle. This is the reason for early Templar churches being circular – as was the Christian cathedral of Aya Sophia in Istanbul and the later Templar church in the Inner Temple of London so that circular perambulations of the church could take place. In masonic ritual, however, it is made rather more obvious that this circling ritual is intended to represent the circuit of the Sun, planets and stars.

It is probably just one of those quirks of coincidence that the great sixteenth century astronomer, Galileo Galilei was named after the circling motion of the moons and planets that he eventually studied. (His father was a mathematician, which may explain the coincidence.)

Bethany

If these two influential characters, Zamaris and Jesus, were related, then this does infer that the biblical Jesus came from the same location as the exiled Thea Muse and Phraataces. It would appear that all of these characters were from Gamala and the lands to the east of the Jordan – in other words, they were from Batanea or Auranitis (Aurania, the modern Hauran). While this assertion may still seem speculative at present,

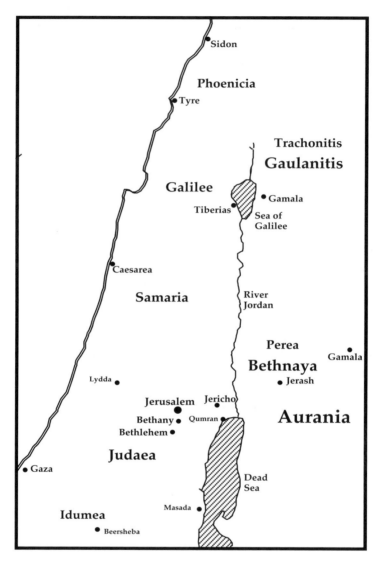

Fig 24.   Map of first century Syrio-Judaea.

especially in regard to the biblical Jesus, the evidence for this claim is to be found once more in the Gospels:

> And being in Bethany in the house of Simon the leper, as he (Jesus) sat among them, there came a woman having an alabaster box of ointment of spikenard very precious; and she brake the box, and poured it on his head. [B4]

As ever with these biblical verses, one needs to understand the background to the story before the correct translation can be made. In this case, the term 'leper' does not refer to a disease, but rather to a religious sect. Simon was actually called *lepros* λεπρος meaning 'scaly', and this is actually a covert reference to a fish – the sign of the later Christian sect. In fact, since the term Nazarene has much the same meaning in Arabic, Simon the 'leper' was just being called the Nazarene here, the same as Jesus was. See the book *Jesus* for more details on this fish symbolism and its connection with the zodiac.

More importantly, however, the woman with the alabaster jar in this verse was, of course, Mary Magdalene. But Mary has already been shown in many works to have been the wife of Jesus and, in addition, I have also demonstrated that Mary was the sister-wife of Jesus. While this may have seemed like a fanciful marital union when I penned this hypothesis many years ago in the book *Jesus*, the links that are being demonstrated here between Thea Muse and the biblical family make this incestuous union a near certainty. Clearly, Thea Muse and Phraataces were adhering to the Egyptian rules of consanguinity, when the mother married her son; and so for this particular royal family, the marriage between Jesus and his sister Mary would have been a perfectly normal (even mandatory) event.

What this sibling marriages does, however, is to strengthen the links between Jesus and this favourite house at Bethany, which was owned by Simon the Leper [Simon the Nazarene]. It is clear that Mary and Martha lived at this house in Bethany and it is also clear that this important but shadowy character called Mary of Bethany was, in fact, Mary Magdalene. It is already obvious from the many biblical citations that this house at Bethany was a favourite place for Jesus and his disciples to stay; but if Mary Magdalene was Jesus' sister then the house at Bethany probably belonged to Jesus' and Mary's brother, Simon.

In short, it would seem that Jesus and Mary Magdalene came from Bethany, and yet the lands that were given to the exiled Parthians (Queen Thea Muse and King Phraataces-Zamaris) were known as Batanea. However, it would only take a simple consonant change from a 't' to a 'th' for Batanea to become Bethanya, or Bethany. Thus Mary of Bethany was not from a Bethany that lay close to Jerusalem, but from Bethanya, the province which had been created and settled by the exiled Parthians. Incidentally, it is likely that Bethanya was the name of an administrative region encompassing all of Gamala, Gaulanitis and Trachonitis, and so it was relatively large in extent.

The classical biblical town of Bethany is said to have been located just outside Jerusalem on the road to Jericho, which is why I have previously said that this was Mary's (and Jesus') Jerusalem residence, within easy commuting distance of the city. But if Jesus was from Gamala, then this house near Jerusalem was a long way from home and a little out of place in the biblical texts. The possibility that Bethany referred instead to Bethanya would clear up this confusion in an instant, for Gamala was a major town in the province of Bethanya. The fact that it was this eastern Bethany that was intended by the gospels, and not the location near Jerusalem, is confirmed to us by the accounts relating to John the Baptist. It is said of John that:

> These things were done in Bethany Βηθανια beyond the Jordan, where John was baptising. [B5]

Readers with a King James Bible will find that this town has been translated as Bethabara βηθαβαρα, meaning 'the crossing over the Jordan'. However, it has been established by theologians that, of all the ancient versions of the Bible that are still extant, the vast majority use the name Bethany instead of Bethabara. This slip of the pen in one or two versions of the New Testament would have been convenient, had it not been spotted and corrected in time (in a more enlightened era); for the incorrect name of Bethabara keeps the biblical events close to Jerusalem and away from their true location to the east of the river Jordan.

Having sorted out this little error, it would seem the true import of the gospels is that John the Baptist was resident at this Bethany (alias Bethanya or Aurania) to the east of the river Jordan – which is why there is a modern tourist trap just east of the river Jordan that claims to be the place of Jesus' baptism. However, this lucrative tourist trap fails to understand that Bethanya was an administrative region, not a specific location or town, and so this location conveniently close to the Jordan is unlikely to be the historical location for the baptism of Jesus. In fact, since the city of Umm el-Jimal contains a number of cisterns, one of which is so large that it looks very much like an Egyptian ritual bathing pool, the baptism of Jesus could have taken place many miles from the river Jordan.

Since Jesus was baptised in this region called Bethanya, it is this region and not the Bethany near Jerusalem that has to be central to the New Testament story. Thus, in one swift stroke of a correction marker, many of the New Testament accounts and stories have been wrenched eastwards, away from Jerusalem and towards the east. In fact, so far eastwards have they travelled, that all of the stories about Mary, Martha and Lazarus are likely to have occurred to the east of the river Jordan in Bethanya (Aurania).

The biblical Concordance has assumed that this location called Bethany was the name of a town. But since it was located to the east of the Jordan, in the province of Bethanya, it could simply have been a reference to the whole province rather than a town. Indeed, since Bethany was supposed to be one of the largest towns in this province, both John and Mary may well have been resident in the town of Gamala, which resided in the province of Bethanya (Bethany). So Mary of Bethany may have been Mary of Gamala. Since we have just seen that the biblical Jesus was sometimes called Jesus of Gamala, and he was also the brother-husband of Mary, this would make a great deal of sense.

When I wrote the book *Jesus*, I did wonder for a long time why I had ended up with a brother (Jesus) whose family home was in Gamala and his sister (Mary Magdalene) whose family home was near Jerusalem. This was simply one of many loose ends that I was unable to clear up at the time, but the rest of the underlying analysis was so convincing that it had to be based on a historical truth. Now, in the light of further research and revelations, it would seem that this separation was not an issue at all, for the location called Bethany has now taken a giant leap across to Syrio-Judaea and into Bethanya or Aurania, the province in which the city of Gamala resided.

That the true home of Jesus and his family should be relocated out onto the plains of Aurania, the modern Hauran to the east of the city of Amman, is reinforced by the Tarmida,* one of the holy books of the Mandaeans, the secretive sect of proto-Christians who now inhabit the marshlands of Iraq (the Marsh Arabs). This rather secretive work is known, by its colophons, to date from the Parthian period; and it begins its narrative just before the life of Jesus. Its opening passages say:

> The interior of the Harran (ie Hauran) admitted them, that city which has Nasurai in it, so that there should not be a road (passage?) for the kings of the Chaldeans (Parthians). [6]

Here, in the first sections of the Tarmida, seems to be an accurate description of the precise situation I have proposed for the city of Umm el-Jimal. The interior of the Hauran (Aurania or Haurania) is where Umm el-Jimal is located, and its function was indeed to act as a frontier town and prevent the passage of the Parthian army into Syria and Judaea. But it would seem that within this city were the Nasurai people, which just has to be a corruption of the Arabic term 'Nasrani' meaning 'Christian'. The term 'Nasurai' was also an early name for the Mandaeans, and since the Mandaeans are vaguely a Christian sect who appear to venerate John the Baptist and regard Jesus as a false prophet (an accusation that we have already seen was rife in the first century AD), the term Nasurai must refer to an early form of 'Christianity'. Now while it may be claimed that a sect that denies the divinity of Jesus cannot be Christian in the true sense of the word, the Knights Templar were

---

* Was the name for the Tarmida derived from the Judaic Talmud?

also reputed to have followed a version of the Mandaean creed, and this belief system formed a part of the reasoning for the Catholic witch-hunt against them. Although their beliefs may not have been wholly orthodox, the Templars would still have considered themselves to be 'Christian'.

As far as the import of this quote is concerned, while we know that the city of Umm el-Jimal was definitely a Christian city during the Byzantine era, as it contains sixteen Byzantine Christian churches, this passage in the Mandaean's holy book comes immediately before the birth of Jesus. If the Mandaean chronology is correct, then they are indicating that the early Christians came from Umm el-Jimal, just as I have suspected. Since Umm el-Jimal lies within Aurania, or the province of Thea Muse Ourania (Aurania), this also links the biblical story with Thea Muse and Phraataces.

Later passages in the Tarmida indicate that the Nasurai (the early Mandaean 'Christians') were very close to the biblical family, as the Nasurai were persecuted along with Jesus' disciples. These passages also claim that some of the ancestors and rituals of the Mandaeans came from Egypt, which would make sense in terms of Thea Muse being an Egyptian princess. However, the evidence then gets even more intriguing, for the texts go on to identify the Nasurai with the Parthians!

> The importance of this document (the Tarmida) lies in the implication that the Nasurai are identical with the Parthians, since the latter correspond with the Ardban Malka (the king of the Nasurai). [7]

Now this is very interesting, for the Nasurai (an early Christian sect) are being described as being Parthian; and their king is said to be Ardban, who we can confidently identify as Artabanus II of Parthia, who ruled from about AD 10 to AD 38. So, this document appears to claim that many of the early Christians were also Parthians, and yet this would only make sense if the biblical family were descended from Thea Muse, as has been proposed. But why, in this case, was the king of the Nasurai identified with Artabanus and not Jesus?

The answer to this question has to be that there were at least three waves of Parthian exiles into Syrio-Judaea – ranging from King Tiridates and King Phraataces to King Vonones I, the prince who Augustus set upon the throne of Parthia after Thea Muse and Phraataces were exiled – and not all of these exiles from Parthia believed that Jesus was a rightful Parthian prince. We know that this is true of the Nasurai (the Mandaeans), for they venerated John the Baptist as a great prophet, whatever his ancestry may have been, but not Jesus, who was regarded as the Egyptian False Prophet. Quite obviously, Thea Muse Ourania and Phraataces were having an uphill struggle to convince everyone, even from among their own exiled community, that their descendants should be the rightful claimants to the throne – a point that the New Testament also makes clear.

Nevertheless, the evidence from these secretive Mandaean texts clearly supports the argument that the early Christians were related to the Parthians, and these texts also support the

Fig 25.   The mountain-top citadel of Gamala.

notion that the original location for these early Christians was the city of Umm el-Jimal in the Hauran (Aurania or Bethanya, the province of Thea Muse Ourania).

Gamala

There is one other point that needs to be cleared up, in regard to the original location for the family of Jesus, and that is the precise location of the biblical town of Gamala; the town that both Judas and Jesus appear to have been most closely connected with. It would seem that Gamala was named after the Hebrew *gamal* גמל meaning 'camel'; and so, just like the frontier town of Umm el-Jimal (Gamal) that was discussed extensively in the last chapter, the biblical town of Gamala was also named after a camel [or Egypt]. So was Gamala the same town as Umm el-Jimal?

Unfortunately for this idea, Josephus Flavius gives us a very good description of Gamala, and the great siege of the town by the Romans in AD 67. Gamala is said to have been a mountain-top refuge to the east of the Sea of Galilee, an invincible Masada of the north. Just such a fortress was recently discovered and excavated by Israeli archaeologists, and this fortress does, indeed, appear to have been Josephus' citadel of Gamala. It even comes complete with a breach in the defensive wall and piles of used Roman *balista* stones, just as Josephus recounts:

> The remains of the city are located on a rocky basalt ridge surrounded by
> deep gorges, with a shallow saddle separating it from the rest of the ridge,

> providing the city with outstanding defensive advantages. The top of the hill
> is narrow and pointed, creating a very steep slope in the north; the city was
> built on the more graduated southern slope. [8]

The geography of this mountain citadel fits Josephus' description of Gamala
like a glove, and the reason it was called Gamala is because it was built upon
two hilltops – like the paired humps of a Bactrian camel. However, it is
always possible that there were two Gamalas (as, indeed, there are to this
day), because although this Gamala to the east of the Sea of Galilee is a fine
location for a citadel, it is a truly terrible location for 500 mounted archers. In
another section, Josephus says of Gamala:

> King Herod Agrippa* also bid Philip to take some horsemen with him, and to
> go quickly to the citadel of Gamala, and to bring out thence all his domestics,
> and to restore the Babylonians to Batanea again. He also gave it him in charge
> to take all possible care that none of his subjects should be guilty of making
> any innovation. Accordingly, upon these directions from the king, he made
> haste to do what he was commanded. [9]

Now this Philip was the son of Jacim and the grandson of Zamaris, the
Babylonian Jew who fled to Syrio-Judaea with 500 mounted archers and
who settled his people in Batanea (Bethanya or Aurania). Note the mention
of Babylonians once more, for this event occurred one or two generations
later and yet these people were still known for being Babylonians (or
Parthians), as were Thea Muse and Phraataces.

    Philip, the grandson of Zamaris, still appears to have had his
cavalry forces, but the mountain-top citadel of Gamala, which was just
mentioned, is most definitely not a place for 500 mounted archers. Cavalry
were the light tanks of the Roman and Medieval army and their whole
rationale was built around their mobility and manoeuvrability; to surprise
the enemy with their speed; to dash in, strike and retire, ready to strike again
at will. To locate such a mobile force among the goat-tracks of a precipitous
mountain – and this citadel of Gamala is truly precipitous – would be
madness in the extreme. I have no doubt that Zamaris would have chosen
the city of Gamala on the plains of Aurania (or Bethanya) for his new capital
city, rather than the inhospitable slopes of the Gamala citadel.

    On the plains of Aurania (Bethanya) there was good grazing for

---

* Herod Agrippa, a son of Aristobulus, reigned in Bethanya (Aurania) after the
death of Herod Philip in AD 37. He also took over the rule of Galilee-Israel after the
death of Herod Antipas in AD 39.

goats and sheep, while the fertile, volcanic soil that covers the undulating hills around Umm el-Jimal is also good for growing grain – despite the low rainfall. Even today, the rolling hills around the city are cultivated with grain; and while the resulting crop-yields would not be as dense as among the south downs of England, there are large areas of land to be farmed in the modern Hauran. In addition, the irrigation systems the newcomers had built around the town of Umm el-Jimal probably afforded the farming of a few cash crops, just as some of the small farming settlements in the area do today. Indeed, the climate, agriculture, economy and architecture of this Gamala of the plains (Umm el-Jimal) was not unlike the city of Marib in Saba. The history of Marib, and its links with Judaism, have already been debated at length in the book *Solomon*.

In addition, the fortress of Gamala on the plains of Aurania would have allowed Zamaris' (and Philip's) mounted archers to sally out across the fast open ground to strike at an approaching enemy, before retiring once more behind the city's secure walls. These rolling hills are ideal cavalry country, and Judaea's eastern borders would have been much better protected by a frontier town like this Gamala of the plains, than a few frightened forces holed up in a remote mountain-top citadel. It may well be that there were two towns to the east of the Jordan called Gamala, but the mountain-top citadel close to the Sea of Galilee was technically in Gaulanitis. The Gamala of Bethanya (Bethany) and Aurania (Ourania) is much more likely to have been the Gamala of the plains – Umm el-Jimal (Umm el-Gamal).

Fig 26. The ruined city of Umm el-Jimal.

The fourth creed

This link between the historical Bethanya and the biblical Bethany means that the whole thrust of the biblical texts shift eastwards. The traditional interpretation of the New Testament is that nearly all of the events took place in either Jerusalem or Galilee. But now it would seem that some of these references to Galilee may pertain to a revolutionary sect, or perhaps even to a circling ritual; and it would also appear that many of the key players in the biblical saga were actually associated with the province of Bethanya, which lies to the east of the river Jordan. This growing and compelling link between the Parthians in Bethanya, Judas of Gamala, Jesus of Gamala and many of the prime characters in the New Testament narrative is very interesting; so perhaps we should look further at the aims and ambitions of this Judas of Gamala.

Perhaps the most important aspect in the accounts, regarding Judas of Gamala, is that he set up an entirely new sect of Judaism. What we were looking for, in our quest to find the true ancestry of Jesus, was a radical secular and religious leader who started a new Judaic philosophy in the early part of the first century AD, and here in the accounts of Judas of Gamala we find exactly such an individual:

> For Judas ... who created a <u>fourth</u> philosophic sect among us, and had a great many followers therein, filled our civil government with tumults ... by this system of philosophy, which we were before unacquainted. [J12]

In his comprehensive account of first century Judaea, the historian Josephus Flavius diligently notes the beliefs of the three main sects of Judaism – the Pharisees, the Sadducees and the Essene. It was always a problem trying to decide to which of these sects the biblical Jesus belonged. However, here we have a new 'fourth sect' that appears to be equally as radical as the Essene and very similar indeed to the creed of Jesus and James. Josephus' discourse on this fourth sect of Judaism indicates that they were similar to the Pharisees, but that they valued liberty and dedication to god and would call no man 'lord'. They were also said to be unafraid of death and demonstrated an indifference to pain. Does any of this sound familiar?

The sect that Jesus and his brother James led has always appeared to have had similarities with and links to the radical Essene sect who resided at the desert 'monastery' of Qumran; especially as a number of Zealots were numbered among the biblical disciples, including Simon Zelotes (Simon the Zealot, who was probably Simon the Leper). However, as we have seen, the principal compatriot of Judas of Gamala was one Sadduc, a name which, in its original Hebrew spelling, is the name Zadok. As it happens, the Manual of Discipline in the Dead Sea Scrolls calls the Essene sect the Sons of Zadok, and so the Essene may have been a later, even more radical, offshoot of Judas' 'fourth creed'. If the Church of Jesus was related to, or the same as, the fourth Judaic sect of Judas of Gamala, then it should be of no surprise that it also displayed similarities with one of its later offshoots. This similarity would also strengthen the links between Judas of Gamala and Jesus of Gamala [the biblical Jesus].

The fourth sect of Judaism sprang from the tax-free province of Bethanya (Aurania) to the east of the river Jordan, which had originally been settled by Zamaris [Phraataces and Thea Muse Ourania]. Given the tax-free status of this province, it is not surprising that the primary complaint of the later Judas of Gamala, the founding father of the fourth sect, was in regard to the new Roman taxes that were being imposed upon the region by the Roman consul Cyrenius. In a similar fashion, when the Jerusalem priesthood tried to entrap Jesus, the primary question was again on the subject of taxes:

> Then went the Pharisees, and took counsel how they might entangle him in his talk. Tell us therefore, What thinkest thou? Is it lawful to give tribute (taxes) unto Caesar, or not? But Jesus perceived their wickedness, and said ... Render therefore unto Caesar the things which are Caesar's; and unto God the things that are God's. [B13]

Note that Jesus did not necessarily believe what he said, he just 'perceived their wickedness' and gave a typical dissembling, political reply. Perhaps a better illustration of Jesus' thoughts on the matter of taxation is to be found in this quote:

> And when (Jesus) had made a scourge of small cords, he drove them all out of the temple, and the sheep, and the oxen; and poured out the changers' money, and overthrew the tables. [B14]

This may have been an act designed to cleanse the Temple of money-changers, but it was also an act against the tyranny of the collection of tax and interest by the Temple authorities in Jerusalem. This philosophy is again directly in line with the philosophy of the fourth sect of Judas of Gamala, who were protesting about taxation.

Having said this, I have no doubt that Judas of Gamala required taxes of his own to maintain the small kingdom of Bethanya (Aurania) and its independent army, but since he had been promised that Bethanya would remain free from Judaean (and Roman) taxes, he was not about to let that tax-free status be revoked just because there was a new king or governor in Syria.

The teachings of this new fourth sect of Judaism seem to be familiar too. As we have already seen, Josephus Flavius says of them that:

> They say that god is to be their only ruler and lord. [J15]

In other words, it would seem that there was a republican element within the fourth sect of Judaism, and that the high priesthood of Jerusalem, and perhaps even the kingship, were being rejected. But this sentiment is exactly the same as the teachings of Jesus, who reputedly said:

> Then saith Jesus unto him ... thou shalt worship the Lord thy God, and him only shalt thou serve. [B16]

There are further similarities between the biblical Jesus and this 'fourth sect' of Judaism to be found in the account of Jesus, son of Ananus (the son of a priest), who I have already identified with the biblical Jesus in the book *Jesus*. It is said of Jesus ben Ananus that:

> Certain of the most eminent among the populace had great indignation at the dire cry of his ... and gave the man a great number of severe stripes (lashes). Yet he did not either say anything for himself or anything peculiar to those who chastised him, but still went on with the same words he cried before. [J17]

This account has a great deal in common with the scourging of Jesus after his trial, but the indifference to suffering this Jesus displayed again fits rather well with the philosophy of the fourth Judaic sect.

These are not the only similarities, for this revolt against taxation by Judas of Gamala was not a trivial event; it was most certainly not a pavement protest that returned to the inn for a few beers when it got dark. No, Josephus Flavius specifically blames this Judas of Gamala for the entire Jewish Civil War and the eventual destruction of Jerusalem in AD 70.

> All sorts of misfortunes also sprang from these men, and the nation was infected with this doctrine to an incredible degree. One violent war came upon us after another ... there were also great robberies and murders of our principal men ... a famine came upon us which reduced us to the last degree of despair, as did also the taking and demolishing of our cities. Nay, the sedition at last increased so high, that the very Temple of God was burned down... [J18]

Likewise, I have already identified the biblical Jesus as one of the authors of the Jewish Civil War, for the New Testament specifically says that Jesus was a rebel with a large army.

> Think not that I (Jesus) am come to send peace on earth: I came not to send peace, but a sword. [B19]

> Then said (Jesus) unto them, But now, he that hath a purse, let him take it, and likewise his wallet: and he that hath no sword, let him sell his garment, and buy one. [B22]

The arming of the disciples of Jesus was not simply for decoration, so that they could pretend to be Knights of God; instead, this was a real armed uprising arranged and commanded by Jesus himself. The plan was to mount a surprise attack on the Jerusalem priesthood and government and so to take over all of Judaea. Presumably this action would then spark a revolt against Rome and so free Judaeo-Israel from Roman dominion.

> And (Jesus) came out, and went, as he was wont, to the Mount of Olives; and his disciples also followed him ... a band of men and officers from the chief priests and Pharisees, cometh thither with lanterns and torches and weapons ... When they which were about him saw what would follow, they said unto him, Lord, shall we smite with the sword? ... And one of them smote the servant of the high priest, and cut off his right ear ... Then Jesus said unto the chief priests, and captains of the temple, and the elders, which were come to him, do ye come out, as against a Zealot, with swords and staves? [B23]

Note that Jesus was being identified here as a Zealot leader, which he tries to deny; but since the disciple Simon was a Zealot, the authorities were probably correct. [24] This biblical account also makes it appear that this meeting on the Mount of Olives was a trivial gathering of the disciples, who happened to be armed with swords for some strange reason, but the complete account of this event paints a rather different picture:

> ... (the Egyptian prophet) got together thirty thousand men that were deluded by him; these he led round about from the wilderness to the mount which was called the Mount of Olives, and was ready to break into Jerusalem by force from that place; and if he could but once conquer the Roman garrison and the people, he intended to domineer them ... But (the governor) met him with his Roman soldiers, while all the people assisted him in his attack ... when it came to battle the Egyptian ran away, with a few others, while ... the rest of the multitude were dispersed every one to their own homes... [J25]

Here is a real historical account of the 'tumult' that the fourth sect of Judaism had created in Jerusalem. The meeting of the biblical Jesus [the Egyptian False Prophet] on the Mount of Olives was not for prayer or meditation (with swords), but for an armed assault on the city of Jerusalem using an army of some thirty thousand men. The Bible echoes the great magnitude of this event when the Gospel of John says that a *speira* σπειρα of men (a band of men) came to arrest Jesus. But a *speira* is more commonly termed as a *cohort*, and both of these are Roman terms for a tenth of a legion – or some 500 - 600 heavily armed soldiers. Clearly, this was a major insurrection being thwarted by the might of the Roman army, and not a small gathering of disciples being rounded up by a few local 'police constables'.

Note also that Jesus was being called 'the Egyptian', and the evidence for this being so can be seen in the following verse from Acts:

> Art not thou that Egyptian, which before these days made an uproar, and led out into the wilderness four thousand men that were murderers? [B26]

This was Saul (St Paul) being mistaken for the Egyptian False Prophet, but the real Egyptian prince in exile in this era was actually Jesus himself. Quite obviously, this verse from Acts is a simple retelling of the well-known 'loaves and fishes' story, and the proof that this is so is to be found in the term being used for a 'murderer', which was *sicarios* σικαριος. This term refers to the Sicarii, and in this era it was Jesus who was the leader of a band of Sicarii assassins, as we shall see in the next chapter. The equivalent, but toned down and more acceptable, 'loaves and fishes' story says:

> And he said unto them, Come ye yourselves apart into a desert place, and rest a while ... And the people saw them departing, and many knew him, and ran afoot thither out of all cities, and they went out, and came together unto him ... And they sat down in ranks, by hundreds, and by fifties ... And they that did eat of the loaves were about five thousand men. [B27]

Thus we have two very similar tales from the Bible and from Josephus; one regarding the Mount of Olives insurrection, and the other about the leading of the 5,000 into the wilderness. The Synoptic Gospels clearly state that Jesus led both of these events, while Josephus and Acts say that the instigator of both events was the enigmatic 'Egyptian False Prophet'.

Note the similarly evasive nature of the accounts in both Acts and Josephus' *Jewish War*, which is one reason why I have stated that Saul-Josephus was the author of both of these texts. Saul-Josephus was normally very diligent in recording the name of every character in his accounts, and so I am certain that he did know the true name of this 'Egyptian'; thus his reluctance to give the Egyptian's true name in his secular books and also in Acts suggests the possibility of a deliberate cover-up. Robert Eisenman, the renowned theologian, says of these two accounts and the suspicious cover-up:

> We will note many such suspicious overlaps in the data available to us. [28]

Eisenman then goes on to make a similar comparison between Jesus and Judas of Gamala:

> Luke's version (of the little apocalypse) is introduced by reference to the destruction of the Temple and generally refers to famine, wars and sectarian strife ... These (are similar to) a section in *Antiquities*, in which Josephus describes the woes brought upon the people by the movement founded by Judas the Galilean (Judas of Gamala). [29]

Again, we can see a direct comparison between the Church of Jesus and the fourth sect of Judas of Gamala. This was not Judas himself creating these woes, as we have moved on a generation here, but it would seem that the sect that Judas had founded was being continued and furthered by the biblical Jesus himself. This would not be so surprising if Jesus was the son of Judas of Gamala.

The obvious reason for Saul-Josephus' infuriating silence regarding the true identity of the 'Egyptian False Prophet' was that this character was actually Jesus himself. But for many reasons it was deemed unacceptable to let the followers of Saul-Josephus, the proto-Christians, know the true heritage of their 'saviour'. But Jesus <u>was</u> Egyptian, which is why the Gospel of Matthew says of Jesus: 'Out of Egypt I have called my Son'. [B30] Once more, the evidence demonstrates that Jesus was of Egyptian descent, and we can now see compelling evidence to demonstrate that this royal heritage was gained via the illustrious line of Thea Muse Ourania.

Philip

The evidence explored so far would seem to suggest that the biblical Jesus was associated with, or perhaps even the leader of, this fourth sect of Judaism that had been founded in about AD 7 by Zamaris (the Parthian or Babylonian Jew), who may well have been one and the same as Judas of Gamala. This sect was then continued by Jesus of Gamala, who I have previously identified as the biblical Jesus. In other words, the fourth sect was the group who are known in the New Testament as the Zelots ζηλωτης. The term *zealos* ζηλος is supposed to refer to those who were zealous for the law (of Moses), but it can also refer to jealousy. An alternative term that was used for the Zelots, according to the biblical Concordance, was Canaanite, a term that can again refer to jealousy. However, the latter word, *canaanite*, was also derived from the Hebrew *quanna* קנא meaning 'possessor' or 'purchaser', with the inference being that this term actually refers to a banker. Since the whole dispute between Judas of Gamala and the authorities revolved around who had the right to levy taxes, the fourth sect may have also been known as 'bankers' for taxes as well as 'zealots' for the law.

We know that Jesus' sect included Zealots in their number, as one of the disciples was called Simon Zelotes, and it was Simon who was also called the Canaanite (because the two terms are interchangeable). We also know that Simon (probably Simon the Leper) was the name of one of Jesus' brothers:

> Is not this the carpenter's son? Is not his mother called Mary? And his brethren, James, and Joses, and Simon, and Judas? [B32]

Even the most eminent of theologians, like Robert Eisenman and Adam Clarke, understand and admit that these were the true siblings of Jesus, and not simply fellow brothers in a cause or society. So the brothers of Jesus were named James, Joses, Simon and Judas, and yet these names were also among Jesus' twelve disciples. But this nominative similarity gives us an interesting possibility and, as I have shown in my previous works, the inescapable conclusion is that many of the disciples were actually the blood-brothers of Jesus. However, these same names give us yet another possibility – a direct link between the biblical Jesus and Judas of Gamala. Josephus Flavius says of the latter:

> Besides this, the sons of Judas the Galilean (Judas of Gamala) were executed; I mean that they were the sons of that Judas who caused the people to revolt when Quirinius (Cyrenius) came to take an account of the estates of the Jews. The names of those sons were James and Simon, whom Alexander commanded to be crucified. [33]

James and Simon were, of course, both names of the brothers of Jesus. But this similarity would imply that Judas of Gamala and Joseph the father of Jesus were the same person. So is this possible? Well, the date of the revolution started by Judas of Gamala was the same as the birth date of Jesus. The next generation of revolutionaries to come from Gamala, as we have already seen, were led by someone called Jesus. Thus both Judas of Gamala and the later Jesus of Gamala came from the province of Bethanya (Bethany), which was a favourite location for the biblical Jesus, and both of these revolutionaries appeared to control a substantial private army.

This may initially have seemed like an impossible condition for the biblical Jesus to have met; however, the biblical account of Jesus' armed assault from the Mount of Olives proves beyond doubt that the biblical Jesus *was* the leader of a substantial army, just as Jesus of Gamala was. Josephus says of Jesus of Gamala (and Jesus of Sapphias):

> Jesus the son of Sapphias, who we have already mentioned as the leader of a seditious tumult of <u>mariners</u> and poor people.

> Simon the son of Gamiel, persuaded the high priests and Jesus the son of Gamala and others of this seditious faction, to cut me down (reduce Josephus Flavius' power).

> A certain Galilean then stayed at Jerusalem whose name was Jesus, who had about him a band of six hundred armed men. [J34]

Thus, Jesus of Gamala (and Jesus of Sapphias) still controlled a large army long after the initial exile of Zamaris to Judaeo-Syria. But since this army was comprised of fishermen (mariners), and the sign of Christianity was the fish, this just has to be a reference to the armed faction controlled and led by the biblical Jesus. Thus Jesus of Gamala (and Jesus of Sapphias) were one and the same as the biblical Jesus.

Likewise, if Zamaris really was one and the same as Judas of Gamala, then we might expect that his sons also controlled a large army. That is exactly what we find, for it is said of Judas of Gamala's grandson, Philip:

> ... there was a firm friendship between him and King Agrippa (Agrippa II of Chalcis, Syria). He also had an army which he maintained, as great as that of a king; which he exercised and led wheresoever he had occasion to march. [J35]

Here was Philip of Gamala in charge a vast army that had free rein over the lands of Syria (Bethanya and Aurania) and also over the lands of Galilee. But a vast army 'as great as that of a king' needs a great deal of funds to maintain it, and these funds were only available because Zamaris [Judas of Gamala] founded a colony in Judaeo-Syria [at Umm el-Jimal] that was free of taxation from both Rome and Jerusalem. This means that Judas of Gamala had to be a tax collector – a collector of his own taxes to fund his private army. It was for this reason that complaints were being made about Jesus being surrounded by tax collectors:

> And it came to pass, as Jesus sat amongst them in the house, behold, many publicans and sinners came and sat down with him and his disciples. [B36]

As is usual, one has to decipher the text to make sense of it. The term being used for a 'publican' is actually a *telones* τελωνης, which means 'tax collector' – and this is a term that seems to have very little to do with the brewery trade, so the translation of 'publican' is highly misleading. In fact, just to emphasise this point, the term *harmartolos* αμαρτωλος for 'sinner' can also mean a 'tax collector'. However, having already noted the possibility of the Zelots being linked with banking, it is likely that these tax collectors were also bankers.

These tax collectors, whom Jesus associated with, probably included his parents. The biblical Concordance says that the name Cleophas κλωπας is exactly the same as the name Alphaeus αλφαιος, which again demonstrates that many of the disciples were actually Jesus' brothers, as I argued in the book *Jesus*. [Alphaeus was the father of James, the brother of Jesus.] However, it also says that both of these names mean 'exchange', from the Hebrew *chelep* חלף meaning 'exchange'. What the Concordance does not do is explain what, exactly, was being exchanged. Bearing in mind the clear inference from the evidence already explored, the exchange referred to has to be of money, and so Alphaeus-Cleophas was an exchequer – a tax collector.

So Jesus was accused by his contemporaries of associating with (and being related to) tax collectors, or moneylenders. It has often been assumed that the people's horror at this association between Jesus and tax collectors was due to tax collectors being a thoroughly nasty collection of people. The theologian Adam Clarke makes this very point when he says:

> It is certain that those who fear god should not associate, through choice, with the workers of iniquity, and should only be found with them when transacting their secular business requires it, or when they have the prospect of doing good to their souls. [37]

However, this new analysis of Jesus' status gives us another possibility entirely. The 'people' who objected were most probably the Jerusalem elders and administrators, and so their 'horror' may have been based upon the fact that Judas of Gamala had not paid any taxes (or Temple dues?) for several decades. Thus Judas and his offspring were in a position to fund their own army and remain wholly independent of the Judaean authorities. The Jerusalem hierarchy had a tax-haven on their doorstep, and they were none too pleased about this situation (except, perhaps, if the Parthian army advanced from the east – then they would have asked Judas of Gamala what he proposed to do about it). But the elders could do nothing about the situation, as this eastern province and its standing army and cavalry were far too strong for them to deal with.

Here was Judas of Gamala's son, Jesus of Gamala [the biblical Jesus], and he too was following in the same tradition of maintaining his own tax collectors, who channelled the taxes of Bethanya and Aurania towards Gamala and not towards Jerusalem. This was probably the reason for Jesus overturning the tables of the moneylenders in the Temple of Jerusalem. Perhaps the Temple was overstepping its remit, by raising secular taxes as well as its own Temple dues. Jesus, as tax collector for Bethanya in Syria, would have had a vested interest in opposing any authority that was encroaching on his own tax collections.

This line of research and argument does seem to make a great deal of sense. But if is true then we need to amalgamate several of the characters in the various texts that deal with this era. These amalgamations are:

Josephus *Antiquities*	Josephus *Life*	Bible
Zamaris, Babylonian Jew	= Judas of Gamala	= Joseph, father of Jesus
??	= Jesus of Gamala	= Jesus, son of Joseph
Simon of Gamiel	= Simon, son of Judas	= Simon, son of Joseph
Jacim, son of Zamaris	= James, son of Judas	= James, son of Joseph
Philip, son of Jacim	= ??	= Philip the disciple

Note that the name 'James' in the New Testament is simply a rather poor translation of the Greek Jacobos Ιακωβος or the Hebrew Jacob יעקב. Thus the name Jacim appears to be a cross between the names Jacob and James.

While it may seem unlikely that Josephus Flavius had mis-identified so many names in his records, this may have been a deliberate deception. Remember that I have previously argued that Jesus of Gamala, Jesus of Sapphias, Jesus Ananus and the biblical Jesus were all revolutionaries from Judaeo-Syria, who led large armed followings during the middle of the first century AD. Can we really believe that so many revolutionaries called Jesus were all competing to overthrow the Judaic authorities in Jerusalem? Or is it more rational to believe that Josephus has used different titles for the same person, presumably to confuse the history of the region and thus to separate the revolutionary aspect of the biblical Jesus from his more orthodox pacific persona. Note also that the different names in the table above occur substantially in different books of Josephus, so the presence of a different team of scribes may well be another factor in this.

However, if these various nominative associations are true, then it would make Jesus a much more important character in the wider politics of this region during this era. But that is what I have been saying all along. Jesus always did appear to have royal pretensions, many influential and well-connected friends and an extensive power base – and now we know why. Had Jesus been the son of Judas of Gamala [Zamaris], then he would have been the son of the leader of Judaea's fourth religious sect. This would have been a powerful position in its own right, but had Judas of Gamala [Zamaris] also been related to, or a pseudonym for, King Phraataces, then Jesus would indeed have had royal pretensions too. Such an ancestry would explain a great deal about the events of the New Testament.

But if the biblical Jesus and his extended family were directly related to and descended from Queen Thea Muse and King Phraataces, then an explanation must be sought for the Judaic-sounding names they chose to use in the New Testament accounts. Thea Muse and Phraataces were of the Egyptian and Parthian royal line respectively, so why would their descendants have used 'Judaic' names? The answer to this problem is that the biblical names we are familiar with may seem to be Judaic to us, as we are conditioned to believe this by the religious authorities. However, in actual fact, these names are not Judaic at all and the vast majority of them can be traced back into ancient Egypt, as we shall see. But this is an extensive topic that will have to be explored in a later chapter.

Stable

We have seen historical evidence that an Egypto-Parthian royal family were exiled to Bethanya (Jordano-Syria) in about AD 4, and also that a new Judaic sect appeared in this same location in about AD 7. It has also been demonstrated that many of these events and characters can be directly linked to the biblical Jesus, whose family was also said to have been forced to travel to a new location in AD 7 because of the taxation by Cyrenius (Quirinius). This forced exile and subsequent long and arduous journey of the Parthian royal family would help explain the reasoning behind the mythology that Jesus was born in a stable. Matthew says that Jesus was born in a guesthouse, but Luke is the author who places the Christmas-card gloss on the tale by saying:

> And she brought forth her firstborn son, and wrapped him in swaddling clothes, and laid him in a manger; because there was no room for them in the inn. [B38]

Whether it was a house or an inn, the general thrust of these stories is that this 'royal' birth was no great state occasion, and so it is entirely possible that the biblical family was on the move. But what was the reason for this great journey? Did entire families really have to travel vast distances across Judaea simply because there was a census and taxation being implemented by a Roman governor?

Initially, the classical biblical story of a 'royal' birth in humble surroundings sounds unlikely in the extreme. But since we now know that Thea Muse and Phraataces were forced into exile at about this same time, the reason for a royal birth in a 'guesthouse' or 'stable' becomes more understandable. Queen Thea Muse Ourania was no longer in her sumptuous royal palace in Parthia, and so the surroundings for this royal birth would indeed have been something to take note of.

Alternatively, the term for 'inn', *kataluma* καταλυμα, also means 'dining room'. As we have already seen, the houses at Umm el-Jimal [Gamala] were made with animal stables downstairs and the dining room upstairs. Since these houses were small rustic abodes, rather than the vast palaces that Thea Muse and Phraataces had previously been used to, it is likely that the upstairs rooms were greatly encumbered with former royal belongings. In the circumstances, it may have been easier to throw the animals out onto the street for a day or two than to arrange for a birth in a cluttered upstairs room.

Either way, the newly exiled and impoverished status of Queen Thea Muse and King Phraataces is one of the few ways we can make sense of the New Testament accounts. I had long suspected that Jesus was of royal blood, but I could not explain exactly why this royal prince would have been born in such lowly surroundings, let alone find a suitable candidate for such a lowly royal birth. However, we now seem to have all the requirements to explain the stable-and-manger birth of a royal prince, with the added bonus that this same birth may well have occurred in AD 7 in Bethanya – or, in other words, at exactly the right moment in history and in exactly the right location.

Magi

Yet again, it seems more and more likely that Jesus was born of the family of Thea Muse and Phraataces, and it is this direct link between Jesus and Parthia that forms the foundations of a very famous biblical event – which goes some way towards finally proving that the true origins of Jesus and his family lie with Thea Muse Ourania:

Now when Jesus was born in Bethlehem of Judaea in the days of Herod the king, behold, there came <u>wise men</u> from the east to Jerusalem. Saying, Where is he that is born King of the Jews? For we have seen his star in the east, and are come to worship him. [B39]

It is entirely possible that this story of the star that the 'wise men' followed to Israel is a simple retelling of the legends of King Solomon, of whom it is said:

And after he slept, there appeared a brilliant sun, and it came down and shed exceedingly great splendour over Israel. [KN42]

These stars or suns seem to be closely linked to the bloodline of Israel, and signify the appearance of a prince of the realm. These allusions are probably derived from the titles of the Judaic kings and queens, as the title 'Sheba' means 'star'. In the book *Solomon* I demonstrate that not only was King Solomon's queen known as 'Sheba' (the Queen of Sheba), but so was King Solomon's father, King David. The title of 'star', especially among the Hyksos-Judaic queens, alluded to the Queen of Heaven, a title that has already been explored in some detail.

Fig 27.   A Zoroastrian faravahar, or depiction of the soul. This motif is obviously taken from the image of the Egyptian flying Sun-disk of Ra.

However, this biblical story about wise men coming from the east has always been a bit of a mystery to me, for these 'wise men' were actually the Persian (or Parthian) *Magus* μαγος: the Magi. The Gospel of Luke has shepherds visiting the birth of Jesus, instead of the Magi; but this term may simply refer to the Hyksos Shepherd Kings. Alternatively, it is also possible that the term being used here for 'shepherd', the Greek *poimen* ποιμην, can be translated as the 'king's counsellors'. Not every shepherd looks after sheep, as the Catholic pope will attest to – and even god is called a shepherd on occasions.

These Magi, or 'wise men' in the King James translation, became the 'three kings' of popular biblical mythology. But this title of 'king' is simply a modern gloss that has no historical foundation whatsoever, and the original designation for the 'wise men' was the three Magi. The biblical Concordance

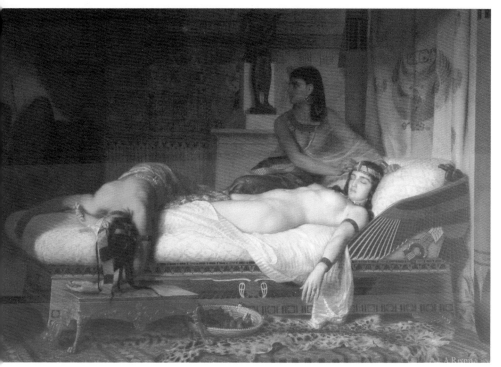

Plate 1. The Death of Cleopatra. Jean-Andre Rixens, Musee des Augustins, Toulouse, France.

Plate 2. Adoration of the Magi. Pieter Aertsen, Rijksmuseum, Amsterdam. Mary wears her traditional blue tunic, representing the Muse Ourania's association with the sky and the Cosmos.

Plate 3. The Virgin Mary depicted as Muse Ourania, Gornji Grad Cathedral, Slovenia. Note the twelve stars around her head and the Moon at her feet.

Plate 4. Virgin Mary depicted as Muse Ourania. Th[e] pose is taken from description in Revelations 12:[1] with the twelve stars on a blue background bein[g] adopted as the emblem of the EU.

Plate 5. Muse Ourania [Mary] and Calliope. Simon Vouet, Samuel Kress Collection, National Gallery of Art, Washington D.C.

Plate 6. The Beth Alpha zodiac, Israel; taken from a third century AD synagogue.

Plate 7. The Sultan Tekesh mausoleum in Kunya Urgench.

Plate 8. The mausoleum of Jubba II and Cleopatra Selene, daughter of Cleopatra VII, in Kolea, Algeria. The design incorporates mathematical allusions to the Sun and Moon.

Plate 9. The ruined city of Umm el-Jimal in Aurania (Hauran) – the 'Mother of Egypt' and the probable birth-place of the biblical Jesus.

Plates 10-17.
Top row 10-12:
Augustus Caesar, Julius Caesar, Vespasian. British Museum, London.

Second row 13-15:
Cleopatra VII, coin of Cleopatra VII, Thea Muse Ourania. British Museum London, and National Museum of Iran.

Coins 16 & 17:
Two coins (obverse and reverse) of King Phraataces and Queen Thea Muse Ourania. Note that King Phraataces wears a triple torq, probably of gold, and has a prominent wart of the forehead. The royal 'wart' on the forehead is a distinctive identifier of the Phraates kings, but no equivalent of this feature appears in the biblical record.

indicates that the Persian original of this Greek word was *meguceen*, or a 'Worshipper of Fire', from which we derive the English word magician. The Magi were said to be the hereditary priesthood of the Medes, who can be identified with the modern Kurds. The Magi have also been linked to the Mandaeans, the Marsh Arabs from southeastern Iraq who were so mercilessly persecuted by Saddam Hussein. E S Drower says of the Mandaeans:

> Arab authors have sometimes confounded the Mandaeans with the Magi or Magicians, and not without reason, since the cults are very similar. [43]

Finally, the Magi are also closely linked with the Zoroastrian priests who were the followers of the Prophet Zoroaster (Zoroastra); or, for admirers of Richard Strauss, the more familiar pronunciation is Zarathustra – hence the symphony *Also Sprach Zarathustra,* which was used so effectively in the film *2001, A Space Odyssey*. It is probably from the Zoroastrian temples of fire in Baku, Azerbaijan – which contain eternal flames fed by natural gas seeping from the ground – that the title 'Worshipper of Fire' was derived. However, the name Zoroaster is more likely to have been derived from the Hebrew *asther* אסתר and the Greek *aster* αστηρ meaning 'star'.

The influential Magi were said to hold profound and extraordinary religious knowledge and, in a similar fashion to the biblical Joseph and Daniel, the Magi therefore became supreme advisors to the Persian kings. In fact, since Daniel became an advisor to a Persian king, he too would have been a Magi. Indeed, the name given to Daniel was Rab Mag רב-מג which is a Hebrew-Persian compound title that refers to a 'Great Magi'. In this civil capacity the Magi therefore became the counsellors of the royal court, the civil administrators and viziers to the king or queen, as was the biblical Joseph. The Magi eventually formed the upper house of the 'Persian Council of the Megistanes', and it is from this latter title and function that the English term 'magistrate' is derived. Thus the Magi became royal courtiers, or 'court officials' in much the same way as we would understand that term – magistrates and judges.

There was one other important function of the Magi or *megistanes,* and that was the selection and anointing of the next king of Parthia. So what, then, were three Parthian (Persian) king-makers doing in Syrio-Judaea, searching for the next King of the Jews? When using the classical New Testament interpretation of Jesus being a lowly Jewish artisan, the presence of Parthian king-makers at his birth makes absolutely no sense whatsoever. Even the novel addition of Jesus' possible Egyptian ancestry adds little light to the situation, for the Egyptians and Parthians were not exactly the best of friends in this era and the Parthian (Persian) Magi would have had no interest whatsoever in the birth of an Egyptian prince. However, if Jesus was descended from Thea Muse and Phraataces then everything suddenly becomes crystal clear.

King Phraataces and Queen Thea Muse Ourania had been the king and queen of Parthia from AD 2 until they were dethroned in AD 4. This may have been a short and turbulent reign, but they were nevertheless king and queen of Parthia (and Thea Muse had been queen of Parthia for about 25 years prior to this), as the numismatic (coin) evidence proves.

Following their exile from Parthia, Rome took the opportunity of installing one of Phraates IV's exiled sons back onto the throne of Parthia. Augustus' first attempt was the installation of Orodes III, but Josephus says that he was deposed within two years due to his extreme cruelty. If Thea Muse and Phraataces were deposed in AD 4 and a year had passed before Orodes III took over the monarchy from them, then the Parthian throne would have been vacant once more around AD 7, when Orodes III was deposed. However, AD 7 is the very date of the Roman taxation of Judaea and thus the very date that the Gospel of Luke claims for the birth of the biblical Jesus. With the dethronement of Orodes III in AD 7, the Parthian Magi would have been on the lookout for a new king from the royal bloodline of the Parthian Arsacid dynasty. While Thea Muse and Phraataces may have been dethroned, due to their unorthodox Egyptian-style marriage, a son (or grandson) of theirs would still have been an Arsacid Parthian prince – and it was for this reason that the Parthian Magi travelled all the way to Judaeo-Syria to see for themselves this new Parthian prince.

So far, so good. We now have a clear and irrefutable link between Jesus and the Parthian royalty, but then something peculiar happens in the biblical accounts. It is said that Herod (the Great) heard of the Magi's visit to Bethanya and desired to speak to them. The Magi said that they had come to worship the 'King of the Jews', which was a deliberate slight on Herod's own kingship, as he was the King of the Jews at the time. As mentioned previously, for these dates to tie up correctly this king must have been Herod Archelous or Herod Philip (the next generation) rather than Herod the Great. Also, the term being used for 'worship' in this verse has been badly translated by some zealous Christian scribes, who were desperately trying to turn Jesus into a godlet. The original word was *proskuneo* προσκυνεω, meaning 'kiss the hand', and this more accurately describes the true intent and actions of the Parthian Magi king-makers. Being loyal courtiers, they would indeed have made their greetings by kissing the hand of the newborn Parthian prince.

But it is said that this Herod was outraged by the news of a newborn 'King of the Jews' and so he ordered the slaughter of all the infants in Bethlehem:

Then Herod, when he saw that he was mocked of the Magi, was exceeding wroth, and sent forth, and slew all the children that were in Bethlehem, and in all the coasts thereof, from two years old and under, according to the time which he had diligently enquired of the Magi. [B44]

Fig 28. The six-sided Magen David.

In the book *Jesus* I have already identified this slaughter with Herod the Great's slaughter of his own children in a bloody royal accession dispute. However, if the Herod in question was actually Herod Archelous or Herod Philip, then perhaps there was another fit of royal rage and retribution, and the accounts of this incident were modelled on the indiscriminate infanticide of Herod the Great.

In this case, the mention of the town of Bethlehem in this verse may be a little misleading, as it may not be the town in Judaea just to the south of Jerusalem. The original name of Bethlehem was based upon the Greek Bethleem βηθλεεμ, which was in turn based upon the Hebrew name Beth-Lechem בית-לחם, which is said to mean 'House of Bread'. However, if we are now assuming that some of the biblical lexicon is being influenced by Egypto-Parthian terms, then we may be looking for a Persian/Arabic equivalent instead. In this case the name of Beth-Lechem may well have been derived from Baith al Chemya, meaning the 'House of Alchemy'.

Alchemy can be explained as the early science of chemistry and physics, and if any of the priests of the primary religions of this era were dabbling in alchemical esoterica, it was the Magi. However, this is not the true origin of this word for it actually goes back into Egypt, where Kam was the original name for Egypt itself. Thus Al Chemy is simply an Arabic term meaning 'The Egypt' and referring more specifically to 'The Egyptian Arts'; because the basics of modern chemistry and physics came out of Egypt. Indeed, it is often claimed that the term 'chemistry' was derived directly from Kam, the ancient name for Egypt. If this were the case, then Bethlehem may actually refer to 'The House of the Egyptians', with the term 'house' possibly referring to the royal family. There was only one Egyptian royal family in Judaea at this time, and that was the family of Thea Muse Ourania.

But if the term 'alchemy' came out of Egypt rather than Persia (Parthia), then so may the term Magi. The biblical Concordance and the

Hebrew dictionary indicate that Magi is not a Hebrew word, and point instead towards Persia. However, I think that this assessment may be in error. In fact, the word Magi <u>is</u> Hebrew, for it forms a part of the 'Star Prophecy' of the New Testament Magi, who followed the 'star' to Jerusalem. The star in question must have been the Magen David מגן דוד or the Star of David, for the Magi were following the *magen*, or star. However, to be more precise, the Hebrew *magen* מגן actually means 'shield', but this word has been translated as 'star' because the Star of David does indeed look like a star.

The answer to this muddle is that the 'star' on the flag of Israel is actually composed of two interlocking triangles or pyramids (one being inverted). In addition, the Hebrew word *mag* is the prefix for the Hebrew word *magdal* מגדל meaning 'tower', which was originally derived from the Egyptian *maktal* *(maktar)*  or *magadal* *(magadar)* meaning 'tower' – and from which the New Testament also derives the title Magdalene.

It was from the symbology of the interlocking pyramids, which form the outline of the Star of David, that the star imagery for the goddess Isis was derived. The star/pyramid symbology of Isis is not so well known; however, a chapel of Psusennes II at Giza was dedicated to 'Isis, Mistress of the Pyramids'. [45] Likewise, it is from the name Isis, who was called Ast or Est in Egyptian, that the Phoenician goddess <u>Ast</u>arte was derived. Astarte may well have been a Lunar goddess but she was also known as the Queen of Heaven and linked to the morning and evening star, Venus. That there must have been a strong association between Astarte and stars can be seen in the Hebrew word *ester* or *aster* אסתר meaning 'star'.

Funnily enough, a related word *eser* אסר or *atsar* עצר means 'magistrate', the same as the Persian Magi, and so *aster* and Magi both relate to stars and magistrates. Thus the Magi in the New Testament were not simply looking for the planet Venus in the (western) evening sky, they were also looking for an incarnation of Isis (Esther or Astarte)

Fig 30. Helen of Sparta wearing a Phrygian (Trojan) cap.

the star goddess. Mary, the mother of Jesus, was that star (or incarnation of Isis) and this is a name that has endured through the ages, even if the etymology does not always fully support it. The true origin of the name Miraim (Mary) is given in a later chapter, but here is a small quote regarding the mythology of Mary the 'Sea Star':

> Here a word has to be added concerning the explanation for *stella maris*, the Star of the Sea. It is more popular than any other interpretation of the name 'Mary', and is dated back to St. Jerome. But the great doctor of the Church knew Hebrew too well to translate the first syllable of the name *miryam* by star; in Isaiah 40:15, he renders the word *stilla* (a drop), not *stella* (a star). [46]

In conclusion, it is likely that the Persian title of 'Magi' was originally an Egyptian term that had been derived from the great 'towers' of Egypt, which still stand on the Giza plateau to this day. I have already attempted to show that the ancient guardians of the pyramids were also the guardians of many of the secrets of Egyptian theology, astronomy, metrology, architecture and science. The Giza temple complex was the cornerstone of Egyptian esoteric knowledge, as it still is today with its peculiar depiction on the Great Seal of America and its strong association with Masonry. If anything was to represent the origins of the Magi's illustrious title, it would have to be the Great Pyramid of Egypt rather than a simple flame.

Liberty

Incidentally, it has long been suspected that the Statue of Liberty was conceived as a representation of Isis-Astarte, the Queen of Heaven. The sculptor of the statue was Frederic Bartholdi, while Gustave Eiffel designed the supporting structure, and the entire sculpture was made in France between 1876 and 1884. However, during the French Revolution a century before, the new Republic had decided that the seal of state would be a female 'goddess' figure complete with spear and Phrygian cap, which was a favourite headdress of Helen of Sparta (Helen of Troy). This mythical French heroine became known as Marianne the icon of liberty, but the link here to the biblical Mariame (Mary) and to Isis is inescapable.

So who was the model for this French (American) icon of Isis, the lady of liberty? The face on the statue is actually that of a rather stern, masculine-looking woman with bold features. It has long been thought that the model for this was Bartholdi's mother, but could there have been an alternative model? Egypt had been opened up by Napoleon a century before this time and the iconography of Egypt was very popular in this era. In addition, the heavily masonic world of American politics and business would have been very happy to push for an icon of Isis to be a national symbol for all America. Was an image of a goddess or a queen from this era of Egyptian discovery used instead? Some of the busts attributed to Cleopatra show a similar masculine profile, while the cloth headdress that she sometimes wears also looks vaguely familiar. Was Isis-Cleopatra chosen to become the face of Liberty?

Fig 31.   Bustof Cleopatra Selene

The face of the Statue of Liberty.

Out of Egypt

Following the visit of the Magi, the very next verses in the Gospel of Matthew relate the flight of Jesus and his family into Egypt:

> And when they were departed, behold, the angel of the lord appears to Joseph in a dream, saying, Arise, and take the young child and his mother, and flee into Egypt, and be thou there until I bring thee word: for Herod will seek the young child to destroy him. When he arose, he took the young child and his mother by night, and departed into Egypt. And was there until the death of Herod: that it might be fulfilled which was spoken of the lord by the prophet, saying, 'Out of Egypt have I called my son'. [B47]

These accounts now give us a new problem, for having decided that Jesus may well have been a Parthian prince, his parents decide to take him to Egypt for safety. Just why would the mother of a Parthian prince, who had been visited by the Magi of Parthia, decide that Egypt was a much safer location for her child than Parthia?

Well, one of the beauties of the thesis that has been explored thus far is that it can easily explain all of these diverse problems. The Persian (Parthian) Magi came to see Jesus because he was a Parthian prince, as we have just seen. However, his mother may well have decided that Parthia was not exactly the safest place for their new child, as the royal family had only just been exiled from that empire. But this royal family did have other options and alternative supporters in other countries – for Thea Muse Ourania was the lost daughter of Cleopatra VII. In the circumstances, perhaps Egypt was the safest place for this royal prince, and this choice would give the double benefit of allowing him to gain a first-class royal education at the great Temple of Heliopolis and to explore the great libraries of Alexandria.

In science, theories are only deemed to be true when they have the power of solving additional problems, both retrospectively and predictively. This thesis is beginning to solve any number of intractable problems that have lain unexplained for millennia. Thus we are on course towards proving that the biblical Jesus was directly related to Queen Thea Muse Ourania.

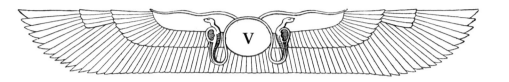

Judaic Names?

The task at the beginning of this book was to attempt to discover members of an exiled royal family who were living in Syrio-Judaea around the turn of the first century AD, who may have had strong links to the great royal dynasties of Egypt and Parthia, and who could be linked to the biblical texts in some manner. That task is now complete, and we appear to have discovered our royal biblical family. However, there is still one rather troubling aspect to this radical new identification – the names traditionally given to the biblical family.

Most readers will be familiar enough with the New Testament to realise that the father of Jesus was not called Phraataces, and his mother was not called Thea Muse Ourania (nor Cleopatra, for that matter). On the face of it, this would seem to be a major stumbling block; for if this entire thesis is true in any way, then it would seem that this Egypto-Parthian royal family would have had to have adopted Judaic names after they were exiled to Judaea. But it is highly unlikely that this would have happened. Thea Muse and Phraataces were not Jews, as such, and it would seem unlikely in the extreme that they would convert to Judaism just because of their exile.

Initially, this might all seem very logical, but only because we have been conditioned into thinking in a very constrained manner. Our perception, which has been fostered and nurtured by all of our educational authorities, is that the Jews were the Jews, and although they lived in a sea of other Middle Eastern nations, they remained completely separate from these other people. This, however, is nonsense. In all of my other books I have tried to demonstrate the close links that once existed between the Jews and the Lower Egyptians – indeed, most of the biblical patriarchs and kings were actually pharaohs of Egypt, who sometimes ruled over a united

Egypto-Judaic nation. Strabo confirms these close links between Egypt and Judaea at the turn of the first century when he says:

> This region lies towards the north; and it is inhabited ... by mixed stocks of people from Egyptian and Arabian and Phoenician tribes ... But though the inhabitants are mixed up thus, the most prevalent of the accredited reports in regard to the Temple at Jerusalem, represents the ancestors of the present Judaeans as Egyptians. [51]

This was why my first book on this subject was entitled *Jesus, Last of the Pharaohs*, for it seemed obvious that the New Testament family was closely related to the Egyptian royal line. The further revelations in this book have only served to increase the historical links between the biblical family and Egypt. But in what way does this link to Egypt help in explaining away these curiously 'Judaic' names? How did Jesus' father become known as Joseph, for instance?

Joseph

The answer to this question lies in the fact that the family of Jesus travelled into Egypt, partly for his safety but perhaps more importantly for his education. If Jesus was indeed related to Cleopatra VII, then the obvious country to go to for his education would be Egypt. In fact, there may have been elements within the Egyptian priesthood who were looking for a bloodline prince of Egypt, so that the Egyptian monarchy might one day be restored.

Having found themselves in Egypt, I think it would be highly likely that this Egypto-Parthian royal family would have been given adoptive Egyptian names that reflected their positions and status. The Egyptian name given to Phraataces may well have been Joseph. While this might sound like a Judaic name, I have already argued that it was, in fact, based upon an Egyptian original. The meaning of the name Joseph (Yoseph) in Egyptian would have been *yah* ⟨𓃟⟩ *sef* ⟨𓋴𓆑⟩ meaning Son of the Moon. All pharaohs of Egypt were the son of one god or another, and so this name would signify the son of the Moon-god, Thoth. Another version of this same name would have been Tuthmoses, which was the same name that was given to the biblical Moses.

However, it is possible that there had been a process of feminisation going on within Egypt. The God's Wives of Upper Egypt had always been a strong faction in Egyptian royalty and theology, but the era of Akhenaton saw the role of the royal wife elevated to an equal of the pharaoh himself. This increased power of the royal wife continued into the era of the biblical United Monarchy, where the royal wife was not only very powerful, but she also became the focus of religious veneration as an incarnation of Isis. This was certainly true of the Queen of Sheba, who became the subject of veneration across Egypt, Ethiopia and the Yemen. I maintain that the Queen of Sheba was an Egypto-Judaic princess, and that she was simply following in the footsteps of Queen Hatchepsut and Queen Nefertiti in adopting the mantle of Isis.

This tradition of powerful queens continued into the Ptolemaic era, and Queen Cleopatra VII proved herself to be no less ruthless than any other monarch throughout Egyptian history in her manipulation of other monarchs in the region and in the disposing of her domestic rivals. Then we have the dramatic life-story of Thea Muse Ourania, the daughter of Cleopatra VII by Julius Caesar. She proved herself most adept at manipulating her husband, the King Phraates, and then when the time was right she murdered him and married her son instead.

Here we can see clear evidence of a line of powerful women who were effectively usurping the role of the male gods of Egypt. Traditionally in Egyptian history, we see the worship of strong male gods, who all happen to have wife goddesses who are portrayed as being in largely subordinate roles. However, the increasing power of the mother goddess, Isis, is readily apparent in the increasing prestige of the Maakare MuTamhat queens of the twentieth dynasty, whom I have linked with the biblical United Monarchy. The huge granite statue of one of these Maakare queens, which is slowly being uncovered at Bubastis in the Nile Delta, is testimony to this prestige; as is the obsessive veneration of the Queen of the Stars in the biblical book of Jeremiah.

With this ever-increasing role of the Isis queens, and the diminishing role of the traditional male deities, it is not beyond the realms of possibility that in the decades prior to the new millennium, the name Joseph now referred to a Moon-goddess rather than to the Moon-god, Thoth. The reason for thinking this is that the sister of Thea Muse was called Cleopatra Selene, or Cleopatra the Moon-goddess. Thea Muse was herself called Ourania, or the Goddess of the Heavens. Mary, the mother of Jesus was also called the Goddess of the Heavens, which is why she is often depicted as standing on the Moon and crowned with a tiara of twelve stars (see the colour section).

There is a definite possibility here that when Phraataces went to Egypt he was known there as the Son of the Moon-goddess (the son of Thea Muse Selene). In the Egyptian, this appellation would have been pronounced as Joseph , and so this became Phraataces' common name.

Jesus

If the name Joseph can be seen to have been derived from an Egyptian title, then so can the name Jesus. It is traditionally thought that the Greek name Jesus ιησους was derived from the Hebrew name Joshua יהושע. But the Hebrew name is actually pronounced as Yehoshuah, and so the similarity between these names looks a little contrived. However, there is an Egypto-Greek alternative that seems much more reasonable.

The Egyptian name for Isis was Ast or Est ⌂ , but when the Greeks got hold of this name they transposed it into Isidos Ισιδος, with the Egyptian 't' being transliterated into a 'd' (a common transposition). Subsequently, all that has happened in later eras is that the 'd' consonant has been dropped from this name, as has happened to the English version, giving the name Isios or Isis. While this may not sound too much like the English name 'Jesus', the original Greek name for Jesus was actually pronounced as Yeaysoos or Ieysoos and so these two names are virtually identical.

However, this argument can be taken one step further, because there is actually another version of Jesus' name in the New Testament. In the book *Jesus*, I pondered over the brother of Jesus called Joses (Ieoses), for he does not seem to have any role within the family. However, this may be due to the fact that Joses is another variant of the name Jesus. The eminent theologian Robert Eisenman says of this character:

> Moreover, this is borne home by looking at the form of the two words in Greek, Ioses and Iesus. What becomes immediately apparent is that these are the same name ... The fourth brother is simply Iesos or Jesus himself! [2]

In other words, when asked to give the names of the sons of Mary, the New Testament authors simply listed them all, and not just those in addition to Jesus (which is how the verse initially reads in Math 13:55). But if 'brother' Joses was actually another name for Jesus himself, then it is apparent that his name can be spelt as either Iesus ιησους (Eeaysoos) or Ioses ιωσης (Eeoses). The latter, I think you will find, is almost an exact duplication of the Anglicised name for Isis ισιος (Eeseos).

Jesus would not, of course, simply have been named as the feminine 'Isis'; rather, his original title would have been Ben-Jesus, meaning the Son of Isis. As in the case of Joseph, as just explained, the matrilineal name may have become more important that the patrilineal. The children of Cleopatra Selene of Mauretania (Thea Muse's sister) seem to confirm this new trend, as both of these children were named after Selene's family rather than her husband's.

V *Judaic Names?*

Had Jesus been a son of Julia Ourania, Thea Muse Ourania's daughter, and had the ancient traditions swung far enough away from the usual Egyptian male dominance, then Jesus would naturally have been called the Son of Isis. Cleopatra VII was considered to be a manifestation of Isis, and since her daughter and granddaughter were both called Ourania, they too were being identified with Isis. As I have already demonstrated in the book *Solomon,* Mary, the mother of Jesus, held the title of Handmaiden of God and Virgin, which were the two primary titles of the Egyptian God's Wife. In turn, the God's Wives, in their bare-breasted portrayals, were also closely associated with the goddess Isis. In the circumstances, it is not so surprising that a son of Julia Ourania became known as Ben Eeoses (Jesus) – the Son of Isis.

James

Once more, we tend to just assume that this is a Judaic name, but it is not. Curiously, the name 'James' is a very badly translated rendition of the Greek name Jakobos (Yakobos) Ιακωβος, which comes directly from the Hebrew Jacob (Yakob) יעקב. While the name Jacob may again seem to be a Judaic name with a long and illustrious ancestry, it is not. The name was originally Egyptian, and it was used by some of the fifteenth dynasty pharaohs of Egypt. These were the Hyksos pharaohs of Lower Egypt, and this was one of the primary reasons for my arguing that the Israelite patriarchs of the Old Testament were actually the Hyksos pharaohs of Egypt, and that the Israelite exodus out of Egypt was actually the historically attested Hyksos exodus out of Egypt.

There are two spellings of the Egyptian Jacob (Yakob) and these are  and , but the meaning of this name is highly uncertain. Since the Bible maintains that Jacob's ancestors came from the east, it may well be that this is a transliteration of a foreign name, just as the Egyptian name Cleopatra is a transliteration of the Greek title 'Muse Cleo Patra', meaning 'My Father's Glory' or even 'Heavenly Muse of my Father'. However, as I have previously argued that the biblical Hyksos-Israelites had always been resident in the Nile Delta, a possible Egyptian translation for the name 'Yakob' is *yakob*  meaning 'weep' or perhaps *yakob*  meaning 'Nile flood'. In effect, both of these names refer to life-giving rain or irrigation of the Nile Delta. Egypt could not exist without the Nile floods, and so a king who could guarantee the flood would be considered to be very powerful indeed. Since one of the pharaohs of the sixteenth dynasty was called Yacobam 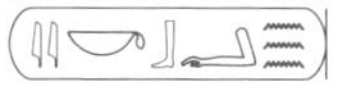, this tentative explanation may be entirely correct. In the book *Jesus* I did argue that the 'm' 'water' glyph at the end of this name was in fact a determinative glyph, which would render the true pronunciation as being Yacob (Jacob), and the meaning as being 'I am the Nile Flood'.

Judas

The Greek name Judas (Eeudas) Ιουδας comes from the Hebrew Judah (Yehudah) יהודה. Again this might sound like a typical Judaic name – indeed, the foundation for the title of the Judaic people – however, this name is again most probably of Egyptian origin. It is likely that this name stems from the Egyptian *yehudjah* meaning 'Seed of the Moon-god' or, in other words, the 'Son of Thoth'. Again there seems to have been a great emphasis here with the Moon-gods, although in this case the deity involved is the male aspect of the Moon and so an equally valid version of this name would have been Tuthmoses.*

---

* Note also that the disciples had the Sicarii dagger men among their number, which is why Judas was also called Iscariot. The function of the Sicarii was the same as the later sect of Assassins, and yet there may be a link here. The Assassins are said to have derived their name from the Hashashin, a part of the Ismaili sect of Islam who were well versed in political assassination. In turn, the word 'assassin' is said to have been derived from *hashish*, the drug that supposedly made these assassinations possible. However, as modern organisers of suicide mission have attested, they prefer their walking bombs to be sane and sober, rather than drugged up to the eyeballs, as they perform their foul deeds.

Since the task of the Assassins was the same as the biblical Sicarii, and their choice of weapon was similar, perhaps there is another origin for the latter's name. Josephus says of the Parthians:

> However they made a conspiracy against Orodes of the Arsacid dynasty, and slew him at a festival ... for it is the universal custom there to carry their swords with them. JA

It would appear that the Parthians of the Arsacid dynasty always carried swords or knives with them, as indeed some sects of Islam still do today, and that they were not above the assassination of the aristocracy. In other words, the name for the later Islamic Assassins may have been derived from the Arsacid dynasty rather than the drug *hashish*. Prince (King) Phraataces was also of the Arsacid dynasty, and so the arrival of a new sect of assassins in Judaea in this era, who were known as the Sicarii, is not so surprising.

JA.   Josephus Ant 18:45

V Judaic Names?

Simon

This was a very interesting and elusive name that took a great deal of tracking down and which provided a couple of competing possibilities for us to ponder upon. The usual explanation is that Simon σιμων is taken from the Hebrew name Shimown שמעון, meaning 'hear' or 'rumour'. However, that is not necessarily so and the clue to this name's true meaning lay in the alternative appellations given to this disciple called Simon [the brother of Jesus].

Firstly, it should be pointed out that while one disciple was called Simon Peter (Simon Cephas), the other was named Simon Zelotes σιμων ζηλωτης. The additional title of Zelotes refers to the fundamentalist, zealous creed of Judaism; and so the name Zelotes ζηλωτης is taken from *zelos* ζηλος and *zeo* ζεο, which are Greek terms meaning 'anger', 'rage' or 'hot' and 'boil'. It would appear that this sect was only suitable for raging adherents to the law who boiled with indignation. That the term Zelotes may have been directly related to the name Simon (Shimon) is evident from the equivalent Egyptian root word for this name, which was *shemm-t* ▭𓄿𓄿𓏌 meaning 'hot'. Thus Simon Zelotes was so-called for his being hot-tempered, or perhaps because he followed the more radical branch of Egypto-Judaism – the Zealots. However, a quote from the Nag Hammadi gospels in a later chapter will confirm that the other Simon, Simon Peter, was definitely known for being 'hot-tempered', and so the name Simon may well have been a true description of both of these disciples' characters.

That the name Simon did refer to a hot temper is also confirmed by another nickname for Simon Zelotes, which was Simon the Canaanite σιμων κανανιτης. Now the term Canaanite may seem to indicate that Simon Zelotes was a Phoenician (a Canaanite), but the biblical Concordance also links this term back to the Hebrew word *qana* קנא, which again means 'jealousy' or 'rage'. The possible roots for Simon's second name or title in Egyptian are *kena* 𓈖𓃀𓏜 and *qendj* 𓄿𓏏𓍯, which both mean 'rage', 'anger' and 'indignation'.

However, this is not the only interpretation that can be placed upon this particular 'surname'. As well as meaning 'zealous', the root for the Greek word *canaanite* κανανιτης is the Hebrew *canaanite* כנען, which means 'merchant', as was pointed out in the last chapter. But this word was, in turn, derived from *qana* קנא meaning 'purchase' and *kanas* כנס meaning 'gather' or 'collect'. So here we come back to the possibility that Simon Zelotes was not so much zealous for the law (of Moses) as he was for the gathering of other people's money. Even the Greek term *zelotes* ζηλωτης, Simon's more usual name, can refer to the desire to gain other people's belongings.

Thus, as has already been proposed, Simon Zelotes, the brother and disciple of Jesus, may not have been a religious fundamentalist but rather a tax collector. Since the entire dispute between Judas of Gamala and the Jerusalem authorities was over the province of Aurania's (Bethanya's) tax-free status, and Judas' refusal to pay the Romans any taxes, I personally think that the latter is more likely.

However, since the Hebrew language is directly descended from the Egyptian language, it is not so surprising that we should also find the original root of the word *qana* קנא in the Egyptian. The term was probably derived from *tennu-t* 𓏤𓃀𓐍 meaning 'numbers' and this was later modified into the word *tennu-t* 𓈖𓃀𓏏𓀀 meaning 'taxes'. The change from the Egyptian *tennu* to the Hebrew *qanna* lies well within the known variations of Egyptian pronunciation.

Mary

In the book *Jesus*, I demonstrated that the name 'Mary' possibly originated with the pharaonic title of Meri 𓌸𓏥, which means 'loved by'. The name generally refers to the pharaoh being 'loved by' a particular deity, hence the common title of Meri Amun (Loved by Amun). As it happens, Queen Cleopatra VII had a very similar title, which was Neteret Merit Se 𓊹𓏏 𓌸𓏥, which probably means 'Goddess Loved by Father'. The 't' at the end of the words *neter-t* and *meri-t* simply confirms that the feminine aspects of god and love were being implied. In Egyptian terms, the 'father' would have related to a heavenly father, but the Greco-Egyptian meaning may have been referring to a mortal father. In many respects, this Egyptian title is a copy of the Queen's better-known Greek name, Thea Cleo Patra, which means 'Goddess Glory of Father'.

In New Testament terms, the primary character who was 'loved by god' – indeed, sufficiently loved that she became pregnant by this same god – was also called Meri. This was, of course, Mary the mother of Jesus. The proof that this Egyptian root was the true origin of this name lies in its alternative meanings and the alternative nicknames that were given to Mary herself.

Orthodox theologians would disagree with the interpretation just given and so the standard biblical Concordance gives a meaning of 'rebellion' for the name Mary, which is hardly suitable as the name for a young lady. As ever, this translation was probably made to draw people away from the true meaning, which has more to do with pharaonic titles than a rebellious child. But this is not the only orthodox interpretation, and St Jerome gave the following alternative:

One of the meanings assigned to the name Mary in Martianay's edition of St Jerome's works is *pikra thalassa* or *bitter sea*. Owing to the corrupt condition in which St Jerome found the 'Onomastica' of Philo and of Origen, which he in a way re-edited, it is hard to say whether the interpretation 'bitter sea' is really due to either of these two authorities; at any rate, it is based on the assumption that the name *miryam* is composed of the Hebrew words *mar* (bitter) and *yam* (sea). [3]

So the name for Mary may have been derived from the Hebrew *meri-yam* מרים meaning 'bitter sea', which was obviously a reference to either the Dead Sea or the Mediterranean. In fact, it is most likely to have been a reference to the latter, because this term is not Hebrew, but Egyptian. The most obvious alternative to the Egyptian *meri* is the word *mer*, which refers to a body of water of any size, or perhaps *merii-t* meaning a 'sea'. In a similar fashion, the Egyptian equivalent of *yam* is *yam* or *yama* meaning 'sea'. Thus, in the Egyptian, the name Meri-yam (Miriam) referred to the Sea-Sea or the Great Sea, which was indeed a reference to the Mediterranean. The Hebrew language has taken this original root and translated it as the Bitter-Sea, and this again refers to the Mediterranean.

However, having said all this I still do not believe that 'Mediterranean' is a suitable name for a young child, let alone a princess. It is always possible that this translation was derived in the first century AD, because of Mary's (probably Mary Magdalene's) well-known journey with her daughter Sarah across the Mediterranean to southern France. Alternatively, this name may be an oblique reference to the celestial seas, over which the great barque of Aton-Ra sailed. In which case, Mary may have been associated with the sky-goddess, Nut.

Certainly, the name Mary, or Miriam in the Hebrew, is not a first century invention, for the sister of Moses was also called Miriam. But Moses was an Egyptian prince, even by the admission of the Christian priesthood, thus even the Catholic Encyclopaedia wonders if the name for Mary was originally Egyptian. Indeed it was – but a reference to a sea was not a typical Egyptian appellation or title for a princess.

The outcome of all this deliberation is that the name Mary is highly unlikely to have meant 'rebellion' and it is almost as unlikely to have originally meant 'sea'. But the fact that the phonemes for her name work best in the original Egyptian demonstrates that this was originally an Egyptian name, and thus the most apt and historically attested meaning of the name is the standard pharaonic title Meri, meaning 'loved by'. However, just as in the case of Cleopatra's name, this name can refer to the person being loved by the gods or the lady in question being a love goddess herself; and the latter interpretation links Mary with Isis, Astarte and Aphrodite once more. Since I have already demonstrated, in the book *Solomon,* that Mary was following in the footsteps of the Maakhah Tamar queens in being a God's Wife, her direct association with Isis and Aphrodite is assured: for the God's Wives were indeed 'Love Goddesses'. In fact, perhaps a better term would actually be 'Sex Goddesses', for the primary duty of the God's Wife was to caress god's penis and allow him to ejaculate.

This epigraphic evidence for Mary's title's direct descent from the Maakhah Tamar queens of Egypt (and the United Monarchy of Israel) underlines Mary's Egyptian heritage once more, undermining any politically correct moves to turn Mary into a negress. Once again, this analysis demonstrates that the name Mary was not Greek, nor indeed was it Hebrew. In fact, the name 'Mary' is pure Egyptian, and so it should not be so surprising that both Thea Muse Ourania and her daughter Julia Muse Ourania became known as Mary.

Talmud

The names that have just been explored are those contained within the biblical accounts. However, the Judaic Talmud gives us an alternative point of view and some very different names for the same characters in this saga, and this gives us a second opportunity to see the true ancestry of the biblical family.

One of the more famous names from the Talmud is that of Pantera, who was reputed to have been the father of Jesus. It has already been demonstrated in the book *Jesus,* that the name Pantera was probably derived from the Egyptian title of Pa-neter-Ra 𓂝𓏺𓂋𓁹 meaning 'Belonging to the God Ra' or even 'My God Ra'. However, following on from this extensive research, it is now possible that we can gain a more comprehensive translation of this name. The full quote from the Babylonian Talmud is as follows:

> 'He who cuts upon his flesh'. It is tradition that Rabbi Eliezer said to the wise, 'Did not Ben Stada bring spells from Egypt in a cut upon his flesh?' They said to him 'He was a fool, and they do not bring proof from a fool'. (Ben Stada is Ben Pandira. Rab Chisda said 'The husband was Stada, the paramour was Pandera'. The husband was Pappos ben Jehudah, the mother was Stada. The mother was Miriam, the dresser of women's hair; as we say in Pumbeditha 'Such a one has been false to her husband')'. (Original brackets) [T4]

The first thing that is abundantly clear from this quote is that the authors of the Talmud knew an awful lot more than they were giving away in their vast biblical commentary, and that their first and foremost objective was to conceal the truth from all but a select few of Judaic initiates.

That this is a fact can be demonstrated by the term 'the mother was Miriam, the dresser of women's hair'. This phrase has been derived from *'Miriam magaddela nashaia'* (or *Miriam magbalah nesaiyr* נזיר מגבלה מרים) meaning 'Miriam the hair dresser'. But if the phrase is read once more, it is apparent that this is simply an obvious play on words for 'Miriam Magdalene Nazarene', or 'Mary Magdalene the Nazarene'. Note here that *nesaiyr* נזיר does indeed also mean Nazarene, and so Mary Magdalene is simply being given the same title as Jesus. The only possible reason for this wordplay has to involve a deliberate cover-up of the characters being discussed.

As has been mentioned by many commentators, Jesus was not 'of Nazareth', for the town did not exist at this time; instead, he was 'the Nazarene'. The term 'Nazarene' actually refers to a 'fish', a sign that became the icon of early Christians and referred to the astrological sign of Pisces. This quote is, therefore, seeming to identify Mary Magdalene as the mother of Jesus, but in fact this jump in the generations is not the problem it may initially seem. The terms 'Magdalene' and 'Nazarene' are both formal titles, and it is likely that Mary the Virgin was also called 'Magdalene', as I have suggested in the book *Solomon*.

Incidentally, it is from this 'dresser of hair' pun that a famous children's story was derived. The name Magdalene is derived from the Hebrew *magdalah* מגדלה meaning 'tower', which was in turn derived from the Egyptian *maktar* or *maktal* 𓎟𓂝𓏏𓏏, which again means 'tower'. The tower in question was actually a phallic symbol, but that is immaterial in this instance. The point of interest here is the linking of the princess who was known for both her hair and a tower, and the result was the ingenious fairy-story known as Rapunzel. The Catholic Church could persecute people for many perceived transgressions of Church doctrine, but writing children's fairy-stories was not high on the list – hence the Illuminati's dependence on tales such as Cinderella, Sleeping Beauty and Rapunzel. ⁵

Following that short digression, it can be seen that the rest of the quote from the Babylonian Talmud is similarly and deliberately confusing in the extreme, and so it may be worth our while dissecting it piece by piece, as there is a wealth of information to be found within its convoluted and secretive folds. Firstly, it should be noted that this quote emanates from the time of Rabbi Eliezer who was a disciple of R. ben Zaccai, who died in old age some time before AD 80. Since I maintain that Jesus died in AD 70 during the siege of Jerusalem, it is likely that Zaccai knew of Jesus, or at the very least was contemporary to all of the events of the New Testament.

In the quote above, the comments of Zaccai or Eliezer are the first elements within quotation marks, while the bracketed comments are the observations of the Judaic Babylonian school of Pumbeditha.* The comments of Zaccai indicate that Ben Stada (the son of Stada) brought spells from Egypt in a flesh-wound, a term that has been interpreted within the Judaean Gemara as a tattoo. However, masonic ritual would suggest that this was indeed a cut in the flesh rather than a skin marking.** The bracketed comments about this statement firstly demonstrate that Ben Stada and Ben Pandira were the same individual (the mother may have been Stada while the father may have been Pandera). The third contention, by Rab Chisda, was that Stada and Pandira were both men – one the husband and the other the secret lover of Miriam Stada (Mary the Virgin). However, since Mary was called Stada, the latter assertion would seem unlikely.

The confusion between Stada and Pandira may have arisen because the title Pandira can be associated with a god. Since Mary and all the queens of Egypt were impregnated both by their husbands and by the gods, the wives of the pharaohs had both mortal husbands and heavenly lovers. In this case, the paramour (or lover) idea may have referred to a god. However, the correction to this statement is that Stada was indeed the mother and the father now gains another name – that of Papos of the Jews. The following table may clarify this situation.

Husband	Wife	Son
Pandira	Stada	Ben Pandira (Son of Pandira)
Papos	Hair dresser	Ben Stada (Son of Stada)

So it would appear that the names Ben Stada and Ben Pandira can be directly associated with Jesus within the Judaic traditions in the Talmud, and so the names Stada and Pandira have to be directly associated with the parents of Jesus. But if this is so, then how can these names be similarly associated with the family of Thea Muse and Julia Ourania?

---

* Pumbeditha was one of the great Central Asian Jewish colleges, of which Nahaiclea and Sora were two others. The version of the Pentateuch known as the Okelos of Babylon emanated from Pumbeditha and was also accepted as authoritative in Judaea.

** Some masonic sects still cut the flesh on their legs or lower backs in recognition of this age-old tradition.

Stada

It has been suggested that the term Stada originated from the Aramaic *satat da*, meaning 'gone astray', which may have been a reference to the quote saying that Miriam had had a paramour or lover. However, since all the other names from the biblical family have had Egyptian origins, perhaps this name does too. If this were the case, then the obvious derivation would be *stata* 𓏏𓂝𓎡𓅓 meaning 'archer'.

Now while the meaning of this term may not have been immediately obvious to classical theologians, it does become more apparent when studying the history of Parthia and the numismatics or coins of this era. As it happens, the Arsacid dynasty of Parthia was carved out and created by forces of mounted archers, and so nearly all of the coins of Parthia show the monarch on the obverse of the coin, while the reverse displays the image of an archer. It was from this archer symbology that the Parthian princely title of Tiridates was coined. Remember also that Zamaris, the Babylonian Jew who fled to Judaeo-Syria, and who may well have founded the city of Umm el-Jimal, had with him 500 mounted archers. In terms of this new interpretation of the biblical family, Jesus would indeed have been the 'Son of the Archer', the son of a Parthian princess or queen.

Pandira

It has long been thought that the name Pandira was derived from the Latin *pantera* meaning 'panther', and so some historians have sought to associate this title with a Roman legionary of the same name. This suggestion gained added impetus when a first century tombstone was discovered in Bingerbruck, Germany, which has an inscription that reads: 'Tiberius Julius Abdes Pantera of Sidon, aged 62, a soldier of 40 years service, of the 1st cohort of archers, lies here.' That Jesus was descended from a Roman legionary may have been a reasonable assumption for the theological fraternity – who continually try to promote the poor carpenter story and thereby undermine Jesus' royal heritage – but if Jesus was the 'King of the Jews' then it is more than likely that he had parents of royal blood on both sides. So is there an alternative rendering for the name 'Pandira'?

Although we do not have a comprehensive history of the events and marriages within Thea Muse Ourania's family, we do have a strong suspicion that her daughter, Julia Ourania, married Ptolemy of Mauretania. (See the family tree in the appendix.) Ptolemy was also a direct descendant of Cleopatra VII, and therefore he was Julia's cousin (their mothers being sisters). Since Ptolemy of Mauretania was the grandson of Cleopatra VII, this marriage was a strategic move that linked Parthia and Libya in a strong dynastic alliance that may not have been greatly approved by Rome.

Since we are looking at alternative names, however, it is worth noting that Cleopatra Selene was obviously the dominant partner in her marriage with Jubba II, at least as far as the naming of their offspring was concerned. Thus it is likely that Ptolemy of Mauretania's full list of titles conformed to the traditional Egyptian Ptolemaic family format. These titles generally included the titles Ieun-Paneter Setepen-Ptah Ir-Maat-en-Ra, ▢⃰ ▢⃰ ◈◈ or various similar permutations on this theme. The meaning of these titles is something like 'Heir of the God, Chosen of Ptah, Carrying out the laws of Ra'. However, the second title could also infer 'Carpenter of Ptah', which is a familiar title in regard to biblical research.

The first part of this title is also interesting, as the slightly different cartouche of Ptolemy VIII demonstrates that the god in question was Ra and this would result in a title that was pronounced as Ieun-Paneter-Ra ▢⃰ instead (the word Paneter is often transliterated as Panedjer). Note that the scribes have positioned both god-flags (neter or nedjer) as facing the god image (Ra), as a mark of respect to the Ra glyph, even though this represents a contravention of the normal rules. But this title gives us an interesting possibility, for if one were simply reading the cartouche from left to right, and ignoring the usual Egyptian conventions regarding the positioning of god-names, the title actually reads as Panter-Ra-Ieun (Pandjer-Ra-Ieun) ▢⃰ meaning 'I am Ra's Heir'. Thus if a scribe had access to the cartouche of a Ptolemy and read from left to right, they would read off the title P.a.n.dj.e.r.R.a, or Pandera. Here is the full reasoning for the Talmudic assertion that the father of Jesus was called Pandera.

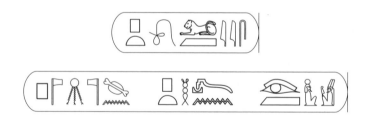

Fig 33. A generic cartouche of a Ptolemy PanterRa-Ieun Setepen-Ptah Irmaat, pharaoh of Egypt.

V   Judaic Names?

About twenty years ago, the author Ahmed Osman [6] determined that Pa-nedjer-Ra referred to the god Ra, which was a revelation in itself, but here we find that PanderRa was used as a formal title by the Ptolemaic dynasty of Egyptian royalty, and that this royal line may well have been the direct ancestor of Jesus (through Thea Muse). This association between the father of Jesus and the god Ra would also explain why the Bible says that Jesus' grandfather was called Helios. The Greek Helios and the Egyptian Ra are, after all, the same deity.

In fact, one can take this argument one stage further in its associations with Jesus, because the full title of Caesarion Ptolemy XV, the son of Cleopatra and Julius Caesar, was (reading phonetically) Pandjer-Ra-Ieun Nehem ⌷⌺ . The final addition to this tile means 'saves', or perhaps more accurately 'saves by water'. Thus Ben Pandira was also the Saviour, as was Jesus himself. In fact, Caesarion would appear to have been the only Ptolemy to have adopted this title. But if Ptolemy of Mauretania, who was the nephew of Caesarion, was inheriting the latter's titles, then he too would have been titled 'Saviour' and may well have passed this title on to his children. Taking all of this into account, the full list of Jesus' titles would have been:

Egyptian title	Biblical title
Setepen Ptah	God's Carpenter
Nehem	Saviour
Ieun Pander Ra	Only Begotten Son (God's heir)
Irmaat Ra	Mediator (God's Judge)

Here, then, we have the intriguing possibility that Jesus was the son of Ptolemy of Mauretania and Julia Ourania. But if this was so, then this would have been another mighty threat to Augustus' leadership of the Roman Empire. In this case, Jesus would have been a direct descendant of the previous emperors and monarchs of Rome, Egypt, North Africa and Parthia; and this would mean that with enough public support, Jesus could have united all of the primary empires of this era. At one stroke, Ptolemy and Julia Ourania could have become king and queen of a united Romo-Egypto-Parthian empire that encompassed nearly all of the known world   and established the most powerful dynasty the world had ever seen. Since the birth of such a well-connected prince to such illustrious parents would have been a grave threat to the reign of Emperor Augustus and King Artabanus II of Parthia, the opposition to Jesus' birth may not simply have come from Herod and the Jerusalem rabbis.

One thing is certain, and that is that the Judaic rabbis knew of Jesus' royal heritage, but chose to deliberately conceal it within convoluted tales and Hebrewised transliterations of Egyptian titles. To have announced to the world that Jesus was descended from Egyptian, Roman and Parthian royalty would have demonstrated that Judaism has a very close relationship with Egyptian theology, and this they could not allow. Instead, in an unlikely collusion between the Judaic rabbis and Saul-Josephus' deliberately vague New Testament accounts, no effort was spared in distancing Jesus and his family from their royal Egyptian and Parthian roots. However, what this process of obfuscation has left us with is a trail of clues that will eventually lead us back to the hidden truth.

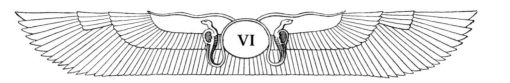

Revised Testament

The evidence shown so far strongly suggests that the biblical family was descended in some manner from the Egypto-Parthian family of Thea Muse Ourania. But a cursory glance at the New Testament accounts will not support that hypothesis in any way, for there does not appear to be any mention of either Persia or Parthia in relation to the biblical family. So how can this be so? If Jesus was descended from Thea Muse, then how was the Egyptian and Egypto-Persian ancestry and culture of the biblical family masked so comprehensively? And, if it has indeed been covered up so successfully, one might also ask how this new theory can ever progress beyond being an unsubstantiated conjecture – for there appears to be no conclusive evidence for this theory within the biblical texts.

However, there may well be a method of seeing through this veil of biblical obfuscation. The first thing to note is that it is highly likely that all of the biblical texts came though the offices of Saul-Josephus, the first century's premier theologian and historian. Although Saul-Josephus was highly prolific in his writing and mostly highly accurate in his endeavours, he was no impartial bystander in this drama. Firstly, Saul-Josephus' historical work had to fit into the Roman perspective of Judaea, for the Romans were his patrons and they expected (on pain of exile or death) that Rome would be portrayed in a favourable light. Secondly, Saul Josephus had serious opposition to his proto-Christian works, both from traditional Jews and also from the Church of Jesus and James: the 'fourth creed' of Judaeo-Israel.

Saul-Josephus' new creed (the fifth way) upset both traditional Judaism and the fourth creed of Jesus and James because it had been opened up to the Goyim – the Gentiles or non-Jews. Saul-Josephus could see that there were more Gentiles in the world than Jews, and if a religion was going to become powerful and influential, it should play to the largest audience. In addition, Judaism was a rigorous religion to follow, while the fourth creed's masonic-style initiatory system meant that only a few selected candidates were accepted. Saul-Josephus saw that the ideal religion allowed anyone in, as long as they put money in the collecting plate. This was the same thought process that eventually initiated the corrupt system of indulgences, or absolution from sin by bribing god, which was nevertheless a reliable road to riches and power.

These tactics worked just as planned, and the Church of Saul-Josephus soon outstripped the parent Judaic belief systems in both influence and resources. In following this strategy, Saul-Josephus also upset the Church of Jesus and James, with his gross distortions of their doctrines. If the Church of Jesus was indeed based upon the Church of Judas of Gamala, it would seem that this sect were primarily libertarians; that is, believers in freedom of thought, expression and will, and also freedom from authoritarian controls and restrictions. As Saul-Josephus says of this 'fourth sect' of Judaism:

> ... they have an inviolable attachment to liberty, and say that god is to be their only ruler or lord. [J1]

In other words, the fourth creed were probably the ancestors of modern Masons. While Masonry has come under attack on many occasions, including from myself, for its policy of nepotism, it is also true that Masonry has attempted to guide Western civilisation away from a state of religious tyranny and towards a society of secular freedoms. The Protestant revolution and the Enlightenment era were both inspired by the Craft, and both resulted in freedoms that society had not experienced for a thousand years or more. The French and American Revolutions were also masonic revolutions, and while these events may have been repressive and bloody in themselves, in each case the goal and the eventual end result was a secular, republican nation guided by the tenets of Liberty, Equality and Fraternity.

This rallying cry to the French Revolution was a masonic phrase long before the revolution began and it underscores many of the aims and goals of Masonry. Liberty: that people should be free from tyranny. Equality: that slavery should be outlawed and all should have an equal chance to progress up the rungs of society. Fraternity: that we should treat our fellow man like a brother, and not an alien or enemy.

Not explicitly included in these three watchwords of Masonry is another basic tenet of the Craft – freedom of religion. As far as Masonry is concerned, while you are supposed to believe in a supreme being, the manner in which you conduct that belief system is up to you. There are no rigid theological doctrines to follow within Masonry, which is why both the French and American constitutions outlawed all religion within the state system. All state functions, from the education system to the courts of law, are supposed to be completely free from religious influences – because religion is supposed to be a personal relationship between an individual and his or her god. As Jesus said:

> And when thou prayest, thou shalt not be as the hypocrites are: for they love to pray standing in the synagogues and in the corners of the streets, that they may be seen of men. Verily I say unto you, They have their reward. But thou, when thou prayest, enter into thy closet, and when thou hast shut thy door, pray to thy Father which is in secret; and thy Father which seeth in secret shall reward thee openly. [B2]

In other words, within the Church of Jesus, the 'fourth creed' of Judaism, there was no need for an oppressive priestly hierarchy and a church in every village keeping a watchful eye on its flock. There would be a great temple for the professional theologians, as was the case in Egypt and the early years of Judaism, but for the common man religion was a private affair. These republican, masonic ethics are the reason why Jesus, Napoleon and George Washington all refused the kingship of their nations, although it was offered to each of them:

> And Pilate asked (Jesus), Art thou the King of the Jews? And he answering said unto him, Thou sayest it [B3]

> Pilate answered them, saying, Will ye that I release unto you the King of the Jews? ... And Pilate answered and said again unto them, What will ye then that I shall do unto him whom ye call the King of the Jews. [B4]

Unlike Jesus and James, Saul-Josephus was not interested in Liberty, Equality and Fraternity, nor was he interested in governing the people wisely and allowing freedom of religion. What Saul-Josephus wanted – and every Church that followed the 'Christian' Church of Saul has wanted ever since – was power and money. Thus the new sect of Christianity was set up with a despotic pseudo-monarch in control of a centralised pyramid of power, and this is what we see today in the Catholic Church and its pope-king. So Saul-Josephus may have used Jesus as an icon for his new Church, but in no way did the fantasy story and the Christian Church that he created reflect the true life of Jesus.

Monarch or republican?

However, if Jesus was indeed descended from the Egypto-Parthian royal family of Thea Muse, it might be countered that Jesus could not simultaneously be masonic, libertarian and republican. This might appear so, but this contradiction may be solved by looking at the evolution of libertarianism and republicanism, for each and every one of these ideals contains its own set of internal contradictions; just as the 'freedom' and 'brotherhood' of Communism was created and maintained by the tyranny of the USSR and the NKVD, Stalin's secret police.

I have a feeling that this kind of libertarianism movement was originally instituted by Pharaoh Akhenaton who, despite his despotic control over the army and the state religion, was decidedly liberal in many other respects. Within the tight straightjacket of his new religion and police-state, Akhenaton allowed many freedoms which allowed a blossoming of new modes of thought and artistic expression that had been unheard of in Egypt for thousands of years. Akhenaton was also so happy – as he and Nefertiti strolled naked around their liberal 'Garden of Eden' [Garden of Aten] in Amarna, like the ancestors of the 1960s hippy movement – that he became distinctly relaxed about his international policy; with the result that vassal states defected and chaos descended upon his borders. Akhenaton may not have been a republican in the true sense of the word, but he was distinctly liberal in many other respects and probably did think he was doing his utmost for the people, rather than the best for himself.

This form of limited liberalism may well have been the role-model for Thea Muse's government. As we shall see shortly, Thea Muse's administration in Parthia was boycotted by the nobility of that empire and so she and her son appealed instead directly to the common people; much as Akhenaton did with his rejection of the traditional priesthood and the creation of his own religious hierarchy. So while Akhenaton and Thea Muse were not real republicans themselves, through their concerted programme of destroying the established aristocracy and appointing a new administrative structure, everything below their status as monarch became fluid and this allowed many of the lower classes to rule instead. So these were both class revolutions, although not exactly in the same mould as the French and American Revolutions. As the ancient Egyptian texts said of an earlier class revolution, which was created during the turbulent Hyksos period:

> The grain is low, the measure is large,
> The weak-armed is strong-armed,
> One salutes him who saluted,

I show you the undermost uppermost,
The beggar will gain riches,
The great will rob to live. [5]

In the first century AD it was to be Jesus who was to lead the new revolution, and this is why he became known as Jesus the Galilean, meaning 'Jesus the Revolutionary'. But the political process of Jesus' administration had moved on a great deal in the twelve or so hundred years since Akhenaton's reign, and masonic-style elections were being held in order to decide upon the new disciple to replace Judas. However, although the levels of political emancipation may initially appear to have increased, I still maintain that the majority of Jesus' disciples were his own brothers. And so, king or no king, it was still the ruling dynasty that controlled the electoral process. Of course, the same is true of modern democracies, despite the illusion that parliaments are controlled by the will of the people. America, for instance, may promote itself as being a true republican state, but it is still a handful of influential families who control the Senate and the choice of president.

So the Church of Jesus may well have been striving for liberty and freedom from doctrine, while the Church of Saul-Josephus was seeking a rigid orthodoxy, oppressive religious laws and a secret religious police-force to enforce this orthodoxy. Of course, it was Saul-Josephus who won this battle and so the Vatican, the Pope and the Inquisition were all created to control our thoughts, to reduce our freedoms and to blight our lives.

It took one and a half millennia to organise, but the Western world eventually fought off this despotic oppression during the Lutherian revolution and the Enlightenment era. However, the Islamic world has never been through this process and so it is still mired in orthodoxy, oppression and tyranny. That Western governments should invite this style of medieval religious repression back into the West – while knowing the level of oppression, tyranny and massacres of the innocents that fundamentalist religions have caused in previous eras – is a grave dereliction of their duty to protect our freedoms and lives bordering on treason. We allow them to continue doing so at our peril.

For Saul-Josephus, back in the first century AD, this difference in doctrine and outlook was probably enough reason to reject and oppress Jesus and Mary Magdalene and the Church they led. But there was another, more important reason for altering the texts of the New Testament in order to excise all references to Thea Muse Ourania and Phraataces, and also those that mentioned Egypt and Parthia. Jesus and Mary Magdalene were descended from the liberal and perhaps slightly hedonistic court of Thea Muse, while Saul-Josephus was a forerunner of the fire-and-brimstone Catholic Church or, indeed, the Puritans.

Similarly, Thea Muse was no doubt a highly independent woman in the direct mould of Cleopatra VII: a woman who was used to power, wealth, ostentatious displays and dominance, not only over the men in her court but also over the men of the priesthood and the aristocracy. Here was a woman who could murder her husband in cold blood, and marry her son in contravention of all the prevailing laws of the land. Thea Muse was obviously not a woman to be trifled with, and for the obsequious, cowardly, craven Saul-Josephus (when faced with his superiors, be they Judaic or Roman), this kind of strong-willed woman probably scared him rigid. Accordingly, when laying out the tenets of Christianity, Saul-Josephus says in his letter to Timothy:

> In like manner also, that women adorn themselves in modest apparel, with shamefacedness and sobriety; not with braided hair, or gold, or pearls, or costly array. [B6]

> But I suffer not a woman to teach, nor to usurp authority over the man, but to be in silence. [B7]

Saul-Josephus' attitude towards women was to provide a conflict of wills, a clash of titans. Whether it was his fear of women like Thea Muse or whether it was simply an opportunity to demonise Jesus and Mary Magdalene, Saul-Josephus outlawed all sexual liberalism and demoted women to the role of priestly assistants. Disgusted with the prospect of incestuous royal marriages in his own backyard, Saul's new sect was to be a Church with strict rules on sexual union and perhaps even a dislike of the whole concept of sex and reproduction. (See the book *Solomon* for another reason for Saul's dislike of sex and reproduction.)

However, it was probably well-known in Syrio-Judaea that Thea Muse had married her son, Phraataces, and so if Jesus was indeed descended from this royal line then none of these court intrigues could be mentioned within the New Testament. The quote from the Babylonian Talmud in Chapter I clearly demonstrates that the Judaic priesthood knew that Mary Magdalene (Jesus' sister) was a royal princess and they were not above making fun of this royal association. Similarly, the Tosephta Sanhedrin says:

> Rabbi Meir used to say ... 'It is like the case of two twin brothers. One ruled over the whole world, the other took to robbery. The one who took to robbery was caught and they crucified him on a cross. And everyone who passed by said "It seems that a king is crucified." ' [T8]

The reference to a twin brother who became a revolutionary and was crucified just has to be a covert reference to Jesus and his twin brother Judas Thomas; especially as the passers-by thought that this man on the cross was a king (of the Jews). This suggestion is reinforced by the commentary on the crucifixion that is recorded in the Koran, where a similar swapping of one twin for another takes place. The Koran says:

> They declared 'We have put to death the Messiah, Jesus the son of Mary, the messenger of God.' But they did not slay him, nor did they crucify him, because he was made to resemble another for them. [K9]

The suggestion is, of course, that it was Judas the twin who was crucified, and not Jesus. Note also that this twin 'ruled over the whole world', which seems to be a reference to a worldly rather then a spiritual realm – a king rather than a prophet. If Jesus was related to Thea Muse, and thus a prince of Rome, Parthia and Egypt, he could indeed have laid claim to being the 'king of the world' – if only he could find a throne to sit on.

The reason for all this covert ecclesiastical sniggering among the Judaic priesthood, which is to be found in the Talmud, was twofold. Firstly, there was the slightly comical plight of a prince with no throne, who tried to muster support to little effect. Secondly, since the royal ancestry of Jesus' family was well known, it was also well known that this royal family had indulged in a court intrigue that included patricide and incest. The Judaic priesthood, who distanced themselves from the fourth sect of Jesus and James, may well have seen an element of humour in all this. However, the puritanical and misogynist Church of Saul-Josephus was founded upon this very same royal family, and so Saul-Josephus had to ensure that all mention of the royal court of Thea Muse and Phraataces was covered up.

One of the methods of masking that Saul-Josephus used was to give Jesus' temporal authority, as a prince of the realm, a spiritual gloss. Thus, the titles Christos and Messiah became synonymous with being anointed by god, as god's son and saviour. But in actual fact these titles referred to the 'anointed one' and they originally denoted the secular authority of an emperor or king. (According to the Gospel of Philip the anointing oil was from the olive, which was called *chrism* and from this was derived the title 'Christ'.) St Clement says of these titles:

> Just as Arsaces was the common title of the Persian king, or Caesar that of the Roman, or Pharaoh that of the Egyptian – so also Christ was the common title for the king of the Jews. [10]

Thus, Jesus the Christ was Jesus the King of the Jews [and Romans and

Parthians and Egyptians], just as the New Testament claims; but Saul-Josephus was not in a position nor in the mood to acknowledge this.

However, masking the entire truth in a historical document is not always possible, especially when the facts are well known. The alternative, as we have already seen from many of the Old Testament texts, is for certain names and locations to be discreetly altered. Change the names, even through the use of local slang and hypocorisms or nicknames, and sometimes the true nature of the events can be utterly shrouded. The only problem with this technique, of course, is that if we can learn the meaning of the slang and the nicknames, then the original historical events suddenly re-emerge from the mists of time virtually unchanged. This is what I shall be attempting in this chapter. As we shall see, the new province of Thea Muse Ourania called Aurania, which lay to the east of the river Jordan, was not censored completely from the New Testament, it was simply and subtly altered to become the 'Kingdom of Heaven'.

Pagan Judaism

Having looked at the reason why the Parthian heritage of the biblical family may have been censored, perhaps the next problem to solve is how the religion of an Egypto-Parthian family could be considered to be in any way Judaic. If the religion of Jesus was based upon Judas of Gamala's, 'fourth creed', it would indeed have been both novel and radical (a revolution or *galilee*). However, this new 'fourth creed' was also supposed to have been based on the creed of the Pharisees – in other words, it was still recognisably Judaic. So in what way was the religion of Thea Muse Ourania, an Egypto-Parthian queen, Judaic?

Actually, perhaps this question should be turned around, for the question should really be 'what exactly was Judaism in this era?' We are all probably aware of what we think Judaism is today, but my previous books have highlighted event after event which demonstrates that Judaism prior to the first century AD was a very different animal. The royal descendants of King Solomon were, for instance, discovered worshipping an erect penis; a phallic fertility symbol. This cult obviously lasted for many centuries because the prophet Jeremiah was fulminating at the Jews for venerating decorated poles. This was quite obviously a May Pole, which is another phallic fertility symbol, and this kind of May Pole dancing used to be very popular in the UK until very recently. Tree worship was also very popular within Judaism, and many a Judaic leader from Abraham through to the kings of the Babylonian exile was guilty of planting sacred groves of trees.

Idolatry was also very popular within Judaism, despite this ritual being entirely contrary to the second of the Ten Commandments. From Moses through to King Solomon, the Judaic people were always being discovered making idols – indeed, King Solomon's Temple seems to have been ornamented with lions and bulls and cherubim, and nobody seems to have minded one iota.

Similarly, the comprehensive history of Judaism provided for us by Saul-Josephus Flavius demonstrates that there was a great deal of astronomical and astrological content within traditional Judaism. The *menorah*, the Judaic seven-branched candlestick, represented the seven known planets, while the twelve loaves of bread on the table (altar) represented the signs of the zodiac – as did the twelve sons of Jacob and the twelve disciples of Jesus. The colourful coats of Joseph and the other Judaic priesthood were also explained by Saul-Josephus in graphic cosmological terms. There were also many synagogues in the third to fifth century AD Israel that had a mosaic zodiac as the primary symbol on the floor of the synagogue. This demonstrates that even in the years following the destruction of the Temple of Jerusalem by the Romans, Judaism still had elements of astrological veneration that were central to the religion. It is unfortunate that debate on the meaning and usage of these zodiacs is largely confined to academic discussion sites, rather than the public arena, Indeed, it is noteworthy that the best analysis I could find of these Jewish zodiacs was written by a Chinese professor from Changchun University in China!

> Our goal is to show that ancient Jews used astrology in much the same way as their neighbors in Palmyra or Nabataea. The Jewish variety of astrology, in turn, will help explain the famous zodiac mosaics. A zodiac in a synagogue meant the same thing as it meant in a temple: it was a symbol of the Supreme Deity, Who ran the universe by the laws of astrology. It is important to emphasize this, for some major scholars of ancient synagogues deny that the ancient Jews did anything as irrational as practice astrology ... In this chapter and the following one, we will show that ancient Jews used astrology in the same ways as their fellow Syrians. [12]

This again demonstrates the ease with which the academic and theological elite can effectively censor the truth about history or a religion. There is no official censorship, as such, but the discussions are rarified and confined to a small academic clique, and so the wider public knows nothing of the true history of their religion. So far, six ancient synagogue mosaics containing images of the zodiac have been discovered in Israel. These pavements date from the third to the sixth century AD and include Hammat Tiberias, Beit

Alpha, Huseifa, Susiya, Naaran, and the recently discovered mosaic at Sepphoris. The Naaran zodiac is described by Dr Ness as being:

> ... a large square, 4.05 meters on a side, containing two concentric circles, 1.6 meters and 3.5 meters in diameter, respectively. The corners hold female figures. They are damaged, but Hebrew labels tell us that they represent the four seasons. Each season was named for one of the Jewish months it contained. Summer is *tebet*, for example. The seasons are also marked with appropriate symbols. Spring, for example, has a bird and tree, while autumn has a star, perhaps for Sirius, the Dog-star, which appears in the autumn.
>
> The space between the two circles is divided into twelve wedges, each just over a meter long. Each held a figure for one of the signs as well as a label in Hebrew. The signs run clockwise, while the seasons run counterclockwise. The signs are not aligned with the proper seasons. Spring, for example, is next to Libra and Virgo, rather than Aries or another of the spring signs. The figures are badly damaged, but they seem to follow the usual Greek iconography of the signs.
>
> The center circle holds a picture of Sol Invictus, the deified sun, driving a four-horse chariot. Two horses are on either side of the chariot. He wears a cloak with stars, a crown of rays, and holds a whip. His face is gouged out, as are those of the horses. [13]

The fact that the seasons are not aligned with the astrological constellations is interesting, and there are two possible reasons for this. Firstly, these zodiacs could be displaying the Egyptian rather than the Syrio-Judaean seasons. The growing season in Egypt was known as *peret*, and this started in October or November, rather than March or April. These Egyptian springtime months coincide with the constellations of Libra and Virgo, just as they do in the Israelite zodiacs, and so this may again point towards an Egyptian ancestry for Judaism.

Alternatively, these zodiacs may have been displaying the millennial precession of the equinox, which I have described in my other works; especially since the seasons are running counterclockwise, as they do in precession. If this is so, then these zodiacs may be designed to show a particular era in history (or in the future). The current zodiac in use in all Western newspapers is significantly out of date as it shows a vernal equinox (March 21st) between the constellations of Aries and Pisces. This means that the 'modern' zodiac has not been updated since the time of Jesus. If these Israelite zodiacs were displaying the usual Western seasons, rather than an Egyptian one, then they are showing a calendar that is 210 precessional degrees, or 15,000 years, before the present time. For the reasons why this era should have been highlighted in this manner, I might refer readers to my book *Thoth:* although it has to be said that this work is decidedly more esoteric than my usual analyses of history.

Fig 35. Mosaic zodiac from the floor of the Hammath synagogue.

Although it may seem strange that the Jews followed astrology, they used to have yet more 'heretical' elements within their creed. The Queen of Heaven was another popular Judaic icon, as can be seen by the veneration of the Queen of Sheba (a name which means Queen of the Stars). The Queen of Sheba was obviously deified in death as being an incarnation of the Egyptian Isis (the Queen of Heaven), but her cult lasted at least until the Babylonian exile, where the prophet Jeremiah was again incandescent that the Jews were worshipping the Queen of Heaven. However, so ingrained was this Jewish cult that the people ignored Jeremiah completely. It is my belief that the exile of these people from Judaea, after the destruction of Jerusalem in 587 BC, was the basis for the emergence of the Sabean empire, and so the Sabeans, or star worshippers, venerated the Queen of Sheba (Queen of the Stars or Queen of Heaven).

There was also the cult of the temple prostitute in Israel, both male and female, and I discuss the similar role of the God's Wife or Temple Virgin at great length in the book *Solomon*. However, the fact that this position did exist in Jerusalem can be seen in the following verse:

> And he took away the male prostitutes out of the land, and removed all the
> idols that his fathers had made. [B14]

The king in question here was King Asa, the great grandson of King
Solomon. However, if there was a pogrom against the male prostitutes at the
Temple of Solomon it was obviously not very successful, because thirteen
generations later we find that King Josiah has exactly the same problem:

> And he brake down the houses of the male prostitutes, that were by the
> house of the lord, where the women wove hangings for the sacred grove. [B15]

Note the mention of the sacred grove once more.

So, from the United Monarchy of King David and King Solomon all
the way through to the Babylonian exile, the Jews were indulging in a
variety of 'pagan' rites, including sacred prostitution, idolatry, astrology,
mother goddess worship, tree worship and phallic worship. Bearing all of
this in mind, what exactly was the creed of Judaism in the first millennium
BC? How do we begin to define it? If Thea Muse of Parthia was indulging in
a little phallus veneration, as she well might have been, was she not
practising Judaism? If Thea Muse consulted her court astrologer, as she most
probably did, was she not following the strict tenets of Judaism? If Thea
Muse gave some money to the Temple of Jerusalem for the provision of
temple prostitutes, was she not being a pious Jewess?

In short, it would seem that the Judaism of this era was very akin to
Egyptian and Parthian belief systems, and thus Thea Muse could well have
been considered to be a Jewess. But if an Egypto-Parthian queen could be
seen as a Jewess, then, conversely, might not some the rituals of the 'fourth
creed' appear to be rather Egypto-Parthian?

The Talmud certainly thinks so of the biblical Jesus, for as we have
already seen it specifically identifies him as being an Egyptian Magi, or
magician:

> 'Did not (Jesus) bring spells from Egypt in a cut upon his flesh?' They said to
> him 'He was a fool, and they do not bring proof from a fool'. [T16]

Likewise we have again seen evidence that Josephus Flavius also thought
that Jesus was called the Egyptian False Prophet. In other words, far from
her Egypto-Parthian heritage making an association between Thea Muse
and Jesus utterly impossible, it would seem that it is absolutely essential for
any claimant to the position of Jesus to have an Egypto-Parthian
background.

Jesus was known in his own era as the 'Egyptian False Prophet', and yet when he was born he was visited by the Parthian (Persian) Magi. It is obvious, therefore, that Jesus had both Egyptian and Parthian ancestry. But Jesus was also demonstrably aristocratic, from a royal family of some nature. There was only one Egypto-Parthian royal family who was exiled to Syrio-Judaea early in the first century AD, and that was the family of Thea Muse Ourania and Phraataces. Ergo, one might say, Jesus and Mary Magdalene must have been descended in some manner from Thea Muse Ourania, the exiled queen of Parthia.

So the ancestry of Jesus may well have been through Thea Muse and thus through Cleopatra VII. However, if we look to the New Testament for an answer to the question of Jesus' ancestry, we are in for a bit of a shock. Unfortunately, the genealogies that these texts provide are entirely contradictory, and so they cannot tell us anything about Jesus' origins. However, it might be worth pointing out that within these two genealogies, the name Sadoc (Zadok) belonged to a colleague of Judas of Gamala, while Heli was the name of Cleopatra VII's son by Mark Antony.

Genealogy of Jesus according to the gospel of:

Matthew	Luke
Jesus	Jesus
Joseph	Joseph
Jacob	Heli
Matthan	Matthat
Eelizar	Levi
Eliud	Melchi
Achim	Janna
Sadoc	Joseph
etc:	etc:

Kingdom of Heaven

The evidence seems to suggest that the ritual and religion of early Judaism could easily have been confused with Egypto-Parthian rituals. Having said that, there still does not appear to be much, if anything, within the New Testament that can be said to directly link the biblical family with the Parthian royal family. But that may simply be because we are conditioned to these biblical events all occurring among a poor artisan's family in Judaea and Galilee, and not among the pseudo-masonic royalty of Bethanya to the east of the river Jordan.

But if we expand our horizons a little and empty our mind of preconditions, it is just possible that an alternative gospel may appear before our eyes. For example, it is said of John the Baptist:

> Verily I say unto you, among them that are born of women there hath not arisen a greater than John the Baptist: yet he that is but little in the Kingdom of Heaven is greater than he. [B17]

If we were to read this verse superficially, it would seem that John is being described as an ordinary man, for we are all born of women; and so a comparison is presumably being made between mortals and semi-divine beings like Jesus. However, the verse goes on to say that anyone who was born in the Kingdom of Heaven would be greater than John. But since Jesus was supposed to have been the unique creation of a singular god, who else in the Kingdom of Heaven could have been greater than John? The verse does not seem to make a great deal of sense, but perhaps we are not reading it correctly.

Those who have 'ears to hear' might have noticed that *gune* γυνη, the Greek term for 'woman', can also be translated as 'widow'. If the latter were the correct reading then John would have been referred to as a 'Son of a Widow', which would make his position much more clear. The term 'Son of a Widow' refers to a Mason, and since I have already demonstrated that Jesus was a Mason, this would make a great deal of sense. With this alteration, this same verse would now read as:

> Verily I say unto you, Among them that are Masons there hath not arisen a greater than John the Baptist: yet even those who are lowly in the Kingdom of Heaven are greater than he.

Contrary to the standard interpretations of the New Testament, John the Baptist actually appears to have been a leading Mason rather than a Neolithic *Stig of the Dump* character, covered in animal skins. Instead of being a humble hermit, he was probably a Past-Master in the esoteric arts and Gnostic theology (and since the Egyptian high priesthood wore the leopard skin as a mark of their high office, perhaps John did wear a few animal skins). This alternative interpretation of John's status is supported by a comment in the Clementine Recognitions, which states:

> It was at Alexandria that Simon (Magus) perfected his studies, being an adherent of John (the Baptist) ... Of all John's disciples, Simon was his favourite. [18]

Again, this verse identifies John the Baptist as being someone far removed from the hairy hermit of popular biblical mythology, for it would appear that he was an influential teacher in Alexandria, the most cosmopolitan city in the Roman empire. In addition, the term *magus* has already been explained as denoting a Parthian astrologer or councillor, one of the Magi 'wise men' who came to visit the infant Jesus. So why, in this case, was John the Baptist the tutor of a (possibly influential) Parthian (Persian) astrologer and councillor?

The answer to this can be found in the verse about John the Baptist we have just looked at. The second sentence of this verse seems to suggest that only those in the 'Kingdom of Heaven' can be greater than John the Baptist, and this is most definitely the theological interpretation of this verse that the Catholic Church would like to promote. But what does the 'Kingdom of Heaven' actually refer to? It may superficially appear to be a common biblical term that refers to the 'Kingdom of God', and not something worth exploring; but in fact this title is only used in the Gospel of Matthew, and it may well have a completely different meaning to the one normally supposed. The true interpretation of this title can be seen if we use the original Greek term for 'heaven', which is *ouranos* ουρανος. Using the original Greek term, the verse now becomes:

> Verily I say unto you, Among them that are Masons there hath not arisen a greater than John the Baptist: yet even those who are lowly in the <u>Kingdom of Ourania</u> are greater than he.

Wow! Surprising as it may seem, the true translation for Matthew's 'Kingdom of Heaven' is the 'Kingdom of Ourania', and it is highly likely that this was actually a reference to the 'Kingdom of Thea Muse Ourania', the exiled queen of Parthia.

The alternative to this title, which is used in the other gospels of the New Testament, is the 'Kingdom of God'. Again, this may seem like a spiritual abode in the heavens, but in actual fact this title is simply using the term *theos* θεος or *thea* θεα; and so the biblical 'Kingdom of God' was called the 'Kingdom of Thea'. When combining the titles of these two common biblical kingdoms, we can now derive the 'Kingdom of Thea Ourania', and this just has to be a reference to the 'Kingdom of Thea Muse Ourania'.

However, it should be remembered that we have already identified exactly where the Kingdom of Thea Muse Ourania was. This kingdom was no longer in Parthia itself, for Thea Muse and Phraataces had already been exiled from that land; instead it was a small province to the east of the river Jordan, and it was indeed called the Kingdom of Aurania, or the Kingdom of Ourania. In fact, this name is the basis of the modern name for this region, which is the Hauran.

Thus, this verse from the New Testament was intimating that John the Baptist was an influential Mason, but that those Masons who had arrived in Syrio-Judaea from Parthia were much more influential than he. Once more, this evidence suggests that Jesus was born from the royal family of Thea Muse Ourania, the queen of Parthia – and so yes, Jesus did understand himself to be of a greater social status and importance than John.

The 'Kingdom of Heaven' is mentioned numerous times within the Gospel of Matthew, so is it possible that the radical new interpretation for this title can be sustained and justified?

> Another parable put he forth unto them, saying, The Kingdom of Heaven is like to a grain of mustard seed, which a man took, and sowed in his field. Which indeed is the least of all seeds: but when it is grown, it is the greatest among herbs, and becomes a tree, so that the birds of the air come and lodge in its branches. [B19]

> Another parable he spake unto them; The Kingdom of Heaven is like unto yeast, which a woman took, and hid in three measures of meal, till the whole was leavened. All these things Jesus said unto the multitude in parables. [B22]

These parables may seem insignificant, but they both indicate that the 'Kingdom of Heaven' was quite small, and that it is destined to grow larger. Theologians will say that this parable pertains to the Church itself, and in the light of these investigations it may well refer to the 'fourth creed' of Judas, which was superseded by the Church of Saul (Christianity).

However, it is also possible that these parables refer to the Kingdom of Ourania once more. Thea Muse's empire had once encompassed all of the lands of the Parthian empire, but the royal family was now exiled in a small province called Bethanya (Aurania), located to the east of the river Jordan. The royal family had arrived in Bethanya with a hundred assorted family members and courtiers, plus a small loyal detachment from the army. The Kingdom of Ourania was most definitely a 'mustard seed', and it was desperately seeking to expand in any direction that it could. This expansion included designs on retaking Parthia, and also on the neighbouring state of Judaea itself.

But if the province of Ourania (Aurania) desired to expand then it needed manpower. The answer to this requirement was to send out the disciples, saying:

> Blessed are the poor in spirit: for theirs is the Kingdom of Heaven.

Blessed are they which are <u>persecuted for righteousness' sake</u>: for theirs is the Kingdom of Heaven. [B23]

This was not a supernatural afterlife that was being offered to the huddled masses; instead, it was a life of toil in the province of Ourania (Bethanya), in return for the basics of food and shelter. Since this has been a successful ploy used by many an emerging empire, it is not so surprising that we should see its reappearance in our modern era:

> Give me your tired, your poor,
> Your huddled masses, yearning to breathe free,
> The wretched refuse of your teeming shore,
> Send these, the homeless, tempest tossed to me,
> I lift my lamp beside the golden door! [24]

As far as America was concerned, the majority of people who arrived on those shores were also 'persecuted for righteousness' sake' – oppressed by the various 'peace loving' religious sects and authorities that still stalked the European continent.

So it would seem that the New Testament disciples were looking for immigrant workers to construct their new city in Ourania. And just in case the poor, huddled masses were afraid of the long journey to the east, the disciples in Judaea also preached:

> And as ye go, preach, saying, The Kingdom of Heaven is nearby. [B25]

While this argument can hardly be construed as positive evidence that the 'Kingdom of Heaven' referred to the 'Kingdom of Ourania', there is another parable that places this interpretation beyond doubt. We shall come to this parable in a minute, but in the meantime the following verse deals with moneylending. The orthodox view is that Jesus was against moneylending and profit, but if he was a son of Judas of Gamala, the collector of the taxes in Aurania, then Jesus should have been in favour of taxation and profit. As we have seen, Jesus often met with tax collectors, but was he a capitalist too?

This is highly likely, for there is a curious parable in which an employer from the Kingdom of Ourania gives money to three of his servants and then departs on a long journey. Upon his return two of the servants had invested their money and doubled it. However, the third servant simply stored the money and just gave it back later, with no interest. At this, the employer from the Kingdom of Ourania (Aurania) had a fit of rage:

> His lord answered and said unto him, Thou wicked and slothful servant ...

> Thou oughtest to have put my money to the exchangers, and then at my coming I should have received mine own with usury (interest). Take therefore the money from him, and give it unto him which hath more money. For unto every one that hath shall be given, and he shall have abundance: but from him that hath not shall be taken away even that which he hath. [B26]

Have readers never wondered why such a strange parable was placed in the New Testament? It is not the sort of thing that gets preached much from the pulpit, is it? ('Dorothy, I would suggest that we take everything from the poor of this parish and, err, let's give it all to the wealthy.' 'Oh yes indeed, splendid idea. More tea vicar?')

This is not exactly the kind of socialist ethos that we are conditioned to expect from Jesus' teachings, but this is entirely the style of government that Judas of Gamala would have been familiar with. Judas was running an independent tax-free province, and he needed good investments to meet his expenses and pay for his standing army, which included 500 cavalry. In addition, the province of Ourania (Aurania) needed an administrative authority, which could carry out the diktats of the ruling family. This topic is also discussed in the New Testament, and the verse in question reads as:

> At the same time came the disciples unto Jesus, saying, Who is the greatest in the Kingdom of Heaven? And Jesus called a little child unto him, and set him in the midst of them. And said, Verily I say unto you, Except ye be converted, and become as little children, ye shall not enter into the Kingdom of Heaven. Whosoever therefore shall humble himself as this little child, the same is greatest in the Kingdom of Heaven. [B27]

At first reading, it might seem impossible that this statement could have anything to do with a royal court, but this is not the case as the term for 'little child' is *paidion* παιδιον, which can also be interpreted as a 'king's servant' or 'minister'. If these same verses were to be interpreted in this manner, then they could be translated as:

> At the same time the disciples came to Jesus, saying, Who is the greatest in the Kingdom of Aurania? And Jesus called a minister unto him, and set him in the midst of them. And said, Verily I say unto you, except ye be converted, and become as king's servants, ye shall not enter into the Kingdom of Aurania. Whosoever therefore shall prostrate himself as this government minister has, will be great in the Kingdom of Aurania.

In this new interpretation, Jesus is looking for chief ministers and courtiers to administer his new kingdom and budding empire. However, if this were the case then it would appear that Jesus was looking for blind loyalty to his regime and complete submission to his authority. So were Judas of Gamala and Jesus of Gamala looking for administrators to assist them with a religious movement, or were they instead looking for cravenly loyal servants and ministers in order to emulate the functioning of the great royal houses of the Parthian east?

> For there are some eunuchs, which were so born from their mother's womb: and there are some eunuchs, which were made eunuchs of men: and there be eunuchs, which have made themselves eunuchs for the Kingdom of Heaven's sake. He that is able to embrace this way of life, let him embrace it. [B28]

Again, the subject matter of this verse is rather peculiar, especially for the lowly Judaean artisan that Jesus was supposed to have been. What were the gawping ill-educated masses supposed to make of this instruction or parable? In fact, eunuchs have little or nothing to do with the Judaean royalty either, so why on Earth did the topic of eunuchs enter Jesus' conversation?

The answer is that this verse is simply a continuation of the discussion about ministers and courtiers (the 'little children') that has just been explored. The eunuch of the royal court was actually a Persian invention and the original duties of this courtier was to attend to the personal needs of the king. Because these intimate duties brought these courtiers into the king and queen's bed-chamber, it was considered prudent that castrated males should be employed, in order to reduce the number of court intrigues and eliminate the possibility of royal bastards. It was from the Greek *eune* ευνη meaning 'bed' that the term eunuch was derived. However, this intimacy with the king allowed the eunuchs to become highly influential and powerful advisers and ministers within the royal court.

The position of royal eunuch was taken to Egypt with the Persian conquest of that country, and once more the eunuchs became very influential ministers within the Egyptian court. Indeed, the eunuch Ganymedes was an adviser and general of Princess Arsinoe, Cleopatra VII's sister. As a general of the Egyptian army, Ganymedes almost captured Julius Caesar himself in the battle of Alexandria.

That Jesus was discussing the role of a eunuch with his disciples is highly illuminating. That this discussion was also combined with his request for ministers in his budding 'Kingdom of Ourania' is nothing short of astounding – for it would appear that Jesus was requesting that some of his disciples should become eunuchs in order to work in his fledgling royal court.

While none of these verses might be construed as positive proof that the 'Kingdom of Heaven' referred to the 'Kingdom of Ourania' (Aurania), the following quote is far more explicit and convincing.

> And Jesus answered and spake unto them again by parables, and said, "The Kingdom of Heaven is like unto a certain king, which made a marriage for his son. And sent forth his servants to call them that were bidden to the wedding: and they would not come."
>
> Again, he sent forth other servants, saying, "Tell them which are bidden, Behold, I have prepared my dinner: my oxen and my fatlings are killed, and all things are ready: come unto the marriage. But they made light of it, and went their ways, one to his farm, another to his merchandise. And others took the kings servants, and entreated them spitefully, and slew them."
>
> But when the king heard thereof, he was angry: and he sent forth his armies, and destroyed those murderers ... Then saith he to his servants, "The wedding is ready, but they which were bidden were not worthy. Go ye therefore into the highways, and as many as ye shall find, invite them to the marriage." So those servants went out into the highways, and gathered together all as many as they found, both bad and good: and the wedding was furnished with guests. [B29]

So what on Earth is this parable all about? The Church takes this as being a parable regarding the Church itself, with the 'king' being a reference to god and the 'son' being Jesus; while the 'marriage feast' was a reference to the Gospels, and the 'invited guests' an allusion to the common people who either accept or reject the Church. But this explanation is all a little contrived, and even if this scenario were true, upon what real events was this parable originally based? A parable only works if the common people can identify with the real social event it describes, as well as with the deeper meaning that it conceals – so who was this king whose nobles and lords refused to come to the wedding feast of his son? Whose day of betrothal turned into a riot? And why was Jesus, the supposed lowly 'carpenter', so interested in the court intrigues of royal dynasties rather than a humble village gathering?

The true answer to this conundrum lies in the fact that this royal family, whose wedding was rejected by the aristocracy of the realm, came from the Kingdom of Heaven. Again, this was not supposed to be a reference to the heavenly kingdom of the gods, but to the terrestrial Kingdom of Aurania, the Kingdom of Thea Muse Ourania. Once we understand this connection, Jesus' peculiar parable becomes fully understandable in each and every respect.

Firstly, the new interpretation of Jesus' ancestry and social standing being forged in this book would ensure that his parables naturally focused upon royalty, rather than the common people, because Jesus was a prince – a prince descended directly from the Egyptian and Persian royal lines, no less.

Secondly, we know that there *was* indeed a disputed marriage within the original Kingdom of Ourania (or Parthia), and this was the highly contentious marriage of Thea Muse Ourania and Phraataces. So despised was this royal Parthian marriage that I have no doubt that the noble guests from across the land did indeed refuse to come to the wedding feast, and it is highly likely that some used violence against the king's servants in order to vent their anger. In fact, the internal strife caused by this wedding was so divisive that the monarch and the prince, Thea Muse and Phraataces, were obliged to go into exile shortly afterwards.

A royal wedding where the honoured guests refuse to attend was hardly a common event in the ancient world, so what other royal marriage could Jesus be referring to? It is an absolute certainty that Jesus' parable must have been alluding to this contentious marriage of Thea Muse and Phraataces in Parthia; and so what we appear to have here is a great deal more information on this marriage than has been given to us by Saul-Josephus. The New Testament is indicating that because the aristocracy of Parthia refused to come to the wedding, Thea Muse and Phraataces dressed up the common people in *kaftans*, the robes that were given to people who are about to have an audience with the monarch, and used the common people as wedding guests instead.

Can you imagine such a scandal? A son of the Queen of England, for instance, getting married in St Paul's Cathedral and the entire congregation being composed of plebeians and beggars from the streets, all dressed in royal and lordly ermine. The aristocracy of the nation would, of course, have felt deeply angry and resentful. Not only had their complaints about the unconstitutional marriage been ignored by the royal family in the first place, but the lords' and nobles' positions of authority had been deliberately usurped and undermined by the common people. And the paupers of the land, all newly dressed up in as much aristocratic finery as could be found, were no doubt cocking a snoot at the nobility, who were probably protesting loudly outside the wedding hall. It is no wonder that the situation descended into chaos and conflict.

Not only were these the common people but there were also undesirables among them, and perhaps we can see in this bizarre marriage ceremony the origins of Jesus' empathy with the common people. The aristocracy opposed the marriage between Thea Muse and Phraataces, a rejection that this Egypto-Parthian royal family simply could not understand, but the common people and the criminals were quite happy to attend the wedding and pay homage to the royal family. The Parthian monarchy were, in short, appealing directly to the common people for their support, rather than using the nobility as deputies and intermediaries in the normal manner. This direct appeal to the masses was a distinctive trait of Jesus and his followers and their subsequent reputation for being revolutionaries or *galileans* may well have stemmed from this very event.

Thirdly, it might be presumed that there is a problem in this analysis, for the parable talks about a king and Thea Muse was most definitely a queen. Actually, this is not a great problem for the New Testament mentions a *basileus* βασιλευς or 'king' while, in a similar fashion, the Parthian coinage of Thea Muse calls her a *basilisses* βασιλεσσες. The similarity between these two terms makes the possibility of a transposition, by a scribe, intent on concealing the unmentionable truth, highly likely. So this wedding was not arranged for the son of the king so much as for the son of the queen, and the queen in question was Thea Muse Ourania.

Fourthly, let us briefly recap the reasons why the noble guests refused to come to the king or queen's wedding in the first place. The account by Matthew makes little comment on this refusal, but in fact the nobility were committing treason here. This was an order by the reigning monarch to attend the wedding of a prince of the realm, and the aristocracy simply refused to come *en masse*. So what made them make this bold stand against the monarch? What was so terrible about this particular marriage that they would risk their titles and perhaps their very lives by refusing to attend? As we have seen, the answer is to be found in Josephus' Antiquities, where he says of Thea Muse and Phraataces:

> (Phraataces) therefore formed a treacherous design against his father (Phraates IV), by his mother's assistance, with whom, as the report went, he had criminal sexual relations also. So he was hated for both these vices, while his subjects esteemed this wicked love of his mother to be no way inferior to his patricide; and he was by them, in a sedition, expelled out of the country before he grew too great. [130]

This was not simply a sexual infatuation between mother and son, for the coinage of Parthia clearly demonstrates that mother and son were married as king and queen. This was the reason for the aristocracy, in the biblical parable, refusing to come to the marriage of their prince – for the prince concerned was Phraataces and he had already assisted his mother in the poisoning of his father, Phraates IV. Not only was the prince condemned for this criminal act, but he was now inviting the aristocracy to a wedding feast to celebrate his marriage to his mother. There are not many events that will trigger a revolt against a royal marriage, or that will foster treason among the aristocracy, but in Parthia this was definitely one of them. Polygamy and incest may have been *de rigueur* within the royal court of Egypt, but it most certainly was not in Parthia, and the result of this clash of customs was a short and decisive civil war and the exile of the royal family to Syrio-Judaea.

Strange as it may seem, the Gospel of Matthew contains a peculiar parable that makes very little sense in its traditional interpretation. However, if this parable is read instead as being a reliable description of the deadly intrigues that occurred within the royal Parthian court, it makes every sense. But Matthew does not just mention this contentious marriage, he places this parable in the mouth of Jesus himself, and so leads us to an inescapable conclusion. For Jesus to have been so concerned about this contentious marriage that he used it in his teachings, he must have been directly related to Queen Thea Muse Ourania and King Phraataces. In other words, Jesus was one of the royal princes of the Egypto-Parthian royal court, who were living in exile in the province of Bethanya ([Bethany] or Aurania.

But if the Kingdom of Heaven (Kingdom of Ourania) and the Kingdom of God (Kingdom of Thea) both refer to the Kingdom of Thea Muse Ourania, then perhaps we can also translate another famous title in much the same fashion. Of all Jesus' titles, perhaps the 'Son of God' is the most theologically evocative – Jesus, the son of the all-powerful deity, the saviour of mankind. However, a more direct and rational translation of this title may again be the 'Son of Thea'. [32] In other words, Jesus was not accused of being the son of a god in the biblical accounts, he was accused of being the son of Thea Muse Ourania.

Seven devils

It would seem that many of Jesus' parables and sayings were related to the Egypto-Parthian royalty of Thea Muse. In an earlier chapter it was confidently stated that Mary Magdalene was the sister-wife of Jesus, but if this were so then she too should betray some similarities to the world of an Egypto-Parthian princess. This is what we find, but again the evidence has been buried deeply within the convoluted terminology of the New Testament. Take the following verse, for instance:

And a certain woman, which had been healed of evil spirits and infirmities,

Mary called Magdalene, out of whom went seven devils. [B33]

και γυναικες τινες αι ησαν τεθεραπευμεναι απο πνευματων
πονηρων και ασθενειων μαρια η καλουμενη μαγδαληνη αφ ης
δαιμονια επτα εξεληλυθει

The evil spirits are the *poneros pneuma* πονηρος πνευμα, or unclean winds, which the Koran has interpreted as the *jinn* or dust devils, the pocket-sized tornadoes that frequently traverse the sands of the Arabias. However, these winds do not have to be quite so large, as they can also refer to a breath from the mouth or nostrils. The term for the devils can also have another interpretation placed upon it, as the *daimonion* δαιμονιον can equally refer to a god or a goddess. Using these and other alterations, an alternative translation for this biblical verse might be:

> And a certain women, who had been healed by separation from bad breath and weakness, Mary called Magdalene, out of whom went seven goddesses.

Humorous as this verse may now seem, I don't think that it referred to halitosis; rather, these bad or evil breaths had some kind of spiritual nature to them. In the book *Eden* I noted that, like Mary Magdalene, the title of Queen Nefertiti also referred to winds or breaths, with her name even including the trachea glyph 𓏏. Several suggestions were made as to why that should be, but no final conclusion was drawn at that time. However, in the Greco-Roman world of the first century AD we seem to have another famous 'princess', of possible Egypto-Parthian heritage, who is again somehow related to breaths or winds. So what does all of this mean, and why was breathing thought to be evil in some circumstances?

While I cannot be certain about this, I am sure that this verse must be an oblique reference to the Nine Muses of Greek mythology, who were minor goddesses of particular human attributes or endeavours. The number of Muses was variable and while the number finally stabilised at nine, it started at three and there may well have been just seven at some juncture. The latter figure would then complement the seven liberal arts or sciences of Masonry.

The initial three Muses were said to be Aoide (song), Melete (practice) and Mneme (memory). In later traditions these were altered and added to, to become the nine (no doubt to fall in line with the traditional *enead*, or the nine gods, of Egypt). The nine Muses were known as Calliope (poetry), Euterpe (music), Clio (history), Erato (lyrics), Melpomene (tragedy), Polyhymnia (sacred poetry), Terpsichore (dancing), Thalia (comedy) and Ourania (astronomy). In comparison, the seven liberal arts and sciences of Masonry are said to be grammar, rhetoric, logic, arithmetic, geometry, music and astronomy. Note that there is an amount of synergy between these two lists, a similarity that may become relevant to this investigation shortly.

The connection between 'bad breath' and the Muses is derived from the fact that the title 'Muse' was derived from the Greek *mousa* μουσα meaning 'song'; as the many attributes of the Muses were often formed into ballads and sung to the audience, as indeed were the great epics like the Iliad and Odyssey. It is from these lyrical Muses that we derive the English term 'music'. But, of course, a song is produced by a breath from the mouth, and so Mary Magdalene's 'bad breath' may well have referred to the Muses of Greece. While this link may seem a little tenuous, in actual fact we still use the same terminology today. The nine Muses were said to be the 'Inspirational Muses', in that their purpose was to inspire, invigorate or stimulate the mind. However, the word inspire also means to 'breathe in', a word that was taken from the Latin *spirare* meaning 'to breathe'.

So the process of education through stimulation of the mind involved breaths of air. I have no doubt that this concept was derived in some manner from the Egyptian opening of the mouth ceremony, where the deceased required their mouths opening in a special ceremony. No doubt this process allowed the *ka* and *ba*, the life and soul of the deceased, to come and go, to and from the body as they pleased. However, a simple extension of this belief-system may well have suggested to the Egyptians that the living can be 'inspired' through a similar process of breathing. So, at a simplistic level, the education of the mind involved the tutor breathing out information and knowledge, and the pupils breathing it in, and this was the reason for Mary Magdalene being associated with breaths (bad or otherwise).

This Egyptian explanation may also be the reason behind the spelling of Queen Nefertiti's name. As has already been mentioned, Nefertiti was associated in some manner with winds or breaths, but the link with the Greek Muses might suggest that this 'breathing' or 'inspiration' should include several different types of knowledge or gnosis. Perhaps this is why we find that Nefertiti's name included five tracheae glyphs – did her title therefore refer to five Egyptian Muses?

As a partial confirmation that these Egyptian tracheae glyphs were somehow related to the breaths of the Greek Muses, it is interesting to note that the Arabic *jinn* not only refers to a 'genie' but also to the 'heart'. It may be from the Arabic notion of the dust-devil being a physical humanoid entity, and therefore a genie of *Aladdin and the Lamp* fame, that the biblical notion of a wind being a spirit (a ghost) was derived. But the Arabic etymology also suggests that breaths are somehow connected with the heart, and the Egyptian *nefer* ⫯ glyph appears to confirm this. For whatever reason, the Egyptians have placed the tracheae on top of a heart glyph, to form the composite *nefer* glyph; and so it seems likely that the Arabic *jinn* and the Greek *muse* were indeed related to the Egyptian *nefer* glyph and thus to Nefertiti.

Fig 36. Cartouche of Queen Nefertiti, or perhaps Neferutiti (the plural).

Bearing in mind all of these diverse arguments, the biblical verse just quoted might now be translated as:

> And a certain women, who had been healed by separation from bad Muses and weakness, Mary called Magdalene, out of whom went the seven Muses.

I was unable to find any suitable translation for the word *poneros* meaning 'evil' and so the reason for the Muses being evil remained a mystery at this stage. So why was Mary only 'healed' when the Muses, or knowledge (gnosis), had been taken out of her? The answer to this is that we may be seeing this verse through the eyes of Saul and his despotic offspring, which is now known as the Catholic Church. I have previously argued that Saul, the founder of the Catholic Church, was not initiated into the higher degrees of the Church of Jesus and James, and so he remained ignorant and fearful of the seven sciences. This was certainly so of the later Catholic Church, which proved to be the second largest millstone around the neck of mankind's technological and educational advancement – the largest millstone being Islam.

The Dark Ages of the first millennium AD were characterised by irrationality, superstition, and theological persecution and tyranny. This was gradually replaced during the Renaissance era by a grudging tolerance of some science and rational enquiry by the all-powerful Church, but the early practitioners of alchemy and astronomy always diced with death as they probed nature for logical, rational explanations. It was not until the early eighteenth century, following the retreat of the Catholic Church in the face of the Protestant revolution in northern Europe, that the true era of the

Enlightenment arose. This was the Age of Reason, as it is sometimes known; the era of freedom from religious tyranny.

It is no coincidence that it was precisely in this era that the Masons came out of the closet and formed the United Grand Lodge of England in 1717. Their daughter institution, the Royal Society, was founded shortly afterwards and this became Britain's premier scientific institution. The Royal Society was a brave new world of enlightenment, where experiments were made and conclusions were drawn that would have warranted burning at the stake in previous centuries. It was through this process of rational enquiry that the technical and industrial revolution was born, and so we owe our present wealth and contentment to both Martin Luther and the underground stream of masonic-type institutions. However, Islam has not had its Renaissance as yet, let alone its Enlightenment, and so the fundamentalist believers of the so-called 'Religion of Peace' will no doubt be murdering freethinkers in the name of the Compassionate and Merciful for some time to come.

The early Church of Saul bore more than a passing similarity to the so-called 'Religion of Peace'. So, when looking at the position of Mary Magdalene from the perspective of Saul-Josephus and his repressive, introspective Catholic Church, perhaps the biblical verse just quoted may now make a little more sense.

The seven sciences of Masonry were evil enough, in the eyes of the Catholic Church, but perhaps the seven Muses were even worse. These were seven women (goddesses) and they were practising music and dancing, while studying history and astronomy. Indeed, one of our primary institutions for learning in the modern era is the museum, which literally means the 'House of the Muses', the house where one was free to indulge in the liberal arts and even the sciences. The famous Museum of Alexandria was constructed by Ptolemy I and was, unsurprisingly, dedicated to the Greek Muses. Queen Cleopatra VII, supposedly a scholar of some ability herself, would have been familiar with the Museum of Alexandria and its association with the Muses – indeed, the queen herself was named after the Muse Clio.

However, as we know from the recent history of the Taliban of Afghanistan, if the fundamentalist theists take control of society, then all of these areas of study and enjoyment are instantly banned – for god does not want his wisdom challenged by mere mortals (or rather the fundamentalist theists do not want independent, freethinkers punching great holes in their unsubstantiated arguments and their illogical assumptions).

This was likely to have been the fate that Mary Magdalene was suffering at the hands of the misogynist Saul. Mary was not a 'sinner', as the New Testament scribes try to impress upon us, she was an educated and liberated woman in the Egyptian and Parthian royal tradition. Music, song, poetry and dancing were encouraged in the Egyptian, Persian and Parthian royal courts, and no doubt Mary was proficient at all these arts, and probably many of the sciences too. The fact that this is true is made perfectly clear in the Gnostic gospels from the Nag Hammadi collection. Here, it is made perfectly plain that Mary was a senior disciple of Jesus, perhaps even his 'right-hand man' *(sic)*, as the *Last Supper* painting by Leonado da Vinci strongly suggests. In the Gospel of Mary it is said:

> Then Mary stood up ... and said to her brethren, 'Do not weep and do not grieve ... for his grace will be entirely with you and will protect you.' When Mary said this, she turned their hearts to the good and they began to discuss the words of the saviour.

> Peter said to Mary, 'Sister, we know that the Saviour loved you more than the rest of women. Tell us the words of the Saviour which you remember – which you know but we do not, nor have we heard them.' Mary answered and said, 'What is hidden from you I will discuss with you.' And she began to speak to them. [N34]

Firstly, it should be noted that Mary greets the disciples as 'her brethren', and while this may be an allusion to the members of a congregation or Church, many of the disciples may well have been Mary's real brothers. In the book *Jesus* I made a strong case that Mary was both Jesus' wife and his sister, and that their incestuous union was derived from the traditions of the Egyptian royalty. The evidence presented in this book can only serve to confirm this assertion, for we know that Thea Muse and Phraataces indulged in a similar incestual union. Were Jesus and Mary to be descended from this Egypto-Parthian royal line, their sibling marriage is not only likely, it is almost a certainty.

Secondly, it can be clearly seen from these two short paragraphs that Mary Magdalene was not only well versed in the secrets of the Church of Jesus and James, but that she was perhaps also its highest initiate. Certainly she was well above Peter, who went on with Saul-Josephus to found the rival Catholic Church, and so Mary must have been fully 'inspired' with knowledge and gnosis. But this deep knowledge caused friction within the uninitiated disciples:

> But Andrew answered and said to the brethren, "Say what you wish about what she has said. I at least do not believe that the saviour said this. For certainly these teachings are strange ideas." Peter answered and spoke concerning these same things. He questioned them about the saviour: "Did

he really speak with a woman without our knowledge and not openly? Are we to turn about and all listen to her? Did he prefer her to us?" Levi answered and said to (Simon) Peter, "Peter, you have always been hot-tempered. Now I see you contending against (Mary) like our adversaries. But surely if the saviour made her worthy, who are you to reject her? Surely the saviour knows her very well. That is why he loved her more than us." [N35]

Note that Simon Peter is being called 'hot-tempered', for this is exactly what his name means in the Egyptian, as has already been explained in an earlier chapter. It is also clear that Mary's deep gnosis and understanding was causing friction within the early Church, and no doubt when the Church of Saul split from the Church of Jesus and James, the education of women was one of the first things to suffer. So, in the eyes of the Christian Taliban, the position of female disciples and saviours was deemed to be desperately heretical, and so Mary Magdalene was denied her gnosis or knowledge. In other words, the seven Muses (the seven evil winds) were chased out of Mary Magdalene, and through this process she was 'healed' of her heretical knowledge (gnosis).

While I cannot say for certain that this is the absolute truth behind this particular verse, my reinterpretation does seem to make a great deal more sense than the original. However, if this is so, then it does mean that there is a tangible and compelling link between Mary Magdalene and the seven (or nine) Muses of Greek mythology. In other words, there is a compelling link between Mary Magdalene and Thea <u>Muse</u> Ourania, the queen of Parthia and Thea <u>Muse</u> Cleo-Patra VII, the queen of Egypt. The precise manner in which Mary was descended from Thea Muse will be discussed in the next chapter.

Who's Who?

The evidence is clear. Mary and Joseph, the mother and father of Jesus and Mary Magdalene, must have been related in some manner to the exiled family of Thea Muse and Phraataces. But if this is the case, then who, exactly, was who?

The first and most obvious candidate for Mary, the mother of Jesus, was Thea Muse herself. However, biology would argue against this association, for to have been a daughter of Julius Caesar, Thea Muse must have been born in 44 BC. But Jesus was most probably born in AD 6, which would have made Thea Muse 50 years old at the time of his birth, and while this is not an entirely impossible age for a mother, it has to strongly count against her, especially if the brothers and sisters of Jesus were his younger siblings, as one might expect. The alternative, and more likely, candidate for Mary must therefore be the daughter of Thea Muse, who was called Julia Muse Ourania. Note again that Thea Muse's daughter used the nomen of the Julia family, which demonstrates that Thea Muse was the daughter of Julius Caesar; for why else would an Egypto-Parthian queen name her daughter after a Roman emperor?

The date of birth for Julia Ourania is uncertain, but perhaps we can confidently predict that she would have been born shortly after Thea Muse's marriage to Phraates IV. The best guess for their marriage is 25 BC, and so we could place the birth of Julia Ourania with some confidence to about 20 BC. This would make Julia Ourania, the biblical 'Virgin' Mary, 26 years old at the time of Jesus' birth (presuming that the Roman taxation of Judaea under Cyrenius represents the true date for the birth of Jesus). So although the biblical name may appear to be 'incorrect', this birth date would certainly suit the daughter of Thea Muse very well.

The reason for the biblical accounts using a different name has already been covered. Firstly, it was not in the interests of either Saul-Josephus or the resulting Christian administration to reveal that their Messiah was born of an Egypto-Parthian princess, for that went against every aspect of the disinformation that they were trying to peddle to the faithful. By necessity, an alternative name had to be used. Secondly, it has already been explained that Mary is not a name but a title, meaning 'Love (Goddess)'. This simply identified Mary as a God's Wife, the high priestess of the temple who attended to the sexual needs of the gods and who was possibly an incarnation of Isis too. Thus, the change from Julia to Mary was not a lie, as such; instead it was a deliberate deception, in order that the links with Egypt and Parthia could be broken.

However, the tradition that Mary was somehow linked to a Parthian queen called Thea Muse must have been very strong in the centuries after Jesus' death, for the Renaissance artists drew upon these ancient traditions and depicted Mary (the 'Virgin') in a consistent and particular manner. The typical imagery of Mary, the mother of Jesus, which evolved in ecclesiastical traditions, was of a young lady dressed in blue and white robes, standing upon the crescent Moon and having twelve stars arranged in a circle around her head. Two versions of this kind of depiction are shown in the colour section, and this imagery is taken from a verse in Revelations which says:

> And there appeared a great wonder in heaven; a woman clothed with the Sun, and the Moon under her feet, and upon her head a crown of twelve stars. [B1]

Although the Bible does not mention the colour of Mary's robes, the Mandaeans do. The goddess in question was called Ruha, and since she was known as the Mother of all Planets, we can confidently identify her with Isis, the Queen of Heaven, and thus with Muse Ourania (the Greek goddess) and finally with the biblical Mary herself. But the Mandaean texts go on to say that the colours of Ruha's robes were sky blue and pale cornflower, which is much the same as the colours adopted by later Western artists for the 'Virgin' Mary's robes.

The twelve stars that were arranged in a circle around Mary's head are perhaps representative of the twelve disciples or the twelve sons of Jacob. However, all of these biblical gatherings that come in dozens were fundamentally based upon the twelve signs of the zodiac, as Josephus makes plain in his accounts. This demonstrates the original astrological and astronomical foundations of Judaeo-Christianity, which have been successfully obscured and covered up in more recent times. Again, this is why Jews in the first centuries AD commissioned mosaics of the zodiac for the floors of their synagogues.

The twelve stars also demonstrate that Mary is again to be identified with Muse Ourania, the Greek goddess of astronomy who was known as the Heavenly Muse Ourania and who foretold the future by looking at the positions of the stars. In other words, Muse Ourania was the original Greek astrologer goddess. Note, however, that the later artistic interpretations of the Greek goddess Muse Ourania, with her blue and white cloak and a ring of stars around her head, are more or less identical to those of Mary the 'Virgin'. See the colour section for an example of this striking similarity. Clearly, Mary, the mother of Jesus, is being portrayed as an incarnation of the Greek goddess Muse Ourania; but why should this be so? Was Mary to be identified with the heavens? Was she being depicted as the Queen of Heaven, an incarnation of the Egyptian Isis? Or was she being portrayed as Thea Muse Ourania, the Queen of Parthia?

The Moon under the feet of Mary may supply us with another clue in this regard, for the Moon is an image of Selene, the Greek goddess of the Moon, the sister of Helios. But Cleopatra Selene, if readers will recall, was the daughter of Cleopatra VII who married Jubba II of Mauretania. Thus this image of Mary standing upon the Moon (Selene), yet crowned with twelve stars (Muse Ourania) can now be seen as an image of Thea Muse Ourania Selene, the first daughter of Cleopatra VII. Just as Cleopatra Selene, the second daughter of Cleopatra VII, was identified with the Moon, I have no doubt that Thea Muse of Parthia was identified likewise. So the image of Mary dressed as the Greek Muse Ourania, but simultaneously standing upon the crescent Moon of Selene, identifies the mother of Jesus with Thea Muse Ourania, the Queen of Parthia; the only caveat to this being that Mary would have to have been the daughter, Julia Muse Ourania, for Thea Muse Ourania would have been past childbearing age in AD 6.

This imagery of Mary is, of course, a very symbolic arrangement that has lasted though the ages and been absorbed into our modern national and political systems. The flag that was chosen to represent the unity of Europe, for instance, comprised a circle of twelve golden stars upon a blue background. For some time the pretence of the twelve stars representing twelve nations of the union was maintained; but as the EU grew ever larger the number of stars did not, and so the pretence quietly faded. In truth, it is highly likely that this EU imagery instead represents Mary, and the continuing bloodline of the biblical family in Europe. However, this symbolism may also be demonstrating a reverence for the cult of the Queen of Heaven that goes back to the veneration of the Queen of Sheba and to Isis herself.

Joseph

The next character that we need to identify in the biblical record is Joseph, the father of Jesus. The first candidate for this position has to be the husband-son of Thea Muse, namely Prince (King) Phraataces. Thea Muse's son would have been born around the same time as Julia Ourania, say about 24 BC, which would make him about 30 years old at the time of the birth of Jesus. Although the Christian Church tends to assume that Joseph was much older than Mary, his wife, there is actually no evidence for this. The only thing we do know is that he disappears early in the story for some reason, perhaps because he died before the main events in Jesus' life occurred.

In the classical interpretation of Jesus' life, this would mean that Joseph died before AD 30, and Jesus' presumed crucifixion at this time. If, however, we assume that this date represented Jesus' third-degree initiation, and that Jesus was still active in Judaea during the run-up to the Jewish Civil War, as Saul-Josephus maintains, then Joseph need only to have died prior to AD 65. If the persecution of the Church of Jesus by Saul-Josephus occurred in about AD 65, then Jesus would have been 59 years old at this time and his mother a not so impossible 85.

We have no historical information whatsoever about the eventual fate of Prince (King) Phraataces, and so there is no way of knowing if he married his sister, Julia Ourania [Mary], or not. However, there is another possible spouse for Julia Ourania [Mary], and that is Ptolemy of Mauretania. If we recall the opening chapters of this book, it was stated there that Cleopatra VII's daughter by Mark Antony, Cleopatra Selene, was taken to Rome as a hostage. She was later betrothed to Augustus Caesar's close friend Jubba II of Mauretania, who was given the kingdoms of northern Africa to rule as a client king of Rome. Jubba II was a wise and reliable monarch who made these provinces relatively prosperous, and who in turn secured the southern borders of the Roman empire for Augustus. It is believed that Jubba and Cleopatra Selene had at least two children, a daughter named Drusilla and a son called Ptolemy. Note that it was Queen Cleopatra Selene who was considered the more illustrious of these two monarchs, for the son's name continued the Egyptian dynasty and not the Mauretanian royal line.

The history of this Mauretanian kingdom is sketchy to say the least, but there is a suggestion that Julia Muse Ourania of Syrio-Judaea married Ptolemy of Mauretania.

> (Ptolemy) probably married a queen (Julia) Ourania, known only through a funerary inscription of her freedwoman Julia Bodina at Cherchel. [2]

As dynastic alliances go, this union would actually make a great deal of sense. Julia Ourania was the granddaughter of Cleopatra VII of Egypt and Julius Caesar, with some intermingled royal Parthian blood as well. On the other hand, Ptolemy of Mauretania was the grandson of Cleopatra VII and Mark Antony. What a glorious mix of bloodlines this union would have fused together; and so this mere suggestion, which was derived from a funerary inscription of a servant in the royal court of Mauretania, just has to be a historical possibility. Such a royal alliance held up the possibility of uniting Rome, Egypt and Parthia under the banner of one illustrious royal family. It would have been an opportunity that was too good to miss.

In Chapter V it has already been demonstrated that Jesus was called Ben Pandera and thus his father, Joseph, was called Pandera or Pa-ndjer-Ra. But it was Caesarion Ptolemy of Egypt, and presumably also his nephew Ptolemy of Mauretania, who was also called Pandjer-Ra in this era, while another of his titles can be read as meaning 'Saviour'. Thus the titles that the Talmud ascribes to Joseph closely match the titles of Ptolemy of Mauretania.

Had the biblical Joseph been Ptolemy of Mauretania, there would also have been a good reason for his disappearance from the biblical accounts. Ptolemy was king of Mauretania between 21-40 AD, initially in a co-regency with his father Jubba II. Upon the death of his father in AD 23, Ptolemy assumed full control of his kingdom. In AD 24 he fought and won several battles against marauding tribes in North Africa, which secured Rome's southern borders once more, and for which he was awarded the ivnry ooopive. However, in AD 40 the emperor Caligula invited Ptolemy to Rome, and Ptolemy made the fatal mistake of wearing a purple cloak. No doubt Ptolemy wore the cloak because he regarded himself as the true successor of the empire of Mark Antony and Cleopatra VII, and so he was displaying himself as the true king of the Roman empire. Had his wife been Julia Muse Ourania, his self-confidence may have been considerably enhanced, as he would have been the founding father of a great new Egypto-Roman-Parthian dynasty. But, in this case, the perceived threat to Caligula's throne would have been proportionately increased.

If Ptolemy thought that the public adulation of Rome would increase his prestige, then he spectacularly miscalculated his status. The much more predictable result of wearing his royal cloak of purple was that, in a fit of rage, Caligula had Ptolemy of Mauretania executed. Thus, according to classical history, one of the last branches of the Ptolemaic dynasty of Egypt had been extinguished. So, if Ptolemy had been Joseph, he would not have been mentioned in any of the biblical accounts that followed the year AD 40, which is what we find. But, of course, if Joseph were a

Fig 37.   Ptolemy of Mauretania.

pseudonym for Ptolemy, then the royal Ptolemaic line had not been extinguished at all, for Joseph had at least four sons and two daughters.

If this was the true ancestry of the biblical Joseph, then there is another reason for sidelining him from the biblical accounts; for in the guise of Ptolemy of Mauretania, he was the only member of the biblical family who was well known in this era and thus well known in the historical record. Thea Muse Ourania and Julia Muse Ourania had been exiled from their former homelands, and so in terms of Roman and Judaean politics and history they were virtually unknown.

Ptolemy, however, was the son of a favourite of Augustus Caesar, and well known in the Roman political arena. Any mention of Ptolemy within the New Testament accounts would have destroyed the popular image of a poor 'carpenter', and so Joseph became a shadowy figure who was almost entirely deleted from this story. In addition, since Ptolemy and any of his potential offspring were obviously a direct threat to the rule of the emperors of Rome, it would not have been in Saul-Josephus' interest to advertise the fact that Ptolemy had a number of surviving sons who were creating a rebellion in Judaea. If Saul-Josephus' texts (the New Testament and *Jewish War*) were to survive in a Roman world, they had to separate the family of Jesus from the Egyptian Ptolemaic royal line.

Another point to make is the resulting status of Julia Ourania. If she had married Ptolemy she would have become Queen of Mauretania, and would have taken up residence in the court of Ptolemy in north Africa. But this presents us with a problem. For Jesus to have been born in Judaea (Bethanya or Aurania), it is more likely that Jesus was actually the son of Julia Ourania and Phraataces. Thea Muse and Phraataces were exiled to Bethanya or Aurania in 4 BC, and since Phraataces had already married his mother, it is not beyond the realms of possibility that he also married his sister. This would place the birth of Jesus in exactly the right location and at exactly the right time. In support of this argument, when talking about Philip of Gamala and the Babylonians of Bethanya, Josephus says:

> Now there was one Joseph, the son of a female physician, who excited a great many young men to join with them. He persuaded (the people of Gamala) to revolt from the king and take up arms. [J3]

However, the word being used for a physician is *magi*, the Magi kingmakers of Parthia. Who else could be the female Magi in this account, other than Thea Muse? The son of Thea Muse was, of course, Prince Phraataces, so this passage would suggest that Phraataces was Joseph, rather than Ptolemy of Mauretania. But the account is interesting nonetheless, as it places the name 'Joseph' in the right context and era.

However, the biblical accounts then insist that Mary [Julia Ourania] and Jesus fled to Egypt. It is said that this was to protect Jesus from King Herod the Great, who did not appreciate a pretender to the throne being born in his own back yard. This is possible, but the king in question at this time would have had to have been 'King' Herod Archelous, the tetrarch of Judaea, and not King Herod the Great. Thus the killing of the innocents, if it did happen in the manner that the New Testament claims, occurred in AD 6 and not 4 BC.

This would imply that Julia Ourania [Mary], the daughter of Thea Muse, fled to Egypt with her newborn son, who we can now call Jesus, in AD 6 or 7. The reason for travelling to Egypt was that, being the granddaughter of Cleopatra VII, Julia Muse Ourania ought to have been reasonably safe there; and her son could also be schooled in the ways of the Egyptian royalty and priesthood at the great temples of either Heliopolis or Alexandria. However, it is always possible that Mary [Julia Ourania] travelled a little further than Egypt and ended up in North Africa – in Mauretania perhaps. The intriguing possibility, once more, is that Julia Ourania became the wife of Ptolemy of Mauretania and not Phraataces.

The possibility also exists that Julia Ourania was married to Phraataces and then remarried to Ptolemy. While it might seem unlikely that a princess of Egypt and Parthia would be passed around from husband to husband in this fashion, this seems to have been a common event in this era. Felix, the procurator of Judaea in AD 54, boasted that he married three queens in succession, including Drusilla, the daughter of Ptolemy of Mauretania. Likewise, Princess Glaphrya of Cappadocia had three husbands, including Jubba II. Princesses appear to have been chattels of the state, to be married off and taken back from neighbouring monarchs and tetrarchs as and when the political situation demanded. Thus it would not have been unusual for Thea Muse to have spotted a dynastic alliance for her daughter, taken her away from her brother-husband, Phraataces, and given her to Ptolemy of Mauretania.

That there were close connections between Mauretania and Judaea is confirmed by Ptolemy's daughter ending up as the wife of Felix of Judaea. So how did this happen? Well, following the execution of Ptolemy at the hands of Caligula in AD 40, the kingdom of Mauretania was completely annexed by Rome. The royal court of Mauretania would, by necessity, have been forced into exile. Had Ptolemy been married to Julia Muse Ourania, as I strongly suspect, then the obvious place for their exile would have been back in Judaeo-Syria and the provinces of Bethanya and Aurania – especially if the latter had still been nominally autonomous from Rome. This is quite possibly how Drusilla, the daughter of Ptolemy of Mauretania [and Julia Muse Ourania], ended up marrying Felix of Judaea in about AD 40.

In other words, the Judaic prophecy was not quite fulfilled as intended. It may well have been that 'out of Egypt and North Africa I have called my son' – for Jesus and his siblings could have followed the same well-trodden path of exile and ended up back in Judaea in AD 40, just prior to the Jewish Civil War. Remember that my previous analysis of the New Testament, in the book *Jesus*, has already claimed that the majority of the New Testament events occurred in about AD 55 - 65, at the time when Saul-Josephus was the military commander of Galilee. Thus the date for the possible exile of Ptolemy's children back to Judaea ties in very nicely with what we know from the biblical accounts of the life of Jesus.

The prophet

Having discovered the true history of the New Testament family, perhaps we can now appreciate the reasons why so many theologians down the ages have sought to cover up the truth. What they sought to portray to the world was an icon of perfection; a role-model family who were supposed to have been related to some great spiritual entity who inhabited the Cosmos. What the diligent theological historians found, however, was a real conspiratorial royal family whose court intrigues shocked all and sundry, let alone the naive Christian priesthood. That these same theologians chose to alter the texts to suit the requirements of their propaganda should not come as a great surprise.

Having said that, it is quite possible that their conspiratorial obfuscation was completely unnecessary. The next prophet from this region was a self-confessed uneducated, self-centered, genocidal, racist and misogynist, whose favourite wife was only seven years old;* and yet the religion he founded is followed by hundreds of millions of people.

If one reads the verses from the Koran, it is blatantly obvious that Muhammad simply invented many of the pronouncements he supposedly received from god – the verses of the Koran – to suit his political, strategic and domestic requirements. Such was the ineptitude of the man that he even had to resort to inventing pronouncements from god to stop his various wives from fighting each other.** This was a man who could not even sort out his own domestic affairs, and yet he holds sway over the domestic living arrangements of all the Islamic world. Here is a man with an insatiable sexual appetite, who sanctioned the use of rape as a punishment, and yet he is taken to be a moral authority of a substantial proportion of the world's population. [4] It is not even as if we can consign this kind of abhorrent behaviour to the moral climate of the era in which Muhammad lived, for even his peers deemed his behaviour and morality to be deeply flawed. As the Edwardian historian Andre Servier said of these ancient commentaries:

> The problem with Muhammad's behaviour is not that he was a bedouin, but that he was a morally degenerate bedouin. [5]

The fact that millions of otherwise rational people will deceive themselves that this is not so, and that Muhammad was a virtuous role-model for society, demonstrates the depths of delusion that otherwise rational people will descend to in order to justify their chosen belief system. Rationality and logic are cast aside in the rush to follow a creed, no matter how

---

* Aisha, one of Muhammad's fifteen wives, was only seven and 'with the dolls' at the time of her marriage. Muhammad was 44 years her senior.

** The verse reads as:

> If you two (Hafsah and Aishah) turn to god in repentance you shall be pardoned; but if you conspire against him (Muhammad), know that god is his protector. ... It may well be that, if he divorces you, the lord will give him in your place better wives than yourselves. [6]

Ibin Warraq says of these and other similar verses:

> The conclusion forces itself upon us that in later life, (Muhammad) consciously fabricated 'revelations', often for his own convenience, to sort out his domestic problems. [7]

contradictory, antisocial or evil it may be. In the process, mankind ends up being governed by the moral equivalents of Sun Myung Moon and Ron Hubbard – the spiritual leaders of the Moonies and the Scientologists respectively. If religion were a democracy, then these degenerate individuals could be consigned to the history books after five years; but it is not, and only a popular uprising like the Renaissance, Lutherism or the Enlightenment can correct the gross errors of the past.

Another mystery of gargantuan proportions is why many within the general population warm to the pronouncements of the uneducated and illiterate. Even within Christianity they try to take an educated prince and turn him into an illiterate pauper, in order to make his pronouncements more acceptable to the faithful. In a similar fashion, Muhammad was unable to read or appreciate the great traditions of Persian and Parthian art, music and poetry; and when the intelligentsia mocked his rustic ignorance, Muhammad's 'god' (Muhammad himself) swiftly forbade the pleasures of the arts.

> Afak mocked Muhammad in verse, especially his desire to control people's lives ... (Muhammad) simply commented "who will deal with this rascal for me?" – and one of his 'weepers' did. That a poet of so advanced an age should be murdered for a verbal sleight would have been inconceivable under the previous Arab custom. [8]

The quote is reminiscent of a famous cry of exasperation from Shakespeare's Henry II, "Will no one rid me of this turbulent priest!". Obligingly, someone in Muhammad's army did just that, and there was no more mockery of the prophet's ignorance. But herein lies a great problem, for instead of humankind being governed by a meritocracy (leadership by the highly educated and most able), we end up with either a mediocracy (leadership by the average) or ignocracy (leadership by ill-educated fools). It is beyond understanding that we should allow the ignorance and envy of a seventh century AD individual to result in the Taliban of the modern era banning song and dance, but it happens nonetheless. Likewise, in modern Britain, we are similarly supporting the destruction of all the nation's best schools, in order to assuage the ignorance and envy of a politician who failed his senior school entrance examinations at the tender age of eleven. How little we have progressed over the centuries!

Perhaps the moral of this whole tale is that it is patently obvious that nations are governed by the whims and desires of men and women, and not by the dictates of any magnanimous spiritual entity. No self-respecting, all-powerful god, should such a thing exist, would play a partisan role in the disgraceful politics of mankind, and any such entity must be observing our world and shaking their head(s) in disbelief. Thus, the many calls for god to bless this or that nation are simply extensions of the age-old propaganda that has been preached from many a bloodstained pulpit over the millennia. That otherwise sane people all over the world should still believe that an unimaginably intelligent and powerful entity would stoop to such levels, and effectively sanction the murder of great swathes of his or her own creation, demonstrates how ignorant and devoid of understanding much of humankind still is. Seneca the Younger, the first century Roman philosopher, said of theology:

> Religion is regarded by the common people as true, by the wise as false, and by rulers as useful.

Were this ancient pearl of wisdom to be displayed above the entrance to every single church, synagogue, mosque and temple across the globe, the world would undoubtedly be a better place.

True Testament

The evidence that has been outlined at length in this book is, in my opinion, the true history and ancestry of the New Testament family. As I had long suspected, the biblical family was indeed of royal blood, and in truth its members were descended from all three of the great empires of the ancient world: the Egyptian, the Roman and the Persian. Had this illustrious family found a vacant throne and seized their opportunity, they would probably have been the most powerful of all the royal lines to rule in the first century AD. But it was not to be.

Josephus records that there was a military foray into Parthia around AD 36, led by another Prince Tiridates, who is said to have been a grandson of Phraates IV. Had Jesus been the son of Julia Ourania, he would indeed have been Phraates' grandson. This Roman-backed incursion into Parthia was obviously instigated by the Parthian (Babylonian) exiles in Gamala [Jimal], and so this military adventure is likely to have involved the biblical Jesus (but Jesus' use of the Roman military as allies must have angered the Parthians and Jews in equal measure). With the backing of several Parthian nobles, Seleucia surrendered and Tiridates III [Jesus] was crowned as king of Parthia. But the presence of Romans in the country angered many Parthians, and so King Artabanus II was able to raise a large army and chase Tiridates III [Jesus] back to Syria. Thus [Jesus'] attempt to re-establish his royal line on a vacant throne was dashed. Likewise, Jesus' desperate attempt to take Jerusalem – both by guile and by force – was also thwarted.

Following the Roman destruction of Judaeo-Israel in AD 70, those who remained of the royal New Testament family were scattered across the Mediterranean, where their descendants would intermittently gain and lose influence and power among the great royal houses of Europe. However, courtesy of the evangelical Saul-Josephus (Flavius), the biblical family's name and a record of their many deeds would spread around the world like a virulent virus. Yet despite this apparent success, the true regal nature of the New Testament family and their precise history and ancestry would be studiously deleted from each and every historical record. Perhaps we should remind ourselves why was this done.

Christianity was the Church of Saul-Josephus, rather than the Church of Jesus and James. It was Saul who took the life history of Jesus and mixed this with some of the basic theology of the Church of Jesus [the fourth sect], and formed a new religion that could be practised by Jews and Gentiles alike. But the new religion of Saul was often at odds with the life and beliefs of its primary icon, Jesus, and so the true ancestry of Jesus had to be glossed over. All Saul-Josephus wanted was an icon for people to worship, not a bloodline that could threaten his own position as Church leader. In a similar fashion, the new bishops of Rome, the Popes, assumed their great power by being the leaders of the Christian Church. The presence of a bloodline directly descended from Jesus could only threaten their position as pseudo-kings of the Church and diminish their massive secular and spiritual power – and so the Catholic Church and the bloodline descendants of Jesus have been at odds with each other ever since.

However, the ancestry uncovered in this book provides us with another reason for the sidelining of the family of Jesus. One of the great assets of Christianity, as it spread around the world, was that Saul-Josephus wove a great morality tale into his narrative. Thus the life and family of Jesus reads as an idyllic fantasy of love, sacrifice and the struggle against adversity and oppression. Mary and Joseph were being portrayed as the Waltons of the first century AD. But if the truth were known, the reality of Jesus' life was very different indeed. In fact, Jesus' grandmother, Thea Muse Ourania, murdered her husband, King Phraates IV. She then embarked upon an incestuous relationship by marrying her own son, Phraataces; a prince of Parthia who eventually became either Jesus' father or his uncle. The couple were then deposed and thrown out of their kingdom by the indignant aristocracy of Parthia, who frowned upon these ancient Egyptian customs of patricide and incest. The royal family were then forced to live in exile in Syrio-Judaea, from where they made efforts to attack Parthia and retake the throne in about AD 36. With this invasion being repulsed, they then planned to take Jerusalem by force, but yet again the efforts were all in vain.

This was the major reason for Saul-Josephus deleting the true ancestry and life of the biblical Jesus. The lack of information regarding Jesus' family was not due to his being totally unknown – it was because the true life of this royal family fell way below the ideals that Saul-Josephus wanted to preach from his pulpits. By all means and all devices, the truth about the court intrigues within this Egypto-Parthian royal family had to be excised from the history of Judaea and from the New Testament accounts. And, of course, it was Saul-Josephus who was in a unique position to actually achieve this, for as the founder of Christianity and the era's foremost historian he controlled the vast majority of the theological and secular history of the region.

It was Josephus, in the guise of Saul, who edited and published the religious history of Joseph and Mary and their family (the New Testament). Likewise, it was Josephus who wrote the secular history of Judaea *(Antiquities* and the *Jewish War)*. Thus Saul-Josephus was able to delete all the references from Judaic history that might have suggested that Mary was Julia Ourania, the daughter of Queen Thea Muse Ourania of Parthia.

Intriguingly, it should also be noted that Josephus was the only historian who wrote anything whatsoever about Thea Muse, which confirms that he did know of this history and wanted us to know something about it. His 'unreliable' testimony was vigorously denied by modern historians and only the later numismatic (coin) evidence from Parthia demonstrated that Josephus had, as ever, his finger on the pulse of Middle Eastern history. Saul-Josephus' reasoning for including Thea Muse in his (secular) history was probably twofold. Firstly, there was probably a little academic pride in that he knew a slice of history that few others did. Secondly, he may have deliberately made this inclusion in an attempt to make a clear differentiation between Thea Muse and the biblical Mary (for he had no idea what other historians in this era would write). His attempts at concealment eventually failed, but he did succeed in covering up the true ancestry of Jesus and Mary Magdalene for over two thousand years.

Having rediscovered the true ancestry of Jesus, after two millennia of obfuscation, the intervening centuries have bequeathed a long and convoluted footnote to this family history. It would seem that Jesus, as a son of Julia Ourania, failed in his first century AD attempt to re-establish his Egypto-Parthian royal family at the vanguard of a unified Romo-Parthian empire. However, through the egocentric and vainglorious, but dogged and diligent, industry of Saul-Josephus, the family of Jesus did eventually conquer all of the Roman Empire and much of the Parthian Empire too. Thus, Jesus' campaign was ultimately successful and he did indeed sit upon the throne of Rome as a god incarnate, just as previous Roman emperors had done. But this conquest was an empty victory, for it was in name only. Despite Jesus' nominative success and world domination over two millennia, the ultimate question remains unanswered – could we yet discover a real family behind the victorious icon?

✠✠✠   End   ✠✠✠

Appendix

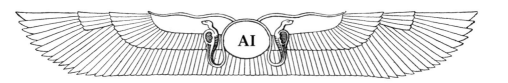

Genealogy of the Biblical Family

The following pages contain a genealogy of the biblical family, which has been linked into the known history of Rome, Egypt and Parthia. Readers may note one or two differences to the family histories that are given in the various text books and web pages that cover this era. However, having looked very carefully at some of these interpretations, it is apparent that some authors are not always taking biology fully into account, with unlikely or unfeasible births and marriages sometimes taking place. Some of these problems stem from the accounts of Josephus Flavius, which contain internal contradictions that may prove impossible to sort out and to square with other historical accounts.

Cleopatra of Jerusalem is a case in point, for she has a separate mention in Josephus, but her offspring appear to equate quite well with those of Miriame II, another wife of Herod the Great. I still think that these two ladies are the same individual, but other authors try to separate them and in the process develop other genealogical inconsistences. Inevitably, these genealogies come down to a personal preference and a best guess, and the following represents my attempt at this.

AI   Genealogy

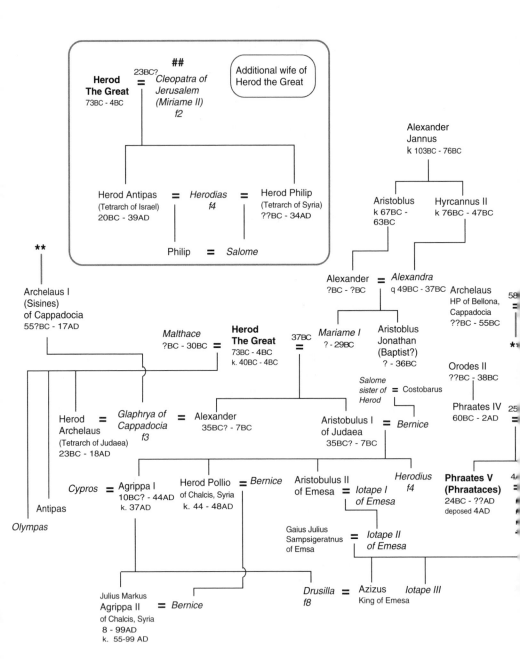

Herod The Great 73BC - 4BC
23BC?
= ## Cleopatra of Jerusalem (Miriame II) f2

(Additional wife of Herod the Great)

Alexander Jannus k 103BC - 76BC

Herod Antipas (Tetrarch of Israel) 20BC - 39AD
= Herodias f4 =
Herod Philip (Tetrarch of Syria) ??BC - 34AD

Aristoblus k 67BC - 63BC

Hyrcannus II k 76BC - 47BC

Philip = Salome

Alexander ?BC - ?BC = Alexandra q 49BC - 37BC

Archelaus HP of Bellona, Cappadocia ??BC - 55BC

58

**

Archelaus I (Sisines) of Cappadocia 55?BC - 17AD

Malthace ?BC - 30BC =
Herod The Great 73BC - 4BC k. 40BC - 4BC
37BC =
Mariame I ? - 29BC
Aristoblus Jonathan (Baptist?) ? - 36BC

Orodes II ??BC - 38BC

Salome sister of = Costobarus Herod

Phraates IV 60BC - 2AD

25 =

Herod Archelaus (Tetrarch of Judaea) 23BC - 18AD
= *Glaphrya of Cappadocia f3* = Alexander 35BC? - 7BC

Aristobulus I of Judaea 35BC? - 7BC = *Bernice*

Cypros = Agrippa I 10BC? - 44AD k. 37AD
Herod Pollio of Chalcis, Syria k. 44 - 48AD = *Bernice*
Aristobulus II of Emesa = *Iotape I of Emesa*
Herodius f4
Phraates V (Phraataces) 24BC - ??AD deposed 4AD

Antipas

Olympas

Gaius Julius Sampsigeratnus of Emsa = *Iotape II of Emesa*

Julius Markus Agrippa II of Chalcis, Syria 8 - 99AD k. 55-99 AD = *Bernice*

Drusilla f8 = Azizus King of Emesa
Iotape III

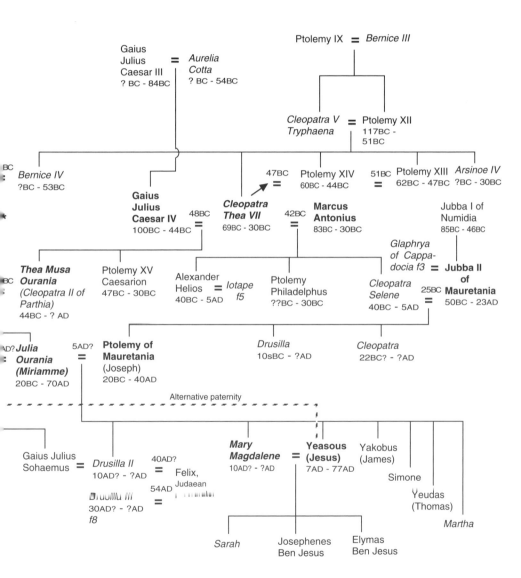

List of diagrams

Photo credits

Plate 1. The Death of Cleopatra, Jean-Andre Rixens.

Plate 2. Adoration of the Magi, Pieter Aertsen.

Plate 3. The Virgin Mary, Gornji Grad Cathedral, Slovenia. Ralph Ellis.

Plate 4. Virgin Mary depicted as Muse Ourania.

Plate 5. Muse Ourania and Calliope. Simon Vouet, Samuel Kress Collection.

Plate 6. The Beth Alpha zodiac, Israel.

Plate 7. The Sultan Tekesh mausoleum in Kunya Urgench.

Plate 8. The mausoleum of Jubba II and Cleopatra Selene, in Kolea, Algeria.

Plate 9. The ruined city of Umm el-Jimal in Aurania (Hauran). Ralph Ellis.

Plate 10-12.

Augustus Caesar, Julius Caesar, Vespasian. British Museum. Ralph Ellis.

Plate 13-15.

Cleopatra VII, Cleopatra VII, Thea Muse. British Museum. Ralph Ellis.

Plate 16-17.

Two coins of King Phraataces and Queen Thea Muse Ourania.

Notes & References

Bible: All references taken from the King James edition, although the text is often modernised for clarity.

Josephus: AA = Against Apion, Ant = Antiquities, JW = Jewish war, L = Life.
Page references are to the Loeb Classical Library system.
Quotes taken from William Whiston's translation, which was first published in 1736; some references are from the Penguin Classics edition by G. Williamson, first published 1959.

Manetho   All page numbers are taken from the LCL edition, editor G. Goold.

Within the referencing system in this book, some of the reference numbers are prefixed with letters. This is to give the reader an idea of the source of the reference, without having to look up that particular reference. This only applies to the more popular reference works, and the following have been prefixed:

B = Bible, M = Manetho, J = Josephus, H = Herodotus,
T = Talmud, KN = Kebra Nagast, K = Koran, S = Strabo.

All references to Egyptian words are taken from:

An Egyptian Hieroglyphic Dictionary, E A Wallis Budge, Dover Publications. The entries in the dictionary are substantially in alphabetical (glyph) order, and so the references are easy to find and have not been listed in the references by their page number.

Notes & References

Chapter I

1. Josephus JW 1:364.
2. Bible 2 Peter 1:16.
3. The history of the early Church, H Lietzmann, vol 3.
4. Bible Re 19:7-9.
5. Ibid Re 21:9.
6. Babylonian Talmud Sanhedrin 106a.
7. Anthony and Cleopatra, W Shakespeare 2:2:200.
8. Plutarch, Caesar 49.
9. Catholic Encyclopaedia. http://www.newadvent.org/cathen/11712a.htm

Chapter II

1. Tombeua de la Chretienne, Marcel Christofle.
2. Josephus Ant 18:39.
3. Josephus Ant 2:47.
4. Hellenistic Queens, Prof Grace Macurdy p189.
5. Myth, History and Culture in Republican Rome; Cleopatra in Rome,
   by Erich Gruen.
6. Cicero, ad Atticum, 14:20:2, 14:20:2, 15:1:5, 15:4:4.
7. J. P. V. D. Balsdon, *Historia* 7 (1958) 80, 86 n. 37.
8. Hellenistic Queens, Prof Grace Macurdy p191.
9. Chris Bennett, Tyndale House, Cambridge UK. Residential Centre
   for Biblical Studies.
12. Chris Bennett, Tyndale House, Cambridge UK. Residential Centre
    for Biblical Studies.
13. Hellenistic Queens, G. H. Macurdy p190.
14. Hellenistic Queens, G. H. Macurdy p191.
15. Cambridge History of Iran, Vol 3a.
16. Metamorphoses or The Golden Ass Lucius Apuleius, Book 11, Chap 47.
17. Josephus Ant 2:232.
18. http://www.thekeep.org/~kunoichi/kunoichi/themestream/
19. C. Settipani, Continuit gentilice et continuit familiale dans les familles
    natoriales romaines: mythe et realit 438f n. 11.

Chapter III

1. Josephus Ant 4:63.
2. Augustus und seine Zeit, V Gardthausen.
3. Monumentum Ancyranum (Res Gestae Divi Augusti)
   See either the Loeb Classical Library or the web site on:
   http://penelope.uchicago.edu/Thayer/E/Roman/Texts/Augustus/Res_Gestae/
   5*.html
4. Josephus Ant 18:41.
5. Florus bkIV.
6. Strabo bk16:28.

7. Strabo, Geography bk 16:28.
8. Monumentum Ancyranum (Res Gestae Divi Augusti).
   See either the Loeb Classical Library or the web address previously given.
9. Josephus Ant 18:39-42.
12. Monumentum Ancyranum (Res Gestae Divi Augusti).
13. The Cambridge History of Iran bk3a.
14. Josephus Ant 17:24.
15. Bible Jer 44:17.
16. Strabo Geography bk16, 2-34.
17. A commentary of the New Testament, John Lightfoot.
18. Dr. De Vries, professor of history at Calvin College in Grand Rapids, Michigan.
    http://www.calvin.edu/academic/ archaeology/uj/publicat/interp/gem.htm
19. Ibid.
22. Ibid.
23. Ibid.
24. Ibid.
25. Ibid.
26. Ibid.
27. Ibid

Chapter IV

1. Bible Lu 2:1-6.
2. Josephus Ant 18:4.
3. Bible Acts 5:34-36.
4. Bible Mk 14:3.
5. Bible Joh 1:28.
6. The Mandaeans of Iraq and Iran, E S Drower bk 1.
7. The Mandaeans of Iraq and Iran, E S Drower bk 1.
8. http://www.israel-mfa.gov.il/MFA/History/Early%20History%20-%20
   Archaeology/Archaeological%20Sites%20in%20Israel%20-%20
   Gamala-%20Jewish%20Ci
9. Josephus Life 184.
12. Josephus Ant 18:9.
13. Bible Math 22:15-18, 21.
14. Bible John 2:15.
15. Josephus Ant 18:23.
16. Bible Math 4:10.
17. Josephus War 6:300.
18. Josephus Ant 18:6.
19. Bible Math 10:34.
22. Bible Lu 22:36.
23. Bible Lu 22:39-52. John 18:1-11. Math 26:47-55.
24. The original Greek text says Lestes ληστης, the primary Greek term for a Zealot.
    The disciple called Simon was known as Simon Zelotes, or Simon the Zealot.
25. Josephus JW 261.
26. Bible Acts 21:38.
27. Bible Mark 6:31-44.

28. James, the Brother of Jesus, R Eisenman pxxvi.
29. James, the Brother of Jesus, R Eisenman pxxvii.
30. Bible Math 2:15.
32. Bible Math 13:55.
33. Josephus Ant 20:100-103.
34. Josephus L 66, 193, 200.
35. Josephus Ant 17:31.
36. Bible Math 9:10.
37. Commentary on the Bible, Adam Clarke 1832.
38. Bible Lu 2:7.
39. Bible Math 2:1-2.
42. Kebra Negast 30.
43. The Mandaeans of Iraq and Iran, E S Drower bk 1.
44. Bible Mt 2:16.
45. The Third Intermediate Period in Egypt, K Kitchen para 225.
46. Catholic Encyclopaedia.
47. Bible Math 2:13-15.

Chapter V

1. Geography, Strabo bk 16 2:34
2. James the Brother of Jesus, R Eisenman   p847.
3. Catholic Encyclopaedia http://www.newadvent.org/cathen/15464a.htm
4. Shabbath 104 b.
5. Woman with the Alabaster Jar, Margaret Starbird.
6. Stranger in the Valley of the Kings, A Osman.

Chapter VI

1. Josephus Ant 18:23.
2. Bible Math 6:5-6.
3. Bible Mk 15:2.
4. Bible Mk 15:9-12.
5. Prophesies of Neferti, Ancient Egyptian Literature, M Lichtheim.
6. Bible 1Tim 2:9.
7. Bible 1Tim 2:12.
8. Tosephta Sanhedrin VIII, 7.
9. Koran 4:157. Many English translations will say 'it only seemed to them' or 'but they thought they did'. However, Prof Dawood, the translator of the Penguin Classics edition, says that the literal translation is 'he was made to resemble another for them'.
10. Recognitions, St Clement, I, 45 p497.
12. Dr. Lester Ness, PhD Foreign Affairs Dept, Changchun University, PR China.
13. Ibid. Extracts from: Sanctuaire Vincent p168; Naaran, Avi-Yonah p893; Symbols, Goodenough VIII.2, p168; Palestine Sukenik p29-30.
14. Bible 1Ki 15:12.
15. Bible 2Ki 23:7.

16. Shabbath 104b.
17. Bible Math 11:11.
18. Simon Magus: An essay 1892, G Mead pp28ff.
19. Bible Math 13:31-32.
22. Bible Math 13:33-34.
23. Bible Math 5:3, 10.
24. 'The New Colossus', a sonnet by Emma Lazarus pinned to the base of the Statue of Liberty.
25. Bible Math 10:7.
26. Bible Math 25:14-30.
27. Bible Math 18:1-4.
28. Bible Math 19:12.
29. Bible Math 22:1-10.
30. Josephus Ant 18:42.
32. Theos θεος refers to a masculine god, while Thea θεα refers to a goddess.
33. Bible Lu 8:2.
34. Gospel of Mary, Nag Hammadi Library in English, James Robinson.
35. Gospel of Mary, Nag Hammadi Library in English, James Robinson.

Chapter VII

1. Bible Rev 12:1
2. Prof Chris Bennett http://www.geocities.com/christopherjbennett/
3. Josephus Life 185.
4. The Sword of the Prophet, Serge Trifovic.
5. Islam and the Psychology of the Musulman, Andre Servier p20.
6. Koran 66:4.
7. Life of Muhummad, Ibn Ishaq. Quoted from The Sword of the Prophet, Serge Trifovic.
8. Life of Muhummad, Ibn Ishaq. Quoted from The Sword of the Prophet, Serge Trifovic.

Index

Index

Auranitis ~ 46, 48, 50, 56, 59. *See also*
Aurania.
Aya Sophia ~ 59.

B

ba ~ 129.
Babylon ~ 8, 43, 44, 45, 46, 56, 57, 66,
110, 112.
Gamala ~ 66.
Judas ~ 57.
Zamaris ~ 56.
Babylonian Talmud ~ 99.
Bactria ~ 66.
Bartholdi, F ~ 85.
Baseirta ~ 29.
Batanea ~ 43, 45, 46, 48, 50, 56, 57, 59,
61, 66, 68. *See also* Bethanya.
taxes ~ 56.
Bathanea ~ 61. *See also* Bethanya.
Bathsheba ~ 20.
Batna ~ 15.
Bedlam, B ~ 17.
Beit Alpha ~ 113.
Ben Jesus ~ 92.
Ben Pandira ~ 98, 100, 103.
Ben Stada ~ 98, 100.
Bethabara ~ 62.
Bethany ~ xv, 60, 61, 62, 67, 68, 75. *See*
also Bethanya.
John ~ 62.
Bethanya ~ 61, 62, 63, 65, 66, 67, 68, 69,
75, 77, 78, 79, 82, 96, 117, 120, 127,
140, 142.
Bethany ~ 61, 62.
Gamala ~ 63.
Jesus ~ 62.
Jesus birth ~ 79.
Bethell, A ~ 21.
Bethleem ~ 83.
Bethlehem ~ 55, 80, 83.
Bicknell, P ~ 27.
Bingerbruck ~ 101.
Bistheibanaps ~ 29.
Bithynia ~ 22.
Brutus, Marcus ~ 24.
Bubastis ~ 91.
Butler, H ~ 52.

C

Caesar ~ 69, 111.

anointed ~ 111.
Caesarion ~ 10, 13, 14, 22, 24, 25, 26,
27, 103, 139.
paternity ~ 25.
Caligula ~ 139, 142.
Calliope ~ 128.
Calpurnia ~ 22, 24.
camel ~ 53, 65, 66.
Cana ~ 6.
Canaanite ~ 74, 95.
carpenter ~ 7, 8.
Carthage ~ 2.
Caspian Sea ~ 2, 15.
Catholic Church ~ 64, 107, 109, 130, 131,
132.
Cephas ~ 95.
Chalcis ~ 75.
Chaldeans ~ 63.
Changchun University ~ 113.
Che Guevara ~ 59.
Cherchel ~ 138.
China ~ 113.
Chisda, Rab ~ 98, 100.
Christ ~ 111.
Christianity ~ 15, 63, 120.
Nasrani ~ 63.
Selene ~ 15.
Christos ~ 111.
Church of Jesus ~ 130, 132, 133, 146.
Church of Saul ~ 107, 133.
Cicero ~ 25, 26, 27.
Cincinnatus ~ 36, 153.
Cinderella ~ 99.
circle ~ 59.
Clarke, Adam ~ 57, 74, 76.
Clementine Recognitions ~ 118.
Cleopatra ~ 23.
Cleopatra of Jerusalem ~ 149.
Cleopatra of Mauretania ~ 15.
Cleopatra of Parthia ~ 29, 89.
Cleopatra Selene ~ 11, 14, 15, 16, 18, 20,
28, 30, 31, 91, 92, 102, 137, 138.
captive ~ 14.
children ~ 33.
Christian ~ 15.
marriage ~ 14, 18, 28.
Mary ~ 137.
sister ~ 16.
Thea Muse ~ 20.
tomb ~ 15, 16.

Index

Index

Index

Index

John the Baptist ~ 62.
Joseph ~ 74, 77, 81, 91, 92, 117, 135,
 139, 140, 141.
 Ptolemy ~ 139, 140.
Josephus ~ xiii, xiv, 11, 19, 142, 146, 147.
 Galilee ~ 142.
 Parthia ~ 11.
 Thea Muse ~ 19.
Joses ~ 74, 92.
Joshua ~ 92.
Josiah, king ~ 116.
Jubba I ~ 14.
Jubba II ~ 14, 18, 20, 28, 102, 137, 138,
 139, 141.
 death ~ 15.
 marriage ~ 14, 18.
 Thea Muse ~ 20.
 tomb ~ 16, 18.
Judaea ~ xiv, 3, 5, 9, 55, 63, 79, 80, 82,
 83, 138.
 Bethlehem ~ 83.
 Cleopatra ~ 9.
 Egyptians ~ 3, 45, 90.
 taxes ~ 55, 79, 82.
Judaeo-Syria ~ 45.
Judah ~ 94.
Judaism ~ 68, 70, 72, 95, 107, 114, 116.
 Akhenaton ~ 45.
 Egyptian ~ 114.
 fourth sect ~ 68, 70, 72, 107.
 idolatry ~ 116.
 Isis ~ 115.
 Thea Muse ~ 89, 112.
 zealots ~ 95.
 zodiac ~ 114.
Judas ~ 57, 74, 94, 96, 109.
Judas Iscariot ~ 94.
Judas of Galilee ~ 57. *See also* Judas of
 Gamala.
Judas of Gamala ~ 56, 57, 58, 68, 69, 70,
 73, 74, 75, 76, 77, 78, 96, 106, 117,
 121, 122, 123.
 circling ~ 59.
 fourth sect ~ 73, 112.
 Gamiliel ~ 57.
 Jesus ~ 58, 73, 74, 78, 106, 121.
 Sadoc ~ 117.
 sons ~ 74.
 taxes ~ 69, 70, 74, 75, 76, 77, 96, 122.
 Zadok ~ 68.

Zamaris ~ 56, 73, 75.
Judas the Galilean ~ 58, 74.
Judas the Gaulonite ~ 55, 56, 58. *See
 also* Judas of Gamala.
 Jesus ~ 58.
 Zamaris ~ 56.
Julia Bodina ~ 138.
Julia Ourania ~ 33, 53, 93, 101, 103, 135,
 137, 138, 139, 140, 141, 142, 145,
 147.
 Africa ~ 140.
 husband ~ 101.
 Jesus ~ 103.
 Mary ~ 98, 141, 147.
 Ptolemy ~ 33, 138, 139, 142.
 Stada ~ 100.
Julianos ~ 54, 153.
 Inscription ~ 53.
Julius Caesar ~ xv, 2, 8, 9, 10, 13, 14, 20,
 22, 24, 25, 26, 27, 29, 30, 33, 35, 41,
 46, 91, 103, 123, 135, 139.
 Alexandria ~ 123.
 bald ~ 46.
 Caesarion ~ 24, 25.
 child ~ 26.
 Cleopatra ~ 10, 22.
 daughter ~ 27.
 death ~ 10, 22, 24, 26.
 Jubba II ~ 14.
 king ~ 24.
 military standards ~ 35.
 name ~ 33.
 Pompey ~ 9.
 son ~ 13, 103.
 Thea Muse ~ 20, 29.
Jupiter ~ 24.

K

ka ~ 129.
Khepri. *See also* Kheper.
King Artabanus II ~ 103.
King of the Jews ~ 80, 82, 83, 101, 107,
 111.
Kingdom of Aurania ~ 119.
Kingdom of God ~ 119, 127.
Kingdom of Heaven ~ 112, 118, 119, 121,
 122, 123, 124, 127.
Kingdom of Ourania ~ 119, 120, 121, 123,
 124, 125.

Index

marriage ~ 125.
parables ~ 121.
Kingdom of Thea Muse Ourania ~ 119, 127.
Knights Templar ~ 63.
Kolea ~ 15.
Koran ~ 128, 143.
Kubr-er-Rumia ~ 15.
Kunya Urgench ~ 15.
Kurds ~ 81.

L

Lagus ~ 2.
Lamb ~ 6.
Lazarus ~ 62.
Leonado da Vinci ~ 132.
Leopard ~ 118.
leper ~ 61.
Lepidus ~ 11.
Levi ~ 133.
Liberty ~ 106, 107.
Libra ~ 114.
Libya ~ 102.
Lightfoot, J ~ 46.
Limes Arabicus ~ 50.
Lincoln, A ~ 38.
Lincoln Memorial ~ 38.
Livia ~ 14.
Livy ~ 2.
Luke ~ 117.
Lupercalia ~ 24.
Luther, M ~ 109, 131.
Lutherism ~ 144.

M

Maachah Tamar II ~ 45.
Maakare MuTamhat ~ 91.
Maakhah Tamar ~ 98.
Macedonia ~ 1.
Macurdy, G ~ 23, 27.
Madonna and Child ~ 23.
Magdalene ~ 99.
Magen David ~ 84.
Magi ~ xiv, xv, 79, 80, 81, 82, 83, 84, 85, 86, 87, 116, 117, 119.
alchemy ~ 83.
meaning ~ 84.
Malchus of Nabatea ~ 4.
Mandaeans ~ 63, 64, 81, 136.
Mankiewicz, J ~ 9, 22.

Manual of Discipline ~ 69.
Marcus Antonius ~ 28. *See* Mark Antony.
Marianne ~ 85.
Marib ~ 67.
Mark Anthony ~ 138, 139.
Mark Antony ~ 4, 5, 7, 11, 12, 13, 14, 19, 20, 24, 28, 35.
Actium ~ 12, 28.
children ~ 14, 28.
death ~ 12, 13.
Julius Caesar ~ 24.
military standards ~ 35.
Parthia ~ 11.
Roman standards ~ 19.
Marsh Arabs ~ 63, 81. *See also* Mandaeans.
Martha ~ 61, 62.
Mary ~ 55, 56, 58, 61, 74, 85, 91, 92, 93, 96, 97, 98, 100, 132, 135, 136, 137, 141, 147.
blue ~ 58, 136.
Europe ~ 137.
gospel ~ 132.
Isis ~ 85, 98.
Julia ~ 147.
Liberty ~ 85.
Muse Ourania ~ 136, 137.
name ~ 96, 97, 98.
Nut ~ 97.
Sea Star ~ 85.
sons ~ 56, 92.
Stada ~ 100.
tax ~ 55.
Mary Magdalene ~ 6, 8, 61, 63, 97, 99, 109, 110, 117, 127, 129, 131, 133, 135, 147.
Bethany ~ 61.
brothers ~ 132.
Gamala ~ 63.
hair ~ 99.
husband ~ 61
Mary of Bethany ~ 61.
Muses ~ 127, 129, 131, 133.
name ~ 97.
princess ~ 8, 110.
Saul ~ 110.
Thea Muse ~ 117.
Mary of Bethany ~ 61, 62. *See also* Mary Magdalene.
Gamala ~ 63.

Scota,
Egyptian Queen
of the Scots

Scota,

Egyptian Queen
of the Scots

Ireland and Scotland were first settled by the descendants
of an Egyptian pharaoh and his queen.

by
Ralph Ellis

Edfu Books

Adventures Unlimited

Scota, Egyptian Queen of the Scots
First published in 2006 by Edfu Books

Published in the U.K. by:
Edfu Books
PO Box 165
Cheshire
CW8 4WF
info@edfu-books.com
U.K.

Published in the U.S.A. by:
Adventures Unlimited
PO Box 74
Kempton, Illinois
60946
auphq@frontier.net
U.S.A.

First edition July 2006

U.K. paperback edition
ISBN 0-9531913-3-8 (978-0-9531913-3-8)

U.S.A. paperback edition
ISBN 1-931882-64-9

Printed in the United Kingdom by T.J. International, Padstow.

Now that is the time when Gaedel Glas,
From whom are the Gaedil born,
Of Scota daughter of Pharao.
From her are the Scots named,
Ut dictum est,
Feni are named from Feinius,
A meaning without secretiveness:
Gaedil from comely Gaedel Glas,
Scots from Scota.

Lebor Gabala Erenn,
(Book of the Invasions of Ireland)

To the morning star, who often rose above the eastern horizon to greet me, and to remind me that it was time I descended into the west and the land of slumber. My thanks also to Andy Power, who assisted in my tour of the monuments at Newgrange and pointed out the strange mummified head in St Peter's Church, Drogheda.

Ralph Ellis
Cheshire
July 2006

www.edfu-books.com

Contents

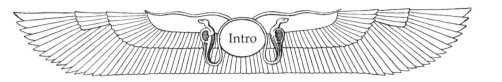

Intro

The Scottish Chronicles

Long, long ago in a faraway land, it is recorded that a prince and princess were enthroned, amongst great pomp and ceremony, as king and queen of their people. But fate was not looking kindly upon either them, or the assembled throng of courtiers and officials who supported them, because many of these people would shortly be forced to flee their homes in search of less turbulent lands beyond the 'Great Sea'. The political turmoil that surrounded this marriage, and its theological implications, took nearly four years to fester and ulcerate. Finally, there was a popular uprising of some kind that forced the abdication of the king and queen; but the revolution was peaceful enough that they were allowed to depart with the majority of their administration and followers.

Hundreds of people were forced to take to the sea in small, precarious vessels, and boldly set off towards the setting Sun and great uncertainty. This was an era in which many of these waters were completely uncharted, but since returning to their homes would mean instant death, they sailed on regardless of the dangers. Eventually, after many trials and tribulations, the royal couple and their small flotilla discovered a new land, which seemed to hold great promise. Like the Pilgrim Fathers in a much later age, these émigrés set about creating a new nation, a new Jerusalem, far away from the political and religious strife of their former homeland in Egypt.

The prince and princess in this Scottish chronicle were called Gaythelos and Scota, and it is from these appellations that the '<u>Gae</u>lic' and '<u>Sco</u>ttish' people are reputed to have been named. And while this harmony in terminology may seem a little convenient, and possibly even contrived, it should be pointed out that this connection was not derived from modern

New Age romanticism, nor was it from a Victorian fairy-tale. In fact, the chronicle of Gaythelos and Scotia was recorded in the *Instructions* and the *Pleading of Baldred Biset*. These were two documents drawn up by the Scottish nobles and intended for submission to the Papal court to demonstrate the great antiquity of the Scottish people. A small element of this history was then appended to the more famous *Declaration of Arbroath*, a document that was drawn up on 6th April 1320 AD, possibly by Abbot Bernard de Linton. This famous document, which is comparable in many respects to the American Declaration of Independence, was likewise signed by numerous earls and barons of Scotland and then sent on its long journey to Pope John XXII. The declaration was made in the wake of Robert the Bruce's victory at Bannockburn in 1314, and like the later American document, it sought to legitimise Scotland's independance from England (Britain).

Abbot Linton may have been drawing on material written six centuries earlier by Nennius, the eighth century bishop of Bangor, Co Down,* whose *Historia Brittonum* contains a similar history of Ireland and Scotland. The one or two paragraphs from the *Historia Brittonum* demonstrate that the entire Gaythelos and Scota story predates the *Pleading of Baldred Biset* and the *Declaration of Arbroath* by a considerable margin.

A later fourteenth and fifteenth century version of this history, by John of Fordun and Walter Bower, is called *Scotichronicon*. This more comprehensive chronicle demonstrates that this popular tale had been told and retold for generation after generation, with little in the way of corruption. As many as half a dozen different sources are cited in Book I of *Scotichronicon*, which all follow a similar story-line about the origins and fate of the royal couple, Gaythelos and Scota. So yes, incredible as it may seem, it has seriously been suggested by the ancient chroniclers that both Ireland and Scotland were first settled by the descendants of an Egyptian pharaoh, his queen and their various courtiers and followers.

Previous authors throughout the generations have investigated this legend, and yet the deductions they have made have been inconclusive to say the least. Many have consigned the story to mythology, and the need for a small nation to have a dramatic and well-connected past. Others have speculated that some aspects of the story are possibly based upon historical events, and suggest that these might belong to the fifth century BC. The author Lorraine Evans saw a possible connection with the Egyptian pharaoh Akhenaton, but did not pursue the matter in nearly enough detail; indeed,

---

* Co is the standard Irish abbreviation for county.

her book *Kingdom of the Ark* was not much more than an introduction to the legend. The task was therefore quite clear – I had to thoroughly research the legends of Scota and Gaythelos to see if there was any historical foundation to this ancient story. For if there was, it would greatly impact not only upon the ancient history of the greater British Isles, but also upon some of its more recent trials and tribulations.

The author has already written four books on revisionary Egyptology, and has already come to the conclusion that much of biblical history and many of the biblical characters were actually based upon Egyptian history and personalities. But since the royal families of Europe were founded by the descendants of biblical families and bloodlines, it seemed entirely plausible that European history was linked to Egyptian history in some respects.

Having researched the subject in more detail, it was apparent that Egyptian and Irish histories met and meshed with uncanny symmetry. This easy synchronicity demonstrated that this was a real history, and not the figment of an ancient scribe's fevered imagination (or, indeed, mine). Not only did the general thesis of *Scotichronicon* appear to be verifiable, but it would seem that real, historical names can be matched with most of the characters too. The history of Ireland, Scotland and the British Isles will never be quite the same again.

Note:

Before we start this adventure, perhaps I should point out that there is no evidence of a link between the Egyptian pleated kilt and its sporran-like flap (sometimes a triangular apron)* and the equivalent Irish and Scottish pleated kilts and sporrans – for all the evidence points towards the Celtic kilt being a relatively recent fashion. [1] It is entirely possible that a link does exist, which may have been passed down through the ages via the covert medium of the masonic apron, which may be why the late seventeenth and early eighteenth centuries witnessed the dual emergence into popular culture of the kilt and Scottish Rite Freemasonry. If readers have any information that places the Celtic kilt back into the pre-Christian era, I would be more than happy to be enlightened. (See the book *Eden* for an analysis of the links between Masonry and ancient Egypt.)

---

* For an illustration of this style of dress, see the many statues and illustrations among the treasures of Tutankhamen. Tutankhamen was, of course, effectively an Amarna prince and pharaoh.

Notes to the reader

a.   This book represents a sequel to six previous titles by Ralph Ellis. While it can be read as a stand-alone title without reference to the previous works, there will inevitably be occasions when it is assumed that the reader has already read, digested and understood certain concepts – primarily that there are innumerable pieces of evidence that point towards an Egyptian heritage for the Israelites, and that their leaders were actually the Hyksos pharaohs of Egypt.

To have read the other titles in advance will prepare the reader for some of the more difficult sections that lie ahead. This is not a hard sell, just a well-intended warning that the history of the greater British Isles becomes rather convoluted at times, and readers need to arm themselves with as much information as possible to understand the full implications of this research.

b.   Because of the radical nature of this book, it has been necessary to highlight the difference between standard orthodox assumptions and those generated by my lateral view of theology. Throughout this book, therefore, I have used curved brackets ( ) to denote orthodox assumptions and square brackets [ ] to denote my radical new assumptions. I hope that this serves to clarify the text.

c.   As readers of the book *Jesus, Last of the Pharaohs* will have noticed, the history of the biblical exodus is not quite as it seems. Not only were the circumstances and nations involved not quite as advertised in the Bible, but, in fact, there were two exoduses from Egypt. Because there is no longer one definitive Exodus to refer to, the term 'exodus' has been left in lower case.

d.   The references in the text are numerous. To ease the problem of continuously referring to the reference section at the back of the book, some references have been prefixed. Prefixes are as follows:

B = Bible, K = Koran, J = Josephus, T = Talmud, S = Strabo
M = Manetho, N = Nag Hammadi, SC = Scotichronicon.

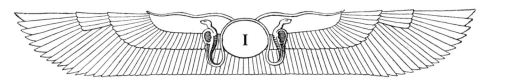

Scotichronicon

Scotichronicon is a vast work set out in sixteen books. It was nominally written by Walter Bower, an Augustinian abbot of Inchcolm monastery in about 1430. Although it was largely his work, he drew extensively on John of Fordun's earlier chronicle of 1360, and quoted extensively from a host of other venerable historians and chroniclers, as was mentioned in the introduction. Of this vast work, only Book I deals with the saga of Gaythelos and Scota, and so the entire chronicle of their and their descendants' exploits are set out in about 80 or so pages.

The interesting part about the story, which has generated so much heated debate and speculation, is that the founding royal couple of both Ireland and Scotland were a Greek prince and an Egyptian princess, who became king and queen of Egypt for a short while. Such fantastic accounts are thought to be the stuff of legend, not historical reality, and so much of the early sections of *Scotichronicon* have been consigned to the fantasy or mythology shelf. It is not either probable nor possible that a royal couple from the eastern Mediterranean could or would embark on an epic journey all the way to the damp, emerald-green coastline of Ireland – especially if this story is supposed to be recalling events from the fourteenth century BC. They simply did not have the technology for such a journey, nor the imperatives to make it. Donald Watt, the translator of *Scotichronicon*, summed up the story in this fashion:

> The story begins with the mythical voyage of Scota, the pharaoh's daughter, from Egypt ... The land that her sons discovered in the Western Ocean was named after her: Scotland.

> It scarcely needs saying that none of this is history in the proper sense ... the name Scota is a back-formation from the name of the people ... She

nevertheless incorporates some features of the mythological sovereignty who figures in Irish and other traditions – the divine partner of the king in a sacred marriage, the successful consummation which confirms his kingship. [SC1]

Here is the usual explanation for the opening chapters in *Scotichronicon* – that it is all mythology. In addition, Watt is making the argument that the Scots have donated their name to their mythological founding princess, rather than her name being the true origin of the Scots' name. In fact, the point being laboured throughout the notes on Watt's translation is that the whole story is a Middle Ages fabrication, designed to impress on readers the great antiquity and cosmopolitan origins of the Scots. However, the evidence that will be presented in this book will conclusively demonstrate that the story is actually a true history, and we shall eventually uncover the identities of all the major players in this ancient tale.

The story itself centers on the royal couple called Gaythelos and Scota, and it is from these two individuals that the Gaelic and Scots people are said to be named. Gaythelos is said to have been a wayward Greek prince who had a dispute with either his father or his brother and so left Greece to look for new opportunities. Being a precocious and fortunate individual, he is supposed to have arrived in Egypt and ingratiated himself with the royal family there. Against all the known customs of Egypt he is said to have married the daughter of the pharaoh, with a view to inheriting the throne of Egypt. However, his successful bid for the throne was not welcomed by the Egyptian proletariat and so he and his wife, princess Scota, were expelled from Egypt and embarked upon an epic voyage across the Mediterranean.

After many short stays and exploits, they are said to have landed on the river Ebro in Spain, where they set up a small fortified town called Brigantia. But, being constantly plagued with attacks by the natives, the new proto-nation looked again for less populated lands to emigrate to. The first of these islands was discovered relatively quickly, and may well have been Mallorca. Finally, after four generations or so, another island home was discovered, and this is more positively identified as being Ireland. It is recorded that both the son and great, great grandson of Gaythelos were called Hiber, and it is from this name that the countries of Iberia (Spain) and Hibernia (Scotland) are said to have been named.

Many of the, by now much larger, population of Brigantia then emigrated to Ireland, which was called Scotia after the name of the people's founding queen. That Ireland was originally called Scotia before the third century AD is fairly well known. Amongst others, Claudian, Orosius, Marianus Scotus, Isidore and Bede all mention that Ireland was called Scotia.

Surelie very much, for Scotland and Ireland are one and the same ... Therefore
yt cometh of some wryters, that Ireland is called Scotia-major, and that which
nowe is named Scotland, is called Scotia-minor. [2]

Of course this name, like the parallel name Hiber, had a habit of moving on
to new lands as the people moved to new pastures, and so it is not so
surprising that when the Scots settled in Canada they called their new
homeland Nova Scotia, or New Scotia. This is compelling evidence that the
names of countries do move to new lands, as significant portions of the
population emigrate.

Fig 1. Map demonstrating that Ireland was called Scotia.
Waddell, The makers of Civilisation, 1929.

The people stayed many generations in Ireland, and it is possible that their
primary necropolis, or burial ground, was either at the megalithic site at
Newgrange or the sacred site of Tara; both of which reside on the river
Boyne to the north of Dublin. After many generations, probably in the sixth
century BC, the Picts came to Ireland from an unknown location. The
venerable Bede has them coming from Scythia (Ukraine and towards the
Caspian Sea), a location which has been amended in recent times to
Scandinavia. However, *Scotichronicon* variously places the Picts in either

3

Aquitaine (southwestern France) or the Basque country. In fact, the southern portion of Aquitaine lies in the Basque region, and an old dialect of Easkal, the Basque language, was called Aquitaine; so it is likely that both of these accounts were referring to the Basques.

The chronicles indicate that the Scotian people were not impressed with these unwelcome (but possibly related) newcomers to their shores; and that the Basques had come with no (or too few) women. A deal was therefore struck whereby the Scotian people of Ireland gave the Basques (Picts) some of their women and advised them to go to Scotland instead. This they did, and the new Scotian/Pictish colony there became rather successful – so much so that many of the Scotians later emigrated to that region by choice. It was through this process that the name Scotia became transferred from Ireland to what we now call Scotland. Likewise, Iberia, the name for Spain that had been derived from the son of Gaythelos called Hiber, was also donated to Scotland, which became known as Hibernia.

Lebor Gabala

This is the story of Gaythelos and Scota, as given by the ancient Scottish chronicles. The task now is to sift through the evidence and try to discover how much of this is a true history and how much is mere fable. However, we might initially start with a few broad-brush assumptions. Firstly, one might observe that the Scots did not exactly have much reason to trace their history back to an obscure Greek prince and an equally obscure Egyptian princess.

Had the Scottish chronicles related that the Scottish people were directly related to Moses of the Torah, Jason of the Odyssey or Ramesses the Great from history, one might have immediately dismissed the story as a complete fabrication. The fact that the proposed Scottish ancestors are so obscure, and the fact that evidence for the pharaoh mentioned in these texts was only rediscovered in the nineteenth century AD, suggests that there is likely to be an element of truth in this ancient history; the only trouble with this suggestion being that none of the other characters involved in the story are easily identifiable within the historical records of Egypt or Greece.

In regard to Prince Gaythelos, it might seem unlikely that we could ever find evidence for this character, as the fourteenth century BC lies in prehistoric times so far as Greece is concerned. We know next to nothing about this pre-Iliad era of Mycenaean Greece, and even the events detailed in the later accounts of Homer are far from certain. With regard to Princess Scota, the records of ancient Egypt do, of course, stretch back much further than in Greece. Unfortunately, however, the name Scota is not known from any Egyptian history, nor is there anything remotely similar. What, then, can be done about this situation? By what method can we start to investigate the traditions of the *Scotichronicon* account?

The first avenue of research might be the origin of the text. *Scotichronicon* is a Scottish chronicle, based upon much older texts that have come from many locations including Ireland (the *Lebor Gabala* from the *Book of Leinster*) and Wales (the *Historia Brittonum*). But this diverse range of chronicles is obviously not the original source, so where did the story originate?

One possibility is given to us by Nennius, the monk who penned the *Historia Brittonum*. He indicates that he used Roman and Ecclesiastical documents to compose his history of Britain, and this seems likely as some of the work appears to be taken from the *World Chronicle*, by Bishop Eusebius. It will be demonstrated in a later chapter that the chronology of Egypt used in *Scotichronicon* was taken directly from Eusebius, so he is definitely a likely source for the Scota story. But, as ever, Eusebius was only quoting others, and it would appear that some of his inspiration was taken from Euhemerus, a Greek historian who wrote a philosophical romance called *Sacred Scripture*. Although it embedded features of the Scota story, Euhemerus' story was largely fictional and what we are really looking for is a true history. So from where and from whom did Eusebius and Euhemerus obtain these details? Since the Gaythelos and Scota story is deeply embedded in Egyptian history, it is there that we must look for the original sources.

It is said that the trail goes cold at this point, but actually there is a very good candidate for the next link in this literary chain back into history. Since Euhemerus lived around 300 BC, there is a very likely candidate for the Egyptian end of this story, and he is the Egypto-Greek historian known as Manetho. Not that much is known about the life of Manetho, but it is thought that he was a priest of Heliopolis, Egypt, who lived at around 300 BC and wrote a long history and chronology of the nation called *The History of Egypt*. The original text has unfortunately been lost to us; however, snippets of his history were copied by other historians, and one of those happened to be Eusebius. Furthermore, since we know for certain that Eusebius' chronology of Egypt was taken directly from Manetho, perhaps the other details about Scota and Gaythelos and their flight from Egypt were copied from the same text. Again this is likely, as a close similarity between the Scota story and Manetho's *The History of Egypt* will be shown later in this book.

The possibility that Manetho was the original author of the Scota and Gaythelos story is interesting, because it gives the whole story much greater credence. It is known, from comparisons with the archaeological record, that Manetho's history of Egypt was quite factual; indeed, his royal chronology of Egypt, and the dynastic separations that he indicated, are still the basis for the modern chronology of Egypt. If the ultimate author of *Scotichronicon* had been Herodotus, one might have been justified in being highly skeptical, but with the originator being Manetho, there is every possibility that there is a great deal of truth in the story.

This hope is considerably bolstered by the constant discovery of small, obscure details from *Scotichronicon* that are known to be correct. Even aspects that are generally unknown today, let alone in a cold and drafty monastery in fifteenth century Scotland, can be shown to be correct. Take, for instance, the general history of Egypt. This is described as:

> The kingdom of Egypt (the name of which was originally Etheria) is the most ancient of all kingdoms except for the kingdom Scythia... [SC3]

Egypt is indeed a very ancient kingdom, as we all know, but that is not the interesting element here. The fascinating aspect of this quote is the unusual name that was given to Egypt – Etheria. Surprisingly enough, Egypt was indeed known as Etheria, and the true spelling of the name in the Egyptian was actually Aturti or Eturti (Ethurti) 𓇌𓂝𓅱𓈖𓏏𓉐 . The name relates to water and to the flooding of the Nile, and the 'ia' on the end of Walter Bower's version is simply a typical Greek rendering of an Egyptian name. In addition, Geoffrey Keating, the venerable historian of Ireland, indicates that this name for Egypt was reduced down to the name 'Aeria' in later generations, and used for the island of Ireland. It is from Aeria that the modern name of Eire was derived. Thus the current name for Ireland is actually a corruption of an original pharaonic name for Egypt. Interestingly, Keating states that this was also the original name for Crete, and we shall be looking at some Cretan connections both with Egypt and Ireland in later chapters.

Perhaps the most important element of this potted history is the fact that the ancient Scottish chronicle is correct, and it accurately records a little-used and very ancient name for Egypt. If this small detail, which is only mentioned in passing, can be seen to be correct, how many other names and events within this ancient chronicle may also be historically correct?

However, while this snippet of information is interesting, we could go one step further than this because it has been suggested that the spelling of Aturt needs rearranging very slightly. If we were to maintain the 'th' in Bower's version of this word, then the original name for Egypt becomes A-th-u-r-t-i, or the land of Arthur. The meaning of Aturti 𓇌𓂝𓅱𓈖𓏏𓉐 is closely linked with the river Nile, as are the legends of Arthur himself and his protective goddess known as the Lady of the Lake (Isis, the 'queen' of Egypt). While this particular paragraph is complete speculation, it is nevertheless interesting that Arthur's city of Camelot translates directly as Kama-ret (Kama-let) 𓂧𓃀𓏏𓂝 𓂋𓏏𓀀 meaning 'People of Egypt'. (The Egyptian 'r' invariably becomes a Greek/Latin 'l', just as Pharaoh Ptoremy was actually Pharaoh Ptolemy.)

If Gaythelos and Scota came from Egypt, as Walter Bower and others maintain, then much of Celtic mythology may have once had an Egyptian flavour. And if the prospect of a heroic Egyptian royalty was not about to excite the Middle Ages populous, what better deception than to dress up this very ancient history in the more contemporary clothes of knightly chivalry. That this was an effective method of maintaining an ancient history is implicit in the success of the Medieval Grail Romances; however, when using propaganda so effectively, one always runs the risk of the story being so successful that it eclipses the true history that lies beneath it.

Was this what happened all those millennia ago? Did an Egyptian queen and her consort arrive in the greater British Isles some thirteen centuries before the Common Era, and establish a society based upon Egyptian culture and principles. If this did occur, one might initially suppose that this would manifest itself in an overtly 'foreign' culture being present in Ireland during the Bronze Age. However, this is not necessarily so.

The author has already demonstrated that Judaism was based upon the creed and culture of the Amarna regime of Pharaoh Akhenaton, and that many of the Old Testament verses have been copied verbatim from ancient Egyptian texts – including large segments of Genesis, the exodus story, Psalms, Proverbs, the Song of Solomon and the Lord's Prayer. We tend to think of our present culture as being a mix of Celtic, Roman and Anglo-Saxon societies that have been heavily influenced by a later blanket of Judaism (Christianity). However, had early Celtic culture been founded upon Egyptian principles (Amarna principles), we would hardly notice the difference, because the Amarna culture of Pharaoh Akhenaton *is* our Judaeo-Christian culture – whether this was derived directly from Egypt or via the indirect transmission route of Israel and Rome.

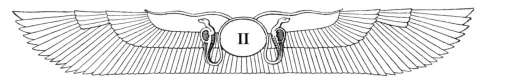

Scota and Gaythelos

This brings us to the nub of this investigation, for if Princess Scota was the daughter of a pharaoh, then evidence for her existence should be available in the relatively well-recorded history of Egypt. Some of the previous research and speculation into her origins has casually identified her as a daughter of Pharaoh Akhenaton, of the Amarna dynasty, but not shown any convincing reason why this should be so. In contrast, this chapter will not only positively identify the pharaoh and his daughter (Princess Scota), but also positively identify her husband, Prince Gaythelos, in the historical record.

This will represent a fundamental turning point in Irish-Scots history, not simply because it will be shown that both Scota and Gaythelos are relatively well known, but also because their discovery turns fiction into fact. The ancient history of these lands and people, as detailed in the great chronicle of *Scotichronicon*, has long been sidelined and dismissed as being unreliable mythology. However, if we are able to show that the names used in these ancient chronicles equate with the known history of Egypt, then these chronicles must be closer to real life than fable. Suddenly, there is the very real prospect that the ancient history of the greater British Isles was conceived and nurtured within the advanced culture of ancient Egypt. And since modern Judaism and Christianity were both born from Egyptian theology, the long-held notion that Ireland originally harboured the secrets of what has become known as the 'Old Church' of Christianity, may not be so far wide of the mark.

So who was this fabled prince of Greece (who briefly became pharaoh of Egypt) who is said to have fled towards Ireland? And which pharaoh from these ancient lands would have dared give his daughter away to a renegade prince from a foreign land? The ancient texts of Egypt clearly state that Egypt never gave its princesses away to foreigners, so how and why would this happen?

> At the height of the New Kingdom, pharaohs regularly took to wife the daughters of Near East princes, but refused to permit their own daughters to be married off to foreign rulers. [1]

Biblical scholars might point towards the marriage of King Solomon and an Egyptian princess, and indicate that the ancient texts were obviously wrong in their boasting. This did indeed remain a bit of a problem, until I deduced, in the book *Solomon*, that King Solomon was also a Lower Egyptian pharaoh himself. In other words, the princess in the biblical accounts had not been given away to a foreigner at all, as King Solomon [Pharaoh Sheshonq] was resident in Tanis in the Nile Delta. But if Egyptian princesses were never given to foreign princes, then the *Scotichronicon* story is already looking suspect, unless we can reinterpret it in some manner.

The name of this pharaoh and the era in which he reigned are debatable too. Some researchers have been led astray by the biblical chronology because of the frequent references to the biblical exodus within *Scotichronicon*, and so they place the era as being just after Ramesses II, the supposed pharaoh of the biblical exodus. One interpretation of *Scotichronicon* even places the era in the sixth century BC, because of a mention of the Persian pharaoh of Egypt, Xerxes. Even the translator of *Scotichronicon*, Donald Watt, is slightly confused. He placed the chronicle's pharaoh in the Amarna era, which is correct, but he could not deduce exactly which pharaoh he should be. Lorraine Evans said the pharaoh concerned was Akhenaton; she was right, of course, but there was no real explanation as to how she came to that conclusion.

In actual fact, the truth about the era and the precise pharaoh concerned is fairly plain and simple. The pharaonic chronology is given in Book I chapter 10 of Walter Bower's *Scotichronicon*, and here the author is plainly following the records of the Greco-Egyptian historian, Manetho. If we list the two chronicles together, readers will clearly see the comparison:

Bower chronology		Manetho chronology	
Amosis	25	Ahmosis	25
Chebron	13	Chebron	13
Amenophis	21	Amenophis	21
Mephres	12	Mephres	12
(Joseph died)			
Mispharmatosis	9	Mispharmuthosis	26
		Tuthmosis	9

Amenophis	31	Amenophis	31
(Moses born)		(Memnon statue)	
Horus	38	Orus	28
Acencris	12	Achencheres	12
		(Biblical exodus)	
Achorisis	7	Acherres	8
Chencres	18	Cherres	15
(Biblical exodus and Scota exodus)			
		Armais (Dannus)	5
		Ramesses	68

Numbers represent the reign lengths for each pharaoh.

Now this list of pharaohs from Egypt is rather interesting, for at the very least it demonstrates that Walter Bower had a copy of Manetho's work with him in his monastery at Inchcolm. Indeed, to be more precise, this is a copy of Manetho's history of Egypt that arrived into the Medieval era via the Armenian version of the Christian chronographer Eusebius. Bower has not only faithfully copied this text, minus one pharaoh, he has also added some other interesting details, which might suggest that he had access to documents long since lost to us.

The mention of Moses' birth is one of these interpolations, and the position in which this is mentioned ties in very nicely with the revised history of Egypt that I have already outlined in the book *Jesus;* namely that Moses was actually TuthMoses, the brother of Akhenaton. If this were so, then the biblical Moses would have been the son of Amenhotep III (Amenophis in Manetho's chronology), which is exactly what Bower indicates. He also, along with Manetho, states that the biblical exodus took place just after the reign of Acencris (Achencheres), which is again perfectly correct according to this same revised 'Amarna' history of Judaism, as we shall see.

To tie all of this into classical Egyptian history, we now need to make a comparison with the standard historical texts, to see how accurate the histories of Manetho and Bower really were. Readers should note that the misplacing of Horemheb in Manetho's version of the king-list was probably due to the Amarna regime having being deleted from most Egyptian records. Having been presented with an entire new dynasty, which was missing from all the other records, it was probably difficult for Manetho to decide where to place that dynasty. He chose after Horemheb, whereas the historical evidence seems to conclusively show that the Amarna era came before Horemheb. There is also the swapping of the position of Chencres and Acencris, possibly due to the two duplicated pharaohs that one of Manetho's lists contains. But the pharaoh of the exodus is clearly stated in Manetho's lists as being the Chencheres (or Achencheres) who immediately followed Orus (Horus), as is denoted in the following list. This list represents a comparison between the pharaonic chronology of Manetho and the chronology accepted by modern orthodox history:

Manetho's chronology	Classical chronology
Ahmos (Ahmoses) (Tethmoses) - 25	Ahmose I - 24
Chebron - 13	
Amenophis - 21	Amenhotep I - 27
	Tuthmoses I - 6
	Tuthmoses II - 14
Amesse (f) - 22	Hatshepsut (f) - 15
Mephres (Misaphris) - 12	
Mephrammuthosis - 26	Tuthmoses III - 54
	Amenhotep II - 34
Tuthmoses - 9	Tuthmoses IV - 33
Amenophis - 31	Amenhotep III - 37
Orus - 38	(See Horemheb) *
Achencheres (f?) - 12	Akhenaton - 17 (12 as co-regent)
(Biblical exodus)	(Biblical exodus)
Acherres (f) - 12	Nefertiti (f) - 14 (all as co-regent?)
	or possibly Smenkhkare - 3
Chencheres (Cherres) - 12	Tutankhamen - 9
Armesis (Harmais) (Dannus) - 5	Aye (Armait) - 4
	Horemheb - 28 (see Orus)
Ramesses - 1 (Aegyptus)	Ramesses I - 2
	Seti I - 13
Ramesses - 68	Ramesses II - 67
Amenophath (Ammenophis) - 40	
Sethos (Ramesses) - 10	(see Seti I, above)

Numbers after the pharaoh's name are reign lengths.   (f) = female.

The accounts of Manetho have arrived via a number of ancient historians: Josephus, Theophilus, Syncellus, Eusebius, and the Armenian version of Eusebius. It is the variations between these different versions that give the differing titles and the extra (missing) pharaohs that were not included in the previous list.

* The names Orus and Horemheb were both derived from Horus (Heru), the hawk-headed god of Egypt.

*   *   *

This list demonstrates the problems involved in equating the known archaeology of the region with the historical accounts of Manetho. Some of the names are obvious equivalents, like Tuthmoses being Tuthmoses IV, and Amenophis being Amenhotep III, although the reign lengths differ significantly. Other names are not so obvious, but many of them can nevertheless be resurrected from Manetho's distorted Greek renderings by using a little common sense.

Central to the present discussion is Pharaoh Chencres, the king who Bower and Fordun *et al* indicate was the father of Princess Scota. Just who was this particular pharaoh? In the other copies of Manetho, this pharaoh (the pharaoh of the exodus) is actually called Achencheres, and this is the name I shall be using to decipher his true identity. You will note that this pharaoh has been placed opposite Pharaoh Akhenaton in the table, and there is good reason for this.

The first syllables of each name are the same in each case, 'Akhen' in the historical texts versus 'Achen' in the records of Manetho; the former being a syllable that has been taken from the ibis glyph 𓅞 , which is pronounced as 'Aakh'. The Greek version of 'Achen' uses either a hard 'k' or a soft 'kh' ('ch') in the different accounts of Manetho and so there is a direct correspondence between these two words or syllables.

The next syllables to these names are merely two variants of a title for the Sun-god, with one version using 'Aton' and the other using the Hebrew 'Cheres' חרס meaning 'Sun'. Several Egyptologists have challenged my interpretation of Cheres, indicating that the Hebrew for 'Sun' is actually Shemesh שֶׁמֶשׁ. This may be so, but the biblical Mt Heres (Cheres - Kheres) חרס was known as the 'Mountain of the Sun', and so Heres (Cheres - Kheres) does indeed refer to the Sun.

Fig 2. Cartouches of Akhenaton Neferkheperura Uinra.

Another challenge to this interpretation, which has been made on numerous occasions in academic circles, is that the Egypto-Greek world of Manetho would not have been influenced by a Hebrew word like Cheres חרס. However, it is a recorded fact that Manetho uses the term Cheres in many of the pharaonic names that include a reference to the Sun-god; be it Aton, Amun or Ra. Thus, it is abundantly clear that Manetho was using the term Cheres for the Sun-god, and during the Amarna era this term would have denoted the Aton. The result of all this deliberation is that Manetho's pharaoh called Achen-Cheres was actually the historical Amarna pharaoh called Akhen-Aton (Akhenaton), and since Bower's pharaoh called Chencres is the direct equivalent of this Acencheres, then the father of Scota must also have been Akhenaton.

In addition to all this, Manetho also asserts that Achencheres was female. While this may initially seem to be a major stumbling block in this interpretation, it is a fact that early Egyptologists were also under the impression that Akhenaton was female. The majority of Akhenaton's images display an overtly androgenous, if not totally female, physique, and so the confusion of both Manetho and later historians is understandable. Indeed, this gender-confusion is likely to have been fostered and encouraged by the victorious Theban priesthood, who sought to denigrate each and every aspect of the 'heretic pharaoh' Akhenaton.

Finally, it should be noted that of all the Amarna pharaohs (including Smenkhkare, Tutankhamen and Aye), only Akhenaton had children during his reign, and so the only pharaoh from this era that could be the father of Scota is Akhenaton. Here, then, we have a definitive resolution to the pharaoh who fathered princess Scota. Whatever the level of truth and fact that resides within the rest of the *Scotichronicon* story, it is fairly certain that the pharaoh it speaks of is a real historical character – he was Pharaoh Akhenaton and, just as the Scottish tale implies, he presided over a pretty unstable regime.

Scota

Having identified the actual pharaoh mentioned in the ancient chronicle, it is worth noting that it is very fortunate that the story it relates takes place during this precise era in Egyptian history. At almost any other time in Egyptian history one might pronounce that it would have been impossible for an Egyptian princess to have been allowed to sail away from her country on such a perilous journey, and so the Scottish chronicle would have to be false. Egypt was the world's superpower, and while foreign princesses may have made perilous journeys to Egypt, the opposite was never true.

However, the Scota story happens to take place during a period of unprecedented social turmoil within Egypt, an era during which even a mighty pharaoh (Akhenaton himself) may have been forced into exile. Of all the dynasties in Egypt's long history, the fact that *Scotichronicon* should focus on this precise period of instability strengthens its claim towards historical veracity. How would Bower, Fordun or any of the previous chroniclers who have handled this history, have known that it was entirely possible that an Egyptian princess may well have escaped from the crumbling Amarna regime of Akhenaton by boat?

If the discovery of Akhenaton being the father of Scota greatly strengthens the chronicle's story, then which of Akhenaton's six daughters could have been called Scota? Unfortunately, this is unlikely to be a true name for an Amarna princess and so what we probably have here is a hypocorism: a nickname. Like many a prince or princess before and after, Scota became known for her deeds rather than her birth name. What she managed to do, together with her husband, was take a whole community out of their comfortable homeland in Egypt and steer them westwards, in a flotilla of small boats, towards the setting Sun.

> So Gaythelos gathered together all his followers and left Egypt with his wife Scota. Because he was afraid to return to the regions from which he had come (Greece), because of old feuds, he directed his course westwards. SC2

Thus the heroine princess became known as Skoti [hieroglyphs] or, when using a Sean Connery accent, Shkoti [hieroglyphs] ; a name which refers to the boat of the setting Sun, the boat on which the Sun-god rowed towards the western horizon. A more fitting name for this queen would be hard to find.

This reasoning is similar to the name given in mythology to Mary Magdalene. She too was exiled from her homeland and she too is reputed to have sailed westwards from the eastern Mediterranean towards France, in a boat with no oars or crew. So, in the legends that describe this journey, the Magdalene is called the Mari Stella, or the Sea Star. And since this legend was so important to the Illuminati, it went on to spawn Sir Arthur Conan Doyle's more modern legend of the Mari Celeste (Mary Celeste), a name that can be translated as Sea Heaven or perhaps Sea Star.

Negra

This voyage of the Magdalene also spawned the cult of the Black Madonna. It is said that several of the New Testament Marys, including Mary Magdalene, were on this voyage to Provence in France. Whether Mary the Madonna was on this small boat or not, she was later portrayed as being black; both in France and across the wider continent. Some enterprising minorities have jumped upon this mention of blackness, as they often do, and argued that Mary was of an African phenotype – which is plain and simple nonsense, born of desperation. That respected authors like Lynn Picknett should follow their lead just goes to show how far this political correctness has spread. There are even some overly zealous types who inhabit archaeological discussion sites on the web and try to convince all and sundry that the beautiful bust of Nefertiti demonstrates that she was a Negress. Such a strategy again smacks of desperation. [3]

The truth of the matter is slightly more cryptic. For a start, the identity of this dusky Mary is not entirely certain, for while she is often assumed to be the Madonna, this could well be a subtle portrayal of the Magdalene. In addition, the Church authorities were not allowed to say, for doctrinal reasons, what the true ancestry of Mary Magdalene and Jesus really was. To the common people Jesus was a carpenter and Mary was a prostitute and that was that, with no questions asked. And if anyone got a little too inquisitive, the overpowering threat of the Inquisition, at the slightest hint of heresy, was a powerful motivation for caution. But, as we are slowly finding out in our more enlightened times, the truth was and is much more complex.

As I have already explained in the books *Jesus* and *Solomon*, Mary Magdalene was not a street prostitute but a temple prostitute, or God's Wife, which was a highly exalted position within Egyptian theology. Similarly, Jesus was not a simple carpenter, but God's Carpenter (Setepenre), which was an old Pharaonic title used by many of the royal dynasties in Egypt. Furthermore, Mary and Jesus were not simply husband and wife, as has been publicly exposed recently in *The Da Vinci Code*; they were also brother and sister, with sibling marriage again being a long-established tradition within the royal dynasties of Egypt. The book *Cleopatra to Christ* also demonstrates that Jesus and Mary were descended from the royal dynasties of Egypt and Parthia (Persia).

As one might imagine, supreme Christian heresies such as these were difficult to discuss back in the Middle Ages, with the ever-present threat of being burned alive hanging over any such discussions. Accordingly, a masonic-type initiatory system was devised, so that only the true and trusted at the core of this particular secret society were told the real truth about Western history and religion. But to place that truth into public view, perhaps as a calculated snub to the Catholic authorities, the Illuminati used a series of secret codes that only the initiated would be able to decipher. In this particular case, they simply painted Mary black. While the Illuminati may have given a host of banal reasons for this choice, from the black colour denoting death to the original statues being made of ebony, the truth is that this colour actually revealed Mary's true ancestry.

The simple answer to this Illuminati code is that in the Egyptian language 'black' is called *kam* , and at the same time the proper name Kam ⟨𓂧𓄿𓏏𓏤⟩ happens to refer to Egypt herself. So the blackness of these Madonnas simply means that Mary (in fact, both Marys) was of Egyptian origin; which is exactly what I relate in the book *Cleopatra*. This is why Mary and the infant Jesus were said to have fled to Egypt when there was a threat to his life. Mary's family was of Egyptian heritage and so it was natural enough for Mary to go to her homeland for safety, and where the young Jesus could complete his education at Heliopolis.

This is why there is also the strange tradition of Saint Mary of Egypt. She was supposed to have been a reformed fifth century AD prostitute who turned to Christianity, but she shares so many similarities with Mary Magdalene that many think she is a secret code for her. But this is a code that again deliberately places Mary Magdalene's heritage back into Egypt. Once again, the Illuminati within the Catholic Church wanted the evidence out there within the public domain, even if it is only obliquely hinted at.

Also on board this small boat, heading towards France, was a young 'servant' called Sarah, who was again said to be black. But the Hebrew name Sarah שׂרה simply means 'princess' and so the true parentage of this young 'servant' should be obvious – she was Mary Magdalene's daughter, fathered by Jesus. This young Sarah, or princess, is especially venerated by the Gypsy people at Saintes-Maries-de-la-Mer in Provence, France, where the small boat is supposed to have come ashore. The Gypsies re-enact Sarah's arrival on these shores every 24th and 25th May, and hold a festival there. This again demonstrates the possible links between this story and Egypt, as the name for the Gypsies themselves is also supposed to have been derived from the name 'Egypt'.

One other point worth clarifying is the peculiar references to Mary's boat having no sails or oars. This lack of propulsive power sounds decidedly odd and so it has to be, as one might expect, an allegorical allusion of some nature. The answer to this little riddle lies in the alternative meaning for a ship's mast. Just as the blade (Λ) and chalice (V) that form the outline of the Star of David are representative of the male and female reproductive organs, so too are the ship and its phallic mast – which is why all ships are said to be female. In a typical piece of Egyptian humanist duality, the ship is the vessel that holds humanity, but it is the mast that propels it along; and so both are required to make a functional vessel or society. Thus the curious reference to a ship with no mast merely implies that Mary Magdalene arrived in France without Jesus and most probably without her sons too. The legends seem to confirm this when they speak only of Mary arriving with her 'Egyptian slave'; that is, her daughter Sarah.

As this explanation clearly demonstrates, many inconvenient facts have been lost from general knowledge and history. This was the fate of the truth during the Middle Ages, to be driven underground and passed on in hushed whispers by the initiated few of the Illuminati. But so strong was the oppression, and so complete was the obliteration of the truth, that much of this information still remains hidden. And yet, just as it would appear that much of this information will resurface and be understood by the general public, another calamity is about to descend upon us.

Unfortunately, when the British government's new Incitement to Religious Hatred law is eventually passed, the truth will once again be made to suffer from the traditional forms of censorship, obfuscation and persecution – even during our supposedly enlightened twenty-first century. We have already arrived at the point where to criticise a religion results in your throat being cut and a message of love and affection from the 'Compassionate and Merciful' deity being pinned to your chest with a dagger; but now the government wishes us to be put in jail too. The repercussions of this new ill-advised law (or any of its pernicious descendants) are all too predictable, for in the eyes of the rabid few it will legitimise their campaign of terrorism against their critics.

Our cherished freedom to question or belittle a peculiar religious proclamation or belief will soon be severely curtailed, and since faith is not based upon rational truth and hard evidence, both the truth and the inconvenient facts that support it will be buried once more within the inner cores of secret societies. Fanaticism and bigotry will become the liberal left's victors, and a new Dark Age of repression will spread across Europe and the entire Western world. Today this repression manifests itself in book burnings, fatwas, murders, death threats paraded openly through the streets of London and widespread religious terrorism in Western capitals; tomorrow the ignorant masses will be building funerary pyres for the infidel unbelievers.

Gaythelos

While it might be satisfying to see that Princess Scota's name was based upon a real Egyptian title, which again indicates that the *Scotichronicon* chronicle is familiar with Egyptian traditions and language, it is disappointing not to find an actual name that can positively identify Scota as a daughter of Akhenaton. Nevertheless, her true identity can be discovered, but the method of deciphering which daughter she was will have to be indirect; through the identity of her husband, Gaythelos.

The information about Gaythelos is sketchy; however, there is enough information in the chronicle to allow us to come to a surprising deduction. It is worth noting that the *Scotichronicon* account is not simply the invention of one scribe, priest or historian, for Walter Bower quotes five or six different chronicles that all relate the same kind of information. Using these different sources, a consistent picture begins to emerge about turbulent times and a royal marriage that occurred at about the time of the biblical exodus:

> In the time of Moses there was a certain king of one of the kingdoms of Greece called Neolas. He had a son who was good looking but mentally unstable, Gaythelos by name. Since he had not been permitted to hold any position of power in the kingdom he was provoked to anger, and with the support of a large number of friends he inflicted many disasters on his father's kingdom. He greatly outraged both his father and the inhabitants (of the country) with his violent behaviour. So he was driven out of his native land and sailed off to Egypt: and there, since he was outstandingly brave and daring and of royal descent, he was united in marriage with Scota the daughter of Pharaoh Chencres. [SC4]

Note here the comment about the prince being mentally unstable, which is an obvious comment about the Amarna dynasty. Akhenaton was known as the 'unstable one', the 'criminal of Akhetaton' (Amarna), or the 'heretic pharaoh'. But while this mental instability was a particular comment about Akhenaton himself, from the Theban Amun priesthood's point of view, it is likely that it also applied to the whole of the Amarna dynasty, and in particular to any of the administration and royal family who publicly supported the god Aten. Professor Watt, the translator of *Scotichronicon*, sees this royal instability as being an unusual feature of the text. He says of this:

> It is curious that (Gaythelos') early life is portrayed in such hostile terms, which have no parallel in the Irish tradition. [SC5]

Having already asserted that *Scotichronicon* is only a local Irish myth, it would now appear that this presumed 'Celtic' mythology does not conform to local literary traditions. However, it does correspond very closely with the literary tradition of the Egyptian late eighteenth dynasty, and the bitter aftermath of the failed Amarna regime. Slowly but surely, we shall see that many of the more unusual aspects of the Scottish chronicle jar with local Celtic traditions, but dovetail nicely with Egyptian history.

There are some differences between the various chronicles that comprise Bower's story, and one says that Gaythelos went to Egypt with an army to help the pharaoh. While it is known that Greece sent mercenary soldiers to help Egypt in later eras, not much is known of such exploits during the Amarna era; and although the Pendlebury papyrus may show Greek mercenaries with traditional 'boar-tusk helmets' fighting in Egypt in this era, this evidence is far from conclusive. The Amarna era was two or three hundred years prior to the Iliad's account of the invasion of Troy, and so Mycenaean Greece may not even have been able to muster an army at that time. Another account in Bower's story says that Gaythelos married his Egyptian princess before he was exiled to Egypt. Yet another indicates that Gaythelos and his army were assisting pharaoh to eject the Israelites [the Hyksos] from Egypt. Finally, one last chronicle indicates that Gaythelos (now called Aegialeus) was actually battling with his brother Apis, rather than his father.

All in all, it would seem that Gaythelos was an Egypto-Greek prince of dubious character who had fought with his father/brother and been exiled to Egypt for his crimes, where he rather fortuitously married a princess with the hope of becoming king of Egypt. However, as has already been explained, the latter point is nigh on impossible, as pharaohs of Egypt never gave their daughters to foreign princes. So who was Gaythelos, and where did he really come from? Well, compare the previous quote from *Scotichronicon* with the following quote from the Greco-Egyptian historian, Manetho:

> This king appointed his brother Harmais (as) viceroy of Egypt, and invested him with the royal prerogative ... He then set out on an expedition against Cyprus and Phoenicia ... (but) Harmais who had been left behind in Egypt, recklessly contravened all his brother's injunctions. He outraged the queen and proceeded to make free with the concubines; then, following the advice of his friends, he began to wear the diadem (crown) and rose in revolt of his brother ...
>
> ... thereafter Harmais was banished from Egypt and, fleeing from his brother, he arrived in Greece, and, seizing Argos, he ruled over the Argives. [M6]

While the tale of a wayward prince plotting a revolt against his father/brother the king is as old as time itself, how many of these stories result in an exile from Greece to Egypt, or *vice versa*? Indeed, apart from the switching of the departure and arrival points, these two stories appear to be exactly the same. But this is not all, for there are yet more similarities to come.

Firstly, it should be noted that it is entirely possible that Manetho was the original source for *Scotichronicon*. If this is so, then it should be expected that there will be areas of agreement between these two histories of ancient Egypt, and the differences may simply be due to the number and variety of historians and scribes through which these chronicles have passed. Thus these two quotes may be from the same history of Egypt.

Secondly, both of these stories occurred at substantially the same time. The Gaythelos story relates to the era of Akhenaton, as we have seen;

while the Harmais story relates to the time of Akhenaton's uncle, Aye, as we shall see later.

Thirdly, the story of Gaythelos eventually ends up in Ireland, where some of the newcomers to that island were known as the Tuatha de Dannen, or the Tribe of Dannen. If this is true, then some of the exiles who left Egypt with King Gaythelos must have been of the tribe of Dannen. However, in a similar fashion, the prince of Egypt called Harmais, in the previous quote from Manetho, was also called Dannus. Indeed, on his arrival in Greece he donated his name to the Athenians, and so Homer's *Iliad* says that it was the Danaoi (the Greeks) who went into battle against Troy. (The book *Eden* conclusively demonstrates that Troy was actually the city of Tanis in Egypt, and the great armada of ships in the Greek confederation was actually the great armada of the Sea People alliance that attacked Egypt.)

Fig 3. Julius Caesar.

Caesar

The two quotes just given demonstrate that there is a possibility of a direct connection between Gaythelos and this prince called Harmais (Armais), who was also called Dannus. So could they have been one and the same person? Was Gaythelos a prince of Egypt who went to Greece, rather than a Greek prince who went to Egypt? This would certainly make more sense of his marriage to an Egyptian princess, and it would also make more sense of the degree of prestige that is being given to a minor princeling from an otherwise unimportant land.

The method of discovering the true identity of Gaythelos partly lies in the meaning of his name. What, then, does the name Gaythelos really mean? Actually, the rather astounding answer to this question is that 'Gaythelos' most probably means 'Caesar' – yes, Caesar, as in the Roman emperor. While this suggestion may initially seem a little peculiar, bear with me a while longer.

The name Caesar is the family name for Gaius Julius Caesar. His birth name was Gaius, his family name was Caesar and his clan name was Julius. So his name should really be given as Gaius Caesar, rather than Julius Caesar. But the more important aspect of his full name, in regard to Gaythelos, is the family name of Caesar – what is the origin of this name?

As with many areas of this research, the etymology of the name 'Caesar' is not known. It is said that it could have been derived from *caesar* meaning 'hairy', hence the jesting and carping about Julius Caesar going a little bald. Alternatively, it could have been derived from *caesar* meaning 'seizure', since some of Caesar's family are said to have suffered from epilepsy. While the name Caesar may have been derived from either of these terms, there is actually a much more satisfactory origin to this famous name.

Firstly, it should be noted that the name Caesar was adopted as a title for subsequent emperors, many of whom were not of the Caesar family at all. So why was this name thought to be so important that it would be used as a title that was almost akin to 'king'? The answer is that the title did refer to a king, but this was not a king of Rome. Instead, the name Caesar was also held by a pharaoh of Egypt and in the Egyptian original the name is given as Kaisares ⬭𓏏𓈖𓊪𓋴 , which is the spelling given for Ptolemy Caesarion, Caesar's son. In the equivalent Greek text this name is translated as Kiasaros Κιασαροσ. Another spelling of this name is Gaysares 𓂋𓆼𓈖𓏏𓊪 , with an initial 'g'.

It is thought by some hardy historians, who don't mind going out on an academic limb, that it is from the Greek title *Kaisaros* that the Latin name and title of Caesar was derived (and not *vice versa*). So Julius Caesar may have derived his family name from an alternative source, rather than his name initiating the common Roman title for 'emperor'. But in what way does this name relate to Gaythelos?

🔻   Well, the Egyptian 'r' was invariably transliterated into the Hebrew and Greek as an 'l', as the Egyptians did not have the 'l' consonant. This would mean that an alternative pronunciation for Kaisares, in the Egyptian, might be Kaisales or Gaysales. There is also the problem of missing vowels, as these were never written in Egyptian, and so the positioning of the correct vowels is always a problem with these transliterations. If we are allowed to make these two common alterations to the Egyptian cartouche given above, we can then derive either the title Caesar (Kaisaros) or the name Gayselos:

Egyptian to Roman	Egyptian to Greek	Egyptian to Celtic
G a y s a r e s	K a y s a r e s	G a y s a r e s
C a e s ar	K a i s a r o s	G a y s a l o s

In addition, the 's' to 'th' alteration is fairly common to many languages, especially among the Spanish, who seem to place a 'th' in every word possible. (Note also the problems that German speakers have with the 'th', which is invariably converted into an 's'.) This final alteration would then make the full transition of this name into the Celtic:

Egyptian to Celtic
Gays alos
Ga y th a l o s

Here we seem to have a direct association between the titles for a Roman and a Greco-Egyptian leader; but the question remains as to which of these names was the formative. Was the name for Prince Gaythelos influenced by the tradition of Roman emperors who bore the name Caesar, or was his name taken directly from the Egyptian title Gaysares?

Fig 4.   Egyptian title of Gaythelos (Gaisalos / Gaisaros).

There are many strands to this question, and the first element is the widespread use of this term or title. As was mentioned in the book *Jesus*, the term Caesar and its equivalents are by no means restricted to Rome. The Germanic tribes used Kaiser, while the Persians used Kasra. The former of these titles was probably derived from Roman usage, but the latter was certainly not, as it was used by successive Persian kings over many generations. Thus, the Persian usage predates the known Roman and Egyptian examples of this title by many centuries.

One Persian example of this royal name is the Persian pharaoh of Egypt called Xerxes, a name which is actually an extremely poor Greek (and English) transliteration of his original name. In the Persian cuneiform, and in the Egyptian hieroglyphs (Xerxes became an Egyptian pharaoh), this king was actually called Khashiarsha ⟨ 𓇋𓈖𓏏𓐍 ⟩ . By picking out the letters 'Kh', 'a', 'sh', 'r' and 'a' from this name, we can derive the Persian title Kh-a-s-r-a (Kasra), meaning 'king'. As an Arabic dictionary says of this word:

> **Kasra**   pl. *Akasirah*. The Khosroes, a name given to almost every king of Persia of Sassanian dynasty). The name is similar to that of Caesar among the Romans and Pharaoh among the Egyptians. [7]

Remember that if Kasra (Kaisars) was a Persian title, then the hieroglyphs in the cartouche for Xerxes may well represent an Egyptian transliteration of this. This, plus the many varied spellings for Kaisars, may point towards this being a foreign title, with no intrinsic meaning within the Egyptian language.

Fig 5. Cartouche of Khashiarsha (Xerxes).

This gives us an interesting new possibility; the suggestion that Gaythelos was actually a Persian prince, rather than a Greek or an Egyptian. If the royal title 'Kasra' originated in Persia, then was Gaythelos Persian? This is a possibility, but on balance perhaps not. The chronology given in *Scotichronicon* places these events squarely within the Amarna era, and the Persians simply did not exist at that time. The ruling empire in the east during this era was the Hittite, and it is unlikely that 'Kasra' was a Nesa (Hittite) word. No, even if the term turns out to be Persian, it must be a more recent title applied to an earlier historical individual.

Instead, what may have happened here is that the term actually originated in Egypt, as many things appear to do. When Cambyses II and Darius I invaded Egypt in the sixth century BC, they naturally took this term back to Persia. There, it spread throughout the Persian Achaemenid dynasty and that is why Xerxes and many subsequent Persian kings were called Kasra (Khashiarsha or Xerxes) meaning 'caesar' or 'king'.

This would mean that the original 'royal' title was the Egyptian Gaysares (Kaysares), and the Persian Khashiarsha was a corruption of this. But these new alternatives mean that the table of transliterations just given can be greatly expanded upon:

Egyptian - Persian I	Egyptian - Roman	Egyptian - Celtic
K ays ares	G ays ares	Gays ares
Kha s ar s	G ays ar	Gaythales
Kha shiar sha	C aes ar	Gaythelos
Khasiarsha	Caesar	Gaythelos

Egyptian - Persian II	Egyptian - Greek
K a y s a r e s	K a y s a r e s
K a s a r e s	K a i s a r e s
K a s r a	K a i s a r o s
Kasra	Kaisaros

As can be seen, the transpositions required from the Egyptian to the other languages are relatively simple, which would strongly suggest that the Egyptian term was indeed the original. And, although it is a slightly circular argument, the evidence linking Gaythelos and the Amarna regime would also lend support to Gaysars being the original form of this title. In other words, the name adopted by the Caesar family in Rome was probably an Egyptian title that may already have been in use for over a millennium by a diverse range of nations; including the Persians.

Perhaps it is also worth noting that some versions of the Gaythelos and Scota saga give the prince's name as Gaedel. The 'th' to 'd' transliteration is well known within the Egyptian language, and so an Egyptian Gaythelos could readily be transposed into Gaydelos and thence Gaedelos or Gaedel. Another factor to bear in mind is the meaning of Kaisares / Gaysares. I have not seen a reasonable meaning in the Persian. Various translations have been proffered, from 'Ruler of Heroes', 'Mighty One', 'House of the King' and an interesting derivation in the biblical Concordance of 'I Will Be Silent and Poor', which sounds highly unlikely. However, none of these offerings come with any explanations, and should be dismissed as guestimations.

In the Egyptian, the title Gaysares (𓍔𓃾𓏤𓈖) may well have been derived from *gaiy-sar(s)* 𓍔𓃾𓏛 𓈖𓍑. This phrase simply means 'anointed prince' and since a prince is only anointed upon becoming king, this term effectively means 'king'. This is the same meaning as is given for the title 'messiah' מָשִׁיחַ, which also means 'anointed one'.

However, if an alternative spelling for this word is used, a similar derivation can be found. The Roman pharaohs of Egypt after Caesarion preferred the title Kaysares (𓂝𓃾𓏛𓈖), which was formed from *kaiy-sar(s)* 𓂝𓃾𓀢 𓈖𓍑 meaning 'exalted prince'. But the Egyptian term for 'exalted' also has strong connotations of a high place or a pyramid, from which we might derive *kaiy-sar(s)* 𓂝𓃾𓊽𓀢 𓈖𓍑 meaning King of the Mountains. While this final derivation might sound unlikely, it is exactly the same as has been previously obtained for the title of the Hyksos (see the book *Tempest* for details). Both of these terms would, of course, be referring to the pyramids of Giza rather than a barren hill in the wilds of the Sinai Peninsular. Thus, the Persians and Greeks were probably following in the footsteps of the Hyksos-Israelite pharaohs of Lower Egypt.

In some respects, all of these translations are related. The exalted individual represents a king or high priest who officiated at the Giza 'cathedral' complex; the anointing refers to the ritual anointing of stone pillars or pyramids, as recorded in Genesis 28:18 (as well as the anointing of the king); while the sacred 'mountain' refers to the Giza pyramids themselves. Since the cartouche of Nero Caesar uses this exact same 'exalt' determinative glyph, of a man with his arms held high, this is likely to have been the exact translation for this name. Determinative glyphs are not often used in cartouches, so this anomaly is very useful (his cartouche uses the short form of the word 'exalt', which is *ka* ⊿⚡).

Fig 6. Nero Caesar, using the 'exalt' glyphs.

Further evidence for this link with the Hyksos-Israelites may also be seen in the name of Xerxes himself. The spelling of his name in the Egyptian is Khashiarsha ⟨𒀭𒈾𒊩⟩, and there is only one suitable derivation for the first syllables of this name, which is *khasut* 𓈉 meaning 'foreign lands'. But this is the very same word that is used for the Hyksos themselves, who were known as the Hyka Khasut 𓋴𓎡, 𓈉, meaning 'Kings of the Foreign Lands', or perhaps more accurately, 'Kings of the Pyramids'. (The three-hills glyph being a reference to the three pyramids of Giza rather than a line of foreign hills, as is explained in the book *Tempest*.)

While it may be true that a Persian king might not want to utilise a purely Egyptian title, to be honoured with a name that invoked the greatest wonder of the ancient world, and the largest and most sacred temple complex in the ancient world, might well be appealing. But there is another reason for Xerxes to be influenced by Hyksos-Israelite traditions, as we shall see.

Esther

The fact that the title Gay Sars (Kay Sars) has such a satisfactory meaning in the Egyptian, again strongly suggests that the word may have originally been coined in Egypt. Also, the Egyptian word *kaiy* ⎦𓈖𓏠𓏤𓀲 , meaning 'exalted' or 'mountain', is very ancient, so it is unlikely that this is a term that has been borrowed from Persia in the sixth century BC. So, the kings of Persia and the emperors of Rome may have been honoured with an Egyptian title meaning 'Anointed Prince', 'Exalted Prince' or even 'King of the Pyramids'.

While this translation is all very interesting, just why should a Persian king use an Egyptian name or title? The reasoning for this has already been given in my books *Solomon* and *Eden*, and the explanation hinges on one of the greatest biblical and historical events in Judaeo-Egypt – the Babylonian exile. In the sixth century BC, the Babylonian king Nebuchadnezzar sacked the city of Jerusalem (wherever that city actually resided), and also raided some parts of Lower Egypt. Following the fall of the Israelite capital city, its royalty and leaders were deported to Babylon as slaves, in what has become known as the 'Babylonian captivity'. But somehow, instead of being incarcerated and subjugated, at least some elements of the Hyksos-Israelite royalty gained high office in Babylon.

Just four decades later the Persians, under Cyrus I, invaded Babylon and, quite incidentally, set the Israelites free. But many of the Hyksos-Israelites had done so well in Babylon that they did not want to return to Egypt/Israel. The Persians, under Cambyses II and Darius I, then went on to invade Egypt proper and became Persian pharaohs of Egypt. Herodotus maintains that the Persian kings waged this second campaign from the Arabias against Egypt because they had requested an Egyptian princess as a diplomatic bride, but had been fobbed off with a commoner. Determined to get a bloodline princess, they invaded Egypt to force the issue.

However, if many of the Egyptian royalty were actually the descendants of the Hyksos-Israelite pharaohs of Lower Egypt, as I have previously explained, then the Persians may well have been requesting a Jewish princess – and so a trace of this diplomatic wrangling may well be visible within the biblical accounts. Surprising as it may seem, this is exactly what we find. The Bible records that Xerxes' chief wife, Vashti, fell out of favour and was divorced. [B8] So Xerxes arranged to see a parade of young ladies and the damsel who caught his eye was a young Jewess called Hadassar הדסה whose ancestors had been exiled in the Babylonian/ Persian-controlled lands since the time of Nebuchadnezzar. Hadassar is better known as Esther אסתר, the heroine of the Book of Esther.

Who was this Esther, who rose from the position of lowly slave to be the queen of the most powerful nation in the world? The Bible tries to make out that Esther was a commoner, but this is simply the usual Cinderella-style fairy-tale for the faithful.[*PTO] For a Persian king to divorce his wife in favour of this young Jewess strongly suggests that she was not only royal, but also of the ancient Egyptian bloodline (the Hyksos-Israelite bloodline) – which was admired and sought after by many of the nations that bordered Egypt. The name Esther means 'star', and after she married Xerxes she would have become the Queen of the Stars, or the Queen of Sheba (*sheba* means 'star' in the Egyptian, and also in the English). The book *Solomon* has already explored the long line of Egyptian 'God's Wives' who were known as Queens of the Stars; they formed a royal line who were honoured in Egypt as incarnations of Isis who were descended all the way through history from Nefertari and Hatshepsut, through the era of King Solomon to the first century AD and Mary Magdalene.

The similarity between the Herodotus' account in *The Histories* and the account of Esther in the Bible strongly suggests, once more, that the theory – that the Israelites were Hyksos Egyptians – is correct. However, the argument can be used in reverse to equal effect; for if Esther was an Egyptian princess, then surely her name or title should be Egyptian. Indeed it is, for the Persian spelling of her name is Aster; a name which was clearly based upon the Egyptian goddess, Ast (Isis) 𓊨𓏏𓆇 . The likelihood is, therefore, that as soon as the aggressively expanding Persian Empire began to come in contact with the Hyksos-Israelite exiles in Babylon and Egypt, the two royal lines began to assimilate. Thus the name for Xerxes, that of Khashiarsha, may well have been influenced by Hyksos-Egyptian custom and language.

Even if the royal title of Kaisares had not been used in Egypt prior to the reign of Xerxes, the Scottish chronicle of Gaythelos was primarily based upon the writings of the third century BC historian Manetho, and Manetho

---

* The Cinderella story may again refer to this 'lost princess of Egypt' story. In reality, Cinderella may refer to Mary Magdalene, the Egypto-Judaic princess who was nearly lost to history because of the Catholic Church's insistence that Jesus was not married to her. But a strong faction within Judaeo-Christianity, who became known as the Illuminati, knew of her illustrious role and status, and preserved her name within the cult of the 'Black Madonna'. This title referred not to the Virgin Mary but to Mary Magdalene, and her strangely black complexion denoted that she was a princess of Egypt (Egypt was known as Kam 𓆎𓅓𓏏𓊖 , meaning 'black'). The Cinderella story is simply another rendition of the story of the lost 'black princess', who thwarts the oppression of the ugly sisters (the Catholic and Orthodox Churches) and eventually finds her lost bloodline prince. This is why Cinderella is portrayed as being the rejected beauty sweeping the cinders from the fire, and getting very black in the process.

Significantly, Cinderella finds her royal prince through the traditional symbol of the lost slipper. Like Jason, of Argonauts fame, the symbol of the missing slipper is a symbol of special status, which is most probably linked to the royal bloodline. Masons use this same symbology in their initiation ceremonies to this day, and are presented before the WM 'slipshod'. See the book *Solomon* for more details of the Magdalene story.

would have been well aware of the Persian twenty-seventh dynasty of Egypt and its two kings called Kaisares (Khashiarsha).

Garland

How Julius Caesar's family managed to inherit this Egypto-Persian name is not known, but there are a few possibilities. The first of these is that the name came directly from Egypt in some manner; but the Egyptian dynasties prior to the Romans, that of the Macedonian Alexanders and Greek Ptolemys, did not use this title. Given this large break between the Persian usage and the Roman usage, it is unlikely that the title came to Rome directly from Egypt. But there is also an outside chance that the name Gaythelos (Kaisaros) had been used in and around the western Mediterranean ever since Scota and Gaythelos landed in this region. Their descendants had spread throughout the islands in the western Mediterranean, as we shall see, and so this name may have been used by the ancestors of Julius Caesar for over a thousand years before it regained the proper status it deserved. If so, then Julius would have been a descendant of this very ancient royal line that originally sprung from the Amarna dynasty of Egypt – as we shall see.

It is also worth noting that the *sar* portion of this same name has been preserved in many languages around the globe to this day. It became Tsar in Russia, Shah in Persia, Sahib in India and Sire in Britain; with all of these titles originally denoting a prince or king. Since Gaythelos was supposed to have been the son of a king, and was later anointed as king himself, his having a title like Gaythelos (Kaisaros or Caesar) was only natural. Even today when we refer to events in ancient Rome, we still tend to say that "Caesar did this", without even mentioning the birth or family names of the emperor concerned.

The etymological evidence we have just seen points towards Gaythelos being an Egyptian prince, or at least someone using an Egyptian title. Likewise, the historical evidence also points towards an Egyptian origin: for the Egyptian prince called Harmais (Dannus) in Manetho's accounts sounds very much like the Celtic character called Gaythelos in Bower's account. So could Gaythelos have been Dannus, an Egyptian prince of the Amarna dynasty?

Well, the genealogy that is given in *Scotichronicon* does not help that much in deciding if Gaythelos was an Egyptian royal, but perhaps it does serve to place him within an Egyptian context once more. In the family tree in fig 7, the father of Gaythelos is variously given as Neolas or perhaps Phenius. However, a third version of Phoro Neus probably gives a better idea of how this name was once pronounced. The Phar (Phor) forename was probably based upon the Egyptian *pa-aa* 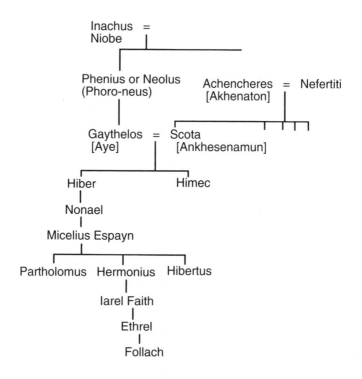 meaning 'Great House', a title that referred to the king or the royal family. In a similar fashion, the last name of Neolas was probably based upon the Egyptian *neru* meaning 'great'.

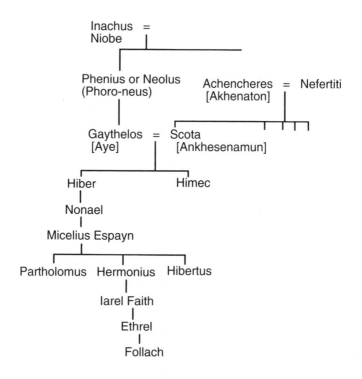

Fig 7. Family tree of Gaythelos.

Thus, the full translation for the father of Gaythelos may well have been Pharo Neoru , which translates as 'Pharaoh the Great' or 'Pharaoh Victorious'. No doubt all the pharaohs of Egypt professed themselves to be the greatest and so although this identification tells us that Gaythelos may well have been the son of an Egyptian king, it does not really settle the question as to who his father was.

Gaythelos' grandfather's name is only mentioned once and it comes courtesy of the scribe who seems determined to place these events during the sixth century BC. He is said to have been called Inachus, and what we possibly have here is a corruption of the Egyptian Pharaoh Antriusha (Inetrush) , otherwise known as Darius I. The familiar name of

Darius is again a poor Greek rendering of the original name for this Persian pharaoh.

Again, Gaythelos is highly unlikely to have been from the Persian dynasty of Egyptian pharaohs, as the general archaeology of the various sites we will shortly be looking at in the western Mediterranean date from the eighteenth dynasty in Egypt (c. 1300 BC). Likewise, the genealogy that is given in the chronicle, and the many references to the biblical exodus, again all point towards the eighteenth dynasty, and more specifically to the Amarna regime of Akhenaton.

The confusion with the sixth century may have come about because some later emigrants came to Scotland in the sixth century. These were called the Picts, as we shall see in a later chapter, but this event had nothing to do with the Gaythelos exodus.

Fig 8. Pharaoh Darius I of Egypt.

Amarna prince

Despite the odd side turning and dead ends, the general thrust of the evidence thus far points towards an unknown prince called Gaythelos (Caesar) marrying the daughter of Pharaoh Akhenaton, and yet this fact narrows down his true identity a great deal. This fact also places Gaythelos' life squarely within the Amarna era, and so there may well be a number of texts that detail such a royal marriage, and so allow us to positively identify Gaythelos.

One potential suitor might be Zannanza, a Hittite prince who was to marry Ankhesenamun   (Ankhesenpaaten), the daughter of Akhenaton. After the death of Tutankhamen, Ankhesenamun found herself without a suitable royal suitor and so she wrote to Suppiluliumas I, the Hittite king, and asked if he had a son she could marry:

> My husband has died and I have no son. They say about you that you have many sons, You might give me one of your sons to become my husband. I would not wish to take one of my subjects as a husband. [9]

Now this request may seem to contradict the assertion that Egyptian princesses never married foreign princes. But not only was this an exceptional circumstance; more importantly, Ankhesenpaaten was not being sent away to marry a prince – rather, Suppiluliumas' son, Zannanza, was being invited into Egypt to become pharaoh. Since the royal line flowed through the female line in Egyptian tradition, this dynastic alliance ensured that no royal blood was being 'lost' to a foreign nation and the royal line in Egypt still remained Egyptian. So was Zannanza the prince called Gaythelos?

Unfortunately not. Zannanza was not Greek, nor was he Egyptian and, as far as we are aware, he never arrived in Egypt. It is thought that enemies within the administration, working either for Horemheb or Aye, assassinated the prince as he entered Egypt's borders; and so this fledgling diplomatic link with the Hittites abruptly ended. This is the only foreign suitor we know of who came to Egypt at this time and who had any chance of being close to a princess, and yet Zannanza could not be Gaythelos. So who was this mythical character who was mentioned so confidently within the Scottish chronicles?

Actually, the rather surprising identification for Gaythelos is inadvertently given in my book *Solomon*. The research in this chapter has closely identified Gaythelos with Manetho's Prince Armais (Harmais), and yet I have already demonstrated that this Prince Armais was most probably the historical character called Pharaoh Armait. And while this identification may sound a little confusing at this stage, perhaps it should be explained that Armait is simply the throne name of Pharaoh Aye $\boxed{\text{𓇋𓎛𓈖 𓏏𓊪𓏤}}$, the pharaoh who followed Tutankhamen onto the throne of Egypt.

Now while this suggestion might seem unlikely, it does have its merits – many of them. Aye is known to have been very close to the royal family at Amarna, and his name closely resembles that of Yuya (Aiuya or Yiuia), the influential noble whose daughters and granddaughters married into the royal family on several occasions. For these marriages to have proceeded, Yuya and his wife Tuyu must have been of the royal bloodline, and perhaps this was even a stronger branch of the bloodline than most of the royals themselves. For this and other reasons, it is presumed that Yuya was also the father of Aye (Armait or Armais). Thus Aye was not simply a usurper of the throne of Egypt, but a member of a parallel line within the royal family that was asserting its historical 'right' to rule.

Even before he became pharaoh, Aye had always been very influential at Amarna and bore the titles 'Commander of the Horse', 'God's Father', 'Vizier', and 'Creator of Laws or Justice'; these were prestigious ranks, some of which were also held by his father Yuya. Aye's first wife Tey also held some impressive titles, being known as 'Favourite of the Good

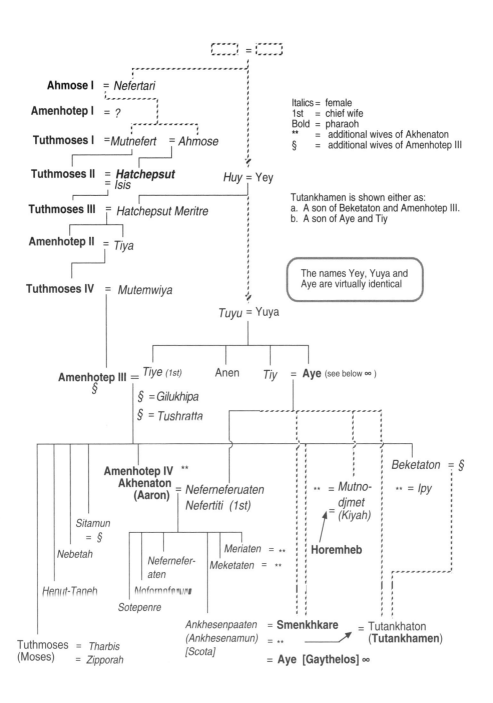

Fig 9. Amarna family tree.

God', 'Nurse of the King's Wife Nefertiti', 'Nurse of the Goddess' and 'Ornament of the King'. Clearly, Aye and Tey were just as well-connected within the Amarna royal family as their parents had been.

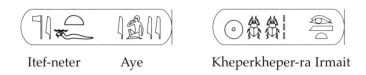

Itef-neter   Aye   Kheperkheper-ra Irmait

Fig 11. Cartouches of Pharaoh Aye.

For Yuya and Aye to have had so many prestigious titles marks them out as possible members of the Amarna royal family. But, as has been mentioned previously, this was not any old distant branch of the family, but a central trunk. Yuya's daughter, Tiye, married Pharaoh Amenhotep III to become his chief wife; and in turn Aye's own daughters are thought to have been Nefertiti and Mutnodjmet, the wives of the pharaohs Akhenaton and Horemheb respectfully. These marriages to three successive pharaohs virtually proves beyond doubt that Aye was of royal blood, so it is highly unlikely that there was anyone in the court of Amarna who was more influential than Aye. A more in-depth look at his life is presented in the next chapter.

It has to be remembered that nepotism was everything within these ancient cultures, because family members provided loyalty, and so all the important ranks and titles in the country were liberally distributed among the immediate members of the family. Tribal links were and are very strong bonds in this region and era, and at its very basic level this loyalty comes down to a question of 'us and them'.

Ankhesenamun

Whatever the political machinations and allegiances within the Amarna dynasty, it is certain that the vizier Aye was influential enough to work his way onto the throne of Egypt after Tutankhamen died – to become Pharaoh Aye (or Aii) Itef-neter Kheperkheper-ra Irmait. He then quickly married Tutankhamen's widow Ankhesenamun, an act which is sometimes said to demonstrate that Aye was not of the royal line and wanted to cement his claim to the throne by taking a royal princess as a wife. However, that argument completely fails to acknowledge that all pharaohs married a bloodline princess, who was often a sister or even a daughter (in the case of Akhenaton and Amenhotep III amongst others). Thus the marriage between Aye and Ankhesenamun in no way invalidates the strong suspicion that Aye was a bloodline prince in his own right – even if that bloodline came through the parallel royal line of Yuya and Tuyu and not the queen herself.

Yuya and Tuyu, as we have seen, must have held the royal bloodline even if they were not royal themselves, and a son of theirs would, to all intents and purposes, have been a royal prince. This observation may give us another possible parentage for Tutankhamen, whose family history is currently uncertain. It has been suggested by many that Tutankhamen was a son of Akhenaton by Kiyah, his second and favourite wife; but that would not explain the complete lack of inscriptions about a son of Akhenaton being born at Amarna. Akhenaton had had six daughters and no sons, and surely the arrival of a cherished son, even if this was through a second wife, would have been mentioned somewhere.

The alternative scenario, which is beginning to look quite attractive, is that Tutankhamen was the son of Aye, who was of royal blood even if he and his parents were not on the throne. This is why Aye was able to claim the title 'God's Father', a title which is normally restricted to the father of a king rather than the father of a queen. Perhaps it is also why the name chosen for this child was Tutankhaton (later, Tutankhamen), which means 'Living Image of Aten', or 'Living Image of the God'. Since the king was a god in his own right, did this name seek to impress on everyone how closely Tutankhaton resembled Akhenaton? In other words his title inferred, 'this may not have been Akhenaton's son, but he is the living image of him and thus just like a royal son in all respects'. That there would have been a physical similarity between Akhenaton and Tutankhamen is not surprising. The line of Yuya and Aye had married into the royal line twice, with Tiye being Akhenaton's mother and Nefertiti being his wife, and so Aye's son (Tutankhamen?) may well have closely resembled the royal children.

This may also explain why it was Aye who was depicted performing the last rites in Tutankhamen's tomb. This has often been explained as Aye's way of increasing his power and prestige, in order to take the throne as the next king; but what if it were simply a portrayal of a father burying his son? The ritual of 'Opening of the Mouth' was a very important aspect of Egyptian funerary rituals, and this was normally carried out by the son and heir to the throne. But since Tutankhamen did not have a son, perhaps his father (and heir) was deemed the most suitable alternative.

Had Aye been the father of Tutankhamen, the ease with which he took the throne on the death of the young king is much more understandable. However, Aye's royal status and his marriage to

Tutankhamen's widow, Ankhesenamun, greatly strengthens the growing links between Aye and Gaythelos [Caesar], because Ankhesenamun was the daughter of Akhenaton. Thus both Aye and Gaythelos are recorded as marrying a daughter of Akhenaton. But these links grow ever stronger when one realizes that very few men married into the family of Akhenaton.

Fig 12. Cartouche of Ankhesenamun.

Of Akhenaton's six daughters, two or three died at a young age, and Akhenaton married three himself.* That leaves us with Ankhesenamun, who had a chequered marital history. She began by marrying her father Akhenaton, then her cousin(?) Tutankhamen, then her uncle(?) Smenkhkare and finally her maternal grandfather, Aye. Out of the two or three marriage possibilities that are recorded for the daughters of Akhenaton, Aye stands out as a prime candidate to be the Celtic King Gaythelos.

Two further aspects of the various Scottish chronicles, as quoted by Walter Bower, are also pertinent to this identification. Firstly, Donald Watt, the translator of Bower, notes that:

> It is important that Scota is the wife, not only of Gaythelos (as here), but in other versions (of the chronicle, she is also the wife) of Gaythelos' father Neolas (and of his descendant and of his son). Her partners may at one time have been numerous. [SC10]

Donald Watt is inferring that these other marriages of Scota, to both her father and her brother, demonstrate that the Scottish chronicles are apocryphal and not to be relied upon, for no Egyptian princess would have

---

* I suppose this does also make Akhenaton himself a candidate for Gaythelos; as Akhenaton was a prince and a king, he argued with his father, he did marry his own daughter and he had as much opportunity to go to Greece after his abdication as did Aye. However, Akhenaton's name was not Armais, and yet Dannus (Gaythelos) was called Armais by Manetho. More importantly, Manetho places two Amarna pharaohs between Akhenaton and Armais, and so it would seem as certain as anything can be in this research that Armais (Dannus, Gaythelos) was not Akhenaton.

endured such a peculiar married life. On the contrary, although the family relationships are not exactly the same, we know that Ankhesenamun [Scota] had had a number of related husbands. Far from these convoluted consanguinity rules consigning this Scottish chronicle to mythology, they may actually confirm that it is historical fact.

Secondly, there is the detailed description of Gaythelos' departure from Egypt. It is reported that Gaythelos was a part of pharaoh's forces who were pursuing the Israelites out of Egypt – again placing this story at the time of the (second) biblical exodus. But then Bower goes on to relate a quite different account where the people of Egypt, not content with ousting Moses and the Israelites, demanded that the pharaoh and his army left the country too! Now while this may sound peculiar, this is exactly what happened. What the Bible fails to mention is that one of the leaders of the Israelites was a pharaoh too, and his name was Akhenaton [Aaron]. So although Bower was possibly confused by the chronicles before him, they were correct. When the Israelites [the people of Amarna] were exiled from Middle Egypt, a pharaoh was indeed exiled along with them. But then Bower narrates a tale which is quite interesting:

> Gaythelos remained behind after the army [Akhenaton's army] had departed, in the city of Heliopolis, as arranged between himself and the pharaoh; with the purpose of possibly succeeding to his kingdom. But the Egyptian people [Horemheb?] ... gathered their forces together and informed Gaythelos that if he did not speedily hasten his departure ... utter destruction would immediately attend himself and his men. (Author's brackets). [SC11]

Again, this is probably what happened. Akhenaton departed Middle Egypt as the Amarna experiment began to crumble, and sought to secure a new power-base in Avaris in the Nile Delta, while Aye remained in Heliopolis and perhaps Upper Egypt to secure the succession for either himself or Tutankhamen. On this occasion, it was Tutankhamen who became pharaoh, under Aye's guidance and patronage, and it was only upon the death of Tutankhamen that Aye [Gaythelos] was able to take the throne for himself. But the Scottish chronicle may well be correct in saying that the rule of Aye was unpopular for his reign ended after less than four years. Since there is no record of his death, Aye may well have been deposed and exiled from Egypt, just as the chronicle suggests.

Curriculum vitae

This line of research and reasoning has not only given us a prime candidate for the character called Gaythelos, it has quite possibly begun to change our entire perception of Celtic history. Where there was once a hazy spectre in a mythological tale, there are now images, texts, statues and tombs. We can now put a face to this mythological apparition; we can divine his motives, strategies, hopes and ambitions. We now know, at last, why Gaythelos and his new royal Egyptian bride would have taken to the perilous seas in search of new lands.

So what is the truth behind the claims and counterclaims about the life of Aye [Gaythelos, Dannus]? In fact, both of his documented life-stories, the Celtic and the Greco-Egyptian, may be true and compatible with each other. Manetho says that Dannus [Aye] was expelled from Egypt for claiming the throne from his brother, the king. If Aye was the brother-in-law of Akhenaton, through Nefertiti, that assertion is entirely possible. We know that Aye was very well placed within the court at Amarna, eventually becoming vizier, and when the regime started to wobble there would naturally have been a scramble for the throne. Before things settled down under Pharaoh Tutankhamen, there was the ephemeral Pharaoh Smenkhkare, who came and went rather suddenly. Was Aye behind his or her (there are claims that Smenkhkare was another name for Nefertiti) claim to the throne? Was Aye also the king-maker who placed Tutankhamen on the throne? This would seem quite likely, especially if Tutankhamen was his son. The latter would mean that Aye was seeking to take the throne from his brother-in-law, and pass it on to his son.

Both of these records mention an exile to Greece, and if Aye had fallen foul of opposition groups at Amarna, it is entirely possible that he exiled himself to Argos (Greece), which was perhaps ripe for picking at the time. At best, Argos was still a land of backward city states during the Amarna era, and perhaps Aye saw the possibility of taking over a fresh new population, and converting them to the Aton religion. Since I have long maintained that Aye must have been of Hyksos-Israelite descent, the new aristocracy of Greece must likewise have become Hyksos-Israelite. This is confirmed in the Torah, which states:

> Arius, king of the Spartans to Onias the chief priest; greetings. It has been found in writing, concerning the Spartans and the Jews, that they are brethren, and that they are of the same stock of Abraham. [B12]

Thus, it is entirely possible that Aye [Dannus] founded the proto-Spartan and Athenian nations some 700 years before they rose to their height of power. Whether Aye aspired to be a king of Argos or a simple evangelist, it is a fact that the prime city in Argos was subsequently called Aten [Athen-s]. The name for Athens is said to have been derived from the Greek goddess

Athene, however further evidence that the Sun-god Aton was the source of the name for Athens is perhaps demonstrated by the Egyptian name for Greece itself, which was Uainn ⌷⌷⌷⌷ . This name was probably derived from *uinu* ⌷⌷⌷ which means 'light', and the reason for choosing this name is simply that the great god Aton ⌷⌷ ☉ was the bringer of all light and thus all life.* So Uinu became the name of the province of Argos and Aton (Athen) became the name of its primary city.

The parallel Greek myths penned by Apollodorus and Hyginus closely follow the life of Dannus, as narrated by Manetho, which demonstrates that this was once a widely held history. In these accounts the father of Dannus [Aye] is said to be King Belus, the king of Chemmis (Egypt). Robert Graves indicates that the *bel* in Belus might be related to the god Bel (Baal); however, since the Hebrew *bel* בעל also means 'lord' or 'master', it is more than likely that this name is being used to denote this person's status. Thus Dannus' [Aye's] father could have been either a king or a senior courtier, like Yuya. These Greek accounts confirm the tradition of a dispute between Prince Dannus (Armais) and his brother King Aegyptus (Ramesses), which resulted in Dannus' exile to Argos (Greece). They also indicate that on arrival in Argos, Dannus took the kingship from the Argive King, Gelanor, by subterfuge, and so the Greeks became known as the Danaoi from that time onwards. [13]

Manetho states that Dannus' brother, Aegyptus, was also called Ramesses. Had Dannus been Aye, as appears likely, then Aye's brother would have been a pharaoh called Ramesses. This initially seemed a little unlikely, as Manetho indicated that Aegyptus (Ramesses) ruled as king at the time that Dannus [Aye] fled to Argos. However, Apollodorus indicates that Aegyptus was primarily the king of the Arabias, and only later subdued the Melampodes (the 'black-feet', or Egyptians). This life-history would actually suit the ephemeral Ramesses I rather well, as he only became pharaoh of Egypt at a late age and his parentage is uncertain. Since Ramesses I was originally from Avaris and was of a similar age to Aye [Dannus], the two pharaohs could well have been closely related. [14]

Aye could have enjoyed himself in his exile in the Greek islands and mountains for a full nine years, until another dramatic event was to change his life once more. The new pharaoh, Tutankhamen, had unexpectedly died young; and while this was a tragedy, especially if Tutankhamen was Aye's son, it was also an opportunity. Most of the Amarna family had died, been killed or dispersed after the fall of Amarna; while the self-imposed regent of

---

* Perhaps it should also be mentioned that the throne name of Akhenaton was Uenu-Aton (or Uenura) ⌷⌷⌷ , meaning 'The Only One of Aton'.

39

Egypt – the army commander Horemheb – was away campaigning in Syria. If Aye could hurry back to Egypt before Horemheb reached Karnak, the throne could be his at last. Helped by the Minoan navy, Aye may well have beaten Horemheb back to Karnak and been crowned pharaoh of the Two Lands in a hurried ceremony. But no pharaoh is complete without a spouse, and so Aye married Tutankhamen's widow Ankhesenamun in a rushed betrothal. Having staked his claim to the throne in this manner, it would have been very difficult for Horemheb, who is not thought to have been of the royal family at all, to have usurped the power of a king and a god incarnate.

This represents a plausible life-history for Aye, and in this fashion both of the records we have considered can be seen to be substantially correct. Yes, Aye may well have had an argument with his brother (in-law), Akhenaton. Yes, he may well have gone to Argos (Greece). Yes, he must have returned to Egypt from Argos. Yes, he did marry a daughter of Akhenaton. Yes, he did become king himself. And finally, yes, he did disappear from the records of Egypt, along with his new wife.

Aye did have a tomb prepared for himself; in fact, he had two. His first was carved into the cliffs at Amarna, but with the demise of that regime it was abandoned. Subsequently, he took over WV23 near the Valley of the Kings, a tomb that may have originally belonged to Smenkhkare. But Aye was not buried in either of these tombs, and both were destroyed by the succeeding pharaoh, Horemheb. No *ushabti* (death figurines) of Aye have ever been found either, and so the evidence suggests that he did not die a normal death in Egypt. So what happened to both Aye and Ankhesenamun? Were they murdered and their bodies disposed of in the Nile? Or were they simply forced out by opposition forces and compelled to go into exile?

Remember that both Aye and Akhenaton were gods, as well as kings. Such people held considerable psychological power over the people, and they were difficult to simply kill off in cold blood. They might well die in battle, of course, but look at the trouble Oliver Cromwell had deciding the fate of Charles I. Having captured the king, he dithered so much that Charles escaped and started a second civil war. Even after Charles' second capture, Cromwell still dithered – simply because of the kings' supposed divine right to rule. Such things weigh heavily on the conscience of a religious man, and so when Cromwell eventually condemned Charles to death he diluted the divine blame (and wrath) with another 58 signatures from all the officials within his regime.

It is entirely possible that exactly the same kind of dithering happened with both Pharaoh Akhenaton and Pharaoh Aye. Both of these kings had tombs prepared for them, but both escaped burial in some manner. The likely scenario in both cases is that they went into exile with a small band of followers. The historian Manetho suggests that Akhenaton was initially exiled to Avaris, in the Nile Delta, but any subsequent destination remains a mystery. Both Manetho and the Greek myths also appear quite certain that Aye [Dannus] went to Greece. Manetho does not give a precise date for this particular exile, but it is likely that this event occurred at the same time that Akhenaton disappeared from history (perhaps Akhenaton went to Greece too).

But if Aye went to Greece, then what about his career during the reign of Tutankhamen? Well, the evidence for Aye's presence in Egypt during this period is equivocal, so we cannot say anything definite on this matter. However, it would appear that Aye was originally a devout Atonist, and so he was unlikely to have stood aside while the complete Aton cult was dismantled around him. His problem was that a senior official called Horemheb had installed himself into nearly every branch of the administration. He was known as 'Overseer of Overseers', 'Overseer of Every Office', 'King's Deputy in Every Place', and 'Overseer of the Army'. Clearly this was the man who pulled all the strings in Egypt at this time, not Pharaoh Tutankhamen.

More sinisterly, Horemheb also adopted the title 'King's Two Eyes Throughout the Two Lands', an ominous title if ever there was one. So Horemheb was also the chief spy-master, and since he was obviously not an Atonist, there is no way in which Horemheb and Aye could have worked together within the same administration. The evidence, be it only circumstantial, is that Aye must have withdrawn from Egypt during Tutankhamen's reign. Sometimes it is better to go into exile, voluntary or otherwise, rather than to see all you have worked for and believed in destroyed.

However, the sudden death of Tutankhamen nine years later was an opportunity not to be missed, and so Aye seized his chance, rushed home and crowned himself king while Horemheb was still away campaigning in Hati. But the renaissance of Atonism under Aye was not to be. The people had tolerated the new cult of Atonism for many years, but perhaps it seemed that this new god just created problems for the people. The taxes grew to pay for the new city at Amarna; priests in Thebes were unemployed on the streets; neighbouring kingdoms were in constant rebellion; there were setbacks in the foreign wars; and a plague may have swept through the country. As deities go, clearly this 'Aton' guy was of the bargain-basement variety. Understandably, the people were fed up with the political turmoil and craved stability. Under the circumstances, it is no wonder that the courtiers, influenced by the army commander Horemheb, were able to steer the boy-king Tutankhamen back towards the worship of the old gods.

As far as many people in the country were concerned, things were now heading back towards the right, traditional direction, when Aye suddenly became pharaoh. One suspects that Aye would have attempted to move back towards Atonism, but the priests, the military and the common people refused to follow, and a leader without followers is no longer a leader. Disillusionment was the real reason behind Aye and Ankhesenamun's probable exile from Egypt. Whatever the political imperatives were, both the historical Egyptian and legendary Celtic records of this era seem to suggest that Pharaoh Aye [Gaythelos] and his new bride Ankhesenamun [Scota] were forced into exile.

But this was no hurried exile, scrambling away for fear of immediate execution. No, to have assembled a flotilla of ships infers that Aye was asked politely but firmly by the administration to leave, and given sufficient time and resources to organise himself. As Bower says:

> So Gaythelos gathered together all his followers and left Egypt with his wife Scota. Because he was afraid to return to the regions from which he had come (Greece) because of old feuds, he directed his course westwards.
>
> Gaythelos with his wife and his whole household and the other leaders were taken in skiffs and embarked on the waiting ships, trusting in guidance of their gods. As their prows cut through the waves of the sea, they headed towards the western regions of the world. SC15

Here was a well-organised expedition, possibly even using the navy of another nation especially hired for the purpose (judging by the sound of the text), taking Aye and a large retinue of courtiers and officials to unknown lands. These also sound like large ships, if the text can be believed in this fine detail, for they required small dinghies to get out to the main boats. This tradition may well reflect the actual event; Aye was already a seasoned traveller and so he would have known that he would need a large amount of supplies, livestock and skilled artisans if he was ever going to survive in a new, uninhabited land. The total population required to set up a viable colony might be as many as 500 or 1,000 people, which would have required a substantial navy to transport.

Amity brig

If you desperately need to transport a large number of people, it is surprising what can be managed and what the people can endure. When a sturdy new ship named Amity was built in Canada in 1816 she was thought to be large, but in fact she was just 23 x 7 meters (18 x 5 meters internal) and grossed just 142 tonnes. Thus her dimensions were about the same as a

Viking longboat in length but somewhat wider in the beam. Perhaps, more interestingly, the Amity was only half the length of the boat that was buried beside the Great Pyramid – which was built at least a thousand years before the voyage of Gaythelos and Scota. Clearly, the ancient Egyptians had the technology to build ships the size of this 'modern' two-masted brig named Amity.

Despite the Amity's modest size, this sturdy brig was built to sail the Atlantic, which she did until 1823 when she sailed to Australia instead. But the voyage that is of more interest to this story is the one she took from Sydney on November 9th 1826, arriving in Albany, Western Australia, on Christmas Day the same year.

> The brig reached Princess Royal Harbour on Christmas Day 1826, but no-one was put ashore until the next morning. The party comprised of 23 convicts – mostly tradesman, 18 rank & file soldiers, a sergeant, a captain, a surgeon, a storekeeper and the commander Major Edmund Lockyer, with stores for six months (including sheep & pigs). [16]

So forty-six people, plus the crew and all their stores and livestock were jammed into a space smaller than the floor area of an average house. But this was not for a cruise around Botany Bay; this was a six-week journey though some of the roughest and most unpredictable seas in the world.

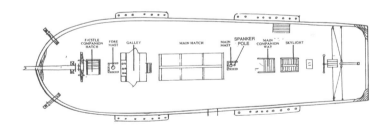

Fig 13. The rotund lines of the Amity brig.

While it is true that the Amity was built of sturdy black birch and American larch, with a high prow and deck to survive the roughest waves, it is also a fact that the Great Pyramid boat was constructed of even tougher Lebanon cedar, and had an equally suitably prominent bow. The only thing that would have detracted from the Great Pyramid boat's design is the shallow draught and low sides; but there again she would only have been dealing with a moderate Mediterranean swell instead of the roaring rollers of the Atlantic or the Southern Ocean. Besides, the Vikings seemed to have coped reasonably well with unpredictable North Sea squalls using a very similar design to the Egyptian one.

So, a small ship the size of the Amity can carry around fifty people and their supplies; but what of the ancient open-deck equivalent? Well, in a very similar fashion the *Lebor Gabala* chronicle, which has occasionally been quoted in *Scotichronicon*, says that each of Gaythelos' boats held sixty people:

> three score (the passengers) of every ship,
> a clear saying,
> and women every third score. [17]

Given this broad agreement in ancient maritime capacity, we now have a pretty good idea of the number and size of Gaythelos' vessels. Further details on the type of ships that would have been available to Aye-Gaythelos will be discussed in a later chapter. But the evidence given thus far demonstrates that even if Aye-Gaythelos' party of exiles had numbered a thousand, only about twenty ships of this size would have been required to transport them across the Mediterranean. A fleet of this magnitude should have been well within the capabilities and technology of the nations concerned, and so is entirely possible that 1,000 people set off from Egypt towards the western horizon, in search of a new homeland.

Less than two decades after Moses and Aaron [TuthMoses and Akhenaton] departed on their exodus to Avaris and beyond, a new exodus was being organised in Egypt. This dramatic event evaded the quills of the Hyksos-Israelites, presumably because they were scratching a living in new lands and had their own survival to worry about. The trials and tribulations of Egypt had been left behind them for a few centuries, and the Hyksos-Israelites had little time for the political machinations in their former homeland. If Aye-Gaythelos was to leave his mark on history, he would have to write his own Day Book or Bible – and he appears to have done just that.

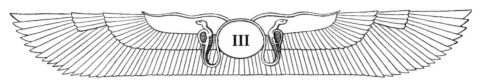

Aye and Gaythelos

If Gaythelos was indeed the Amarna Pharaoh called Aye, perhaps we should take a short detour at this point and look a little closer at the man and his motives.

As we have seen, Aye was probably quite old by the time he came to the throne, and the new wife he then took was actually his granddaughter, Ankhesenamun. It is often said that Aye was a commoner, but since his daughters, Nefertiti and Mutnodjmet, both became queen, this is highly unlikely. Aye was honoured and decorated under Akhenaton, presumably for his role as army commander in keeping law and order in Egypt during Akhenaton's religious reforms. These would have been hugely unpopular amongst the powerful, traditional priesthood, and no doubt Aye's heavy hand kept a lid on any unrest.

The traditional honour given to officials in Egypt was the golden collar or torq, and Aye is portrayed as receiving dozens of these torqs. Since Scota was a daughter of Akhenaton, it is not so surprising to see this same tradition migrating across Europe, and so in Ireland and Britain we see Bronze Age torqs turning up in many burials. The later chapter on Ireland will uncover some interesting aspects about this Irish tradition, which will link directly back to the Amarna era and to Aye himself.

The name Aye was probably derived from *a-iy* or *a-yi* 𓄿𓇌 meaning 'I Am'. This is a contraction of his full name, which was Aye Atif-neter 𓄿𓇋𓏏𓆑 𓊹 meaning 'I Am God's Father', with the 'god' in question probably being a pharaoh. It is generally thought that this title referred to Nefertiti, who was probably Aye's daughter, and so the title actually meant 'I Am Pharaoh's Father (In-Law)'. However, it is entirely possible that this title referred to Tutankhamen instead, as we shall see shortly. This claim was important to Aye, because he needed to be of the royal bloodline to be a legitimate claimant to the throne. As already mentioned, since the bloodline in Egypt was maternal, Aye must have been very closely related to the bloodline for the royal bloodline holder – Nefertiti, not Akhenaton – to have been his daughter.

However, within the framework of the new, revisionary Egyptology that has been forged within this series of books, Aye is also known to have been a chronological contemporary of the biblical Moses. So it may or may not be significant that when Moses asked 'god' for his real name, he replied:

> And god said unto Moses: I AM, it is I AM. Say unto the children of Israel that I AM hath sent me (Moses) unto you (the people). [B1]

חE ויאמר אלהים אל-משה אהיה אשר אהיה ויאמר כה תאמר לבני
ישראל אהיה שלחני אליכם

It would appear that both Aye and the Hebrew god were called 'I Am'. But, just as with the Egyptian term for 'god', the Hebrew equivalent can also be translated as 'leader' (pharaoh, vizier or president). So the 'god' in this verse could easily have been a person. Interestingly enough, the Hebrew word for this individual called 'I Am', is actually *hayah* היה; while at the same time an alternative vocalisation of Aye's name might be Aya. So the names for these two leaders, H-aya and Aya, appear to have very similar meanings and pronunciations. If these characters could, just for the sake of argument, be considered to be the same, then this verse from the Book of Exodus may actually be saying:

> And Moses said unto (the vizier or president), Who am I, that I should go unto Pharaoh [Akhenaton], and that I should bring forth the children of Israel [the people of Amarna] out of Egypt [Amarna]? And Moses said unto the vizier, When I come unto the children of Israel [Amarna] ... they shall say to me: What is his [the vizier's] name? What shall I say unto them? And the vizier said unto Moses: **Aye**, it is **Aye**. Say unto the children of Israel that **Aye** hath sent me (Moses) unto you (the people). (Author's brackets.) [B2]

While this is a radical suggestion, the context of this verse would suit this interpretation too. The era in question was just before the second biblical exodus [the Amarna exodus] and Moses, the high priest of Heliopolis, was getting advice from a leader [the vizier, Aye] as to what should be done about the children of Israel [people of Amarna]. The advice from the leader [Aye] was that he had seen how bad life was getting in Egypt [Amarna] for these people, and he would tell pharaoh [Akhenaton] to bring the people out into the land of the Canaanites (meaning 'lowlands') [ie: the Nile Delta].

Since I have already established that Moses was TuthMoses, the brother of Akhenaton, his acting as an intermediary between Aye and Akhenaton would be entirely understandable. Since we know that Akhenaton's regime became unstable towards the end of the Amarna era, it is highly likely that influential administrators, like the vizier Aye, would have been advising Akhenaton as to his best exit strategy. One option would have been the abandonment of Amarna, and an exodus of the whole population to a safer region – perhaps in Lower Egypt or even elsewhere.

Aye   Yuya

Fig 19. Spelling of the names of Aye and Yuya.

Although some readers might not like the analogy, this is a bit like the last days of the Third Reich. Despite the fact that Hitler's empire had almost entirely collapsed around him, and his command stretched not much further than his bunker in Berlin, all of his courtiers were either so in awe of him or so afraid of him that no one would give him an honest assessment of the situation, let alone any honest advice. The apparent exception to this was Albert Speer, Hitler's chief architect, who seemed to be able to disagree with Hitler without suffering serious harm.

This biblical quote seems to be indicating that the same was true of Akhenaton, and everyone bar Aye was afraid to give him a true assessment of the political situation in Egypt. Again readers may think this assessment of Akhenaton's character unwarranted and unfair, but just think of what he had achieved in about five years (assuming a co-regency) Akhenaton had assumed control of the army and taken on the most powerful institution in the land, the priesthood, and closed them down. Likewise, he had taken on the hearts and minds of the people and convinced them, either through persuasion or fear, that their entire belief system was wrong and heretical. A weak, ineffectual leader, as Akhenaton is often portrayed as being, just could not have achieved this.

In the book *Jesus*, a comparison was made with England's Henry

VIII and Oliver Cromwell, two leaders who dared take on the might of the Catholic Church. They faced the same problems that Akhenaton faced, in terms of the power and influence of their opposition. They both battled through and succeeded in their campaigns, but neither of these leaders could be portrayed as politically weak, as Akhenaton has often been.

Exodus

We know that the people of Amarna fled somewhere after the fall of this regime, and it is likely that Akhenaton and many in his immediate family fled too; as no trace of their deaths have been discovered, either in Amarna or Thebes. So the context of the biblical account fits the known historical facts, and it is possible that here in the Book of Exodus we have a verbatim record of a conversation between Akhenaton's brother, TuthMoses, and Aye (Aya). Having seen so many convergences and connections between biblical and Egyptian history, this suggestion is entirely probable.

Remember that this is the second exodus from Egypt, as the major mass-migration event of some 500,000 people travelling to Jerusalem was actually the Hyksos exodus that had occurred some 250 years earlier. The biblical account has contracted these two exodus events into one story, with Moses as its leader – although the pitched battle between the armies of the biblical Jacob and Esau (as reported by Josephus Flavius) may well represent another biblical memory of the earlier great exodus.

It is not always wise to build speculation upon speculation, but this argument can be taken one stage further. If Aye was indeed the biblical character who conversed with Moses, and who was sometimes referred to as 'god' (or vizier), then it should be recalled that the next major meeting between these two characters was at (or in) Mt Sinai. Wherever this location may actually be, the purpose of the meeting was for Moses to collect the 'divine' commandments and give them to his people:

> And the lord (vizier) said unto Moses, Come up to me <u>into</u> the mount (Sinai) ... and I will give thee tablets of stone, and a law, and commandments which I have written; that thou mayest teach them (to the people). [B3]

So it is possible that this verse could be translated as Moses [TuthMoses] receiving the laws or commandments from the vizier Aye, and not from the god-figure. As it happens, the throne name of Aye was Kheperu-ra Ir-maat ⊙𝕞𝕞𝕀 ≅ , which means 'Image of Ra, Creator of Laws'. So once again, the titles of Aye dovetail precisely with the biblical accounts of Moses' meetings with this 'vizier' (or god). Aye was known as the Image of the God and the

Creator of Laws, and this 'Image of God' (Aye) was giving those 'Created Laws' to Moses during the exodus [from Amarna].

If both of these verses have been translated in the correct manner, then it would appear that both the high priest of Heliopolis (Moses) and the king of the Two Lands (Akhenaton) were showing deference to Aye, and that in many respects Aye was the senior ranking individual. Actually, this is not so unlikely as it may seem. Aye was not only the elder of these three, but he was also a son of Yuya (Yiuia) 〔〕 ; hence the similar names.

The meaning of Yuya's name is not fully known, but bearing in mind the translation for Aye, it is likely that the initial y (i) 〔 means 'I' once more. The yu (iu) 〔 syllable was probably derived from the same root as Aye's double reed suffix 〔, which means 'am' or 'to be'. The final part of Yuya's name, the ia or ya 〔 , may mean 'praise' or it may simply be an exclamation. Thus Yuya's full name may well mean 'I Am Praised' or perhaps 'Hail, I Am'. In other words, Aye's name probably echoed his father's (Yuya's) and so Yuya would also have been regarded as a god-figure in the same way that Aye may have been.

The precise relationship of Yuya to the royal family is not known, but he did provide a daughter and two granddaughters as bloodline queens of Egypt, and he did manage to end up with one of the most prestigious burials ever discovered in Egypt. This was also a burial that was not disturbed during the government-sponsored looting of the Valley of the Kings during the later twentieth dynasty, and that may not have simply been a fortuitous accident. Whatever the power-base of Yuya and Aye really was, it was very influential and very effective.

Dannus

The biblical assistance we have had in identifying the meaning of these names is very useful, and perhaps it can shed some light onto the other name that was given to Aye – Manetho's alternative name of Dannus. Manetho is often derided as being unreliable, but we can be reasonably certain that the name Dannus was given to Aye because Manetho's Dannus was exiled to Greece and the name subsequently became the primary title for most of the Greek people – the Danaoi Δαναοι. As Strabo recounts:

> Dannus, the father of fifty daughters, on coming to Argos (Greece) took up his abode in the city of Inarchos and throughout Hellas (Greece). He laid down the law that all people hitherto named Pelasgians were to be named Dannans (Danaoi). [54]

So the name 'Dannus' eventually referred not simply to a person, but to an entire nation. So what did Danaoi mean? Since this was obviously not a Greek name, I have not seen any attempt at a translation from the Greek. In Celtic traditions, the similar title of 'Tuatha de Dannan' was said to refer to the 'People of the Goddess D-Anu'. If the term D-Anu had been derived from the Egyptian, then this may have been from the word D-Anu ⌒ 𓉐𓊖 meaning 'The Heliopolis' or even 'Heliopolis!'.

However, there is an alternative to this translation because the exact Egyptian spelling of Aye's alternative name appears to have been preserved in the ancient records; for the Danaoi Greeks were referred to by the Egyptians as the Djainiua ⌒𓏭𓇌𓈖𓇌𓏥. The hieroglyphic spelling of this title would seem to preclude any association with the city of Anu or On (Heliopolis).

The precise meaning of 'Djai-niua' has never been resolved, but the first thing that was evident was that the 'n' glyph seemed to be optional. So, the task was to look for a word that also had an optional 'n'. The result, for the center portion of the name, was *au* 𓇌𓃭 or *niu* 𓈖𓇌𓃭𓏥, which both mean 'us' or even the genitive, 'our' (this word also retains the same 'red crown' determinative glyph). The prefixed *a* 𓇌𓏭 may refer to an emphatic particle, and so *a-niu* 𓇌𓏭 𓈖𓇌𓃭𓏥 probably means 'Our!' This seemed rather similar to the names for Aye and Yuya, which also referred to 'me' or 'I'. The only difference here being that *a-niu* was in the plural, because it referred to a whole nation – perhaps it was no longer 'I Am', but 'We Are'. This would leave the initial *da* ⌒𓏭 or ⌒𓏭𓇌, which simply means 'the' or, perhaps more likely, 'seed' (offspring). So it is likely that the name for Dannus and the Djainiua (Danaoi) people means 'Our Seed' or 'Our People'. If Dannus was Aye, who was called 'I Am', then the name 'Our Seed' for the nation as a whole would be quite appropriate.

What was this peculiar title of 'I Am' trying to indicate? It tends to sound a little self-important; a mark of these people's special status: 'I Am', but you are not. Actually, while there may be a bit of self-indulgence in this name, the true meaning can only be teased out by looking at the biblical equivalent. As was noted before, the name used for this important person (god) in the Bible was 'I Am', which is the same as Aye's and Yuya's names. However, in the Bible we have a further translation in a closely related language – Hebrew. The Hebrew version of this name is Hayah היה, which was derived from Havah הוה, with both meaning 'exist', 'to be' or 'I Am'. Note once again that if the initial 'h' is dropped from Hayah we can derive Ayah, or the name of Pharaoh Aye.

Much more interestingly, both of these words are very closely related to Khavah הוה meaning 'life'. Obviously to 'exist', one needs to have 'life', and so we can presume that the similar spelling indicates that these were originally the same word. However, the Hebrew ה and ח are too similar for copyists to always transcribe them correctly (yes, they are supposed to be different consonants), and no doubt two variations of the same word have crept into the language through such errors.

Readers who have digested the book *Eden in Egypt* will now see in which direction this argument is going. In this book, I have already argued that the biblical Eve was Akhenaton's second wife, Kiyah . As it happens, the Hebrew name for Eve is Khavah חוה, which was derived from Khayah (Khiyah) חיה, with both of these words meaning 'life'. But now it would appear that we have a very fortuitous and convenient meeting of terms and people.

a. Kiyah may have been a daughter of Aye, and Aye was called 'I Am' both in the biblical and the historical record.

b. Kiyah was possibly the biblical Eve, who was called Khavah חוה or Khiyah חיה in the biblical record. (Note the similarity in spelling to Havah חוה and Hayah היה meaning 'I Am'.) Thus Khiyah's nickname may have been 'I Am', exactly the same as her father's was.

Is it really possible that Kiyah was another daughter of Aye, a sister to Nefertiti? Certainly, the Egyptian royalty liked to keep marriage within the family and this was especially true of Akhenaton, who married three of his daughters. Aye did have another, younger daughter called Mutnodjmet, but she seems to disappear from view at Amarna after the fourth daughter of Akhenaton was born. Could the rather reclusive daughter called Mutnodjmet have had the nickname of Kiyah?

Incidentally, this is not the only confusion in regard to Mutnodjmet's name. Having spent many hours pondering the original spelling of her name, it seemed most likely that she was using the flat-topped seedpod ⌠, rather than the domed and multi-

Fig 20. A vastly improved version of Queen Kiyah's portrait, by Lena Wennburg.

51

seeded pod ⸢, both of which mean 'sweet smelling'. This may seem like a trivial point, but it would mean that the true pronunciation of her name would be Mutbenrit ⸢⸣ instead of Mutnodjmet, and this is a significant difference if one is looking for connections between names in differing languages.

This discrepancy remained a mystery until the *Rock Tombs of El Amarna* was referenced, and there it can be seen that Professor Davies calls Aye's daughter Benretmut. What he has done here is to place the god-name, Mut, at the end of her name, as perhaps it should be anyway; but essentially, Mut-benrit and Benret-mut are the same name. Despite Mutbenrit probably being the true pronunciation of her name, this book will continue with the standard pronunciation of Mutnodjmet to avoid confusion with other reference works.

Fig 21. Glyphs of Mutbenrit (or Mutnodjmet).

For Akhenaton to have married two sisters is actually quite likely, and it would explain a great deal about the role and position of Kiyah within the royal family. Certainly Mutnodjmet was the younger sister to Nefertiti, just as Kiyah also appears to be the younger wife of Akhenaton. In short, there is nothing to prevent this association, and it would also go a long way in explaining the rivalry between Nefertiti and Kiyah. The two wives would obviously have been sisterly rivals for Akhenaton's affections, but if Kiyah was Mutnodjmet there may have been a theological split too.

Mutnodjmet was quite pointedly not conforming with Amarna traditions by keeping an old god-name in her name, and she is also never shown participating in the ceremonies of the Aton. Basically, she was pointedly saying, 'I do not believe in your Atonist rubbish, and I want nothing to do with it.'

Despite this overt rebellion against the Aton, Mutnodjmet was still shown with the royal family as a friend of the elder princesses, and even had her despised and banned name (the goddess Mut) etched into many scenes. For this to have happened, she must have had the protection and sympathetic understanding of the king, Akhenaton, for everyone else in Amarna appears to have changed their names to delete the old god-names and to mention the Aton instead.

Indeed, so contentious was Mutnodjmet's name that someone, at a later time, chiselled out the Mut portion of it from many of her depictions. Now while there has been a great deal of ancient desecration of the Amarna tombs, with Theban Amun supporters hacking out the name of the Aten and Akhenaton from every location possible, this particular piece of damage would not have been their work. For a start, a stranger from Thebes would have been unlikely to have spotted a minuscule reference to Mut within these large tableaus; and even if they did do so, as a supporter of the traditional gods they would have had no problems with this particular god-name. It was the Aton they despised, not Mut. No, the vandal who chipped the Mut out of Mutnodjmet was obviously an Aton supporter, and so this little piece of desecration must have been performed before Amarna was abandoned. That someone would creep into Aye's tomb and cut out just this particular hieroglyph demonstrates how contentions Mutnodjmet's name really was, and how peculiar it is that she was allowed to keep this name.

There is also the question of why a devotee of Amen and Mut would want to stay in the Atonist capital of Amarna. While it is true that Mutnodjmet's sister and parents resided there, would she not have felt more comfortable in Karnak with a relative? Her unique, aloof position in Amarna was even being ridiculed by the Amarna artists, who gave her two dwarf companions in some of the scenes:

> These servants (dwarfs), for whom ridiculous titles and names are invented, and their mistress (Mutnodjmet), who stands apart without participating in the worship of the Aten, invite comment. Were it not for the youth of the princess and her Egyptian aspect, I would venture to suggest that (she was foreign)... [5]

In fact, one of the dwarfs was called 'Vizier of the Queen' and the other 'Vizier of his Mother', with the term 'vizier' normally referring to a governor or even prime minister. It is not clear which 'queen' and 'mother' were being referred to by these titles but if the intended subject was Mutnodjmet, as Professor Davies maintains, then this may be important in linking Mutnodjmet with Kiyah – for the latter lady most certainly did become queen. What is actually intended by these comical dwarfs is not entirely clear at this stage, but it can hardly be complimentary to Mutnodjmet to have these two dwarfs constantly in tow. However, since all of this tomfoolery was displayed within the tomb of her father, perhaps the intended ridicule was not too onerous.

Nevertheless, the conventional wisdom is that Mutnodjmet was a nonbeliever, aloof and alone, with constant ridicule and sniggering behind her back; and yet she stayed at Amarna. Why? One possibility is that she was rapidly becoming the king's favourite, the pretty younger sister of Nefertiti with an alluring rebellious streak, and so Akhenaton would not allow her to leave. There might also have been scheming Theban priests who were taking advantage of Mutnodjmet's favoured status and theological rebellion to undermine Akhenaton's religion. This is exactly what happened with Anne Boleyn, whose anti-Catholic opinions and favoured status at the royal court of England were used by the Lutherans to undermine Henry VIII's nominally Catholic religion.

Fig 22.   Mutnodjmet is standing, with her two dwarfs, in the register above the three daughters of Akhenaton. Note that Akhenaton may well be wearing a garter in this picture. The book 'Eden in Egypt' has a chapter on the Order of the Garter.

Mutnodjmet was older than Akhenaton's daughters, and would have reached maturity in the middle of Akhenaton's reign, which is exactly when Queen Kiyah rises to power in the royal court. It is also about this time that Mutnodjmet disappears from the scenes and texts, so did she have a name-change and reappear as the king's favourite, Kiyah? Certainly it would have been completely unacceptable for the devout Atonist, Akhenaton, to have married someone with a name like Mutnodjmet, which mentions the banned goddess Mut, so was 'Kiyah' invented as an acceptable nickname? Was the name Kiyah adopted as a compromise, because it did not mention the Aton and simply and playfully echoed her real name? Certainly Kiyah, like Mutnodjmet, seems to have been a reluctant Atonist, as Professor Aldred points out:

> On a separate register Kiyah, followed by an infant, presumably her daughter, also makes an offering (to the Aton). But despite the single ray of the Aton, which brings an ankh to her nostrils, and the fact that this is a major icon from her own chapel, her position seems merely incidental compared with the princesses ... In the writer's opinion, this indicates that the princesses are of superior status to Kiyah. [6]

That may be one possibility, but it does not explain why Kiyah was lovingly described as the King's Favourite Wife. Would such a favoured consort still be portrayed as having low status? Another explanation might be that Kiyah, like Mutnodjmet, was actually a reluctant Atonist, and did not want to be shown making offerings to the Aton, especially within her own chapel. So the possibility exists that Kiyah was actually a daughter of Aye, the younger sister of Nefertiti, and perhaps she was even Mutnodjmet herself.

As was explained previously, the meaning of Kiyah's name is not known, but it is thought to have been derived from *kiy* meaning 'monkey'. While this derivation initially sounded to me like a professional wild guess, it may not be that far wide of the mark. Readers will recall that Mutnodjmet's real name was actually Mutbenrit, and the suffix to this name, that of *benrit*, means 'sweet smelling'. However, the very similar word *benet* just happens to mean 'baboon'; and so Mutnodjmet and Kiyah may both have been known as 'little monkeys'.

This similarity demonstrates that Kiyah could indeed be a nickname for Mutnodjmet, but it would also pose a serious question about the courtiers' and scribes' intent here. It has been assumed that 'monkey' was an affectionate pet-name for Akhenaton's second and favourite wife, but with all the previous ridicule surrounding Mutnodjmet, could this term actually be yet another carping remark about her traditional beliefs? If so, it would seem strange that Akhenaton would allow such open disrespect of his favourite wife, Kiyah; but then it is equally strange that such an important official as Aye would allow similar disrespect for his daughter, Mutnodjmet.

All in all, this is quite a muddle, but there is a way of making sense of it all. Professor Davies is certain that the title of the dwarf who was called 'Vizier to the Queen' was made in reference to Mutnodjmet. But he then faces a problem, because Mutnodjmet was not a queen at this time, and she would not be so for another ten or so years (depending on when exactly this scene was carved and painted). Davies then toys with the idea that Mutnodjmet was a pseudonym for Tadukhipa, a princess of Mitanni who had entered the harem of Akhenaton's father, Amenhotep III. Tadukhipa was a queen, as is required, but she would have been much older than the images of Mutnodjmet portray. So what is the answer to this conundrum? Why was Mutnodjmet being feted as a queen?

The answer is that Mutnodjmet not only *eventually* became Queen Kiyah, as has already been suggested, but she was actually betrothed to Akhenaton even at this young age. While it is known that the pharaohs took child brides, as did the biblical patriarchs and indeed Muhummad, there was one Israelite sect that did things slightly differently. The Jewish Essene – who resided on the shores of the Dead Sea in the first centuries BC and AD – also took child brides, but unlike their contemporaries they were not allowed to have sexual relations with their betrothed until the girl had had three menstrual periods. Was Akhenaton adhering to this same ancient law? Was Mutnodjmet a child bride who was not yet allowed to consummate her marriage?

This is certainly a possibility, and it may well explain why Mutnodjmet is always depicted as following the royal couple, rather than her parents, Aye and Tiy. Even when Aye was being given honours, Mutnodjmet still stands behind the royal couple rather than her father. It would also explain why hints to her queenly status were being made by the dwarfs, but there was no official recognition of this – because she was not officially a queen as yet. She was betrothed, but not yet married and certainly not yet consummated.

This might also explain the strange appearance of the 'comical' dwarfs. Perhaps they were not court jesters, designed to ridicule Mutnodjmet; instead, they were representative of the courtiers and officials who served a real queen but, because Mutnodjmet was only a child-queen, she only received childlike courtiers. The dwarfs were like a child's toys or dolls – playthings to amuse her until she could handle the responsibility of running a real queenly office with real courtiers. This scenario would also explain the lack of embarrassment over this 'ridicule', for it was not ridicule at all, but simply a child playing with her real-life dolls.

That said, Mutnodjmet still appears to be a theological outsider, always standing on the periphery of the worshipping scenes and never participating, as Akhenaton's daughters do. Is it possible that such a young individual could have made such a fundamental and radical theological choice in life at such a tender age? Well, I personally did, and vigorously rejected any association with Church ritual from the age of seven onwards.

Fig 23. Hieroglyphic spelling of Kiyah.

Downfall

The precise chronology of the end of the Amarna era is not certain; however, the following will not be too far from the truth. Nefertiti appears to disappear from the records in about year 14 of Akhenaton's reign, and is often presumed dead; although an alternative scenario is that she became more powerful and metamorphosed into Smenkhkare, who became a co-regent pharaoh with Akhenaton in year 15. Since the female pharaoh Hatchepsut had done something similar a few generations previously, and since Smenkhkare and Nefertiti held many names in common, this is actually quite likely.

However, as Cyril Aldred points out, the only *shabti* (funerary figurine) of Nefertiti named her as a female Nefertiti, not a 'male' Smenkhkare. If Nefertiti did metamorphose into Pharaoh Smenkhkare in later life, it is very unlikely in the extreme that she would then be buried as 'Nefertiti'. Thus, in Aldred's opinion, Smenkhkare would have to be a young son of an Amarna royal, and not Nefertiti herself. However, if that is true, it is peculiar that Nefertiti could die during the relatively well-documented year 14, and nobody mentions a word about it. The great, influential queen dies and nobody depicts her funeral, anywhere? This does seem rather unlikely and the only other possible suggestion is that she went into exile somewhere.

If Nefertiti was not Smenkhkare then this would mean that this ephemeral pharaoh was a young Amarna prince, aged about 16 to 18 years, in Akhenaton's year 15. This makes Smenkhkare's parentage highly uncertain. For Smenkhkare to have become pharaoh before Tutankhamen indicates that he must have had a greater claim to the throne. However, since Smenkhkare was too old to have been a son of Akhenaton, this would, in turn, make it highly unlikely that Tutankhamen was a son of Akhenaton – for any son of Akhenaton would surely have had primacy, even if he was only an infant. So the age and short reign of Pharaoh Smenkhkare strongly suggests that Tutankhamen was not a son of Akhenaton. The alternative and more likely suggestion is that Tutankhamen may have been a son of Aye, and in this scenario it is entirely possible that Smenkhkare and Tutankhamen were brothers.

This argument may actually make more sense of the tombs in the Valley of the Kings, as there has long been a heated discussion as to who the occupant of KV55 was. This pharaoh was buried in an unfinished tomb in a modified sarcophagus that had once belonged to Kiyah. It is likely that Queen Kiyah had 'eloped' with Akhenaton in year 17, leaving her pre-prepared sarcophagus unused. Smenkhkare died just one year later without any funerary furniture having been made by that time, so the mortuary staff borrowed the sarcophagus that had been prepared Kiyah and other furniture taken from the tomb of the late Queen Tiye, who is likely to have been moved (minus her funerary furniture) to a small annex in the tomb of Amenhotep II for some strange reason.

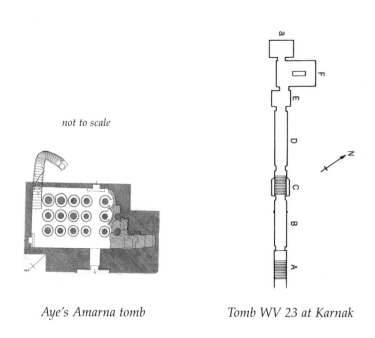

not to scale

Aye's Amarna tomb   Tomb WV 23 at Karnak

Fig 24. The two unused tombs of Aye.

Smenkhkare was probably buried in the West Valley (instead of the King's Valley) in tomb WV23, but this tomb was later commandeered by Aye, and so Smenkhkare was finally laid to rest in the rather bare surroundings of

KV55. By the time that Aye emigrated, leaving his tomb empty, the cult of the Aten was already finished and so either during this move or perhaps during a later raid on Smenkhkare's tomb, all the king's cartouches and most of those of the Aten were excised. Hence we are left with an unidentified Amarna pharaoh who is too young to be Akhenaton himself, lying on the floor of a bare, unprepared tomb known as KV55.

Regarding the other Amarna royals, Akhenaton's daughters Meritaten and Ankhesenpaaten (Ankhesenamun) were very much alive in year 14; but Kiyah seems to disappear from the scene at this time, and her small temple at Amarna had been usurped by Meritaten, Akhenaton's daughter-wife, with Kiyah's names and images being altered accordingly to suit the new owner. Since Kiyah was still being sent wine from her estate up to year 16, it is thought unlikely that she was dead, but perhaps she was in disgrace. Of course, had Kiyah been the biblical Eve it is likely that she was indeed in disgrace. The precise events and reasoning regarding Eve's fall from favour in the Book of Genesis are difficult to decipher, but if Kiyah were the rebel princess Mutnodjmet then perhaps we may have a better understanding of this affair.

Mutnodjmet [Kiyah] had always been an unwilling participant in the new Atonist theology of Amarna, and so it would have been very easy for her to fall foul of enemies within the administration. One possible enemy would have been her sister, Nefertiti. There may always have been social tensions between the two of them, resulting from sharing a king and husband, but it is highly likely that there were theological tensions too as Nefertiti was a devout Atonist, whereas Mutnodjmet [Kiyah] was not. Whatever their differences, both Nefertiti and Kiyah disappeared from Amarna at about the same time; although there is little evidence of a link between these two events.

Iconoclasm

It was at about this time, in years 15 to 17 under the co-regency rule of Smenkhkare and Akhenaton, that the destruction of the cult of Amun intensified, and the image of Amun was erased from every temple in Thebes. [7] But this orgy of destruction was perceived as being the final straw, especially by the unemployed Amun priesthood at Thebes, and so there was a popular revolt against these onerous religious reforms.

Conventional wisdom has it that Akhenaton died in year 17, as his small but influential empire was crumbling around him; but there is no evidence for this death at Amarna, apart from a couple of 'magic bricks' (funerary bricks) in KV55 that may have belonged to him. What is more certain is that Smenkhkare dropped the epithet of 'Beloved of Akhenaton' at this time and became the sole pharaoh ruling Egypt. Smenkhkare then married Meritaten, who then must have unexpectedly died or moved away because Smenkhkare then hurriedly married Ankhesenpaaten (Ankhesenamun).

Whatever the precise circumstances were in Amarna at this time, it is fairly certain that both Akhenaton and Kiyah were now gone, presumably into some kind of exile, while the young Smenkhkare was desperately trying to patch up a rapidly failing regime, and the revolutionary Amarna experiment was rapidly drawing to a close. Manetho mentions that Moses [the brother of Akhenaton] retreated from the 'quarry on the east-bank of the Nile' [Amarna] to Avaris with 80,000 followers and managed to hold the army of the next pharaoh at bay. Presumably this was more of a reference to general Horemheb than the boy-king Tutankhamen, as it was Horemheb who was effectively running much of the administration and was the army commander of Lower Egypt. Significantly, it was Horemheb who became the next pharaoh after Aye, and it was Horemheb who subsequently married Mutnodjmet, Aye's daughter and Nefertiti's sister. Had Mutnodjmet been Kiyah, as has been suggested, she would have been a doubly suitable candidate for a diplomatic marriage with Horemheb. She would have been the wife of a previous king (Akhenaton) and also a known sympathiser of the traditional gods of Egypt.

Significantly, Mutnodjmet was then given the title of Heiress; but heiress to what exactly? Since this title is thought to have legitimised Horemheb's claim to the throne, it is likely that this title was referring to a royal heiress. But how could humble Mutnodjmet, who was just the daughter of Aye and a peripheral figure in the Amarna court, be a royal heiress? As Mutnodjmet this is highly unlikely, but if the same lady was also known as Queen Kiyah, then she could indeed be legitimately titled as a royal heiress.

While the parallel royal family of Yuya and Tuyu were obviously very important people who were of the royal bloodline, they were not royal themselves. So neither Nefertiti nor Mutnodjmet [or Kiyah] could claim the title King's Daughter; and neither could Kiyah [Mutnodjmet] claim to be King's Great Wife, as that title went to her older sister, Nefertiti. However, upon the death of Akhenaton [in Avaris], Kiyah-Mutnodjmet could indeed claim to be the heiress to the throne – the king's sole surviving bloodline wife.

Kiyah-Mutnodjmet would have been middle aged by the time she married Horemheb. She was certainly older than Meritaten, Akhenaton's oldest daughter, as she was always portrayed as being taller than the princesses at Amarna. Meritaten was born in year 1 of Akhenaton's reign, so this would make Mutnodjmet at least four or five years old at this time, and therefore about twenty-two years old by the time Akhenaton abdicated in year 17. A suitable chronology for the life of Khiyah-Mutnodjmet might be as follows:

Event	Kiyah-Mutnodjmet's age
Co-coronation of Akhenaton	5
Birth of Tutankhamen	15
Coronation of Akhenaton	17
Co-coronation of Smenkhkare	20
Abdication of Akhenaton (reign 5 full yrs)	22
Coronation of Smenkhkare (reign 1 full yr)	22
Coronation of Tutankhamen at (age 8, reign 9 yrs)	23
Coronation of Horemheb	32
Kiyah-Mutnodjmet's marriage to Horemheb	32

The above assumes that two years of Smenkhkare's reign was in a co-regency with Akhenaton.

If Kiyah was one and the same as Mutnodjmet, then the former would also need to be five years older than Meritaten. This is more or less what the images of Kiyah at Amarna seem to show; surprisingly enough, it would seem that the probable ages of both Kiyah and Mutnodjmet match very nicely, so Kiyah-Mutnodjmet could indeed have been the wife of both Akhenaton and Horemheb.

Nubia

In the last chapter it was noted that Gaythelos [Aye] was supposed to have headed a Greek army that came to the aid of Pharaoh [Akhenaton]. While it was stated there that the use of Greek mercenary forces in this era has not been documented historically, the identification of Gaythelos with Aye sheds a great deal more light on this story. Bower quotes one of his many sources as saying:

> The Ethiopians had overrun the whole of Egypt in those days from the mountains right to the city of <u>Memphis and the Great Sea</u>. So Gaythelos ... was sent with a great army to help his ally Pharaoh [Akhenaton]; and to cement this alliance the king gave him (Gaythelos) his only daughter in marriage. [SC8]

If these events did indeed occur in the time of Akhenaton, as is likely, then this 'overrunning of Egypt' has to be taken with a pinch of salt, as no historical evidence for a Nubian incursion on this scale exists; but it could be an exaggerated account of some of the periodic Nubian advances into Egypt. However, Professor Watt, the translator of *Scotichronicon*, goes a stage further and indicates that this account has no basis whatsoever, and is simply a literary device invented to explain why Moses should have had an Ethiopian (Nubian) wife:

> And Miriam and Aaron spake against Moses because of the Ethiopian woman whom he had married: for he had married an Ethiopian woman. [B9]

Watt goes on to say that there is also 'no biblical basis' for this myth of a battle between Moses and the Ethiopians, and for Moses marrying a Nubian. However, this merely exposes the deficiencies in Watt's theological education, for there *is* a biblical-type record of a dispute between Egypt and Ethiopia (Nubia); and this story is to be found in the parallel accounts of Josephus Flavius, the historian who compiled his own version of the Torah. As has been explained in my previous works, Josephus had access to the Torah from the ruined Temple of Jerusalem, and so his version of biblical history is far older and much more authoritative than the Torah used in both Judaism and Christianity. By using this more authoritative source, Josephus says of this incident:

> The Ethiopians (Nubians), who are the next neighbours to the Egyptians, made an inroad into their country ... (the Egyptians were) overcome in battle, some of them were slain, some ran away in a shameful manner ... the Ethiopians proceeded as far as <u>Memphis and the sea itself.</u>

> The Egyptian under this sad oppression ... (decided) to make use of Moses the Hebrew, and take his assistance ... the king commanded his daughter (Thermuthis)* to produce him, that he might be general of their army.

> (Moses) came upon the Ethiopians (Nubians) before they had expected him and joining battle with them He beat them and deprived them of hopes they had against the Egyptians ...and (Moses) gave (the Nubian princess Tharbis) an oath to take her to his wife; and that once he had taken possession of the (Nubian) city he would not break his oath to her. No sooner was the agreement made ... when Moses had cut off the Ethiopians (Nubians), he gave thanks to god, consummated his marriage and led the Egyptians back to their own land. [J10]

This series of quotes is interesting in many ways. Firstly, the obvious similarity between Bower's source and the works of Josephus demonstrates that the Scottish chronicler was very familiar with the works of Josephus, as well as those of Manetho. Both accounts indicate that Egypt had been overrun from Memphis to the Mediterranean and both indicate that a foreign prince became an Egyptian army commander who led the battle for freedom. Josephus says that this foreign prince was Moses, while Bower says that it was Gaythelos.

Another striking similarity between these two accounts can be seen in the role of the pharaoh's daughter, Thermuthis.* The Moses story, as we all know, has Moses being discovered as a baby in an ark (basket) on the Nile by pharaoh's daughter. Pharaoh then orders his daughter to bring Moses to him. In reality, the biblical symbolism of an 'ark on the Nile' is a retelling of the Osirian myth, and so Thermuthis was probably Moses' biological mother. This is why Moses was regarded as a prince of Egypt, because that is exactly what he was [and thus he was TuthMoses, Akhenaton's brother]. However, in both accounts, we now have a pharaoh's daughter who is closely associated with the Moses-Gaythelos hero figure. In the biblical account she is possibly his mother; in the Scottish chronicle she is said to be his wife. However, the general thrust of the two stories displays a very common theme and, when taking Josephus' version into account, both texts indicate that the hero figure (Moses-Gaythelos) married a royal princess.

This demonstrates the wide variety of sources available to Walter Bower *et al*, and that these documents have been distilled and transcribed reasonably faithfully into his chronicle of the Scots. This gives us some confidence that the other sources he used, which are no longer available to us, were also transcribed reasonably faithfully into his account.

The second and more important reason for the interest in these two accounts is the curious fact that Josephus says it was Moses who pacified the Nubians and married the princess; whereas Bower indicates that it was Gaythelos who did this. This close similarity between these two sources would seem to indicate that Gaythelos was actually another name for the biblical Moses, rather than the historical Pharaoh Aye. However, in my previous works I have already argued that Moses was TuthMoses, the elusive elder brother of Akhenaton, and so at the very least this alternative link between Gaythelos and Moses would place the Scota story within the Amarna era once more, which would confirm many of the arguments already made.

Is it possible that Gaythelos could have been Moses, the brother of Akhenaton? TuthMoses [Moses] was the elder brother of Akhenaton, but by

---

* Thermuthis is an alternative Greek name for the goddess Isis. See the book *Cleopatra* for further details.

how many years we do not know. Aye was the father-in-law of Akhenaton, through his daughter Nefertiti, but if we presume that Nefertiti was a child bride of around fourteen years of age, then Aye need not be that much older than Akhenaton. Thus TuthMoses [the biblical Moses] and Aye could well have been of the same generation in the extended Amarna family.

This gives us an intriguing possibility. Aye seems to be the most likely candidate for the character known as Gaythelos, and yet Moses is also now a candidate who shows similar attributes. Could, therefore, TuthMoses [Moses] and Aye have been one and the same character? Both Gaythelos and Moses are being intimately linked to an exodus event, and Aye also seems to be connected in some manner, so were all these names originally connected to the same individual? Was Aye also called Moses?

Whilst this proposal is intriguing, on balance it does not stand up to scrutiny. Gaythelos became a king, and yet Moses never claimed the throne. Perhaps the most important reason why this comparison fails, however, is the fact that Gaythelos is not named in the Scottish chronicle as being Moses. Had there been any hint of the biblical Moses being the founder of the Scottish people, this triumph would have been trumpeted from every rooftop; but it was not. Also, *Scotichronicon* makes a clear distinction between Gaythelos and Moses; and in many places the chronicle indicates that Gaythelos was a part of the Egyptian regime who was chasing Aaron, Moses and the Israelites [Akhenaton, TuthMoses and their followers] out of Egypt. Although it might seem historically unlikely, the latter assertion may actually suit the role of Aye.

Although Aye was a follower of Aton and vizier to Akhenaton, it is known that towards the end of the Amarna regime, Aye made a break with much of Amarna theology. In the reliefs in the tomb of Tutankhamen and in the remaining reliefs in his own Theban tomb, WV23, Aye is shown in the company of the traditional gods, not the Aton. Whether this was due to a religious conversion or because of political pragmatism, Aye had effectively turned his back on the Aton and the Amarna theology. It is possible that Aye was trying to save the remains of the Amarna dynasty in the only way he knew how, but to any pious Atonist he would have been seen as a traitor. In their eyes, Aye would have been an integral part of the oppressive Theban regime who had thrown Akhenaton and TuthMoses [Aaron and Moses] out of Amarna – just as *Scotichronicon* indicates Gaythelos did.

On balance, therefore, the link between Moses and Aye does not work, and Gaythelos was most probably Aye. The confusion between Aye and Moses in these two accounts has probably occurred because they both held similar positions. If a skirmish with Nubia had developed during the Amarna era, it is possible that TuthMoses (the brother of Akhenaton) would have been called upon to command the military, as he is known to have held the title 'Commander of the Horse'. However, this is also a title that was held by Aye; and since Aye is likely to have been the senior of the two commanders, it would have been Aye who was ultimately in charge.

This may be the reason for the differing accounts as to who married whom. Josephus says that the hero married the defeated Nubian princess, while Bower indicates that the hero married the princess of the victorious Egyptian pharaoh [Akhenaton]. With two commanders on the field of battle, both accounts may have been correct. It was the younger Moses [TuthMoses] who married the Nubian princess, Tharbis, while the more senior Aye eventually married the daughter of Akhenaton (although by the time this latter marriage occurred, Akhenaton would have been in exile for many years). However, following the fall of Amarna and the exile of Akhenaton, relations between Aye and the two brothers, Akhenaton and TuthMoses [Aaron and Moses], are likely to have deteriorated significantly.

Despite all of Aye's desperate diplomatic, marital and theological manoeuvreings, it is likely that he, like Akhenaton before him, was also pushed out of Egypt in another exodus event. This is where the valuable extra material within *Scotichronicon* fills in a few of the missing historical details, for the Scottish chronicle explains that:

> Gaythelos remained behind after the army (of pharaoh) had departed the city of Heliopolis, with the purpose of (Gaythelos) possibly succeeding to his kingdom. But the Egyptian people ... gathered their forces together and informed Gaythelos that if he did not speedily hasten his departure from their kingdom, utter destruction would immediately attend himself and his men. SC11

The chronicle is quite clear in saying that there were two exoduses at this time. Firstly, the [Amarna] Israelites were being chased out of Egypt [out of Amarna towards Avaris] by a pharaoh. The pharaoh indicated here would have been a reluctant Tutankhamen, who was being manipulated by General Horemheb. But Gaythelos stayed behind with the intent of becoming pharaoh, which is exactly what Aye did in the historical record. Then, at a later date, Gaythelos [Aye] was also advised by the people to leave Egypt, and this may well be historically true too. Thus Gaythelos and Aye seem to have had similar intentions and appear to have led similar lives, which again suggests that Gaythelos was Aye.

This history rather makes Aye-Gaythelos appear to be an antihero figure, a 'traitor' who turned upon his own (Amarna) people when the odds were stacked against them. This uncomfortable fact was probably noted by Walter Bower, and so later chapters of *Scotichronicon* begin Aye-Gaythelos' transition from an unstable adventurer-prince into a wise king and leader.

Subtle parallels are then drawn between the wanderings of Gaythelos and Scota and the wanderings of the Israelites. Then, again like Moses, Gaythelos dies after seeing his people's initial promised land (which lay just off the coast of Spain) from a hilltop. These parallels are not being built into the story to indicate that Gaythelos was Moses, but to renovate the former's tarnished image and to portray him as having equal standing with the legendary lawgiver. Anything Moses could do, Aye-Gaythelos could do better.

The final thing to note in this section is that since Aye-Gaythelos left Egypt on an exodus, it is imperative for this explanation's integrity that this character was not buried either in Amarna or Thebes. Accordingly, Aye's Amarna tomb was completely unfinished, and while his Theban tomb (WV23) was finished, there is no evidence that it had ever been used. Upon initial examination by Belzoni in 1816, it was noted that many of the wall paintings in WV23 had been deliberately hacked out in antiquity, as had the images of all the Amarna pharaohs and queens apart from Tutankhamen; and likewise, Aye's sarcophagus had been pulverised. It wasn't until 1972 that Otto Schaden made a thorough inventory of all the remnants in the tomb, and during this investigation he noted a few fragments of artifacts and some plaster blocking from the entrance to one of the rooms. The latter was taken as being evidence that the room had been sealed after a burial, but the sparse remains of plaster blocking did not have any royal seal impressions, which would have been stamped on the blocking of any completed royal burial. So, as is the case for Akhenaton, Kiyah and Nefertiti, there is no evidence for Aye's burial either at Amarna or Thebes.

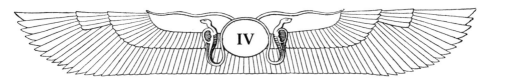

IV

Ebro River

The small ship ploughed through the crashing waves on a stiff easterly breeze, the small square-rigged sail tugging and heaving on the yards. Every now and then a puff of spray swept across the open deck and soaked all of those huddling within. In a small, hastily-erected cabin, Aye-Gaythelos and Ankhesenamun-Scota sat shivering on a small, ornate couch, feeling decidedly queasy.

What a turn of events for a once proud royal family and all of their senior courtiers and officials. Here were the pampered elite of the most powerful nation in the world, and they were reduced to a couple of square meters on the deck of a heaving ship. Here were officials, whose idea of a long 'sea' voyage was crossing the Nile from Karnak to the Valley of the Kings, and now they were crashing though a rough swell and could not see the land on any horizon. Half of them may have been convinced that Aton would look after them in their hour of need, and perhaps the other half thought Aton had deserted them, and so they cowered in the bowels of the small ship hoping that their deaths would be swift and painless.

But perhaps the Aton was still smiling on these refugees, if weakly, for the Scottish chronicle states that the royal flotilla did not flounder in the open seas. Instead, they landed in several ports along the North African coastline. But these were not the ultimate destination of these refugees, just short stops to rest, recuperate and to gather provisions and water. It is likely that their destination was uncertain, and the flotilla was blindly searching for a likely place in which the people could settle, but they found nothing but desert scrubland along the North African coastline and so they soon pushed on once more. It is also thought that Minoan ships of this era never deliberately sailed at night, and so many stops would have been made each evening along the coast.

Eventually, after seeing the Spanish coastline across the straits of Gibraltar, they altered course and travelled eastwards and northwards, heading up along the eastern coast of Spain. Once more they dropped of at several spots *enroute*, but found nothing to match their former homelands along the Nile valley and the fertile Delta region.

Bower makes a comparison here with the fate of the Hyksos-Israelites, who were wandering around the Sinai peninsular in a similar fashion at this very same time. The Aye-Gaythelos exodus would have taken place just twelve or thirteen years after Akhenaton and TuthMoses left Egypt, in about 1320 BC, and so the Aye-Gaythelos exodus can rightfully be equated by Walter Bower with the biblical exodus. Time after time, the Hyksos-Israelites seem to have been pushed out of Lower Egypt, and on each of these occasions they took their culture, hopes and ideals all across the Mediterranean. More importantly, they also took their technology and leadership skills and imposed or instilled those attributes onto more primitive populations in many diverse locations. One of those locations was now going to be Spain.

> In this way the wandered for a long time over unknown seas in various directions, passing though many places, enduring many perils and various vicissitudes according as they were driven about by the violence of opposing winds, until forced at last by lack of food they landed safely on the shores of Spain beyond all their expectation. [SC1]

But Spain was not an uninhabited land, and their arrival caused a bit of a stir amongst the local population:

> The local inhabitants rushed together on all sides in resentment of their arrival. Their aim was to oppose them in armed warfare; soon a fiercely contested battle was joined and the inhabitants were defeated and turned to flight. Then, after he had won the victory, Gaythelos pursued the inhabitants and plundered a considerable part of their territory. He returned to the shore and pitched his tents on a small mound on higher ground. [SC2]

It should be borne in mind that the Egyptians had a professional standing army that was quite well equipped. They had chariots, horse, bows, spears, swords, daggers, armour, shields and decades of experience fighting the Hittites and other nations. The Spanish tribes, on the other hand, were probably farmers and hunters with a mixed bag of agricultural and hunting weapons and no experience of fighting a disciplined army. For the Egyptian soldiery who accompanied Aye-Gaythelos, this was probably a turkey-shoot.

The battle was quickly won and the chronicle then goes on to relate how Aye-Gaythelos and his followers established themselves and built a strong town called Brigantia, in the middle of which they constructed a large tower. Now this tower could have been a defensive keep, but a following chapter will discuss the possibility that this was actually a religious shrine of some nature.

Fig 14. *Map of Spain, with the Ebro river flowing through Zaragoza. (Courtesy Tourizm Maps.)*

Balearics

The chronicle states that the new town of Brigantia was situated on the river Ebro. Now this is the modern name of the river in the north east of Spain, which runs from just south of Bilbao to an exit a hundred miles or so south of Barcelona. Since this is the modern name for the river, it has largely been discounted as a true account of Aye-Gaythelos' landing in Spain, but it will be shown shortly that this was indeed the location at which they landed. Further confusion has arisen because the chronicle then goes on, confusingly, to assert that Ireland could be 'seen' from a hill near the town of Brigantia.

> On a certain clear day as he was looking out from Brigantia he saw land far out at sea. So he armed some energetic and warlike young men and sent them off to explore in three small ships. SC3

Note that the chronicle does not mention Ireland at all, just that land could be seen. It would seem that Orosius, a Spanish historian and theologian of the fifth century AD, has taken this account rather literally, and since the ultimate destination of Aye-Gaythelos' followers was Ireland, he indicated that Brigantia was the 'lookout' for Britain (Ireland). It is probably this suggestion that has led some modern historians, including Professor Watt, to speculate that Brigantia was actually located on the northwest tip of Spain at La Corunna, a point in Spain where there is no landmass between the Spanish and Irish coastlines. But this argument defies logic. I suppose that it could be argued that the chronicle was using a literary allusion, but the fact of the matter is that it is impossible to see Ireland from Spain no matter how clear the day was, as it lies well below the horizon.

What, then, was the text meaning when it stated that an island could be seen from Brigantia? From where on the Spanish coast can you see an island? The solution to this is given in every nautical manual where it is stated that the distance to the horizon (in nautical miles) is 1.17 times the square-root of the height of the observer (in feet). The hills just to the west of the mouth of the Ebro river rise to some 4,000 feet (1,200 m), and so from the top of these peaks you would be able to see 74 nautical miles (nm) or about 150 km. But the distance to the nearest island, Mallorca, is about 120 nm, so at first glance it would appear that Aye-Gaythelos would have been able to see nothing but water from his salient near the Ebro river. But, the mountains on Mallorca also rise to some 4,500 feet, which alters the calculation considerably. In fact, the top 3,000 feet (900 m) of the Mallorcan mountains may have been visible to Aye-Gaythelos on a fine clear day, although to the naked eye these rocky pinnacles would have been very small indeed.

The view from the top of the El Port mountains above the river Ebro is as impressive today as it was in the era of Aye-Gaythelos; the only difference being that one can now drive to the top in about half an hour. The only problem on the day that I visited the area was the usual Mediterranean haze; so it was not simply a few isolated island peaks that were lost from view, but the entire horizon. As the chronicle says, it would have to have been an exceptionally clear day to see the minuscule tops of the Mallorcan ranges.

But perhaps Aye-Gaythelos never saw the mountains at all. All one would need to see was a range of cumulus clouds springing up in the morning in the same location, day after day. Any sailor worth his salt would know that one of the prime initiators of cumulus clouds is land, especially a mountainous land adjacent to the sea. Regular cumulus clouds building up in the morning would strongly indicate that there was an island out there in the Mediterranean, even if the island itself was well over the horizon. The reason that these nearby islands had not already been discovered by these exiles' roving ships is that sailors in this era only ever hugged the coastline. Thus a trip from Egypt down the North African coast would have shown the peninsular of Spain, across the Gibraltar strait, but these nervous navigators would never have seen the islands of Mallorca and Ibiza.

The chronicle then goes on to relate that the young bloods in the exiled community did make this hazardous journey to the nearby islands (knowing that something was there) and started another settlement in the Balearics; and that the people made the crossing so often that this stretch of water became known as the Sea of Hibernia, after the son of Aye-Gaythelos. It is now called the gulf of Valencia:

> They put into a nearby harbour on this island and after beaching their ships went all around exploring the island. After seeing as much of the island as they could they sailed back to Brigantia, reporting to their king Gaythelos on the very beautiful tract of land that they had found in the Ocean. [SC4]

> So because Hiber (the son of Gaythelos) sailed so frequently to that island and so often returned ... he bequeathed his own name for all time to that sea and island. Just as the sea was called Hiberic, so also the island was called Hibernia. [SC5]

There are several confusing and contradictory statements about this newly discovered island. It is said to be in the boundless ocean, which is thought to refer to the Atlantic; but the people of Brigantia sail regularly to and from this island, which sounds like a nearby island (for Ireland is a very long way from the Ebro). Likewise, the island could also be seen from the mainland, which reinforces the view that the island was not that far away. This really does not sound like a commentary on the discovery of Ireland at all, and the simple answer to this dichotomy is that two groups of islands were eventually discovered by the Brigantians. The later accounts in *Scotichronicon* do indeed relate to Ireland, so this island was discovered at some point in time, but it would appear that the first island that they discovered – the island that was seen by Aye-Gaythelos from Brigantia – was Mallorca.

If this is so, then the chronicle supports the idea that Aye-Gaythelos first landed on the mouth of the river Ebro, as the chronicle states, and not along the remote and wild Atlantic coast of Spain at La Corunna. This argument is supported by the very name that this river has been given. It has been assumed by some historians that Ebro is a relatively modern name for this river, and so it cannot be related to the original story of Aye-Gaythelos in any manner. But this is not so. In a similar fashion, Professor Watt argues that this river was included in the chronicle because its name sounded similar to Hibernia, the original name for Ireland (the name for the river Ebro having the same epigraphic root as the name H-<u>iber</u>nia):

> The name (of the river) in its Latin form 'Hiberius' resembles 'Hibernia', or Ireland; hence its inclusion (in the chronicle). SC6

In other words, like the name for Queen Scota, the name of the river is a 'reverse inclusion' that was fabricated by Walter Bower to entwine mainland Spain into the story-line. However, neither of these assertions is true.

Firstly, the name Ebro is a very ancient name for this river indeed, and its original Roman name was Hiberius (Iberius). Likewise, the Catalonian museum in Barcelona states that the Phoenician and Greek explorers who plied these waters in the seventh century BC called the local people Hibers, because that was the local name of the river that flowed through the region. In other words, the name for the Ebro is at least 2,700 years old.

Secondly, the name of the river was not inserted as a 'reverse inclusion', to link the Scottish chronicle to Spain, as the origins of this name are not native Iberian at all, but native Egyptian instead. *Scotichronicon* looks way beyond the environs of northeastern Spain towards Egypt, and so the word for a river in the ancient Egyptian language is Eebre (Eebro) 𓈖𓏤 .

This word has also found its way into the Hebrew, where it became Yebel יבל, which can also be pronounced as Eebel. Remember, however, the standard 'r' to 'l' transliteration that often takes place between the Egyptian and the Hebrew – due to the fact that the Egyptians did not have an 'l' consonant in their language. In other words, the Egyptian original of Eebere (Ebro) has become the Hebrew Eebele. So Professor Watt is most likely to have been wrong in his assertion. The Scottish chronicle clearly states that these names were brought from Egypt to Spain and thence to Ireland and Scotland, and having researched the situation that is exactly what we find. That this intricate and ancient Scottish chronicle could somehow link Egypt, Spain and Ireland through mere chance and coincidence is unlikely in the extreme. That this story could have been fabricated in a Scottish monastery, long before the Egyptian language had been deciphered by Francois

Champollion, is simply not credible; and so the only remaining option is that the chronicle is probably true, and a people did migrate from Egypt to Spain and thence to Ireland and Scotland.

There is always the possibility that the alternative name for the Israelites – the Hebrews or Ebriy עברי – also came from the same epigraphic root. The biblical Concordance maintains that the name 'Hebrew' was derived from Eber עבר, the son of Salah. However, the Nile was a sacred river of Egypt, the lifeblood of the nation, and for the nation (of Hyksos-Israelites) to be named after the sacred Eebere river would be quite logical. The leading 'h' may be due to this being the Hebrew word for 'the', and so the H-Eberews (Hebrews) may well have been called 'The Nile People'. But, as we have seen, Spain was called (H)iberia and Ireland was once called (H)ibernia; thus many brothers from the Orange Lodges in Northern Ireland claim that both Spain and Ireland were originally known as the 'Land of the Hebrews'. This is said to be the reason for the Star of David appearing on the flag of Ulster, as we shall see in a later chapter.

But if some of these Egypto-Hebrews were exiled to Catalonia, what would be more natural than to take this name, which may well have been used for the Nile itself, and to bestow it upon the river they had just discovered in this new land. This was the New Nile, just as the most influential American city became New York. Thus the name of the river Ebro itself strongly indicates that a people who were using the Egypto-Hebrew language landed and settled in this very location, and what better candidate do we have than the royal couple – Aye-Gaythelos and Ankhesenamun-Scota? In addition, the location they found in Spain was absolutely ideal for a party of renegade Egyptians. I have long maintained that the Amarna regime was allied to the Hyksos, and so their main power-base outside Middle Egypt was situated in the Nile Delta, at Avaris. Thus the emigrants, in their flotilla of small boats, would have drawn heavily upon Delta farmers and Delta livestock to sustain themselves in their new lands.

What they found, when they arrived at the river Ebro, was a delta region that was very much like the one they had left behind in Egypt only a few months previously. Although it is much smaller, the Ebro Delta would have had much the same topography, plant life, sunshine and annual floods as the Nile Delta in Egypt. The only difference was that the floods came in the spring, rather than the summer/autumn inundation in Egypt, as the snows of the Pyrenees melted.

One can imagine these refugees calling in at each and every major river system that they found along the North African and eastern Spanish coastline, just as the chronicle suggests. Each time, the farmers would have leaped out of the boats, run their fingers though the parched soils and shaken their heads in despair. Most of the rivers, even in eastern Spain, are seasonal, and dry up during the long hot summer. Few, if any, of these sites would have been suitable for farming without major irrigation projects, which these refugees did not have the time nor the equipment to build. Then, at long last, the migrant farmers laid their eyes upon the Ebro Delta, fell to their knees and blessed Aton for his deliverance.

The Ebro gets its waters from the Pyrenees, and the snow on these high peaks slowly melts all though the long, hot Iberian summers. This supplies the Ebro with a spring flood, just in time for the spring planting, and a steady flow of water throughout the summer. In the autumn and winter the rains return and replenish the supply of water and snow, so that the Ebro stores up its stocks of water once more for the coming growing season. The Ebro was manna from heaven; it was deliverance for Aye-Gaythelos and Scota.

Ebro river

As the surging Ebro river pours into the Mediterranean, it takes with it tons of silt every day that have built up, over the years, into a sandy promontory, or delta, that juts out from the Spanish coastline. The land itself is reasonably fertile, but perhaps the modern irrigation of the region masks a more hostile environment. Away from the river channels and freshwater lagoons, the land can be dusty, arid and barren. Perhaps deep-rooted trees once covered this region, but today the fallow areas of the delta well away from the river are reduced to sandy scrublands.

However, any Delta farmer from Egypt worth a bushel of grain would have seen the opportunities of this delta region. Areas of the Nile Delta can be similarly barren, without man's intervention, but the perfectly flat fields and the adjacent river – which is actually slightly higher than some of the surrounding land – makes for an ideal irrigation system. All that needs to be done is to create small clay-lined field walls across the flat landscape, perhaps add a *shaduf* at one end to lift the water from the river, and the irrigation system is complete. For very little expenditure in labour, an Egyptian farmer could have had several fields up and running within a few weeks; and all of these are capable of producing two crops a year. Most of the current Ebro Delta is given over to paddy-fields for rice, but there were other crops of many varieties growing in the same field systems, which demonstrates the fertility and versatility of a delta region.

Had Aye-Gaythelos and Ankhesenamun-Scota landed in the Ebro Delta, they would certainly not have gone hungry. Apart from the rapidly expanding field system, the river itself teems with fish, even in the modern era; while the lagoons are similarly populated with wildfowl of every description. In fact, the Ebro river is a major destination for modern European fishermen, looking for a river untouched by pollution and rich in aquatic life. Only last year one of the largest fish ever caught in Europe was reeled in on the banks of the Ebro – a 2 m long, 95 kg carp. In short, there would have been plenty of protein available for the tired refugees from Egypt, to tide them over until the first crops were harvested. And there would have been good scope for population growth too. There are over 300 square kilometers of Ebro Delta that can be irrigated and farmed, with each field producing two crops a year – enough to feed a vast population.

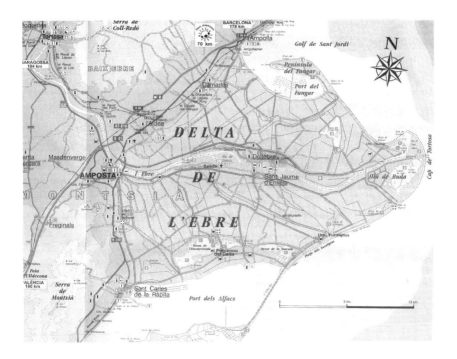

Fig 15.   Map of the Ebro Delta.

The area would have been ideal for transport too. The Ebro is plenty wide and deep enough for Minoan-style boats to navigate upstream for miles, should they have needed to. At the very least, the armada of boats from Egypt could have been taken deep into the delta to protect them from storms at sea; rendering them safe for future generations to use in their travels across the Mediterranean. The river may also have given a degree of protection to the community, as there may well have been small eyots, or river islands, on which a small settlement could be built. There is just such an eyot in the river now, but since these features can shift and change over the years there is no certainty that this particular eyot is an ancient feature.

Brigantia

There is only one spot on the west coast of Spain that a sensible Egyptian leader would declare as 'home' and that is the Ebro Delta – and thus the settlement of the Ebro region displays its origins with an Egyptian name. Here, Aye-Gaythelos and his followers built Brigantia, a small fortified town that was dangerously exposed in a faraway land.

There are two possibilities within the Egyptian language as to how the name of this new town was derived. The first is somewhat tentative, but it is possible that Aye-Gaythelos was influenced by the wetlands that surrounded his new town, and so the name that was chosen was Baregta 𓄿𓊖𓈗 meaning 'pool', a word which evolved into Bregta (Brigantia). Pools were not only necessary for life in otherwise hot and arid lands, they were also a central component of every Egyptian temple complex. The priesthood underwent a ritual cleansing in these pools before any ceremony commenced, and it is probably from this ancient tradition that the immersion rituals of John the Baptist evolved. Thus every Christian baptism is a vestigial re-enactment of this ritual priestly cleansing in a large sacred pool. We shall be exploring the settlement of Ireland in a later chapter and, of course, one of the largest cities in that land became known as Dub-linn, or the 'black-pool'.

However, perhaps the second option for the name of this town is the more compelling of the two. Brigantia was set up as a fortified town, in order to repel attacks that were being carried out on a daily basis by the local population. From the evidence at Avaris, Yehudiyeh and Tanis – the fortified Hyksos cities discovered in the Nile Delta – the favoured way of fortifying a city was to build a slope all the way up to the top of the city wall, which is called a glacis. This may seem like a counterproductive thing to do – to build a nice wheelchair-friendly slope all the way up and over your fortifications – but the logic behind this feature is actually quite sensible. The slope was made as smooth and as slippery as is possible, which is why it became known as a glacis, as in glacier: from the French *glacier* meaning 'ice' or 'slip'. So, the enemy is disadvantaged by trying to climb up a steep, slippery incline, while the defenders at the top of the ramp have a clear field of vision for loosing off their arrows. A wall offers an attacker the opportunity of hiding at the bottom of the wall under a wooden shield, and undermining the wall (which was invariably made of mud-brick in Egypt, and easily undermined). A glacis slope, on the other hand, presents no such

Fig 16.   Osiris sitting on a sacred pool, denoted by the zigzag lines.

opportunities for the attacker.

Bearing all of this in mind, another possible translation from the Egyptian is *b-rigata-t* meaning 'glacis', the inclined ramp around a fort. This sort of name for a city also has a precedent within Egypt, for Tanis was once called Thar , meaning 'fortress', as well as Tchan (Greek, Tchanis) which referred to the surrounding dyke or moat. It is uncertain if the city of Tanis was in existence at this time, but it is more certain that Tanis was a city constructed by the descendants of Hyksos-Israelite refugees. So too was Yehudiyeh, which was also a Hyksos-Israelite city in the Nile Delta, as the name suggests. Interestingly, the defences at Yehudiyeh included a glacis.

Since the people of Brigantia eventually migrated once more to the greater British Isles, it is probably from the name of this city that the name for the Brigantes people was derived. The Classical Gazetteer of 1851 says of these people:

> **Brigantes** *(Celtic* 'plunderers'), a people of Britain, occupying the whole of Maxima Csesariensis, with the exception of the portion occupied south of Alaunus, l. by the Otadeni *Durham, Cumberland, Westmoreland, Lancashire, and Yorkshire.* II. of Hibernia, s. *Waterford and part of Tipperary.* [7]

Interestingly enough, the capital city of the British Brigantes tribe is given as being Eboracum, modern York, a Roman name which is strangely reminiscent of the river Ebro. Note that this venerable reference book uses the classical names for cities and countries, and so Ireland is called here Hibernia. Interestingly, the Brigantes people of Britain were also settled in southern Ireland, which was the eventual destination of the River Ebro Brigantians. The derivation given for the name Brigante is also interesting, as we still use the term 'brigand' today to refer to a 'bandit'. The Gazetteer then goes on to describe Hibernia (Ireland) as:

> **Hibernia.** an island in the Atlantic, west of Britain. Its principal people, the Hiberni, would appear to have come from Iberia (Spain), and it was their name which Caesar extended to the whole island. The Scoti, who formed a portion of its later population, were Scandinavian immigrants, and were called by the natives Daoine Gaul or Gaulte, meaning 'foreign or barbarous men' whence Donegal. [8]

Note the general acceptance that the people of Hibernia (Ireland) came from Iberia (Spain) – and brought the name of their former country with them. The Scandinavian origins for the Scoti is less convincing as they are also being called the Daoine, and any classical scholar would know that the Danaoi came from Greece, from whence Aye-Gaythelos is also supposed to have originated.

Stratigraphy

With a secure settlement on a river island and food being produced in quantity, Aye-Gaythelos may well have felt quite at home in Brigantia. However, farmers have to go out into the fields, fishermen need to sail the river, carpenters need to find forests, and hunters have to travel to the lagoons; and no doubt the resentful aboriginal population along the River Ebro were harassing each and every movement these new immigrants made. Had Aye-Gaythelos a sizeable army with him, it would have been relatively easy to stamp his authority on the region and pacify the locals. However, with perhaps less than a thousand citizens, including women and children, the community was dangerously exposed, and it is no wonder that a voyage was contemplated to the less well-inhabited Balearic Islands, and a new colony started there.

But Brigantia, by all accounts, was still active over many generations, and so a sizeable town with many deposition layers may well have been left somewhere in the Ebro Delta. Another obvious location for Brigantia, apart from an eyot or river island, would be Deltebro, a small rise in the land to the north of the river that lies just 4m higher than the rest of the delta lands. Had this location been defensible, with a mud-brick glacis fortification, it would have stood above the flood-level of the river and been a favourable location for a town. However, it is *still* a favourable position for a town and so the whole area is currently occupied. Unfortunately, the chances of doing any archaeology in this region are pretty remote, and so the true location of Brigantia may well remain hidden under this town for centuries to come.

In fact, Bronze Age archaeology for this entire region is surprisingly minimal. Besides a few flint shavings and a deposit of bronze axe heads, the museum for the Catalan region, located in Barcelona, has no artifacts whatsoever prior to the seventh century BC. Likewise, the charming small museum of the delta, situated in Amposta, has nothing from the Bronze Age for the delta region. However, the historical scenario being described in this chapter may well have resulted in this archaeological situation. The native tribes were described as being primitive, and so are unlikely to have joined the Egyptian Bronze Age. Aye-Gaythelos and his community were certainly well within the Bronze Age, technologically, but their community was so small that it probably left few clues to its existence. Only on the Balearic Islands did a Bronze Age culture really start to flourish, and on these islands there are many clues that point towards the Minoan Empire, if not the Egyptian Empire.

Some Bronze/Iron Age burials have been located in the south of Spain, at Granada, but no great settlements. Nevertheless these burials are interesting, for they are pot burials and one of these alabaster pots is engraved with the cartouche of Pharaoh Takelot II (Meriamun Hedjkheperre) of the twenty-second dynasty (c. 850 BC). The inscription on the pot says that its owner was from a foreign land and travelled through many countries, which is undoubtedly true. But what this man was doing in Granada is not entirely clear. Even the size and duration of stay for this band of hardy Egyptian exiles is a matter of conjecture, although I would presume that they were actually of Egypto-Phoenician origins.

Fig 17. Burial pot from Granada inscribed with the cartouche of Takelot II.

Back towards the Ebro, in

Catalonia, the only early archaeological remains date from the Iron Age, about 600 BC, when small, fortified villages were being constructed all around this region. Typically, they were located on hill tops, built in an oval fashion, with the rear walls of each house being used to form a contiguous defence wall. This is the same design as is to be found in Israel, another location in which the Hyksos-Israelite exiles from Egypt found themselves. Although it has to be said that the similarity between these two designs could be due to coincidence rather than common ancestry, it is interesting enough. The appendix has a short dissertation on the similarities between these Israelite settlements and Hyksos Egyptian settlements.

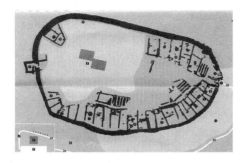 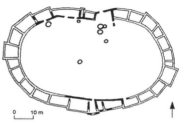

Fig 18.   La Moleta del Remi   Isbet Sartah fort,
*   fort, Catalonia   Israel*

Mallorca

As was discussed earlier, although the natural environment along the Ebro Delta was very productive and benign, Aye-Gaythelos grew concerned that his fledgling empire was being attacked so often in Brigantia that it may never grow and prosper as he had hoped. He needed to find an alternative, more suitable location:

> Gaythelos suffered many kinds of calamity in that place (Brigantia). His whole mind was intent of the protection of his people, as befits a practical and careful leader ... Although he had been successful in inflicting heavy losses on the enemy on many occasions, he never gained a single victory without some loss to his tiny nation, which he saw would grow smaller as a result of daily and unending decrease instead of increase in numbers. [SC9]

Plate 1.
View from the
El Maestrat
mountains in
Catalonia, looking
across the Ebro
Delta.

Plate 2.
Satellite image of
the Ebro Delta.
Courtesy of the
Earth Data Analysis
Center.

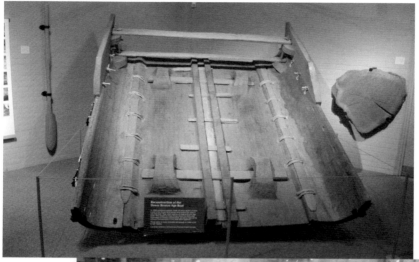

Plate 3. Top. A reconstruction of the Dover boat. Dover Museum.

Plate 4 Center. The Dover boat. Dover Museum.

Plate 5. Lower. Model of the Ferriby boat. Hull Museum.

Plate 6. Right. Bronze Age cartwheel employing the same construction techniques. Dublin Museum.

Plate 7. Solid gold cape, discovered at Mold, Flintshire, UK. Thought to be Early Bronze Age and dating from 1600 BC. British Museum.

Plate 8. The Ring of Minos, from Minoan Crete. Dating is estimated to be about 1500 BC. Iraklion Museum.

Plates 9 & 10. Left. Two golden torqs from the Gorteenreagh hoard, Co Clare, Ireland. Possibly dating from 800 BC. Dublin Museum.

Plate 11. Right bottom. Ornate spiral torq from the Iron Age Snettisham hoard, UK. Probably dating from 75 BC. British Museum.

Plate 12.
Reconstructions
Minoan Knossos
Crete.

Plate 13. Right.
Helen of Troy, by
Evelyn De Morgan.

Plate 14. Far right.
Mary Magdalene, by Carlo Crivelli.
Note that while the 'Virgin' Mary's
traditional colours are blue and
white, Mary Magdalene's are red
and green.

Plate 15. Lower left.
Bull-leaping fresco, of
Minoan inspiration, from
Avaris in the Nile Delta

Plate 16. Bottom left.
Bull-leaping fresco from
Minoan Knossos, Crete
Iraklion Museum.

Plate 19.   Truncated round-tower at Torello, Mallorca.

Plate 17 & 18.
Top and Middle left.
Truncated round tower at Parale,
near Santanyi, Mallorca. Note the
ramp leading up to the raised
doorway, and the exposed and
vulnerable position of this so-
called 'fortress'.

Plate 20.   Top right.
Pillar room, Santanyi, Mallorca.

Plate 21.   Middle right.
Pillar room, Phaestos, Crete.

Plate 22.
The Mound of Hostages; a part of the complex of tombs and henges at Tara, in the Boyne valley, Ireland.

Plate 23.
The truncated round-tower inside the Cahergall amphitheater, Ireland. Note the steps, picked out by the shadows, leading up to four levels of terraces. The photo does not show them very well, but each set of steps has a symmetric partner leading in the other direction, forming a 'V' shape.

Plate 24.   The Gallarus Ossuary near Dingle, Co Kerry, Ireland. This upturned boat design is identical to the *navetas* on Minorca, which demonstrates the close links that exist between these two cultures. The Scottish chronicles say that the descendants of Gaythelos and Scota travelled to Spain and Ireland, and so the mythology and the archaeology dovetail precisely.

Plate 25.   The Tudons Naveta, near Ciutadella, Minorca. Clearly, this design is the inspiration for the Irish *navetas*. The Scottish chronicles indicate that the Irish *navetas* would have been built one or two centuries after the Minorcan examples.

Plate 26. Top left.
The Rattoo round-tower, near Ballyduff, Co Kerry. The upper windows point to the cardinal points, and the doorway is raised above ground level.

Plate 27. Top right.
Scota's grave, near Tralee, Co Kerry. Unfortunately, this is just a natural outcrop of rock and not a tomb of any kind.

Plate 28. Bottom.
Last Supper carving in St Peter's Cathedral, Drogheda. The disciple on Jesus' right is female (she is Mary Magdalene).

Plate 29. Above.
North Molton necklace, containing lignite and faience beads from Egypt. The faience beads are virtually identical in design to the Tara faience beads. Photo, Exeter Museum.

Thinking that he had offended the gods by taking over land that had been given (by the gods) to other nations, Aye-Gaythelos determined that they must search again for uninhabited lands. So he sent out his boats and scanned the horizon from a large hill, as already discussed. There, on a particularly clear day, he saw cumulus clouds over Mallorca, and realised that there must be an island out there in the deep ocean. But it would appear that Aye-Gaythelos died not long after this discovery, which would not be so surprising given that he was already quite old when he left Egypt. However, this account may have been a literary allusion to link Aye-Gaythelos with Moses, as this was the same fate that befell the Hyksos-Israelite lawgiver – to be able to see the promised land from Mount Nebo, but never reach it. So, like Moses, it was to be Aye-Gaythelos' sons who went in search of new lands in and around Brigantia.

> So after he heard his father's words Hiber sailed to the aforesaid island with his brother Hymec and took possession of it, not by force but finding it empty and completely uninhabited, as certain authorities claim. After taking possession of the island he entrusted it to his brother and his family and returned to Spain. SC12

The mention of an island at this stage in the chronicle must again refer to Mallorca and not to Ireland. One cannot, of course, see Ireland from Spain, and the mention of regular travel between this island and Brigantia again favours the Mallorca identification.

River and Sea

The importance of the names being used in *Scotichronicon* is once again highlighted by the names of Aye-Gaythelos' sons. One of these sons was called Hiber and the other was called Hymec, and both of these names are quite interesting as they too appear to have been Egyptian titles. The name Hiber is obviously a derivation from Ebro (Yibro) 𓇋𓃀𓂋𓈖 , meaning 'river'. Conversely, the name Hymec (Heemec) is most probably derived from the Egyptian Eema (Yima) 𓇋𓄿𓈖 , meaning 'sea'. Both of these names are prefixed with an 'h' meaning 'the', as in 'H-ebrew'. Like Eeber, the name Eema has also filtered down into the Hebrew, where it became Yam (Eam) ם‎ meaning 'sea'. Interestingly enough, the word Yam more specifically refers to the Mediterranean, and also refers to the west. Since Aye-Gaythelos was heading westwards across the Mediterranean, such a name for his son would have been doubly fitting.

Incidentally, having identified so many Hebrew words that have been derived from the ancient Egyptian, I have already proposed that Hebrew is simply a later dialect of the Egyptian language. This should not be so surprising, since the Hebrews were in fact the Lower Egyptian Hyksos and so they and their leaders (pharaohs) would have spoken perfect Egyptian. Some of these words have also found their way into the English, and in this particular case we still use the term 'immerse', which was derived from the Egyptian *eema* or *yima*. See the book *Eden* for further details.

So the two sons of Aye-Gaythelos were called River and Sea in the Egyptian language, which is quite fitting considering that Aye-Gaythelos and Scota were delivered from Egypt by river and sea. In fact, if one were to add to the speculation here, it should be noted that Ankhesenamun-Scota was Aye-Gaythelos' new wife, who he married when he was crowned pharaoh of Egypt, which was just three or four years before they both made their exodus to Spain. Thus these sons of Aye-Gaythelos may well have been born during this great exodus from Egypt, and if one had been born while at sea and the other delivered as they reached the great river in Spain, it would only be natural that their names would have become Sea and River (Eema and Eebro).

That these may well have been Egyptian-influenced names is also supported by the conveniently opposing nature of the names. One of the central planks of Egyptian theology, which was later inherited by Hebrew theology, was dualism. To the Egyptian priesthood the universe, the world and all life was created in a dualist fashion. Thus the gods in their great wisdom formed the male and the female, king and queen, day and night, light and dark, desert and marsh, chaos and order, and Sun and Moon (which are identical in apparent size), amongst many other dualist features. Even the gods themselves came in symmetrical pairs, who complemented or opposed each other. While the complete answer to life, the universe and everything was unknowable, you can be sure that it would be dualist. While it is true that the new theology of Akhenaton dampened many theological concepts in Egypt, this dualism remained intact, and so the fact that a king like Aye-Gaythelos chose the names River and Sea for his sons is completely in line with standard Egyptian theology and culture.

Ireland

The tale thus far appears to be marooned upon the Balearic islands, so where does Ireland come into this story? What probably happened is that Hiber went to Mallorca first, as that was the closest island and could be seen (by his father Aye-Gaythelos) from the mainland. It would have taken a number of years to settle and build up the population, but after a generation or three there may well have been a vibrant enough population to expand out to other locations. The texts mention that there were constant battles with the indigenous Spanish tribes, as we have already seen, so spreading out across Spain was not the easiest option. Instead, they went island-hopping to Mallorca, Minorca and Sardinia, as will be discussed in the next chapter, and only then did they undertake the long and hazardous journey around the Iberian peninsular to Ireland. In fact, the chronicle says:

> Supreme power at last fell to ... King Micelius Espayn. One of his predecessors (Gaythelos) had acquired for himself and his peoples a place to live in freedom that was independent but too small for such a numerous population ... Micelius had three sons called Hermonius, Partholomus and Hibertus. He prepared a fleet and sent them across to Ireland with a sizable army, knowing that they would find there extensive but practically uninhabited land to cultivate. [SC13]

Micelius was the great grandson of Aye-Gaythelos, through Hiber. So this account indicates that it had taken the people of Brigantia just four generations to become powerful enough to build and crew a fleet capable of sailing to Ireland. If they had started with just 1,000 people in Brigantia and trebled the population each generation, they would have become 80,000 strong in four generations. This is assuming that each couple had six surviving children, which is just about possible given the high birth rate of the time. This population of 80,000 would have been at least doubled by a large number of captured slaves and newly converted citizens from the native lands. Assuming there were no major catastrophes, the potential total population after four generations of 160,000 would just about be large enough and vibrant enough to construct a fleet of ships to go looking for and colonising new lands.

These simple demographic calculations indicate that Aye-Gaythelos could not really have started in Brigantia with much less than 1,000 followers, otherwise the colony would not have been large enough to achieve the kind of expansion that has been recorded. The *Lebor Gabala* indicates that there were about 60 people on each ship, which would equate to a fleet of about 16 ships. The Irish chronicle goes on to indicate that there were just three or four ships on this exodus to Spain, all tied together to prevent them from getting dispersed; but this figure seems to be unreasonably low, given the subsequent battles and history that the various chronicles relate.

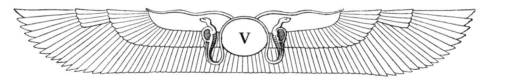

Minoans and Phoenicians

An important question that has not, as yet, been addressed is how a king and queen of Egypt assembled this large flotilla in the Nile Delta and how they navigated the largely uncharted waters of the western Mediterranean. Although the Egyptians possessed boat-building skills for their extensive Nile fleet, they were not exactly renowned in this era for their seafaring skills. Although Aye-Gaythelos and Ankhesenamun-Scota were fleeing an unstable political situation, and necessity is the mother of invention, a long voyage without the necessary knowledge and skills might be foolhardy in the extreme.

The alternative option is that the Egyptian royalty were able to employ the skills from other nations that bordered the Mediterranean, and an obvious candidate for this might be the Phoenicians, the Mediterranean's most celebrated seafaring nation. But this suggestion is not as straightforward as it may at first seem. The reign of Pharaoh Aye has been classically dated as 1325 - 1321 BC – the late fourteenth century – while the rise of the Phoenicians as a seafaring nation has been traced only to the eleventh century BC onwards. However, there must have been the nucleus of a seafaring empire extant in the Mediterranean at an earlier date than this, because the vast armada of the Sea People invasion of Egypt took place in the mid twelfth century BC.

This gives us the tantalizing possibility, already explored in my books *Solomon* and *Eden*, that the earlier voyages of Aye-Gaythelos and Scotia were related to, and laid the foundations of, the Phoenician empire. My researches thus far have unearthed evidence that points towards the Sea People invasion of Egypt in the twelfth century BC being masterminded by Hyksos-Egyptian diaspora royalty, who were trying to utilise mercenary armies from all over the Mediterranean to regain control of Egypt. These military exploits, and the need for subsequent reinforcements and materials, may well have laid the foundations for a maritime trading empire which, I believe, may have evolved into the separate empire of the Phoenicians.

To investigate this suggestion further, perhaps a review of the origins of the Phoenicians is required. Unfortunately, the history of the Phoenicians is shrouded in mystery, and it is only through mythology that a tentative homeland in Scythia, modern Ukraine, is implied. Certainly some early sculptures show distinctly Caucasian attributes, but that observation merely places the Phoenicians within a broad swathe of territory from Iran through to Spain.

Whatever their origins, the Phoenicians eventually took residence along the Levantine coast, with their main port cities of Tyre, Byblos and Sidon. Utilising their maritime skills to the full, new colonies were established from the eleventh century BC onwards, at diverse locations across the Mediterranean. Eventually, the Phoenicians were to establish cities in nearly every Mediterranean coastal nation bar modern Italy and Greece. But where did this maritime tradition come from? What were the imperatives that drove the Phoenicians onto the capricious seas?

The most probable answer, to which classical history subscribes, is that military and political pressures forced these people out into the Mediterranean. But the new twist to this history is that this was not pressure from the Hittites upon the peoples of the Levantine coasts; instead, this was a few centuries earlier, the pressure came from Upper Egypt and it was applied to the Hyksos pharaohs of Lower Egypt. This very early wave of migrants would have set out from Egypt circa 1580 BC, as Ahmose I swept to power in Lower Egypt, and settled in coastal settlements all across the eastern Mediterranean. Being seaborne migrants, they would no doubt have met and had close links with the other major maritime nation in this early era, the Minoans, but more of that later.

This, however, was not the only civil war in Egypt, and the religious reforms of Akhenaton in the fourteenth century BC destabilised Egypt in a strikingly similar fashion. Once more, sections of the Lower Egyptian Hyksos people and monarchy were being pushed out across the Mediterranean in a flotilla of small craft.

None of this explains where the maritime expertise, utilised by Aye-Gaythelos, came from. Undoubtedly the fourteenth century BC Egyptians had the boat-building skills necessary, and this is amply demonstrated by the impressive cedar boat that was buried next to the Great Pyramid at Giza. Any nation capable of constructing such a leviathan would be amply equipped to build boats capable of circumnavigating the Mediterranean. But what of the navigational skills for open-water sailing?

Santorini

The source of this maritime expertise in this pre-Phoenician era may come from a surprising location – Thera (Santorini). Between 1625 and 1600 BC, the great volcano on the island of Thera erupted with devastating violence. The force and fallout from this eruption were sufficient to create the biblical plagues in Egypt, which resulted in the Hyksos-Israelite exodus, and yet it may also have provided some of these Hyksos exiles with their means of deliverance.

Luckily for the inhabitants of Thera, the volcano must have given them a reasonable amount of warning about its intentions, for no buried population was ever found in the ruined city of Akrotiri. Apart from a priest and his assistants (or sacrificial victims), it would appear that the population had all fled the island. This exodus and the subsequent destruction of the island of Thera actually formed the basis for Plato's story of Atlantis and a fresco of the city of Atlantis is actually on display in modern Santorini, as is related in the second edition of the book *Tempest*. But the destination of these exiles from Thera is unknown, and it is presumed that they fled to the Minoan empire in Crete, whose society and nautical technology were virtually identical to the Theran's. However, around this same time, in the city of Avaris in Lower Egypt, a number of Minoans begin arriving; and their distinctive artwork has been discovered in the remains of this city.

The excavations of Avaris by Manfred Bietak uncovered some exceptional frescos that were undoubtedly Minoan, both in their design and execution. The fresco, or secco, painting technique was unknown in Egypt and the Levant at this time, but many fine examples of this type of artwork have been discovered at Knossos in Crete. In addition, the characters in the Avaris frescos wear distinctive Minoan costumes, and the subject matter in the frescos – that of bull-leaping – is uniquely Minoan. Indeed, the styles employed are more typically Theran than Minoan, indicating that the artists came from Thera (Santorini).

The colours used in these paintings are also interesting, as the bull-leapers' skins are invariably depicted in lighter tones, which range from yellow though to white. Archaeologists have speculated that the lighter toned athletes may be female, but that is contradicted by a similar image of a yellow skinned young boy and a white skinned prince (with feathers) at Knossos. It is not entirely clear if these skin-tones represent a fashion or genuinely fair-skinned people, but there is a similarity here with Egyptian depictions from around this era.

In the tomb of Userhat, a royal scribe who worked under Amenhotep II and was buried at Thebes, many of the people in the wall scenes are depicted as having blonde hair. This is not simply artistic licence, as some of the people in these scenes have black hair. So was this a new fashion for light coloured wigs or were there pockets of other nationalities living and working among the general population? [1]

While the prospect of a tribe of blonde-haired people living in the Near East in this era may seem unlikely, it would appear that the later Greeks also had a number of blondes in their midst – despite the predominant Greek phenotype having wavy, raven-black hair. I have already identified Helen of Sparta as being related to the Hyksos-Egyptian royal line in some manner, in the book *Eden*; however, surprising as it may seem, Helen is also said to have been blonde. The poems of the Spartan poet Alcman were inspired by the legends of Helen, and yet despite the typical Greek beauty being raven-haired, these poems acclaim the beauty of blondes. Thus, Helen has traditionally been viewed as being a blonde or perhaps a blonde-ginger-haired beauty, which is how she was portrayed in the recent film *Troy*.

This portrayal caused howls of protest from the politically correct brigade, who declared this to be yet another Hollywood distortion of the truth. However, while I could not find a direct reference to Helen's hair colour in the *Iliad*, Homer does mention many a golden-haired Greek in his epic, including Achilles, Meleager and Agamede. In addition, Helen was married to the 'yellow-haired' King Menelaus; and while Homer gives Helen a gloriously erotic and supernatural parentage, she was probably closely related to Menelaus, and thus also blonde. The historian Bettany Hughes says of Helen:

> We hear of a female poet (rare in Greece) called Megalostrata who, like Helen, was 'golden-haired'. [2]

In a similar fashion, the biblical Mary Magdalene was also envisioned as being blonde or blonde-ginger, although descriptive evidence for this within the Bible is lacking. Nevertheless, many a Renaissance painting portrays her as being blonde-ginger, just like Helen; and the crypt of Mary Magdalene under the church at Saint-Maxim has her (supposed) relics crowned by a distinctive blonde wig.

Fig 26. Blonde Egyptians, from the tomb of Userhat.

If there were blondes in Egypt, it is entirely possible that some of those people could have been related to the (possibly) lighter-skinned Minoans. However, having done all this meticulous work on the possibility of Minoans living in Egypt, the conclusion of Manfred Bietak was:

> I have proposed very cautiously, as a working hypothesis, the possibility of an inter-dynastic marriage between the Hyksos [Israelites] and a Minoan princess. [3]

While Bietak suggests the possibility of a dynastic alliance, the obvious link to the destruction of Thera cannot be ignored. This is made perfectly clear in the following quote:

> Excavations conducted by the Australian Institute ... at Avaris, have now revealed thousands of fragments of wall-painting apparently stripped from the walls of the Hyksos palace when it was overthrown by (Ahmose I) who founded the eighteenth dynasty. There on Egyptian soil were wall paintings which were unmistakably Minoan in character. What were they doing there? Who painted them and why? [4]

The answer to both of these conundrums is more than obvious. Modern dating of the Thera eruption places the exile of the population of Akrotiri and the other cities on Thera to about 1620 BC, while the classical date for the destruction of the Hyksos capital city of Avaris by Ahmose I is around 1580 BC. Thus the exiles from Thera could have been resident in Avaris for some forty or so years before the city was overrun by the forces of Ahmose I. Forty years would have been quite sufficient for the exiled royalty of Thera to have created their palace in Avaris, and decorated it with scenes that reminded them of their abandoned and destroyed homeland. So, to be more precise, these were not 'anomalous' Minoan frescos in Avaris, but Theran-Minoan artwork which was created by the refugees from the island itself.

Despite this obvious chronological connection, academics still seem confused on the precise origins of this artwork, and one researcher says of the Avaris frescos:

> Whether we are seeing Knossians (Minoans), as suggested by the sport, or Therans, as suggested by the blue hair ... the people from (one of these islands) came to Egypt and brought with them images of their religious practices ... The mystery of what they were doing there and why the paintings were commissioned remains unsolved. [5]

Why is there any mystery? There are two options for the origins of this artwork, given in the previous quote: Thera or Knossos. We also know that the era for these paintings being commissioned in Avaris was just before the attack by Ahmose I or, in other words, just after the Thera eruption. We also know that one of these islands was destroyed, but the entire community was evacuated just before the Thera eruption, as no decimated population has ever been discovered in the well-preserved ruins of Thera.

It would seem to be perfectly obvious that a substantial number of the Theran population must have been evacuated to Lower Egypt, where they reconstructed a palace full of classical Theran artwork. But this flowing naturalistic style of artwork was so different to the formal religious artwork of Egypt that it was probably considered to be revolutionary. In fact, this naturalistic artwork was so progressive that it was to greatly influence a later pharaoh from Lower Egypt and thereby cause a complete religious reformation within Egypt. That later pharaoh also happens to be central to this story, for he was the revolutionary iconoclast, Akhenaton – the father of Ankhesenamun-Scota.

As an aside, the bull-leaping imagery that is so familiar to us from Thera and Crete may not simply have been a circus trick for the entertainment of the royalty. Instead, it may have had stellar and thus religious connotations. The era for these depictions was just after the constellation of Taurus had given way to Aries, in the precessional cycle of the Cosmos. Thus the standard image of the leaper on the back of the bull's neck can be directly compared to the stars that stream off from the 'neck' of

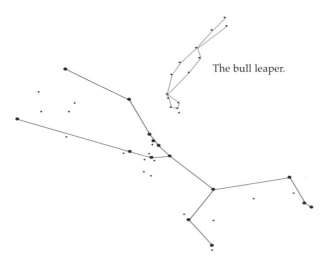

The bull leaper.

Fig 27.   Taurus, with Minoan bull-leaper.

the constellation of Taurus. In which case, the acrobat's display in the arena would have had subtle and mystical undertones for the assembled priesthood and royalty. In the stellar diagram in fig 27, only the neck and horns of the bull can be seen in the constellation of Taurus, but the outline of a 'bull-leaper' jumping over the horns of Taurus can be clearly seen in the layout of the minor stars of this constellation. The image this projects is strikingly similar to the artwork of the Minoans, and this may be the inspiration for this athletic display.

Fig 28. Seal-stone of Gournes.

While some will claim that stellar imagery is not at all common in Minoan art, the seal-stone from Gournes does exhibit circular 'buttons' on the limbs of the bull, that can readily be interpreted as stars, as can be seen in fig 28.

Minoan Amarna

The reason for some of the Theran exiles siting their new colony in Egypt, rather than Crete, is uncertain. It is known that the Hyksos retained close links with the Minoans, as many artifacts from Egypt have been discovered in Crete and *vice versa*. Examples are the Egyptian sistrum discovered in Arkhanes Phouri in Crete, and the decoration of the tomb of Hepzefa in Egypt, which follows Minoan principles. [6]

Both of these similarities date from the twentieth century BC, which demonstrates that there were close contacts between the two cultures long before the Thera eruption in the seventeenth century BC. It is possible that this close connection was based upon a common heritage, as has been suggested, although direct evidence for this is somewhat lacking. It is thought by many historians, including the venerable Manetho, that the Hyksos people were a Semitic people who migrated into Egypt from the lands to the east; in other words, the lands that had also been occupied by the proto-Minoans. It is not beyond the realms of possibility that the Hyksos and Minoans shared a common heritage, if not a common ancestry.

Oblique evidence in favour of this suggestion is to be found in the previous quotes. All of these historians are indicating that the Hyksos people of Lower Egypt had allowed the Theran-Minoans into their country, and that they may have even adopted some of the Minoan's revolutionary artistic styles. However, when Ahmose I captured Avaris in about 1580 BC, both the quasi-religious naturalistic scenes of bull-worship and the naturalistic scenes of the Nile Delta wildlife were hacked off the walls and destroyed. Clearly, the Theran-Minoans were far more closely allied to the Hyksos-Israelites in Lower Egypt than they were to the Upper Egyptian regime of Ahmose I.

This similarity between the Therans and the Hyksos-Israelites was most probably intensified after this exodus, as they now had the significant bond of a common tragedy and thus a common heritage and history. Certainly, this bond must have endured through the following generations, because some two hundred years later another pharaoh of Egypt was again adopting and promoting the naturalistic art forms of the Theran-Minoans. As we have already seen, this pharaoh was Akhenaton, who I have long argued was related in some way to the previous Hyksos-Israelite regime in Avaris. Akhenaton's artistic reforms have often been said to have been unique and revolutionary, but this is not at all correct. While Akhenaton's artistic preference was unique to Middle and Upper Egypt, it has exact parallels and similarities with the Theran-Minoan artwork of Avaris:

> Much comment has been made on the Minoan character of the nature scenes at Amarna, which along with the large quantities of Mycenaean pottery found at the site has suggested to some (that there was) an Aegean influence in the art. However, nature scenes are not typical of Mycenaean art but of Minoan art; and Minoan painting was a thing of the past by the time of Amarna. [7]

In this quotation, Vivian Davies is pointing out that although the artwork at Amarna looks distinctly Minoan, the Minoan empire had all but collapsed by this time. So how did Minoan artwork suddenly appear at Amarna?

The answer to this is a simple continuation of the arguments that have already been put forward in this chapter. There were probably strong cultural links between the Theran-Minoans and the Hyksos-Israelites, who may both have originated from lands along the eastern Mediterranean coastline. The two strands of these people forged a diverging empire in different lands, in Egypt and Crete/Thera. But when the island of Thera exploded in about 1620 BC, many thousands of Therans emigrated to their related cousins in Avaris, in Lower Egypt. Although these lands and the city at Avaris were overrun in about 1580 BC, during the civil war with Upper Egypt, the common bond of these privations ensured that these two peoples stuck together in whatever lands they were exiled to. When the Hyksos-related Amenhotep pharaohs again rose to power in Egypt a century or more later, these Theran-Minoan influences were still strong within this community. Hence the style of Theran-Minoan artwork survived the slow demise of the Minoan empire on Crete, and hence Akhenaton (Amenhotep IV) had a strong appreciation for this 'unusual' naturalistic artwork.

It should perhaps also be pointed out that some aspects of Minoan culture were definitely *not* supported by Akhenaton, and that included bull-worship. Akhenaton was the brother of the biblical Moses (TuthMoses), and so he was closely linked to the (second) exodus from Egypt. Yet the biblical accounts make a great play on the difficulties that Moses was having with bull worshippers.

I had long been puzzled as to why Apis-bull worshippers would have been allied with the Hyksos-Israelites on the exodus out of Amarna. That the Upper Egyptians still worshipped the Apis is well known, but why any of these people should wish to follow Moses and Akhenaton's Atonist regime on the exodus remained a complete mystery. However, if these renegade bull worshippers were not Egyptian Apis worshippers but the remnants and descendants of the Theran-Minoans, who had long venerated the bull in their own idiosyncratic way, then the mystery may well be solved. But if this is so then the alliance between the Therans and Akhenaton must have fallen apart during this (second) exodus, because the Bible reports that many battles were fought between the followers of Moses and the bull worshippers who accompanied them.

Script

Perhaps at this point it might be useful to look at the unique script of the Minoans. There are three stages in the development of the Minoan script and language, and although the dates of these stages are far from certain, they appear to mimic the major periods of civic unrest in Egypt. The first stage is notable for the usage of pictorial symbols, which represents the simplest form of writing possible. It is presumed that these glyphs and symbols have meaning, but none has yet been deciphered.

Then, in about 1650 BC – which is more or less at the same time as the Thera eruption and the resulting Hyksos-Israelite exodus from Egypt – the first usage of symbolic letters of a rudimentary alphabet were used, which is called Linear A. Unfortunately, although some of these alphabetic characters are similar to the later Linear B characters, the precise pronunciation for this alphabet and the nature of the language it represents are both unknown.

Finally, in an era variously described as being between 1400 BC and 1325 BC – which is more or less at the time of the Akhenaton and Aye exoduses from Egypt – Linear A was superseded by the more sophisticated Linear B script.

The exact language represented by the Linear B script was unknown for a long time, but then a nonspecialist in the field of etymology, Michael Ventris, demonstrated that the Linear B was a syllabic alphabet and that the tablets that had been discovered were written in an archaic form of Greek. At first this discovery did not go down too well with the establishment, especially those from Greece who were effectively being told by a non-academic Englishman that the artifacts in their museums were actually written in their own language. However, despite all the protests, it became abundantly clear that Ventris was correct, and that the Linear B tablets in both Mycenae in Greece and Knossos in Crete were all written in an early form of Greek. Fired on by this discovery, many have subsequently tried to show that the earlier Linear A script tablets were also written in Greek, but that attempt has so far failed, and the Linear A texts remain undeciphered.

Thus far, the evidence seems to show that Linear A was used by the Minoans for their own language, of which we have no knowledge. However, the fact that the Minoans started using a proper script around the time of the Hyksos-Israelite exodus from Egypt may imply that they were influenced by the more sophisticated Egypto-Hebrew script, which in its cursive demotic form is akin to a modern alphabet. The language that the Minoans were recording with this Linear A script is unknown. At some later date, it is thought that the Mycenaean Greeks adopted the Linear A alphabet and adapted it for their own language, and this became the Linear B script and language. Both the new script and the new Greek language subsequently supplanted the original Minoan script and language back in Knossos. At a much later date, the Greeks then adopted the simpler Phoenician script but maintained the same language; and it is this Phoenician alphabet that we recognise as the foundation for all modern Greek and Latin scripts. [8]

The general thrust of this chronology and argument is that there may well have been Egyptian influences upon the Minoan and Greek languages, which were provided by the many exiles fleeing from Egypt; including Aye-Dannus. It is not the intention of this book to look into this concept in any great detail, but the idea occurred because some similarities had already been noted in the second edition of the book *Eden*. The primary similarity was the name for the Trojan horse, which was called, in Classical Greek, an *h-ippos* ιππος. However, due to a rather dramatic historical misconception, the Trojan *ippos* (a horse) was actually a Greco-Egyptian *appis* (a bull), which was a Greek rendering of the Egyptian *hep* (the sacred Apis-bull).

I had initially thought that this Greek adoption and alteration of the term for the Egyptian Apis-bull had been a comparatively recent event, perhaps dating from the Classical Greek era. However, the Mycenaean word for a horse (in Linear B) was *iqo*, which Michael Ventris has identified with the Greek *h-ippos*. Since the Egyptian word is the more ancient of the two, it must have been from the Egyptian *hep* 𓎛𓄿𓃒 that the Greek *iqos* or *h-ippos* was derived. It might seem unlikely that the Mycenaeans would confuse a bull with a horse, but such linguistic changes are far from uncommon; as can be seen with the similarly named but physically unique hippopotamus ιππο ποταμοσ, or 'river horse'.

Another interesting word in Mycenaean Greek is *eqeta*, which became the Classical Greek *heqetai* ηεψεται. This denoted a special leader who was closely allied to the royal court and performed a prestigious but largely honorary role in the Mycenaean army. This position has proved to be a bit of a mystery, especially as the *eqeta* used the prestigious and expensive chariot for transport, and so John Chadwick says of these leaders:

> The 'Followers' *(eqeta)* are important men, presumably followers of the king and members of his household ... Why does each unit have a royal officer *(eqeta)*, not apparently in charge, but attached? My guess is that he is the communications section. [9]

While that may be entirely possible, a more tenable scenario is that the royalty of the Mycenaeans were not of the same culture or nationality as the common people. Indeed, they may have been of exiled Hyksos-Egyptian stock, and had taken over the Mycenaean people by force and become their *de facto* leaders. In this case, each army unit would require a member of the new Hyksos-Israelite royalty to oversee it and ensure its loyalty. While this may seem to be a tenuous suggestion, the name for the Mycenaean *(h)eqeta* may well have been based upon the Egyptian *heqa* 𓋴𓄿𓀀 meaning 'ruler' or 'royalty'. Indeed, the related Egyptian title of Heqetai 𓋴𓄿𓏏 means the 'Ruler of the Two Lands' or the 'Ruler of Egypt'.

Further similarities are to be found in the two classes of Mycenaean royal landholdings, which are given as the *te-menos* and the *te-ret*. Since these two terms are paired in this fashion, they are very likely to have been taken from the equivalent Egyptian words *ta-meh* 𓇉𓏏 and *ta-resi* 𓇌𓏏 , which mean 'land of the north' and 'land of the south' respectively. Actually, these were rather important Egyptian titles, and should really be read as 'Lower Egypt' and 'Upper Egypt' respectively. For the exiled leaders of Egypt to adopt these familiar titles in a foreign land would be quite logical. Likewise, if the Mycenaeans had been influenced to this degree by the exiled Hyksos-Israelites (c. 1580 BC) then this would indeed have been a logical destination for the exodus of Aye-Dannus some three centuries later (c. 1330 BC).

Of course, this is not to say that the language of the Mycenaean Greeks is going to prove to be a complete derivation of the Egyptian language, as Hebrew appears to be. As was mentioned previously, more often than not a ruling elite in a new land has to adopt the language of the native people and not *vice versa*. However, it is also common that some phrases and customs of the new ruling class become established within the native language, and no doubt these words would include mention of the ruling elite itself, their right to occupy the land and the names of their gods.

The navy

The primary point to be made in these discussions of the Minoan empire is that the Theran-Minoans, many of whom were resident in the Hyksos-Israelite capital of Avaris in 1580 BC, appear to have had a close relationship with the Lower Egyptian monarchy. More importantly, perhaps, they would also have had the maritime experience that the Hyksos-Israelites may have needed during their first (great) exodus from Egypt. So, during this first exodus out of Lower Egypt, some of the refugees may have taken to their boats and established colonies elsewhere in the Mediterranean. Some may even have gone to Crete and Greece, and spread their culture and language there; perhaps even aspiring to positions of power and influence.

The legends of Greece herself indicate that this transfer of culture from Egypt to Greece came in a later era. The Pseudo Callisthenes, for example, indicate that Pharaoh Nectanebo II (Nakhthoreb) of the thirtieth dynasty fled to Macedonia (Greece) where he 'established himself as a magician'. It was from an illicit union between Nakhthoreb and Queen Olympias that Alexander the Great was supposed to have been born. [KN10]

Now this fabulous account of the paternity of Alexander is the stuff of pure legend, but it does indicate a strong desire for Alexander to have been of Egyptian royal blood, which is probably correct, as one of the primary goals of his great military expedition was to conquer Egypt and become Pharaoh. But although it is entirely possible that Nakhthoreb fled to Greece, there was probably a great deal of Egyptian royal blood already in Greece, which was taken there during the first great exodus from Egypt.

Moving on two centuries from the first exodus, we arrive at another exodus of a 'Hyksos' pharaoh from Egypt – that of Akhenaton and his followers. The evidence from the archaeology and from the naturalistic artwork of Akhenaton's regime, suggests that the Theran-Minoan influence among the Hyksos-Israelites was still strong, even within the city of Amarna, and so Akhenaton may also have retained the seafaring skills of his Minoan cousins. If so, his rapidly failing regime may have had all the maritime skills necessary for building a seaworthy fleet and navigating a long voyage; skills that Aye-Gaythelos was going to rely upon some 15 years after Akhenaton's exodus.

It is also worth noting that the demise of the Minoan empire in mainland Crete (as opposed to Thera) was suspiciously concurrent with the demise of the Amarna regime, and again one may suppose that there was a link between the two. The Minoans had retained close contacts with the (exiled) Hyksos regime, and may have depended to a great extent upon them for trade, as the latter regained their power base within Egypt. But as the Amarna regime rapidly collapsed, and the influence of Mycenaean Greece in the Mediterranean grew in equal measure, so the traditional economy of the Minoans had to rapidly evolve and adapt. Instead of looking south to their colleagues and cousins in Egypt, they now had to look towards a new and possibly threatening empire in the north. But this transition was obviously painful, for the Minoan empire appears to have finally collapsed at this time.

It is entirely possible that the link between these two failing empires, in Egypt and Crete, was even closer than this. Although it is merely speculation, Aye-Gaythelos and Ankhesenamun-Scota required dozens of ships to evacuate their proto-nation out of Egypt, and the Minoans were still a reasonably powerful maritime nation at this time. Were dozens of Minoan ships either commandeered or purchased by Aye-Gaythelos and Scota, leaving the Minoan mainland susceptible to Greek raiding and maritime dominance?

Phoenicia

We have looked at the Minoan empire in some detail and witnessed its eventual demise. However, nothing in human history is static and, where one empire fails, a new nation normally rises to fill the strategic and commercial vacuum. The seafaring economy of the Mediterranean was to be no different, and so as the last of the Minoans ebbed away, the mainland Greeks rose in maritime power and influence. But such was the scale of the available commerce that there was room for another player in this market and so a small nation from the Levant began to make inroads into this Greek dominance of the seas. This new nation was, of course, the Phoenician nation. However, one researcher in the field reports that the rise of the Phoenicians may have been closely and causally linked with the demise of the Minoans:

> The Phoenicians and the Celts may have originated in the Indus Valley, and
> also from the Knossos Civilization of Crete. [11]

As mentioned previously, a cultural link between the Minoans and
Phoenicians would make a degree of sense, as both were major maritime
empires and the latter simply seem to have taken over when the former
declined. That the Phoenicians may have been linked to the Minoan's allies,
the Hyksos-Israelites, is implicit in their original name, as they appear to
have called themselves the Kenaani or Canaanites כנעני. This term is
traditionally said to mean 'merchant' and the land of Canaan כנען referred
to 'lowlands'. The adjoining book *Cleopatra* translates the term 'merchant' as
more accurately meaning 'banker'.

The Book of Leviticus then relates that the land of Canaan was given
to the Israelites after Joshua conquered it, and since Joshua was of the next
generation after Moses, this event would have been just after the exodus of
Aye-Gaythelos and just before the major rise of the Phoenician empire. This
account, and the previous arguments that have been discussed, therefore
demonstrate possible links between the Hyksos-Israelites, the Minoans and
the Phoenicians. These may have been simple trading links, although it is
much more likely in this kind of era that any such links were also cemented
with a royal alliance, with Minoan princesses being packed off to Avaris and
Amarna. The offspring of these diplomatic unions would then be free to
travel back to Crete and take with them the intermingled Egyptian-Minoan
culture.

Further evidence that the Phoenicians and Minoans were closely
related can be seen in the name given to a Phoenician boat, which was *kefti*
. But the Egyptian name for the Minoans was the Kefti ,
and the Bible calls them Kaphtor כפתר. Thus the Phoenician boat and
perhaps the Phoenician people themselves were easily confused with the
Minoans. The biblical accounts say that the Kaphtorites (the Minoans) were
none other than the Philistines, which it actually calls the Pelesheth פלשת.

The Pelesheth (Philistines-Minoans) are obviously the historical
Peleset, who were one of the many tribes of the Sea People alliance who
attacked Egypt during the reign of Ramesses III. Since I have always
maintained that this Sea People alliance was organised by the exiled Hyksos-
Israelites (and thus also the exiled Amarna regime), and used as a mercenary
force to destabilise the Upper Egyptian Theban regime, the Hyksos-
Israelites and the Peleset (Pelesheth-Philistines-Minoans) should have been
allies. Why, according to the biblical accounts, their presence on the Levantine
coast sometimes led to friction and skirmishes it not entirely clear. However, the
biblical Concordance, in its usual circuitous manner, does confirm that all these
tribes were much the same or at least very closely related:

Kaphtor: the original home of the Philistines, perhaps on the southwest coast of Asia Minor, maybe in Egypt or close by, or more probably on the island of Crete.

Philistine: an inhabitant of Philistia; descendants of Mizraim who immigrated from Kaphtor (Crete) to the western seacoast of Canaan.

Canaan: the fourth son of Ham and the progenitor of the Phoenicians and of the various nations who peopled the seacoast of Palestine. [12]

The result of these observations is that Kaphtor was Crete, the Egyptian Keftiu; the Philistines came from Crete; the Minoans came from Crete; the Canaanites were the Phoenicians; the Phoenicians came from Canaan; Canaan and Philistia were neighbouring countries; both the Canaanites and the Philistines were immediate descendants of Ham; and the Philistines were the descendants of Mizraim. However, in the Bible, Mizraim means Egypt, and so the Philistines were descendants of Egypt. Whew!

Thus it would seem that the Minoans, Phoenicians, Canaanites and Philistines were pretty much one and the same people – with the Philistines (the Minoans) being separated from the rest by just one biblical 'generation'. The Concordance also implies that the Philistines (Minoans) were of Egyptian origins. Although it is not clear if this refers to Upper Egyptians or the Hyksos-Israelite Lower Egyptians, the strong links between the Minoans and the Lower Egyptian monarchy in Avaris would strongly suggest the latter.

It has already been demonstrated that the Canaanites were substantially an Egypto-Israelite nation, as has been discussed in the book *Solomon.* That their descendants, the Phoenicians, may well have been similarly descended from Egyptian exiles (the Hyksos-Israelites) is confirmed by the overtly Egyptian nature of their artwork. Time and time again, the artwork and motifs of the Phoenicians are demonstrably based upon Egyptian antecedents. The excavations at Phoenician Carthage, for example, unearthed the following trinkets:

This material is of undoubted Egyptian inspiration   The most common figurative themes are the *wadjet eye, ujat, uraeus,* and the Ptah-Patechus. We also have the hawk, Horus, Bes and Thoth. Less frequent are certain divine beings like Isis, Min, Khonsu, Shu, Khnum or Amon-Ra, Sekhmet, Anubis ... [13]

In other words, nearly every Egyptian deity can be found within the sparse remains of the city of Carthage. Even Phoenician architecture is overtly based upon Egyptian styles, with the typical Egyptian cornice at the top of a building being a favourite theme. These cornices were even adorned with multiple *uraei* and the winged solar disk, rendering them almost indistinguishable from their Egyptian equivalents, except perhaps in the quality of their workmanship. But if Phoenician art was based upon Egyptian styles, then their language also shows great affinity to Hebrew:

> The affinity with other languages of the first millennium is considerable, and seems to show a strictly parallel development, particularly as far as Hebrew is concerned ... The comparison between Phoenician and Hebrew does indeed show autonomy, but above all it shows coexistence and parallel development. [14]

In other words, these two languages were closely related, and their development was closely related and in step with each other. However, in the book *Eden* it has already been demonstrated that Hebrew was a direct descendant of the Egyptian language, and so this equivalence and parallel development of the Phoenician language suggests that it too was a dialect of ancient Egyptian. For a nation like the Phoenicians, who had adopted the majority of Egyptian customs, architecture and theology, this would not be too surprising.

While the Hebrew and Phoenician languages may have been based upon ancient Egyptian, their script was not – although some historians do maintain that the Phoenician script could have been based upon the cursive Egyptian demotic script. What is far more certain is that this new Phoenician script became the basis for the later Hebrew, Greek and Latin scripts, and so this aspect of Phoenician culture has become a central component of all Western cultures. This topic is discussed in more detail in Chapter VII.

Purple palms

As we have seen, the historical Greek name for the Canaanite people was the Phoenicians, and the traditional reasoning for this new name for the Canaanites is that the word was derived from the Phoenician word *phoinikhon* meaning 'purple', which was derived from the Mycenaean or ancient Greek word *poniki*. This name was supposed to be a reference to the purple dyes that were made from the *murex* snail in Phoenicia. This may be partly true, but the Phoenician reference to purple may also be an oblique reference to the Lower Egyptian royalty, who were distinguished by the Red Crown. In addition, the *murex* purple dye was so expensive that it was the preserve of the royal family, a tradition that survived into the Roman era and the emperor's cloak of purple.

This meaning for their name also links the Phoenicians directly with the Minoans once more, for the origins of the *murex* dye trade actually lie in Minos. In her recent excavations, Maria C. Shaw discovered evidence for *murex* purple extraction at Kommos, a port in southern Crete. She says:

> I have excavated part of what seems to be an installation for extracting purple in a MMIIB context at Kommos ... In the area involved I found crushed *murex* and some channels carved in the ground filled with *murex* shells. [15]

The Knossos tablets refer to the purple dye being called *po-pu-ro*, [16] and this term is more or less identical to the Greek *porphyry* πορπηιρι, which is in turn the origin of the English term 'purple'. One would presume that the Minoan term, *po-pu-ro*, was the original here and it is the Greeks who have adopted this word. But it is unlikely that the Phoenician equivalent of *phoinikhon* has been derived from *porphyry*, which leaves the true origin of the latter name rather uncertain. In other words, the Phoenician word for purple may simply have been derived from the Phoenician's eventual monopoly of the purple dye market, and not the other way around. In which case, the Phoenician's well-known title may have predated their entry into the lucrative purple trade, and so we may have to look for another origin for their name.

One possibility is that the name for the Phoenicians was derived from the *phoenix*, the fabulous bird from Egyptian mythology that was capable of regenerating itself. This attribute, of dying and being reborn anew, may have been considered to be quite fitting for this nation's name, especially if the Phoenicians were the reborn descendants of the Minoans. But there is a flaw in this argument, because the traditional Egyptian name for the *phoenix* was the *bennu* ⌐〰️👁️🐦 . So how did the Egyptian *bennu* become the Phoenician *phoenix*? The answer to this probably lies in the tree with which the *phoenix* is associated.

The traditional observation is that the *bennu* (*phoenix*) is associated with the persea or avocado tree, as that is where it is supposed to have perched. However, the *bennu phoenix* is more closely related to the *benra-t* ⌐〰️👁️🌴 tree, which is actually the date-palm. The reason that this strange association has come about is due to the graphic symbology of the palm frond. The *bennu* bird was, in essence, a representation of the Sun, and its regeneration after a long time-span denoted the movement of the Sun through the heavens. The most likely event that this story was trying to explain was the rising of the Sun in a different astrological constellation

every 2,000 years or so, due to the
precession of the equinox (the slow
wobble of the Earth around its central
axis). This was the 'regeneration'
event in the cyclic life of the *bennu
phoenix:* when the Sun faded from one
astrological house and was born
again into the next.

In Egypt, the Sun-god Ra was
invariably depicted as a flying sun-
disk, as can be seen at the beginning
of each chapter in this book. These

Fig 29. The phoenix.

flying Sun symbols were normally
placed over doorways, no doubt so
that Ra could see all who entered the
building. However, in a changing religious environment, the flying Sun-disk
may have become an unacceptable motif, and so we see the later Judaeo-
Israelite invention of the 'flying scroll'. Zechariah is said to have had a vision
of a huge flying scroll that was the width of the porch of the temple, which is
probably an exact description because this was actually the winged Sun-disk
of Ra that was displayed above every entrance-way in Egypt, and probably
over the doorway to the Temple of Jerusalem too. The symbolism of this new
flying scroll imagery is identical to the winged Sun-disk, but the theology
can now omit any references to the Sun-god Ra, if that is expedient to the
new Judaic priesthood.

> Then I turned, and lifted up mine eyes, and looked, and behold a flying roll.
> And he said unto me, What seest thou? And I answered, I see a flying roll; the
> length thereof is twenty cubits, and the breadth thereof ten cubits. [B17]

In ancient Israelite iconography, the scroll is normally portrayed as being
rolled up and seen edge on; in other words we see just a circle with two
wings attached, or the symbol of Aton-Ra. However, the rectangular
dimensions given in this verse convinced some ancient scholars that the
scroll had been unwound and opened, thus presenting a rectangular image.
It was from this ingeniously revised symbology that the mythology of the
Persian flying carpet was derived.

But this is not the only way of covering up the Hyksos-Israelite
veneration of Aton-Ra, and an alternative to the flying scroll might well be
two palm fronds. These innocent-sounding palm fronds happen to look
rather similar to a pair of bird's wings, so the image of Aton-Ra can be
overtly displayed once more, but again the true symbology is hidden. A

good example of this is to be seen in the Peitavas synagogue in Riga, Latvia. This synagogue happens to be one of the few synagogues in the world that are decorated in the Egyptian style, and above the pylon-styled doorway there are two palm fronds in just the same position and layout as the Egyptian flying Sun-disk. Again, the symbology remains hidden, and none of the congregation need know that Adhon, the Judaic god, is actually a reference to Adon (Aton-Ra), the solar deity of Akhenaton. See the book *Eden* for a colour picture of this synagogue and the golden palm fronds above the doorway.

It seems highly likely that the Phoenicians have gone though exactly the same process of obfuscation as the Israelites, and the evidence for this lies in the terminology that is used. While most classical interpretations will still maintain that the Phoenicians were named after the word *phoinikhon* πηοινικηον, meaning the colour purple, the biblical Concordance does not agree with this analysis at all and uses the Minoan/Greek term *porphura* πορφυρα for 'purple' instead.

Fig 30. The palm-frond symbol of Ra in the Peitavas synagogue, Riga.

So if the term *phoinkhon* was not readily used for a colour, from where did the Phoenicians derive their common Greek title? In fact, the Concordance refers to Phoenicia as Phoinike φοινικη, or the 'Land of Date-Palms'. So the Phoenicians were actually named after the Greek term for a date-palm, which was called a *phoinix* φοινιξ. So it would seem that the fabulous *phoenix*-bird was closely related to the date-palm in both the Egyptian and the Greek languages. But this was probably not any old date-palm symbolism. As has already been explained, this is likely to have been a reference to the two 'palm fronds' (or wings) that were placed over the entrance-way to all the temples in Egypt, in an image of the flying Sun-disk of Ra. So, it would seem that the Phoenicians were named after the Sun-god Ra, but they used the covert symbology of the palm frond to display this, just as the Riga synagogue does to this day.

This same symbolism is also probably the origin of the Christian Palm Sunday; a festival which is supposed to celebrate Jesus entering Jerusalem on a donkey and palm fronds being strewn in front of him by the faithful. So, Jesus was just about to be crucified and 'resurrected' (reborn) and the people of Jerusalem are said to be spreading *phoenix* fronds (palm fronds) in front of him, and yet nobody within the establishment bothers to mention the obvious symbolism. It is strange that theologians do not mention the fact that Jesus was being overtly identified with the self-regenerating *phoenix* in these verses, but presumably this is because the authorities do not wish to admit to the more 'pagan' elements that lie behind classical Christianity. Instead, it is sometimes said that palm fronds were used in this manner because the palm was a symbol of victory; but why would a humble palm frond be a symbol of victory? The simplest answer is that the palm frond was also a symbol of the almighty Ra, who led armies to victory in battle. Accordingly, the Christian palm frond festival is celebrated on Palm Sunday, the day of the Sun.

However, the humble palm frond has another epigraphic twist that connects the Phoenicians with the Hyksos-Israelites, and thus with the collapsing Amarna empire. The Phoenicians rose to power in the eleventh century BC, when the Hyksos-Israelites were re-establishing their dominance in Egypt under the leadership of the twenty-first dynasty pharaohs, which included Pharaoh Psusennes II. The wife of Psusennes II was a lady called Maakare MuTamhat, who has already been equated with the biblical Maakhah Tamar in the book *Solomon*. This queen was deified after her death and became a tremendously influential figure of respect and worship, much as the Virgin Mary has achieved within the Catholic world today. However, an alternative Hebrew name for the date-palm is *tamar* תמר, and so through their title the Phoenicians may also have been paying their respects to the great mother-goddess of the Hyksos-Israelites.

At the end of the book *Solomon*, it was argued that Tanis in the Nile Delta, the newly established capital city of Psusennes II, may have been called the 'City of Palms'. This may be true for several reasons. Firstly, since Queen Maakhah Tamar resided in this city, its name would have been (in the Hebrew) the City of Tamar עיר התמרים, which actually means the City of Palms. Secondly, the entire temple complex at Tanis is comprised solely of the most beautifully carved, pink-granite date-palm columns imaginable. Thirdly, it is mentioned in the Bible that the Israelites were driven out of a City of Palms for a period of eighteen years, an event that appears to coincide with the aggressive campaigns of Ramesses II (Ramesses the Great), who did indeed take control of Avaris and the Nile Delta lands for a while.

But that is not the whole story, for the city of Tanis may have had an alternative name in another language. The Hyksos-Israelites were unceremoniously kicked out of Avaris in the Nile Delta (on the first occasion, c. 1580 BC) several centuries before the reign of Psusennes II. It is likely that Pharaoh Psusennes was related to the Hyksos-Israelites, and they were now in the process of building a new capital city further north than Avaris, a city which we know today as Tanis. This city was rising, *phoenix*-like, out of the sands of the Delta, and Psusennes II was physically using building materials from the abandoned city of Avaris to construct his new capital city. The comparison between the *phoenix* myth and the founding of the new city of Tanis upon the ashes of the old city, could not be more fitting.

This comparison is greatly reinforced when it is recalled that the temples in the new city of Tanis were made from hundreds of finely carved, pink-granite date-palm columns taken from Avaris, and in the Phoenician/ Greek languages the date-palm is known as a *phoinix* φoινιξ. Thus the city became known as the Phoenix (Phoinike φoινικη), or the City of the Date-Palms, as has been suggested. This convenient synergy – between the *phoenix*-like rising of a new city that was made from the ashes of its old self, and those ashes comprising *phoenix*-shaped (palm-shaped) granite columns – is striking to say the least.

What this may infer is that the Greek name for the Phoenician people may have been derived from this very city. When the reborn City of Palms (Tanis) rose majestically from the sands, the Phoenician/Canaanite observers in the Levant may have made the obvious link between the palms and the mythology of the fabulous *phoenix* bird rising from its own ashes. Thus the Egyptian *bennu* became known as the Phoenician/Greek Phoenix. There is only one problem with this scenario, and that is the troubling fact that this would make the Phoenician people more closely linked (or originally linked) to Tanis and the Nile Delta than to the cities of Palestine and the Levantine coast.

Now this might have been a huge and immovable stumbling block, were it not for the fact that a very strong argument has already been put forward in the book *Solomon*, that the original city of Jerusalem was actually located at Tanis. While that theory was put forward quite tentatively in the first instance, more and more evidence keeps turning up to support that original idea. Here again there is further independent evidence, from the history of the Phoenicians, to suggest that the Nile Delta was the most important biblical location from the time of the Judges all the way through to the era of Nebuchadnezzar.

Ashtoreth

That the Phoenicians may have had links to the Hyksos-Israelites is hardly surprising. They sprang from the same geographical location as many of the Hyksos-Israelites, and they worshipped the same gods. Although there were strong movements against polytheism within Judaic culture, Baal was still worshipped throughout the Levant and by the Phoenicians. The scale of the undercurrent of polytheism within Judaism can be glimpsed in this biblical quote from Kings:

> And the high places that were before Jerusalem, which were on the right hand of the mount of corruption, which Solomon the king of Israel had builded for <u>Ashtoreth</u> the abomination of the <u>Zidonians</u>, and for Chemosh the abomination of the Moabites, and for Milcom the abomination of the children of Ammon, did the king defile. [18]

Here are three 'pagan' gods and goddesses whom King Solomon had built temples for; a list that includes Ashtoreth, which is the biblical spelling of the Phoenician mother-goddess Astarte. This is being made clear in the quote above because the temple of Astarte was made for the Zidonians, the inhabitants of the Levantine city of Sidon, who were also called the Phoenicians. But the gods of the Phoenicians were not only the same as the gods of the Hyksos-Israelites, they were, of course, also the same as the traditional Egyptian gods. Astarte is only a Phoenician version of the Egyptian Ast (Est), or Isis ⌂ : the wife of Asar (Esar or Osiris ⌂) and the mother-goddess of fertility.

It is also likely that the cult of Isis was present within the Minoan empire. During the excavations of Knossos, a carefully broken and interred figurine of a goddess was discovered in the produce-storage areas. These finely crafted goddess figures are distinctively bare-breasted and cloaked with the winding coils of a huge serpent. Because of her attire, this goddess quickly became known as the snake-goddess, and there was much speculation as to whether the prominent snake signified duplicity as in the biblical Eve or perhaps the wrath of a Seth-like deity.

If the direct links between Minos and Egypt were more readily accepted, it would seem much more likely that the snake-goddess is actually a depiction of Renenutet 〰🐍⌒◠𓎛 , or the goddess Isis in the form of a snake. Since I have already demonstrated, in the book *Solomon*, the links between Isis and the bare-breasted symbology of the God's Wife, these figurines depict Isis in every detail. In her serpent guise, Isis is said to represent youth, fecundity and, more importantly, the fertility of the harvest. It is thought that these two figurines were deliberately buried during civil disturbances in Knossos following the Thera eruption and the associated failure of Minoan agriculture. With Renenutet-Isis being the goddess of the harvest, who had probably failed to do her duty for several seasons, it is not surprising that they were broken and buried in the now empty Knossan food magazines.

Although Renenutet-Isis had failed the people of Keftu (Crete), there were many nations around the Mediterranean who still revered her. Such was the status of her cult by the end of the first millennium BC that even the Christian religion could not suppress her, and so she is represented in the modern Christian world by the Madonna and Child. Moreover, she is also represented by the celebration of Christian Easter [Ast-er]. The primary fertility symbol of Ast (Isis) 𓊹𓏏 was the egg, as can be seen from the spelling of her name, and so the primary symbol of Easter has always been the Easter-egg. Christianity has long dodged tricky questions by upstart youngsters about where in the Bible the Easter-egg symbolism came from, as this subject is not covered in the New Testament, and so the priesthood have sought solace in fairy-tales about not being able to eat eggs during Lent and other such nonsense. The truth is infinitely more believable: Easter is the festival of Ast or Est (Isis-Astarte) and it celebrates the spring equinox and the springtime generation of new life – which is symbolised in Pharaoh Akhenaton's Hymn to the Aton by the hatching of an egg.

This egg symbology was also important in Minoan theology. One of the enduring mysteries of Minoan culture is the beds of beach-smoothed pebbles that adorn their ritual centers. When discussing the Theran-Minoan artwork in Avaris, it is said that:

> Other fragments (of the frescoes) depict the ground in terms of pebbles or gravel, a characteristic of Minoan art ... and the so-called 'Easter-egg' pebbles, which are very much a Minoan iconographic form. [19]

The Easter-egg pebble is not only classically Minoan, its precise symbolism is unknown. However, in the light of Phoenician worship of Astarte (Ast or Isis), and the latter's close association with the Easter-egg, the symbolism of these beds of 'eggs' becomes more obvious. Finally, it would seem that some of the Phoenicians also worshipped Aton (Adon), the one and only god of Akhenaton:

> The name 'Adon' appears in a number of Phoenician inscriptions in Cyprus, including one from Idalion. [22]

The quote is actually referring to Adhon, the Judaic god. However, Adhon is not only the name of the Judaic god, it is also the title of Akhenaton's new god of Egypt, the Aton ⎝☉ . This deity and his name was not only taken and adapted by the Hyksos-Israelites into their all-powerful god, it was also taken by the Greeks and turned into the god Adonis; where only the Aton's regenerative properties were retained.

Here we might also glimpse the reason for the Phoenicians adopting the palm imagery for the Sun-god Ra. The reforms of Akhenaton had expunged all the other gods and idols from Egypt, and his people were expected to worship only the one hidden god (Aton) through Akhenaton himself. This meant that all the images of the gods were erased, and that included the flying Sun-disk too. If a core of early Phoenicians had been influenced by Akhenaton's religious reforms, it would have been expedient to replace the flying Sun-disk with the flying scroll or even with two palm fronds – the *phoinikhon* or *phoenix*.

Bronze Age boats

Both the Minoans and the Phoenicians were great maritime nations, but what type of boats would they have been using during this early era? It is known that the Minoans had seaworthy boats in this era as they are mentioned in several texts. However, their precise method of construction was not known until quite recently, since no plans or records of their construction technique have ever been discovered.

Because of this lack of data, early reconstructions were based on guesswork and a few frescos from the ancient city of Akrotiri, located on Thera. A replica boat has been assembled in Heraklion, but it has been assumed here that the design was lightweight, with the majority of the hull being cloth stretched over a wooden frame. While this might be fine for inshore sailing, I am not convinced that this design would be strong enough to withstand the long journeys that we know were made to Greece and Egypt. [23]

A more likely alternative is that the Minoans were using the traditional sewn-plank boat, of which the Giza pyramid boat is the finest surviving example. In this type of construction, massive planks of wood are closely fitted together to form the shape of the hull, and then they are sewn together using withies or ropes. Once the hull is formed, some internal ribbing can be added for additional strength. But, unlike in a modern clinker-built boat, the main strength in the Giza boat – which was built at least 4,500 years ago – is formed by the hull itself rather than the framing. The gaps between the planks would then require a lot of caulking to keep the hull watertight.

Although this is a primitive construction technique, the sheer size of the Giza boat, which is some 43 m long and 6 m wide, demonstrates that a large vessel can be made using these early techniques. All that would be required to make the Giza boat perfectly seaworthy is the addition of some gunwales or elevated sides, to keep out the larger swell of the Mediterranean. Since the next quote seems to indicate that these gunwales were a later addition to a boat, presumably a river boat could be transformed into a seagoing vessel with very little extra work.

At some point between the early dynasties of Egypt and the middle of the Minoan era, maritime construction techniques changed and improved. Although little written evidence is available, it is known that mortise and tenon joints replaced the earlier sewn-plank technique at some unknown time during this period. Perhaps the best description of this from antiquity is from Homer's Odyssey. This account says:

> (Odysseus) shaped the planks to fit one another and bored mortises in them all. Then he hammered the ship together with tenons and dowels ... he worked on, laying the decking planks and fastening them to the close set frames, then finished the ship with long gunwales. [24]

The Odyssey epic dates from about the twelfth century BC, which means that this 'hull first', mortise and tenon technique had probably evolved during the Egyptian eighteenth dynasty (c. 1580 - 1290 BC) , and lasted through to the Roman era. The technique seems to have been adopted by many nations and used all across the eastern Mediterranean, until it was eventually supplanted by the 'frame first' technique.

In Odysseus' 'hull first' technique, the planks that formed the hull were placed adjacent to each other, and joined together by a line of mortise holes along the edges of the planks and short tenon rods that completed the joint. The hull of the boat was built up in this fashion, and only when it was complete were some internal frames added for rigidity. The mortise and tenon joints, together with the frames or ribs, were all held in place with dowels (wooden nails). Confirmation that Homer was correct in his description was found in the Kyrenia ship, which was discovered off the coast of Cyprus in 1967. This ship dates from the much later fourth century BC, but still used the techniques described in the Odyssey. However, in following this ancient construction technique, the boat ended up with a total of about 8,000 mortise and tenon joints throughout its hull, which demonstrates how labour-intensive this design was. Nevertheless, a reconstruction of the Kyrenia boat, made in 1985, showed that the design made an eminently seaworthy craft which required very little in the way of caulking and achieved a remarkable speed of 9 kts with a favourable breeze. A $^1/_5$ scale model of the Kyrenia boat was also made by Coventry Boat-builders in Britain, and is now located in the Manchester Museum. [25]

Although Odysseus was a Greek hero, it is known that he travelled to the prime Minoan base of Crete. Had this technology been available to the Greeks, it would certainly have been available to the Minoans (and *vice versa*), who would immediately have noted any new methodologies and techniques being used. However, the original date for the Iliad and Odyssey is said to be around the twelfth or eleventh century BC, so a question-mark still hangs over the type of vessels used on the voyages of Aye-Gaythelos and Scota, which would have been in about 1320 BC. Had these vessels used the sewn-plank technique or a mortise and tenon construction?

The answer to this question was finally discovered in 1984, with the uncovering of the Uluburun wreck just off the southern coast of Turkey. There, over a period of ten years, a remarkable Bronze Age ship was slowly uncovered that still contained its complete cargo. The sheer wealth of this cargo was astounding, and it led the archaeologists on site to declare that this was a royal cargo. The most notable artifacts were the raw materials, which were cast into ingots, with some ten tons of copper, a tonne of tin and a ton of coloured glass being discovered. Since copper and tin were required for the manufacture of bronze, and the latter was a very useful and expensive material in this era, this cargo must have represented a king's ransom. In fact, this is just the sort of cargo that Aye-Gaythelos would have needed for his first trip (or exile) to Greece – raw materials for establishing a new colony in Argos.

So, was this wreck anything to do with Aye-Gaythelos and his many exiles and travels? Well we are never going to find a letter penned by Aye on board, as written confirmation, but the other evidence that was uncovered was interesting nonetheless. Firstly, this ship was dated by dendro-chronology to 1306 BC (+/- 25 yrs), a date that fits Aye-Gaythelos' first exodus to Greece (c. 1330 BC) and his second exodus to Spain (c. 1320 BC) rather well. This date has been disputed recently, but it is a fact that the only definitively datable artifact found on the wreck was a gold scarab beetle that was inscribed with the cartouche of Queen Nefertiti. While this artifact could have been a family heirloom, still being carried around in later generations, the chances are that this final cargo was being transported during, or shortly after, Nefertiti's reign. Thus the presence of this scarab links the cargo with the Amarna dynasty and also with the Amarna era.

Secondly, there is the sheer variety of the cargo on this vessel. In addition to the raw materials, there were oils, incense, musical instruments, ostrich eggs, bowls, cups, ceramics, lamps, thousands of beads, trinkets, cosmetics, jewelery, ivory, fishing nets and fishing equipment, hooks, harpoons, axes, saws, chisels, adzes, spears, arrows, and swords etc. Either the intention of this voyage was to trade anything and everything possible, or this was instead a cargo that contained everything that a new colony in a foreign land would need for the next decade or so. So the date, the cargo, the link with Amarna and the location of the wreck all favour an association with Aye-Gaythelos.

Finally, the method of this boat's construction should also be mentioned. Although the Uluburun ship had largely rotted away, it was established that she was of the 'hull first' construction technique with mortise and tenon joints – just as Odysseus' and the much later Kyrenia ships were. The only thing that was not determinable was the ship's origins – from the cargo discovered she could have been Mycenaean, Minoan, Canaanite (proto-Phoenician) or Egyptian.

The boat illustrations in fig 35 show the progression in technology from the Giza boat through to the

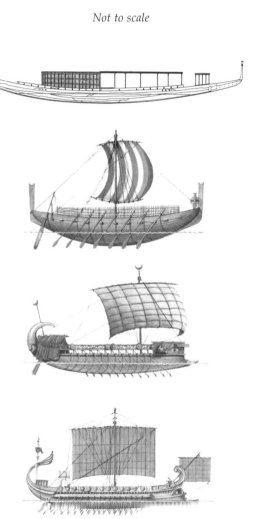

Not to scale

Fig 35. The evolution of the trireme.
a. Early Egyptian 2500 BC
b. Minoan 1500 BC
c. Phoenician 600 BC
d. Roman 100 BC

Roman trireme. Note that the early Minoan boat has much higher gunwales than the Giza boat, to allow for the larger swells of the Mediterranean. The next vessel is perhaps more accurately termed as a bireme, rather than a trireme, as it has two banks of oars. The third illustration is of the better known trireme with three banks of oars. However, since descriptions of these vessels go up to five banks (a quinquereme), it has been suggested that this number may be related more to the number of men per oar rather than the number of banks of oars. Since no remains of a trireme have been discovered, and the available images on pottery and in inscriptions are confusing, argument still rages as to how the oars were arranged.

Note also the high prows on all of these boats, which demonstrates that no sensible designer would send a boat to sea with a low prow that would easily ship water. The bireme and trireme prows were subsequently modified in later eras to permit the offensive ramming of enemy ships, but they still maintain a seaworthy high prow.

Ferriby

The options for the boats that formed Aye-Gaythelos' fleet are the Egyptian sewn-boats or the later Mycenaean mortise and tenon boats. But if Aye-Gaythelos had used such vessels to sail to Spain, and his descendants then further migrated to Ireland, some of this technology would surely have been spread throughout the greater British Islands. Unfortunately, the museum exhibits at Newgrange in Ireland do not support this suggestion, for the boat technology displayed there consists of a coracle – a simple animal-skinned stick-and-string tub.

However, the same museum exhibit then goes on to say that thousands of tonnes of quartz were brought from the Wicklow Mountains, which lie to the south of Dublin, up to Newgrange; a distance of about 90 km or so. It is highly unlikely that a coracle could have been taken out onto the Irish Sea loaded with quartz without being swamped; so it is highly likely that a more seaworthy vessel was available when this henge was constructed, or when any additions to this henge were made. So there must be a gap in the maritime archaeological record of Ireland. Since wood is highly perishable, this is not so surprising, and so most of the evidence for better transport vessels has long since deteriorated and faded away.

But not all of the evidence has disappeared; it is just a matter of striking a lucky find in the anaerobic muds of the major river estuaries around the greater British Isles. In recent years there have been two major chance discoveries of Bronze Age boats in Britain, and these are the Ferriby boats at Hull and the larger Dover boat from Kent.

V   Minoans and Phoenicians

The first of the Ferriby boats was discovered by Ted Wright in 1931, on the north shore of the river Humber, England. The course of this river had altered slightly in the early part of the last century, and had begun to scour silts and muds that had been laid down thousands of years ago. Encouraged by a local archaeologist, two teenagers began a 'shore watch' to see what successive tides uncovered. They were suitably rewarded for their diligence, as the boats that they eventually found were one of the major archaeological discoveries of the twentieth century.

The first of the boats uncovered was formed from three planks of oak. There was a long center-plank and two side-planks, which were bound together with yew withies to form the bottom section of the boat. When the full structure was exposed, it was found to be 13 m long and nearly 2 m wide, giving it a reasonable load capacity. The sides of the boat were missing – they may have been deliberately removed for recycling onto a new vessel – which was disappointing, as the original layout of the boat now becomes a matter of conjecture. Unfortunately, the excavation of the site was a bit of a shambles and the boats were largely destroyed. The few remains that have been salvaged from the site are not on show at present, which is again quite disappointing.

The presumed archaeological era for these three craft was deduced to be in the Bronze Age, because of a bronze adze blade discovered in the same strata; a blade that closely matched the cutting marks on the boats themselves. It was deemed that this type of construction was far too advanced for the Early Bronze Age, and so they were consigned to the Middle Bronze Age, or about 1300 BC. Eager to get a scientific date for the boats, the new technique of carbon-dating was employed in 1951, and this gave a much later date than expected, with a range of 750 - 150 BC being determined. Further testing in 1958 pushed this date back to around 1300 BC, which seemed more archaeologically acceptable.

These tests were both conducted while carbon-dating was in its infancy, and so more testing was carried out in the 1980s and these tests rendered dates of 1890-1700 BC and 1930-1750 BC for the two main boats. These dates were much earlier than expected and present distinct archaeological problems, for the construction technology of these boats appears to be far too advanced for this date.

However, one does have to wonder about the accuracy achievable for carbon-14 testing in such circumstances. The wood of these boats had been soaked in the Humber muds for over 3,000 years, and when they were discovered the wood had the consistency of soft butter, which is why their excavation was so difficult. In other words, the wood was nearly 80% contaminant and only 20% original material; so in trying to establish a date for these boats, are we dating original wood or the absorbed contaminant?

Dating such a find must be a bit like weighing a large, wet bathroom sponge, and agreeing that the sponge itself weighs one kilo. Similarly, dendrochronology was not possible on these remains; not simply because the wood was in such a poor condition, but also because the planks that made up the hull were so thin. If there are not enough growth-rings visible, then dating by dendrochronology becomes impossible.

Dover

The same was true of the Dover boat, which was discovered during the construction of a pedestrian underpass in 1992. This time, the boat was successfully removed and conserved by the more radical technique of cutting it up into sections, and it is now on show in the Dover Museum. The construction technique of the Dover boat was almost exactly the same as the Ferriby boats, except that on this occasion two keel-planks were used instead of one, making the boat much wider. The Dover boat was a fortuitous and important discovery, because it demonstrates that this exact same design was in use across much of Britain during the Bronze Age. Of course, it is always possible that the two vessels were manufactured in the same location and exported around the country, but at the very least this remarkable and advanced sewn-plank design must have been a familiar feature in many British coastal Bronze Age communities.

Not all of the Dover boat was recovered from the site as some of the boat continued under neighbouring shops, and so a debate still rages as to exactly how long this vessel really was. The favoured solution is that it was not much longer than the 9 m that was recovered, and had a truncated back-end, with what is known as a transom-plank across the back. This, it is said, would make the boat more rigid and more seaworthy. An alternative design is for a symmetric, tapered shape to form the back-end immediately after the recovered sections, which would result in a vessel some 13 m long. This is also said to be a practical design, but less seaworthy than the first option. The outside contender in this list of options is that only half of the boat was recovered, and so its full length would have been an impressive 18 m.

The problem that the archaeologists have in deciding and reconstructing the probable design of the boat is that the longer the boat gets, the less structurally sound it becomes. The design of the boat, as it is presented to archaeologists, looks more like an estuary cruiser than a seagoing vessel; and if this type of low-sided vessel were too long, it would flex in rough seas and fall apart. However, there are a few points that may favour the longer option.

Firstly, if the 2.5 m wide Dover boat had been constructed to the full 18 m length, it would have had almost exactly the same length to breadth ratio as the larger of the Ferriby boats; which had a 13 m length and a 1.7 m beam. This would make it appear as if the two boats came out of the same boat-yard. If the Dover boat was designed to be rowed, as is highly likely, the designer would want to make it as long as possible; both to cram in as many oarsmen as possible per tonne of boat, and also because a long, thin craft – like all modern racing rowing boats – goes much faster through the water. In other words, there would be evolutionary pressures that would push the design to its absolute limits in length.

In addition, the longitudinal strength of the boat lies not simply in its length, but also in the strength of the planks' joints and the depth of the boat's sides. The current perception, that the boat is a weak design, is based upon the notion that these boats looked like low-sided river punts; but if they had taller sides, like a Viking longboat, they would be much more rigid, longitudinally. Although their construction technique was more advanced than the Dover boat, it is known that the Vikings were able to make equally long and narrow boats, which were more than capable of withstanding the punishing and unpredictable North Sea. The Imme Gram, for instance, is a reconstruction of a longboat that was excavated at Ladby, Denmark, and she measures 21 m by 3m. Likewise, the Athenians also made their trireme war vessels as long and as slim as possible, to make them fast and deadly. The reconstructed trireme called Olympias had a total length of 37 m and a breadth of 5m, giving exactly the same length to breadth ratio as the longest option for the Dover boat. The various length to breadth ratios for these different boats are as follows, and the evidence would seem to indicate that the Dover boat could easily have been constructed to the full 18 meters.

Boat	Length (m)	Width (m)	Ratio
Imme Gram	21	3	7:1
Olympias	37	5	7.4
Ferriby	13	1.7	7.6
Dover	18	2.5	7.2

Was the Dover boat originally 18 m in length? The keel-planks so far recovered on the Dover boat were created from single lengths of hewn logs, and so the question remains as to whether there were any new sections added and jointed down the length of the hull to increase the length. One of the Ferriby boats did have a keel-plank formed from two jointed sections, so this was a possible solution to increasing the Dover boat's length. However, it would be inadvisable to have the keel and side planks all jointed in the same place amidships, as this would weaken the vessel considerably; if there were joints in these planks, they would need have been staggered, and all presumably towards the aft end of the boat. However, these Bronze Age shipwrights would have had a much better selection of trees to choose from than we have nowadays, and so it is just about possible that a straight plank could have been taken from an oak log that was 18 m in length. So, the keel-planks may have just about been created in one piece, and the length of the boat thus determined by the maximum height of the oak tree.

The other question, in terms of the vessel's rigidity and strength, is exactly how high did the sides of the Dover boat go? Again, we are working in the dark here because the sides of the boat have been removed in antiquity. Since this is the same fate as that of the Ferriby boats, one presumes that this was a common procedure – perhaps the bottom of the boat rotted before the sides, and so the sides were removed and reused on a new vessel. Had there been two or more side-planks, which are now missing, this would have made the entire structure more rigid and more seaworthy. The current reconstructions of the boat have a single side-plank added, resulting in low sides that look fine for river use, but are hardly suitable for cross-channel services.

However, it is a fact that the Athenian trireme, Olympias, also had a high length to depth ratio for its hull, as it appears to show a design using a 16:1 ratio. Since Lloyd's of London's nineteenth century limit for this ratio was 10:1, the shipyard building Olympias was skeptical that she would be strong enough not to break in half during a large swell (which is known as hogging – the boat bending in the middle like a hog's back). However, it was pointed out that with the hull-planks of the Minoan and Greek designs being pinned together, as well as some internal ribbing being in place, the ancient hull may actually be stronger than the later frame-only vessels. Accordingly, Olympias was built with the original 16:1 length to depth ratio, and the structure has proved to be seaworthy in all the conditions she has met thus far. If this same ratio were adopted for the Dover boat, the hull would only need to be 1.1 m in depth (from the top of the gunwale to the bottom of the keel). In which case, only two side-planks would need to be added to the hull section that has been found in order to turn this into a seagoing vessel. For really heavy weather, the Minoans added curtains of cloth or reeds to the gunwales to increase their height, and so deflect the spray without adding to the weight of the vessel. [26]

Another technique, which was used to strengthen these boats longitudinally, was the *hypozomata*, a tensioned rope that ran from bow to stern over a pillar in the center of the boat. This acted like the cables in a stayed suspension bridge, and prevented the ends of the boat from sagging (hogging) in a large swell. This technique was certainly in use during the Greek era, but the design is much older than this as it is known that even the

Egyptian reed boats utilised a similar type of device. This became all-too evident to Thor Heyerdahl during his pioneering voyage on a traditional reed boat, named Ra I, from Egypt to America in 1969. Drawings of these ancient Egyptian reed boats clearly showed a rope that led from the high stern of the vessel to the center section, and so this rope was installed as per the original design. However, having tripped over this rope countless times during the voyage, it was decided that it should be done away with – even though the rope was obviously under tension. Having cut the rope, the stern of the vessel promptly, but gracefully, slid below the waterline. There is no evidence that the Dover boat had such a tension cable, but there are plenty of possible attachment points at the front of the boat had they been in use in British vessels.

The other crucial aspect of the sewn-boats at Ferriby and Dover, which may have a bearing on their original design, is their origin. Were these indigenous designs, which had evolved and been improved in total isolation within the British Isles over centuries or millennia, or was this construction technique an import from the Mediterranean? The earliest sewn-boat designs are from ancient Egypt, as has been explained, and although similarities between the British and Egyptian sewn-boats are sometimes acknowledged in passing, the current thinking is that:

> Boats of Ferriby type have no known ancestors or descendants but are obviously of a long lineage. [27]

In other words, these Egyptian and British boat designs evolved completely independently of each other. But here are two very similar construction techniques, both involving sewn-planks and internal ribbing, and the only real thing that separates them is geography. Although there are differences between the massive sewn-boat that was discovered beside the Great Pyramid (at Giza) and the Bronze Age British boats, there are a number of similarities too. Both boats were made from rough-hewn planks that were sewn together with rope; both used flat keel-planks, rather than a true keel; both used a variety of grooved edges to the planks to aid their jointing and sealing; both used internal ribs; both used thwarts, or cross-benches; and both were constructed in the Bronze Age. Is it so improbable that the Egyptian technology could have reached Bronze Age Britain, and that this option should be dismissed so lightly?

The one major difference between these vessels is the cleats and bracing-struts (dowels) that run across the keel-planks of the British boats, but this additional cross-bracing may simply be an adaptation to rougher northern seas. Both the Ferriby and the Dover boats used short struts that were placed through cleats on the bottom of the boat. Although this might look like a primitive technique, in comparison with the sleeker Egyptian hull, since each cleat is an integral part of the keel-planks, this method is actually much stronger than using additional sewn ribs. This strengthening of the keel would be especially useful when coming ashore onto rocky ground, which could split an unbraced plank. Conversely, it is unlikely that the bottom of the Giza boat had to deal with anything other than soft silts and sands.

The cleats along the bottom of these boats also give us a direct link with Irish construction technology. Although no Irish sewn-boats have been discovered thus far, one of the major discoveries of Irish Bronze Age technology was an ancient wagon-wheel. Rather than using spokes, the wheel was formed from large planks of wood; and to link these together in a strong enough fashion the wheelwright has used cleats and dowels in exactly the same fashion as the Ferriby and Dover boats. Thus it is certain that the technology and techniques required to make a sewn-boat were available in Ireland.

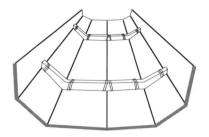 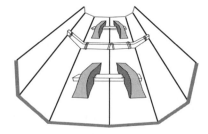

Fig 36.   Ribs in the Giza boat   Cross-bracing in the Dover boat.

It has to be said that the British sewn-boats were more roughly made than the Giza boat, but this should not be so surprising. The economy of Egypt was far stronger than that of Bronze Age Britain, and so the latter could not afford the luxury of finishing off every detail to perfection. Besides, the Dover boat is likely to have been a commercial boat, whereas the Giza boat was probably ceremonial – a no-expense-spared government enterprise.

It is worth noting again that sewn-boat technology in Britain has no known ancestry, and the technique was not used by all the communities in Britain. This fact was dramatically illustrated by a more recent find in the Humber river. It would seem that around 450 BC, just 1,000 years after the Ferriby boats were abandoned on the north shore of the Humber estuary, another type of craft was plying these same estuary waters. But this new vessel did not represent an improvement on the Ferriby design, nor an adaptation of it. This was no clinker-built, fully ribbed wonder-vessel with iron rivets and billowing sails – instead this was a dugout 'canoe'. Perhaps canoe is the wrong term here, for this single, hollowed-out tree-trunk was nearly 13 m long and weighed in at over six tonnes. This was the Hasholm boat, which was recovered from the Humber in 1984 and is still undergoing preservation in the Hull Museum. So why did the technology in this region regress so dramatically, from the stable, seaworthy, high-technology sewn-boats of Ferriby and Dover, to the rough-hewn hollowed-out log of Hasholm?

Fig 37.   Bronze Age wagon-wheel, Dublin Museum.

One possibility might be that the sewn design was not indigenous to the people of this area, and when the designers moved on or died out, the technology went with them. It is known that any high technology in these early eras was tightly controlled by families or clans, and so the continuation of that technology was highly dependent on their survival or continued occupation. Even in the thirteenth century AD, the same kind of cartel was flourishing within the cutting-edge Venetian glass industry. Exclusive access to a new technology was a valuable commodity, and so everything was done to protect the industry and its lucrative income:

> However, it has been plausibly suggested that the move (to Murano) was made in order to isolate the master glassblowers and prevent their sharing their valuable glass-making know-how with foreigners. In fact, the glassblowers became virtual prisoners on Murano, insulated from any

contacts who might divulge their production secrets to potential competitors abroad. [28]

The possibility exists that the sewn-boats in Hull and Dover were an imported design, suitably adapted to the rougher waters of the English Channel and North Sea, but their manufacture was based upon a few skilled artisans working in a limited number of locations. Other communities, either not blessed with living next to a sewn-boat yard or not being able to afford the enormous barter-cost to purchase one, had to make do with low-tech solutions for river navigation.

However, if this sewn-boat building technique did indeed come from Egypt, then we might just be able to make some alternative suggestions as to how these boats originally looked, and thus how they performed in the open sea. Take a look at the Ferriby boat design in the following plan-view diagram, where it will be seen that the keel-planks protrude a long way beyond the side-planks. It is thought that this protrusion represented a ramp at the front of the boat, a design that is again similar to a river punt. The additional side-planking would have met this extended and upturned keel-plank, and so only two more side-planks would be necessary to finish off the vessel.

This low-sided, flat-prowed design would be fine for river work, as the cargo could easily be dragged over the front of the boat, and there would be no problem with waves crashing over the bows and swamping the vessel. However, the discovery of the very similar Dover boat changes this perception completely. It is unlikely that the Dover boat was an estuary cruiser, as there are no large-sized estuaries in this region, and so it must have been a seagoing vessel; even if this was only a matter of hugging the coastline down towards Dorset. Indeed, shale from the Dorset region was found inside the Dover boat, and so it is likely that she had been at least this far down the coast.

But a wide, flat, punt-like prow is not very good in even the slightest of swells. The sea would batter the boat's wide, flat prow, slowing her progress, and the spray would pour over the prow and rapidly swamp the vessel. All in all, this kind of blunt-prowed, low-sided design would not be that sensible on the open waters of the English Channel. Even the dumbest of Bronze Age designers would have spotted the fact that his perfectly acceptable river-boat design was being rapidly swamped as the wave height grew. It would not take a great leap in imagination for this same designer to realise that a seagoing vessel required a higher bow and sides. In the aftermath of a single mishap in the open sea, the design could and would have been quickly changed.

The evidence from Minoan archaeology is that the boats being used in the Mediterranean in this era did have seaworthy high prows, and the Greek myths of Dannus [Aye-Gaythelos] confirm this view. In fact, it is said of the vessel that took Dannus to Argos (Greece) that:

> With Athene's help (Dannus) built a ship for himself and his daughters – the first two-prowed vessel that ever took to sea – and they sailed to Greece together... [29]

It is not entirely certain what is meant by a two-prowed vessel, but perhaps Dannus had lashed two ships together to increase the load-carrying capacity for his voyage. But it would seem clear that one of the most prominent parts of a ship's construction was the prow, and this should have been evident to designers of every nation.

Hence, if one looks at the design of the Giza boat, it will be seen that the bow has been made to curve up substantially. A colour picture of this boat can be seen in the book *Tempest*. But the manner in which this has been achieved is interesting, as the following plan-view of the boat demonstrates. Here, it can be seen that the keel-planks on the Giza boat extend well beyond the initial few side-planks, just as they do on the Ferriby boat. But this extension was not so that a flat, stumpy prow could be made, it was so that a high, curving prow could be added to this extension. Note that the prow and stern sections of the Giza design are almost completely separate units, which were not a part of the primary structure, and they were simply attached to the keel-plank extensions. This would make the upturned bow quite weak and one wonders if they could stand a battering from reasonable-sized waves, but perhaps this was not a top priority for a vessel that cruised the Nile and rarely went to sea.

Now take this Giza design and apply it to the Ferriby boat's hull, and it will be seen that exactly the same can be achieved. Instead of the upturned end of the keel-plank representing the bow of the boat, it could instead have been the extended attachment point for a raised prow. In turn, the number of side-planks would then have to have been increased to mate with this new bow section, increasing the depth of the sides of the vessel as well. All in all, these two changes to the design would have made the boat far more seaworthy and turned an estuary cruiser into a coastal trader.

The same may also be true of the Dover boat. Instead of a protruding extension on the Ferriby boat, the keel-planks of the Dover boat form a recessed 'U' shape. Into this recess, it is thought there may have been a flat wooden board, making a flat, inclined bow that is again reminiscent of a modern river-punt. As before, this is not exactly a seaworthy design. However, given the large amount of reinforcing that is present around this recessed area, perhaps this was instead the attachment point for a tall bow section. Once again, this new design would have required further side-planking to meet up with this raised bow, and this would again greatly increase the seagoing capabilities of the vessel.

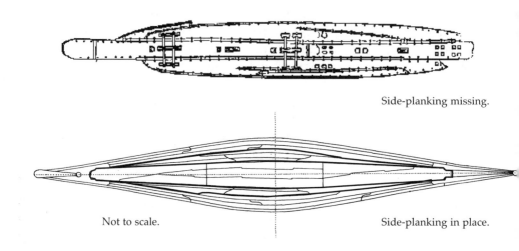

Side-planking missing.

Not to scale.   Side-planking in place.

Fig 38.   The Ferriby boat design (top) and the Giza boat (bottom). [30]

The rather flat bottom of the Dover boat, which is good for an estuary vessel that spends a lot of time sitting on the mud when the tide goes out, would now sport a more streamlined and pointed bow section. Now the boat would be suitable for loading in the shallows of the estuary and also pushing through the moderate swell of the English Channel. The traditional view of the Dover boat never did make much sense, but with this small alteration, perhaps the designer was actually a Bronze Age genius. That this was the intended design can perhaps be deduced from the later experiences of Julius Caesar, when he fought his way through Gaul towards Britain in 50 BC. Caesar, or his biographer, was a great observer of local customs and technologies during his many campaigns, and one of his descriptions was of the standard Breton seagoing vessel:

> Their hulls were somewhat more flat-bottomed than those of our ships so that they may more easily approach shoal water and tidal flats. Their prows, however, were quite high, and their sterns too; well suited to the magnitude

of the waves and storms. The ships were made completely from oak, very resilient to any forceful blow or rough treatment ... In an encounter with these ships the only advantage ours had was speed and the use of oars; in all other respects their ships were better suited to the character of the region and the force of its storms. To this was added, that whenever a storm began to rage and they ran before the wind, they both could weather the storm more easily and heave to securely in the shallows, and when left by the tide feared nothing from rocks and shelves: the risk of all which things was much to be dreaded by our ships. [32]

This is not a description of a British vessel as such, but one of the Veneti from Brittany, in northwest France. But, of course, the Bretons were substantially a Celtic nation who had very close cultural and trading links with greater Britain, as their name might suggest. However, in addition to Caesar's description, we have a similar description of a British seagoing vessel from the accounts of Strabo. His *Geography* was written just after Caesar's campaigns in Britain and some of the text may have been drawn from his accounts, but Strabo nevertheless includes some interesting additional observations:

> Because of the great tidal variation, they make their ships flat-bottomed and beamy (wide), with high sterns and prows, and they use oak, of which they have an abundance. For this reason, they do not match up (mortise and tenon) joints in the planks but leave open seams which they caulk with tree-moss. [S33]

These two description match the design of the Ferriby and Dover boats rather well. The flat bottoms, the oak fabrication, the open seams and the moss caulking are all features of the Ferriby and Dover boats. Indeed, the similarity is so great, it is almost as if Strabo were standing in the Dover Museum and describing what he saw.

His additional comments are of even more importance, however, as he also illuminates the rationale that lay behind the designs of these boats. The flat bottoms were not designed so these boats could cruise up rivers, but rather so that they could beach as far up the tidal flats as possible. In the Mediterranean, which does not have high tidal variations, the tides do not present a great problem. But, as Julius Caesar mentions, the boats of Brittany could sail through estuary shallows without fear of being beached or toppling sideways on rocky outcrops. Caesar also discovered another problem with tides during his invasion of Britain in 55 BC, when his ships were caught out by a high tide and a storm and were 'dashed to pieces and cast upon the shore'. Tides can be highly destructive, and so coastal boats need to be dragged as far up the beach as is possible, which is what a flat bottom achieves.

Strabo also comments on the jointing technique used in the planking. His argument is not that the sewn-boat is more primitive than the mortise and tenon design, but that the oak planks precluded the use of mortise and tenon joints. The only reason I can suppose for this is that the oak planks may have been too strong to easily drill out the mortise holes. While this might be so, it may also be true that the plain butt-joint was a much quicker method of construction, and as long as the boat held together why bother with the more complex mortise and tenon joints? Certainly, the reconstructed section of the Dover boat seems to be adequately strong for its purpose.

While the sewn-boat may seem to be a rough and ready method of construction, it was not just the British shipbuilders who opted for this simpler technique. In 1497, the Portuguese explorer Vasco da Gama was sent out to discover a sea route through to India. After a long and eventful voyage he landed at Calicut in India, where he was coolly greeted by Arab merchants who were fearful of Portuguese competition in the valuable spice trade. However, the point of interest in this present discussion is that the Arab vessels all had sewn-plank hulls. Either the Arabs had not updated their shipbuilding techniques, or perhaps they too found the sewn design simpler and cheaper.

The last and most important point, which is made by both Julius Caesar and Strabo, is the shape of the Breton/British boat's prows. Each and every aspect of the Ferriby and Dover boats matches their descriptions of British boats except, of course, the orthodox interpretation of how the prow was formed. This is why I think that both of these British Bronze Age boats had separate, high prows, which were added onto the keel-planks rather than being an integral part of the keel. Why these ancient shipwrights should make the prow and stern separately I do not know, but the example of the Giza boat suggests that is exactly what they did. This separate prefabrication would also explain why these prows and sterns were missing from the Ferriby and Dover boats as, like the missing gunwales, they could be easily removed and reused on a new vessel.

Here, then, is the evidence that the advanced Egyptian or Minoan shipbuilding techniques were available in greater Britain during the Middle Bronze Age period. While I suppose it is possible that there were parallel and independent advances in technology, which produced similar or identical boat-building techniques in Britain and the Eastern Mediterranean, I personally think that this is unlikely. The Hasholm dugout demonstrates that some tribes in Britain were still in the Stone Age, as far as shipbuilding was concerned, and yet others had progressed onto elaborate seagoing vessels. Indeed, the British tribes that had the superior technology preceded the Hasholm dugout by about 1,000 years.

The simplest way of explaining this dichotomy is through technology transfer from one nation to another. But in this early era, and with such a complex industry as shipbuilding, it is more than likely that this transfer of technology also involved the transfer of significant numbers of artisans. The Dover boat would have required significant improvements in the technology for rope-making, adze-fabrication, metallurgy, transport, scaffolding and caulking, in addition to the overall design of the vessel. If there was a significant transfer of artisans and technology from Egypt or Crete to Britain, during the fourteenth century BC, the chronicle of *Scotichronicon* would provide all the necessary explanations and reasons for this transfer.

Navetas, Talayots and Nuraghi

We now come back full circle to the Minoans, for there is evidence that links the Minoans directly to the adventures of Scota. Shortly after Aye-Gaythelos and his people landed in Spain and founded Brigantia, they supposedly went on an expedition to Mallorca, where it would seem that they founded another colony. But again we have to ask ourselves if this is historical fact or romantic mythology.

In the historical reality of the region, a new people did arrive in the Balearic Islands around the thirteenth or fourteenth centuries BC. We are pretty sure that they were immigrants from overseas because they built boat-shaped stone monuments called *navetas*. Whoever these new people were, they were quite industrious because, on Minorca and all of the other Balearic Islands, a number of ancient monuments were suddenly constructed.

The first of these structures that need to be researched are the halls of pillars. To the south of Mallorca, near the town of Santanyi, there is a large complex of Bronze Age monuments. Within this complex there are several large rooms that are not functional rooms, because the available floor-space is ruined by a large pillar. From the surviving (but smaller) Minorcan versions, it is clear that this pillar once held up a stone roof, but since the rooms themselves were not large enough to be practical, it was the pillar that must have been the most important element in this design. Similar pillar-rooms can be seen in the eastern Mediterranean, where they are said to be religious shrines of some kind. The other location to the east is, of course, the island of Crete and more specifically the Minoan empire that was based there. In my travels to Knossos, Phaestos, Tripodo, and in many other

Minoan cities, I was able to confirm that special rooms were built which contained a single pillar.

I have speculated in the book *Tempest* that these pillars were not simply phallic, but they may also have had metrological significance. It is known that the Egyptians and the subsequent Hyksos-Israelites were fascinated by metrology, the study of measurements, and that certain measurement systems were regarded as sacred. The god of modern Freemasons, a society that inherited many of these ancient Egyptian traditions, is known as the Great Architect, and so it is to be expected that measurements would be sacred to an all-powerful architect. The pillars in Minos seem to have been constructed using the Egyptian Thoth cubit (Royal cubit) measurement system, and so their function may have been to venerate and preserve a standard of measure. They could also be phallic symbols, and when looked at in that light they do have similarities to the eastern (Indian) lingam.

Whatever their function, these halls of pillars at each end of the Mediterranean are quite obviously the same in every detail, bar one. It is clear that the technology being used in Crete was far in advance of that used in the Balearic Islands, but that is perhaps understandable. When Aye-Gaythelos landed in Iberia with his small proto-nation, they would have had to struggle for their very existence, without spending precious time and energy on religious monuments. They would also have lacked a toolmaking industry for many years, and may not have been able to carve the blocks as neatly as we see at Knossos. Nevertheless, the evidence seems clear – there is a physical and religious link between the Minoan empire and the budding empire in the Balearic Islands, and yet this is where the descendants of Scota and Aye-Gaythelos are reputed to have lived.

The second structures of interest in the Balearics are the truncated round towers, which are called *talayots* in the Balearic Islands and *nuraghi* on Sardinia. An entire chapter has already been written on these strange structures in the book *Jesus*, and this conclusively demonstrated that these towers were not intended as defensive structures, as archaeologists maintain. They are simply too numerous, too small and too vulnerable to defend a population. Their siting it not defensive either, for instead of being at the center of a conurbation, as a castle's keep would be, they are often situated at the more vulnerable extremes. This 'defensive structure' would be the first part of the citadel to fall, not the last. No, these towers are not defensive structures in any way, shape or form. Instead they are religious monuments once more – churches, temples or shrines, call them what you will.

Undoubtedly there is a phallic symbology involved here, and comparisons have already been made with the Egyptian Benben tower which once stood at Heliopolis. A local historian from Sardinia has suggested that the *nuraghi* towers there were originally taller and finished off with a conical roof structure, and an ancient model of a tower seems to confirm this. However, having reviewed the available evidence, I no longer think that this is possible for the similar *talayots* on Mallorca and Minorca. Although the majority of the *talayots* are now ruined, there are many of these towers that retain most of their structure. Looking at the remaining ruins, it is apparent that there is not enough fallen material to account for a taller structure or for a stone roof. If it is claimed that stone-robbers have been at work, then they must have been very careful to strip the tower down symmetrically, and not just attack one side. In addition, the upper surface on some of the virtually complete towers have suffered upper-surface erosion, whereas the underlying layers have obviously not; so it is certain that these *talayots (nuraghi)* have stood in this truncated form for a very long time. In fact, all the evidence points towards the round-towers on Mallorca being designed in this fashion from the very start.* So what, in this case, was their function?

One possibility was graphically suggested by the form of the Erismanzanu *nuraghi* on Sardinia. In modern times this round-tower has acquired an olive tree within the body of the tower, and this tree erupts out of the top of the tower in a rather pleasing fashion, as can be seen in the colour section of the book *Jesus*. Could the towers have been constructed to contain sacred trees? Certainly the towers could easily have had a small layer of earth at the bottom, and some in Mallorca have small conduits running through them that could have been used for watering the tree. The size of the tower looks right for this suggestion; the function appears logical; and we know that the cult of the sacred tree was widespread in both early Egypt and the subsequent culture of the Hyksos-Israelites. But although the idea had its merits, there was no evidence for this proposal whatsoever, as any sacred tree in these towers would have long since died and decayed. Besides, any modern archaeologist is likely to have removed any remains of a tree and discarded it as a sign of the site's later abandonment.

Then, just as it seemed that the true function of these towers could never be discovered, a breakthrough was made in the city of Iraklion, Crete. There, in the museum was a new display of the Minos Ring, which had

---

* Many of the *talayots* on Minorca are actually solid, rather than being empty cones. I rather think this is due to the Minorcan versions being made of rough boulders, rather than the cut blocks that were used on Mallorca. Without their in-fill of material, the Minorcan *talayots* would have quickly collapsed; as the one or two examples that were empty – like the smaller of the two *talayots* at Torello near the airport – have clearly demonstrated.

recently been rediscovered. The ring has led a charmed life, for it was buried some 3,500 years ago, rediscovered in 1928, but then lost again. It spent the next seventy-odd years in the bottom of someone's drawer until it came to light again in 2002, when it went on display in the city's museum.

The Ring of Minos is a remarkable piece of workmanship. Crafted in gold, it is a finger-ring with an oval face upon which is engraved, in the most intricate detail, a scene that portrays the travels of a typical Minoan goddess – through the air, land and sea. What this scene actually signifies is not fully understood; however, the main element that caught my eye was the truncated round-towers that were depicted on the ring. For out of the top of two of the towers there sprang trees, and these trees were clearly being attended to by special attendants. Indeed, one of these attendants is picking a fruit from one of the trees, which is clearly a significant event for a fertility mother-goddess.

Fig 39.   Expanded view of the Ring of Minos.

Here, then, is the likely function of these round-towers. Within their protective shield there grew a sacred tree, and the inference from the Ring of

Minos is that the tower was indeed a protective shield rather than an overgrown 'pot'. The tree on the left of the ring can be seen to be leaning against the side of the tower. This could be artistic licence, but it is also the exact form we would expect if the roots of the tree resided much lower down at the bottom of the tower.

The type of tree involved is open to speculation. The image on the Ring of Minos portrays a broad-leafed tree, which may be the persea or avocado. This tree was particularly sacred to Heliopolis, as it was in this tree that the *phoenix* sometimes perched. However, if the detail of the image can be regarded as accurate then this may not be the persea, as the leaf portrayed on the ring is too blunted and the fruit is in the wrong orientation (the stalk should be on the other end).

However, whatever the species of tree involved, the symbolic value of the tree is rather better understood. The sacred persea tree in Egypt was used to record the names of the pharaohs. There is a marvellous representation of this to be found in the Temple of Karnak at Luxor, where Thoth is shown inscribing the cartouche of Seti I on the fruits of this tree – a colour picture of this scene is to be found in the book *Eden*.

It would appear that the tree was recording the names of the royal family, so it was not just a sacred tree, it was a family tree; a record of the royal family's history. When a person dies, their body normally decays and their soul can be taken up by the roots of a tree; so the tree absorbs the person's Ba or soul. It was for this reason that the soul of a person was often regarded as residing within a tree. Clearly if a tree could contain a soul and record the names of successive generations of the royal family, it would be very sacred indeed.

Whatever the symbolic value of these trees, it is a fact that here again we have a direct and unmistakable similarity between the Minoan empire and the new civilisations that were growing on the Balearic Islands, and also on Sardinia. Classical chronology places the beginnings of the Minoan empire some 500 - 700 years before the culture that suddenly blossomed on the Balearic Islands, and the Balearic Islands also have boat tombs that point towards an inward migration following a long voyage. So it would seem highly likely that it was the Minoan culture that travelled westwards, and not *visa versa*. If this is so, then we are looking for a history of a people that travelled westwards from Crete towards the Spanish coast, and in the history of Aye-Gaythelos and Scota we have just such a history.

Why look for any other explanation? We have the history, handed down from generation to generation, and we have the equivalent physical evidence that confirms the story. Moreover, the written history can be shown to be historically accurate, in regard to its terminology and numerology, and so it must have been based upon some kind of historical reality. Once more, the simplest solution to the cultural and archaeological evidence that we see around us is that the chronicle of *Scotichronicon* is based upon true history. Aye-Gaythelos and his wife Ankhesenamun-Scota did travel to Spain to escape the political turmoil of late eighteenth dynasty Egypt.

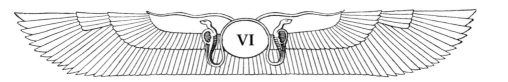

Evidence in Ireland

Having landed in Ireland, these new immigrants from Iberia named their new homeland after their founding queen, Scota. And so the original name for Ireland was Scotia, as the following map confirms. This naming of a new land after a queen was not so unusual and it has occurred more than a few times in recent history. A later example occurred in about the sixth century BC, when the Babylonian king Nebuchadnezzar invaded both Judaea and lower Egypt. As is related in the book *Solomon*, a party of refugees from this invasion, under the command of Johanan and the guidance of the prophet Jeremiah, left the smouldering wreck of Jerusalem and went to the southern quarter of the Arabian peninsular. There, they set up a new nation that was called Saba, which was named after the long-since departed but greatly respected and deified Queen of Sheba (Saba).

Back in Ireland, an earlier queen was also conferring her name on a new nation. Although this association is sometimes disputed, it does seem likely that the original name for Ireland was Scotia, and that this title was derived from the name of the legendary exiled Egyptian queen who lived in Spain. Professor Watt, the translator of *Scotichronicon*, indicates that this royal name has been 'back engineered', and so John of Fordun or Walter Bower must have derived the queen's name from the Scottish nation, in order to weave their 'fictional' chronicle into the history of the land. The evidence to demonstrate that this was not so is to be found in the other term that was applied to both Ireland and eventually Scotland – that of Hibernia. This name was said to have been derived from Aye-Gaythelos and Scota's son, Heber. While this latter point is a matter of speculation, it is certain that the ancient name for Spain, Iberia, has the same epigraphic roots as Hibernia (and Heber). Neither Fordun, Bower, nor any of the previous Scottish chroniclers could have 'back engineered' the original name for Spain into the history of Scotland, and so this name demonstrates a positive link between Spain and Ireland, and later Scotland.

Fig 42.   Map of Europe, by L Waddell 1929.

If there are known epigraphic links between Spain and Ireland, a means of transference needs to be sought. The obvious vehicle for this transference is the chronicle of Gaythelos and Scota, and all that needs to be done to facilitate this process is to understand that this chronicle is more history than fiction. But if one name for a nation could have been transferred in this manner, then why not two? Under the circumstances, the tradition of the name Scotia being derived from Queen Scota does not seem quite so fanciful.

If names can be transferred from one land to another, with the assistance of thousands of emigrants, then perhaps the same may be true for their customs and technology. If so, then further evidence for the *Scotichronicon* chronicle may be found in some of the traditions and archaeology of Ireland.

VI *Evidence in Ireland*

One of the enduring symbols of ancient Scotia (Ireland) is the frequent use of golden torqs, or necklaces, by the ancient Irish royalty. The Dublin Museum has a fine collection of these gold torqs, which all appear to have been made locally to a number of different designs. The majority of these torqs have been dated to the Iron Age, but since they were not discovered in clearly stratified locations, this date is based more upon guesswork than science. Similar torqs found on the British mainland, like the Snettisham hoard, are again said to date from the Iron Age. However, none of these have been discovered in reliably datable strata.

But where did the custom of wearing golden torqs ultimately come from? Examples of torqs appear in various locations all across northern Europe and similar designs in copper and bronze even turn up in the Baltic states. But the latter, especially, are quite obviously more recent examples of a much earlier tradition. To look for the origins of this type of artifact we really need to look south, towards the eastern Mediterranean; where the strongest candidate for the true origins of the golden torq is, of course, Egypt. It is in Egypt, and more specifically the Egypt of the Amarna era, that we find the earliest depictions of the golden torq.

Although none of these golden torqs appears to have survived in Egypt, the evidence for this custom can be seen in the tombs at Amarna. That we have this evidence at all is due, in no small part, to the less formal artistic style that pervaded the Amarna regime; and a good example of the new artistic style that had swept through Amarna during this period is to be found in the tomb of Aye-Gaythelos, which is the southernmost of the southern tombs at Amarna. Aye was in the process of excavating a grand tomb at Amarna that was to have had twenty-four pillars in its main hall, and an impressive array of wall paintings around the perimeter. Instead of the usual formalistic scenes of the deceased meeting the gods and being raised into the afterlife, we instead have a series of cartoon-like vignettes that portray the main events in the life of Aye-Gaythelos and the Amarna royalty.

One of these delightful depictions is of an award ceremony, where Aye and his first wife, Tiy, are shown being presented with a vast array of precious goods. The royal couple, Akhenaton and Nefertiti who are giving out these awards,

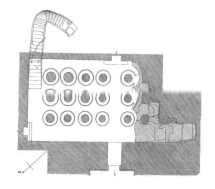

Fig 43. Plan of Aye's tomb at Amarna.

can be seen standing in the window of appearances along with three of their small daughters. As can be seen in the following diagram, all of the royal family are depicted as being naked, which may seem odd for an award ceremony, but this is quite in line with Akhenaton's naturalistic views – views that also influenced the narrative in the Book of Genesis and the similar naturism of Adam and Eve. If one can imagine the scandal that would erupt if the British Royal Family all appeared on the balcony of Buckingham Palace completely naked, then the full impact of Akhenaton's religious reforms can perhaps be envisaged. Although the God's Wives of Egypt were invariably clad in long, revealing gowns, for the royal family to be completely naked was still a quantum leap in social etiquette.

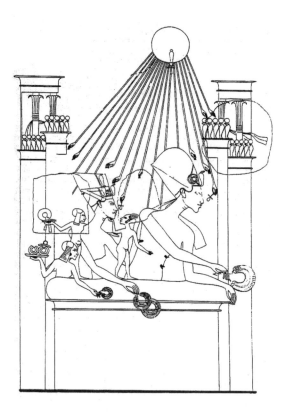

Fig 44. *Akhenaton, Nefertiti and family (all naked) giving golden necklaces to Aye-Gaythelos and his first wife Tiy.*

In this particular scene, the royal couple and their children are all depicted in the act of giving out golden rewards to both Aye-Gaythelos and Tiy, and most of these happen to be in the form of gold torqs. Aye-Gaythelos already has six torqs while his wife Tiy has five, and both are shown reaching out for yet more. This ceremony was obviously one of the highlights in Aye's career, for he is eventually shown with eighteen golden torqs and a host of other valuable goods. Since Aye could not possibly have worn quite so many necklaces, some of these torqs may have been used by Aye to reward a few of his favoured subordinates. Just as Akhenaton derived some of his status from the giving of these awards, so Aye in his turn would derive status if he could reward his favourite subordinates.

Whatever the final fate of these torqs, it is clear from this imagery that gold torqs were an important symbol of wealth and status in Amarna. So it is likely that Aye-Gaythelos would have recalled this event in later years, and perhaps recreated its potent symbolism during his own reign. This would not necessarily have been a ceremony in Amarna or Thebes, but a quieter event in the remoter periphery of the Mediterranean, at Brigantia in Iberia. No golden torqs have been discovered as yet in Catalonia, but since the prime location for the fortress-town of Brigantia has had no archaeological investigations, this is not so surprising. The descendants of Aye-Gaythelos moved on some generations later to Ireland, and it is here that many examples of this style of decoration are to be found. The cultural link here, between Amarna Egypt and ancient Ireland, is unmistakable.

There is, however, one small mystery that remains, and that is the source of the gold used in the Irish torqs. Unfortunately, there is no evidence whatsoever for Bronze Age gold mining in Ireland. Gold-bearing seams are to be found in a range of hills that stretch from the Sperrin mountains in the north of the country through to Croagh Patrick in the central west. If anything, the composition of the gold in the Irish torqs is similar to the composition of the Croagh Patrick gold, but the comparison is not definite by any means. But the quantity of gold discovered on this sacred mountain of Ireland is minuscule and this, coupled with the lack of evidence for mining and smelting, has led many to speculate that the gold for the torqs must have been imported.

However, if this was all foreign gold, from where would the early Irish royalty have imported it? And with what would they have bartered for it? Since early Ireland was not known for its great wealth, the number of gold artifacts that have been discovered is both surprising and perplexing. One simple solution that would solve all these problems would be the suggestion that the descendants of Aye-Gaythelos brought this gold with them.

Although money was not used in the Egyptian eighteenth dynasty, gold was known for its intrinsic value and it was being demanded from Egyptian pharaohs by all the minor kingdoms that surrounded Egypt. In essence, golden artifacts or gold bullion was being used as money, even if this was not minted currency. Aye-Gaythelos and his advisors would have known the value of gold and would surely have taken as much of it with them as they could. Gold is of high value and easily transportable in ships, as it can be used as ballast in the hull. Kilos of gold could have been smuggled out of Amarna as the regime of Akhenaton collapsed, and similarly Aye-Gaythelos could have diverted much of the remaining national assets into his safekeeping before he was exiled.

We know that something like this was indeed happening at Amarna because a number of caches of gold bullion have been discovered in the remains of the city. But this was not the normal gold assets of the treasury, this was gold trinkets that had been hurriedly melted down and poured into small hollows in the sand to form very rough bars of gold. The hurried nature of this process has led to speculation that this gold represented emergency assets for a group that was making a quick getaway. This was not a city in a slow decline because the center of power had shifted to Thebes; this was more like a population fleeing for their lives.

While the evidence for the use of gold bullion at Amarna is compelling, even likely, the evidence in a later era in Israel is unmistakable. One of the most interesting of the Dead Sea Scroll finds was the Copper Scroll, which was not discovered until 1952. The Copper Scroll details the locations of 64 caches of gold and other precious objects, amounting to a staggering 4,630 talents of gold alone. Since a talent is supposed to weigh in at about 30 kg, this would equate to about 140 tonnes of gold. This just has to be in error, and so we have the same situation that has been discussed at length in the book *Solomon,* regarding the treasures of King Solomon. In this previous discussion, having looked at the Egyptian accounts of their treasury, I finally decided that the true weight of a talent had to be about 200 g, which would result in a total inventory for the Copper Scroll of about one tonne. While this is still a massive amount of gold, it is at least within the realm of possibility.

Debate still rages over when this hoard was buried and whether it is a true account or not. Some commentators regard it as an extension of the tales of treasure being buried just before the destruction of the first Temple of Jerusalem. However, as John Allegro pointed out, the Copper Scroll is not a story at all; just a list of locations and amounts buried, which was recorded on an extremely expensive roll of pure copper. Having looked at all the arguments and counter-arguments, it would seem likely that this list was a real attempt to record the locations of treasures that were buried just prior to the destruction of Jerusalem by the Romans in AD 70. Indeed, these hidden caches of gold in Jerusalem may have been a part of what the Knights Templar were looking for during the twelfth century AD. Had there been a copy of the Copper Scroll, which had been kept and handed down within one illustrious family, a thorough search of the newly captured city of

Jerusalem may well have revealed a king's ransom in gold (plus some very interesting written accounts, histories and genealogies).

Whatever the case, all of this evidence points towards a long tradition of gold being buried or hidden away prior to an impending disaster, presumably to facilitate the founding of a new city and a new empire in the future. In other words, despite the fact that the concept of tradeable money had not been established during the Amarna era, gold *was* being thought of and used as an asset. It may seem an obvious point that does not need labouring, but if a royal family was exiled from Egypt during the fourteenth century BC they are likely to have taken substantial amounts of gold with them, to assist with the purchase of materials from local tribes and to reward their own commanders and leaders.

If Aye-Gaythelos and Ankhesenamun-Scota did take a huge cache of gold from the Thebes or Memphis treasuries before departing to Brigantia, it may well be that much of this still remained some generations later when the subsequent move was made to Ireland. That Aye-Gaythelos would have had time to arrange all of this is implicit in the chronicle, which says of their journey:

> And as Gaythelos wandered through many provinces, stopping at various places which he considered suitable (along the North African and Eastern Iberian coastline) ... he knew that the people he led, burdened as they were with women, children and <u>much luggage,</u> were distressed beyond endurance. [SC1]

It would seem that this was no emergency evacuation from Egypt. Like the Hyksos-Israelites some centuries before, Aye-Gaythelos left Egypt on his own terms and in his own time; which was sufficient to allow for the collection of all their belongings and probably much else besides. All of these assets would have ended up in Brigantia, and at a later date some of these assets would naturally have been transferred to the new colony that was being established in Ireland, and it was this treasure and bullion that probably formed the basis of the Irish gold hoards. Much of this Egyptian gold may have been transported as ingots, and reworked into new forms to suit new fashions and tastes, but it is entirely possible that some of the torqs in the Dublin Museum may even represent original Amarna workmanship – one of the very golden torqs depicted in the tomb of Aye, perhaps.

Here we have a very plausible answer to a very intransigent problem. Ireland has produced a large number of finds of professionally made and intricately worked gold, and yet there is no evidence of gold mining or smelting in Ireland at this time. Conversely, we have a long tradition of gold being hoarded and used as emergency capital, or finance, during turbulent eras in Egypto-Israelite history. Similarly, we also have a persistent tradition that some of the ancient Egyptian royalty landed in Ireland and set up a colony there. The archaeological and literary evidence of Ireland seems to dovetail rather well, if only *Scotichronicon* is taken to be more history than mythology.

Tara prince

The same argument can also be made for the discovery of faience beads in a burial at Tara, north of Dublin. In the spring of 1955, a team of archaeologists led by Prof Sean O'Riordain discovered a burial at the ancient royal burial site at Tara. One of the skeletons uncovered in the upper levels of this cairn was rather interesting, as a Bronze Age dagger and pin were discovered in the grave and the skeleton of this young man still wore the remains of a bead necklace around its neck. The really interesting thing about this necklace was that it comprised alternate amber, jet, bronze and long, segmented faience beads. So unusual was this find that the skeleton became known as the Prince of Tara. [2]

Faience is not a natural mineral; instead, it is a man-made silicate material that is made in a similar fashion to glass manufacture, with a blue-green copper glaze on the surface of the bead. (In fact, the Tara beads are more glass than glazed.) Quite simply, this type of material had not been manufactured in Ireland in the Bronze Age, and the most likely source for these beads is Egypt or perhaps Minoan Crete. Dr J Stone, who led the examination of the faience beads, thought that the closest match to these beads was from finds that had been made in Abydos, Egypt and Tell Duweir in Israel. [3] Certainly, the considered opinion was that these beads were not of local manufacture and must have been imported. While the favoured argument was that these beads must have arrived in Ireland through a series of random trading links that stretched all the way across Europe, it is also possible that they arrived in the same flotilla that brought the descendants of Aye-Gaythelos and Scota to the shores of southern Ireland. These links with the Aye-Gaythelos exodus are further strengthened by some of the other artifacts that were discovered. Prof O'Riordain says of these:

> The occurrence of segmented bone objects similar to those in Iberia might be taken as indicating the route along which these trinkets came... [4]

And this was indeed the most probable route along which these faience beads travelled, because they were brought to Ireland by the descendants of Aye-Gaythelos, and the intermediate stop-off point for these exiles was on the river Ebro in Iberia. That these beads were considered to be highly valuable is perhaps confirmed by there only being four such beads on this necklace. Unlike Egyptian necklaces, which might have hundreds of faience beads on them, the Tara Prince could only afford four, and this is exactly what we might expect from the arrival of a flotilla that contained a limited amount of treasures.

Interestingly, from the burial artifacts that were discovered in this grave, the favoured date for this burial is the late fourteenth century BC; while the date of the Aye-Gaythelos exodus to Spain would also have been the late fourteenth century BC. Despite the exodus from Spain to Ireland occurring some generations after this period, the treasures that were carried onwards towards Ireland would have been the same late fourteenth century artifacts that had been taken from Egypt, and so the burial of the Tara Prince (if this was the necklace's true provenance) would have appeared to have been late fourteenth century BC even if it actually took place several centuries years later.

Incidentally, the passage grave that lay underneath this burial was excavated a year later, in 1956, and this turned out to contain a great hoard of some 250 assorted burials and cremations that had been interred there over a great span of time ranging from the Neolithic (c. 4000 - 2500 BC) to the early Bronze Age (c. 2500 - 1800 BC). Clearly, the Tara mound was a sacred site that contained the bones of many an early Irish leader or king, and it was no doubt for this reason that the Tara Prince was buried within the earth mound that covered this passage grave.

The subsequent history of this necklace is also interesting. During a visit to the Dublin Museum, which is a fine classical edifice modelled on the British Museum in London, I could not find this necklace anywhere. I was told that it was in storage, and I would need to contact the keeper of antiquities by post. Having done so, I was then told that no such necklace had ever been discovered in Ireland, let alone stored in the museum itself. After much searching on the internet, I eventually discovered a reference to the original excavations and asked again for a photo of the necklace; to which the reply was:

> Although this necklace was excavated in the 1950s, it has only recently come into our possession and has not, as yet, been photographed. [5]

Here we have one of the most interesting finds in Irish archaeology, and it appears to have been sidelined and ignored. This necklace is a dateable artifact that was important enough for the corpse to have become known as the Tara Prince, and it is one of only two such artifacts that demonstrate that Ireland had trading links of some nature with the eastern Mediterranean during the Bronze Age. The other find of faience beads was at the Dundrum Sandhills, Co Down. Despite the import of the find at Tara, it takes the Dublin Museum fifty years to get a photograph of these beads! As the University of Dublin admits, in its newsletter of March 2006:

> The findings ranging from about 3500 BC were catalogued and stored at University College Dublin's School of Archaeology. And there they have rested, undisturbed for nearly 50 years, until Dr Muiris O'Sullivan and publisher Nick Maxwell took the initiative to share this treasure trove from the oldest visible monument on the Hill of Tara. [6]

Luckily, while the reports on the Tara excavation were dragging their collective heels, there was an excavation of a similar necklace in 1889 in North Molton, Exeter. This was a chance discovery of a Bronze Age tomb of a similar age to the Tara Prince. Once more, the burial goods associated with this tomb included a fine necklace containing lignite and faience beads, which were obviously not of local origin. One necklace might indeed be the result of fluke trading and bartering across the whole of Europe over many generations, with the necklace finally ending up in Tara, north of Dublin. However, two or three necklaces from the same era places a completely different perspective on these discoveries. That three necklaces have been discovered means that it likely that many more await discovery, and this proliferation of artifacts either means that there were good trading contacts between greater Britain and the eastern Mediterranean, or that an expedition from the east arrived in northwestern Europe with a hoard of jewellery on board.

The first option would mean that the Minoans, the Bronze Age's primary trading nation, were sailing regularly to Britain with supplies of gold and jewellery from the eastern Mediterranean; and possibly returning with copper mined at the huge Bronze Age copper mines near Llandudno, North Wales. While this would make some sense, there is no direct evidence for constant trade links with the eastern Mediterranean in this early era. Had this trade been this regular, with ships arriving every year perhaps, one would have thought that there would have been an abundance of Minoan, Mycenaean or Egyptian goods to be found in Britain. But there is not; there are odd finds from Egypt and Mycenae here and there, but there is no evidence of the abundance of goods and the kind of regular trade that was obviously present during the Roman era, for instance.

The first option also does not account for the surprising amount of trade that was conducted with Ireland, which appears to have received large amounts of gold (perhaps pre-manufactured torqs) and now also faience beads from the eastern Mediterranean. While North Wales had valuable copper to trade with any possible Minoan explorers, Ireland has always been short of valuable raw materials with which they could have traded for high-value Egyptian goods. So how, then, did Ireland receive all these luxury goods?

The alternative explanation is, of course, that all of these valuable goods arrived with Aye-Gaythelos and Scota – and so this was a limited, one-off arrival of gold and jewellery that had to last for many generations. Subsequent trading allowed some of this Egyptian jewellery to slip into England, but this would have been trading from an otherwise impoverished Ireland to wealthier England, and not *vice versa*.

Incidentally, an obvious Egyptian translation for the royal burial site at Tara would be Ta Ra [hieroglyphs] meaning 'Land of Ra'. And while we are looking at epigraphic links with Egypt, it should also be noted that the primary goddess for Tara – who may also have been the wife of King Eremon, one of the first Milesian kings of Ireland – was called Tia or Tiye. Strange as it may seem, this Celtic name just happens to be the same as the names for the wife, sister and the mother of Aye [Gaythelos]. [7] The second component to this title (a name that is sometimes said to be the sister of Tiye) was Tephi, and this may have been derived from *tepia* [hieroglyphs] meaning 'noble ancestor'. Thus, the full title for Tiye Tephi may well refer to 'Our Noble Ancestor Tiye'.

It is said that Queen Tiye Tephi came from the east, across the seas, which (as a descendant of Tiye of Egypt) she would indeed have done. It is from this Celtic Queen Tiye that the alternative Gaelic name for Tara, that of Tea-mair, was derived. But since Tiye came from across the seas, this may well have been derived from Tiye-Mer [hieroglyphs] meaning 'Tiye of the Sea'. This is a similar title to the one given to Mary [Magdalene] who was sometimes known as Marie Stella (the Mary Celeste), or the Sea Star.

Gold cape

Another striking similarity between Egyptian and Celtic jewellery is the golden shoulder collar or cape. In 1833, workmen digging for stone in Mold, north Wales, uncovered an early Bronze Age grave containing a number of ornaments and artifacts. Among these was a crumpled sheet of gold which, when it was finally unfolded and restored, turned out to be a golden cape that covered the entire neck and shoulders. Arguments have raged as to how the cape should be worn, because it would radically restrict any arm movement, but the obvious solution is that the dead need no arm movement. In other words, the cape was designed and fabricated as a funerary artifact, to bejewel and glorify the dearly departed.

This type of funerary decoration is also to be found in Egypt. More specifically, a very good example of this type of cape can be found among the few remains of Kiyah's burial goods. As has been suggested before, Kiyah and Akhenaton, the two naked lovebirds from the Book of Genesis, eloped to Avaris just prior to the fall of Amarna. This left unused a large number of grave goods, which had been destined for the royal couple's tomb; and so they were reworked and reused in other burials.

Queen Kiyah's Canopic jars, which would have held her internal organs after her death, had her name expunged from them and this left just her husband's name, Akhenaton, on them; which has caused an amount of confusion. They were then deposited – along with the mummy of an unknown male pharaoh inside Kiyah's modified and reused coffin – in tomb KV55, and this has led some to claim that this burial was for Akhenaton himself. Unfortunately, although recent dental analysis has indicated a slightly older corpse than was previously thought, the general opinion is that this mummy is still too young to be that of Akhenaton, and so the most likely candidate has to be Smenkhkare.

Fig 45. Statuette of Kiyah, with golden shoulder cape.

Whoever this burial was eventually intended for, Kiyah's reused Canopic jars portray Akhenaton's favourite queen as being dressed for her future burial in a (golden) single-piece cape that covered the entire shoulder and upper torso. While some of these capes were made from a multi-coloured array of small beads, others were made of solid gold; as the capes worn by Tutankhamen's *ushabti* funerary figurines clearly demonstrate.

It has to be said that the similarity between this distinctive type of funerary decoration from Amarna and the Bronze Age example from north Wales is remarkable. (See the colour section for an image of the Mold cape.) Once again, this similarity demonstrates that there must have been close cultural or trading links between greater Britain and Egypt during the Amarna era – a link that is best explained by the *Scotichronicon* account.

Red hand

Another interesting symbol, which later became a prime emblem of Northern Ireland, is the red hand. Now this is a peculiar symbol that has only the most tenuous of myths associated with it. As Andy Power relates in his book *Ireland, Land of the Pharaohs*, the myths describe a race in which the first to reach land would win the throne of Ulster. A certain prince called O'Neil was losing the race but cut off his hand and threw it to the shore, ensuring that his hand touched land first.

This is supposed to explain the adoption of the red hand – and the drops of blood that are said to be dripping from its wrist – as an emblem of Ulster. But this kind of supernatural mythology is rarely even close to the truth and the true reasoning is likely to be more complex and have a much deeper symbology. Bearing in mind the strong possibility that the first Irish tribes may been the descendants of Aye-Gaythelos and Ankhesenamun-Scota, and that the biblical accounts were descended from the history of the Amarna regime, the true reason for the redness of this hand may lie in the Egypto-biblical accounts.

As has been pointed out in my previous works, there is a thread of redness that runs through the biblical narrative and many of the patriarchs and kings are said to be strangely red; including Adam, Esau and King Solomon. This red thread is quite literally expressed at the birth of Pharez and Zarah in the Book of Genesis:

> And it came to pass, when she gave birth, that the one (child) put out his hand: and the midwife took and bound upon his hand a scarlet thread, saying, This came out first. [B8]

Fig 46. *Red hands (each with three drops of blood) on a bank in Bangor, N Ireland.*

This strange propensity for redness is likely to be an oblique reference to the Hyksos-Israelite royalty, and the Red Crown of Lower Egypt. In a similar fashion, this same redness may well explain why the hand of Ulster is red.

This is indeed an alternative explanation that is sometimes given for the adoption of the red hand in Ulster symbolism. The mythology in these alternative accounts indicates that Jacob's pillar (the Stone of Destiny) was taken into safekeeping by Jeremiah and that it somehow ended up in Ireland. This is how, so it is said, the Star of David ended up on the flag of Ulster. (I relate much of the history of Jeremiah in the book *Solomon*.) Another strand of the same mythology says that Pharaz and <u>Zarah</u> were exiled to Spain and founded the city of <u>Zaragoza</u>, and at a later date their ancestors sailed to Ireland. Since Zaragoza lies on the river Ebro in Catalonia, this is a very similar story to the *Scotichronicon* account, and the symmetry between these two mythologies again links biblical and Egyptian history.

If the red hand of Ulster is somehow connected with Egypto-Hebrew culture and mythology, then the disembodied hand may be better explained as a component of the great Osirian myth. During a battle with his brother Seth, Osiris was killed and cut up into pieces, which were scattered around Egypt. Isis, Osiris' sister-wife, was said to have searched for these body parts and reassembled the late Osiris. However, the tradition of a dismembered Osiris and the various appendages being linked to the temples of Egypt was still a strong part of this mythology. In other words, the presence of a dismembered holy relic does have a satisfactory explanation in Egyptian mythology. As with the later Catholic churches, no cathedral of the gods was complete without a holy relic, which was often a body part of some saint or disciple. Likewise, no self-respecting Egyptian temple would be complete without a piece of Osiris, and perhaps the exiled Brigantians claimed to have one of his hands. This link with Osiris may not sit very well with the theology of Akhenaton, but in a similar fashion the story of Moses and Aaron's [TuthMoses and Akhenaton's] exodus from Egypt is littered with complaints about the people reverting to alternative belief systems.

Further evidence that this red hand may be a component of the Osirian mythology may be seen in the three drops of 'blood' that sometimes issue from the wrist of this hand. The original symbol for Osiris in Egypt was the piece of flesh glyph ⟩ , which spelt out the name Asar ⟨glyphs⟩ , or Osiris. So what we may be seeing here, on the red hand of Ulster, is a direct link to Osiris, and in the Ulster version his name was spelt as ⟩⟩⟩ . The next chapter deals with this question in greater detail, and shows that this Osirian symbolism may well have travelled from Iberia to Ireland with the Pictish immigration.

Fig 47. Star of David on the flag of Ulster.

The other direct link between the red hand of Ulster and this same royal Egyptian couple is to be seen in the symbolism of the red hand itself. If some of these Irish traditions were derived from Aye-Gaythelos and Scota, then one might expect to see some direct similarities between the Amarna royalty and the resulting society in Brigantia (Iberia) or Scotia (Ireland). Indeed, if Gaythelos were really Aye, then we might expect that this similarity would involve Aye himself. Strangely enough, one of the similarities we do see is the startling fact that Aye was the proud possessor of a pair of red leather gloves. They were presented to Aye-Gaythelos at the same award ceremony that has just been discussed; but these particular gloves were obviously something rather special. As Professor Davies says:

> At any rate, the picture would lead us to think that Aye was intensely proud of this rare possession (the gloves). As soon as he is outside the gates of the palace he puts them on and exhibits them to his friends ... the bystanders press round to see and stroke them, lift up their arms in wild astonishment, and are ready to fall down and do homage to him and them (the gloves) indiscriminately. (Author's brackets.) [9]

Davies does not give the colour of these gloves in his report, but Professor Desroches-Noblecourt specifically states that they were coloured red on the tomb's wall-paintings. [10] Clearly, the special depiction and recording of this event demonstrates that this was not any old pair of red gloves. Aye-Gaythelos had just been given 18 gold *shebu* necklaces (torqs), 12 gold armlets, 11 semiprecious bead necklaces, 4 gold cups, 5 signet rings, 2 metal vases – indeed, everything bar a partridge in a pear tree. So great was his booty that the bottom of this particular tableau shows an excited courtier exclaiming, in the fashion of a modern cartoon, "Aye ... along with Tiy. They have been made people of gold!" Another bystander shouts, "Pharaoh has given Aye and Tiy millions of loads of gold and all manner of riches!" Indeed he had, but for some reason the item that most pleased Aye, in amongst all this bounteous treasure, was his pair of red gloves.

Fig 48. Aye-Gaythelos showing off his red gloves.

Aye's excited reaction to the presentation of these gloves is rather odd, for it is not as if gloves were an unknown commodity in Egypt; they were used by the royalty for horse-riding, and Tutankhamen owned several pairs. While it is true that Tutankhamen's tomb postdates Aye's Amarna tomb by a few years, are we to believe that these were the first pair of gloves that Egypt had ever seen? No, there must have been something especially symbolic about these gloves, and one is reminded of the similar fuss made about Moses' possible use of 'gloves':

> And god said unto him, Put now thy hand into thy bosom. And he put his hand into his bosom: and when he took it out, behold, his hand was leprous, as white as snow. And god said, Put thy hand into thy bosom again. And he put his hand into his bosom again; and when he took it out of his bosom, behold, it was turned back like his other flesh. [B12]

This strange display was intended as a symbol that would somehow impress the assembled priests of [Upper] Egypt, and place them in such awe of Moses' powers that the pharaoh would let the Hyksos-Israelites leave Egypt [on their own terms]. It is difficult to derive any real logic from this event, but the respective colours being used in these two 'glove' scenarios, that of red and white, are representative of the national colours of the Two Lands of Egypt. In which case, these 'gloves' may have been symbolic of the land and the nation of Egypt. In other words, they may have been similar, perhaps, to a modern-day high official being given the keys to a city. We know that Aye-Gaythelos was made vizier, or prime minister of Egypt, so were these gloves symbolic of his office in any way? Alternatively, since these gloves were often used for horse riding and Aye was also made Commander of the Horse, perhaps these gloves symbolised his position as supreme army commander.

One other possibility, is that the glove symbology was linked in some manner to the hands of the Aton. The Aton Sun-disk was always portrayed as having rays that ended in small hands, which caressed the royal couple or offered them the *ankh*, the symbol of life. It is entirely possible that this imagery turned the humble hand into a potent symbol of god, and the power of the gods to protect and give life. It may have been through this route that the symbol of a governor or army commander became linked to a glove. The red colour used for these gloves no doubt reflected the redness that was always associated with the Lower Egyptian royalty.

Whatever these red gloves really symbolised, the fact of the matter is that a simple red glove could and did have a significant symbolic value within Egyptian culture, and especially within Amarna culture. Thus, it is likely that the descendants of Aye-Gaythelos would have likewise honoured this same symbology and made it an important component within their culture. This is exactly what we see in Ulster, where the red hand or glove and the Judaic Star of David have become fundamental symbols of the province and its people. Thus, both the golden torq and the red hand symbology appear to have made their way from Amarna to Ireland, a fact that strongly supports the Gaythelos and Scota story.

Round-tower

As we saw in an earlier chapter, one of the prime architectural forms to be seen in the Balearic Islands is the truncated round-tower. It is likely that these Bronze Age towers were based upon earlier Minoan and Egyptian designs and so the cult of the round-tower could well have been brought to the Balearic Islands during the Aye-Gaythelos and Scota exodus. The Minoans were still the primary source of sea trading and ship design during this era, so it is likely that Aye-Gaythelos would have needed their expertise to organise and execute his exodus plans. It is also known that there were strong Minoan elements within the early Avaris and later Amarna eras of Egyptian history, and no doubt some of their theology and traditions could have been transported upon this same exodus. In addition, the Minoan cult of the round-tower could well have been a local version of the much earlier Benben tower veneration at Heliopolis, and so the round-tower monument would have already been familiar to most Egyptians.

It is not known exactly when the descendants of Aye-Gaythelos made their subsequent jump from Spain to Ireland as the various chronicles give differing accounts, but at some point after the twelfth century BC a strategic move to Ireland was made. Along with the golden torqs, faience beads, bone artifacts and the red hand, any number of other traditions may well have been transported to Ireland, and one of these may have been the cult of the round-tower. Ireland has about seventy-three round-towers still standing, which were all associated with monastic centers. They are variously described as being bell-towers, defensive positions or safe locations for valuables; however, these orthodox arguments have already been demolished in the book *Jesus*.

The general layout of these towers is for a tubular construction in stone and lime mortar, with walls that are battered (inclined and tapering) and a conical top. The upper windows, if they are present, are aligned with the cardinal points and not with topographical features or the adjoining monastery. One interesting aspect is that the tower's entrance doors are all situated above ground level, and wooden ladders were required to reach this entrance. It is said that this was for security, but in the majority of cases the first room in the tower was not tall enough to receive the ladder inside it. Thus, if a retreat to the 'safety' of the tower had ever been made, with enemies in hot pursuit, the ladder could not be drawn up into the tower. However, leaving your ladder up against the door rather defeats the strategic advantage of having an above-ground-level entrance. As has already been demonstrated, these towers were far from being places of refuge.

If these round-towers were not places of refuge, and if the windows at the top were often poorly suited to the ringing of bells,* then what was their function? Well, since they were all situated within monastic centers, they are likely to have had a religious function. Since the monastic traditions of Ireland are reputed to have been derived from Egyptian monastic customs, it is likely that the tradition of the round-tower also came from Egypt, either directly or through Iberia. In which case, these Irish round-towers would originally have been based upon the Benben tower at Heliopolis, and would have represented phallic symbols. The phallic Benben tower of Heliopolis was a Lower Egyptian complement to the feminine uterine temples of Upper Egypt. Likewise, the monastic towers of Ireland complemented the feminine uterine henges of Ireland, like Newgrange and Knowth; the only problem with this argument being the differing eras for these structures. The henges of Ireland are said to be prehistoric, whereas the round-towers only date from the 6th century AD at the earliest.

One of the difficulties in dating these ancient sites is the long periods of time during which they were in use and during which time they may have been significantly modified. An obvious example of this possible modification lies in the significant difference between the megalithic circles and kerb stones at Newgrange, Knowth and Dowth, and the much smaller boulders and grass-turves that were used to construct the mounds themselves. Bearing in mind the open designs of Stonehenge and Avebury in England, it is not unreasonable to suppose that there were two building

---

* The Rattoo round tower in the colour section is a later example of these Irish designs, which dates from about the twelfth century AD. This round-tower has four windows at the top which face the cardinal points, as do many of these towers, a fact which may suggest that they were designed as bell-towers. However, other round-towers either have much smaller windows or none at all – as at Clonmacnoise, Co Offaly and Donaghmore, Co Meath – and so the generic function of these round-towers cannot be for bell-ringing. In actual fact, the tower is a representation of a phallus and originally this would have been the phallus of the Egyptian god Atum; although the rituals and the god being venerated may have changed over the centuries.

phases involved in the Irish henges. The earlier henge design may have resulted in an open area surrounded by megaliths, exactly as at Stonehenge and Avebury, and only in a much later era did the population decide to cover over this exposed area to properly imitate a uterine passageway. However, this second phase employed just small stones, earth and grass-turves; a technique which is significantly different to the earlier megalithic building phase.

Newgrange, Dowth and Knowth are said to be some 5,000 years old. However, since the carbon-dating for this assertion was conducted at a very early point in the development of this technique, these dates must be treated with caution, as the wide variation in the carbon dates for the Ferriby boats has clearly demonstrated. Even the modern dates for the Ferriby boats, using the latest carbon-dating techniques, were far earlier than the site archaeologists had predicted. However, the megalithic rings at Newgrange are certainly from the Stone Age and so I am fairly certain that none of the designs, technology and decoration used in the megalithic portions of the various henges in the Newgrange area had anything to do with an Egyptian influence. However, the mound and passageway was possibly a later construction, and whether this may have included some influence from the descendants of Aye-Gaythelos and Scota is open to speculation.

The next question is: could there possibly be any connection between the round-towers of Ireland and the truncated round-towers of Mallorca and Minorca or, indeed, the original towers at Knossos and Heliopolis? Although all the examples of round-towers in the Balearic Islands were most certainly truncated – and thus probably based upon the Minoan concept of a truncated tower and a sacred tree – it is said that some of the similar towers on Sardinia did once have conical tops, as do the Irish towers, and may have been more influenced by the design of the Egyptian Benben tower. But there is still a large span of time between these Bronze Age Sardinian towers and the much later towers in Ireland, which date from the sixth century AD. So were there any earlier Irish round-towers that have not survived into the modern era?

Evidence for the possibility of earlier round-tower designs lies in the magnificent Iron Age 'fortresses' that appear in the west of Ireland. Remaining forts include Grianan near Aileach, Co Donegal; Staigue near Catherdaniel, Co Kerry; and Cahergall near Cahirsiveen, Co Kerry. These 'fortresses' are essentially large, squat, truncated round-towers, and they appear to display all the features that were later absorbed into Irish round-tower construction. They are circular, with battered walls and a lintelled doorway. The only primary difference, one that may have limited these forts' height, is that they were made from drystone walling.

Fig 49.   The Cahergall, Grianan and Staigue amphitheaters.

However, as is usual with my lateral investigations into history, we have to question the established explanations given for these monuments. The traditional perception is that these impressive constructions were forts, and the literature gives graphic illustrations of these massive forts containing a couple of mud huts: an image indicating that a fearful estate-owner had resorted to massive fortifications to protect his meagre possessions. On the surface this might seem like a reasonable view, but does it stand up to closer scrutiny?

While these monuments are large, they are certainly not big enough to contain a village. Conversely, these 'forts' appear to be much too large for a solitary fortified farmstead – these were definitely community construction projects that would have required a great deal of labour to build. What they look like is a castle-keep, or the Motte from a Norman Motte and Bailey village fortification; the only trouble with this explanation being that we have a Motte and no Bailey: the castle-keep with no castle. So would a community build a keep for its valuables, and leave everything else – including the village – unprotected?

There is another problem with the castle-keep theory, and that is the internal design of the 'fort'. Firstly, there is no evidence of hinge-points for a door at the entrance. Now the Gallarus Oratory, which will be mentioned later, had door hinges, so why not these 'forts'? Just how was the entrance closed? More alarmingly, there are a large number of stairways up and down the inner wall of the fortification (eighteen at Cahergall and twenty at Staigue). But this is far too many to defend the fort, as any enemy who reached the top of the wall would have a very convenient choice of descent routes. A much more secure arrangement would be to have just three narrow stairways down from the wall, which could be defended with the minimum number of soldiers.

So, if the fort explanation looks somewhat dubious, then what were these huge great monuments built for? Well, the first time I stepped into one, I was immediately taken back to Rome and my recent tour of the Colosseum. All around the circumference of these 'forts' are staggered stairways leading to terrace after terrace, which are built into the sides of the walls. This terracing has no logical function, for a fort, but make every sense in terms of a stadium. Now while this terracing is rather precipitous, and would give a modern Health and Safety Officer palpitations, there would have been no such qualms a few thousand years ago. Each and every terrace could have provided seating for scores of people, and the entire stadium could have seated several hundred people. This, I believe, was the true function of these monuments; and yet this simple observation changes our entire perception of these Irish communities. Out goes the image of a fearful, huddled population living behind vast fortifications due to rampant lawlessness throughout the land, and in comes the view of a confident and prosperous society that was able to entertain hundreds of people in some kind of social celebration. This was the true function of these monuments and, after much research, I was at last able to find an author who might agree with this proposition. Jack Roberts, an author of Celtic mythology, says of these monuments:

> This type of enclosure is often misnamed a 'ring fort', but they were not defensive structures, their purpose being as places of assembly where people met for civil and religious purpose and to enact important ceremonies. [13]

Precisely. But what kind of shows would have been staged in these stadiums? Did the local population hope to see a Greek tragedy, or a religious rite? The answer to this lies at the Cahergall stadium, because upon entering its enclosure I received another shock. Inside this monument was not a large open-plan space resembling a circus arena, as I had expected; instead, there was a large truncated round-tower. Momentarily this was a bit of a puzzle, for why should the standard Mallorcan or Minorcan round-tower have been placed inside a large stadium?

The answer to this was more than obvious on the respective days that I visited these monuments. In Mallorca and Minorca I was able to sit below the round-tower and consume a sandwich and a small beer while idly contemplating the size and form of the sacred tree that would have once erupted from the mouth of the tower. A priest, in ancient times, could easily have stood tens of meters away from me and explained in measured tones the function of his ritual. In Ireland I was only just able to stand up and could not even hear my own voice, let alone that of a distant priest. The wind howled, the rain skidded horizontally across the sodden turves, the windchill made it feel like -10 °C, and it was all I could do to keep the camera steady. (I had to wait three hours for a break in the weather to take proper photos.) However, inside the stadium there was a small sanctuary of calm and normality. The air was relatively still and quiet, the temperature was almost tropical in comparison, and a voice echoed from wall to wall almost as well as in a Roman amphitheater.

Here then is the reason for the ancient traditions being modified and for the construction of great circular stadiums. In the Balearic Islands, the only problem was watering the sacred tree during the hot and dry summers. On the western fringes of Ireland, no self-respecting tree dares put a leaf above ground, and the foolhardy specimens that try are stunted, gnarled and blown into horizontal hedges. The cult of the sacred tree could not exist on the west coast of Ireland without some degree of protection and climate-control. In addition, the stadium allows for a large number of people to witness these sacred rituals in relative comfort. So, the Cahergall fort is actually the Cahergall stadium.

There is one final problem, and that is even when including these stadiums into the equation, there still remains a large expanse of time between the construction of the round-towers in the Balearic Islands and the Iron Age era of the Irish Grianan and Cahergall amphitheaters. However, there are so many similarities between these monuments, including their construction techniques, that it is likely that there is a common heritage here. The round-towers in Ireland, Mallorca and Minorca all sport a truncated, circular layout; they all have battered walls and a lintelled doorway; they are all drystone constructions, and the Mallorcan and Minorcan towers even show evidence of the raised doorway design which is such a common feature of the later Irish round-towers. In the Balearic design, the raised doorway was sometimes accessed by an inclined ramp, but was often suspended in midair – just as we see with the Irish round-towers and the Egyptian pyramids.

Can this difference in dating between the Balearic and Irish round-towers be overcome in any way? Well, as ever with these monuments, stone cannot be dated and so the age of these constructions can only be inferred by other artifacts on the site. But if the site has no occupation stratification, which is a common feature of religious rather than domestic monuments, the dating of the site becomes more problematic. Thus Brian Lalor, an author on the history of Irish round-towers, describes the Grianan amphitheater as being 'variously dated'. In other words, nobody can give a precise date for these monuments and the dates we are presented with are based upon pure guesswork. The earliest suggested date I have seen in a historical text is 500 BC; however, the tourist guide to Ireland says that these stadiums date from 1400 BC. Indeed, the fact that these stadiums have so little in the way of stratification and other artifacts with which to date them, again strongly suggests that these constructions were religious amphitheaters and not secular forts.

Given the uncertainty within the *Scotichronicon* chronicle regarding the date of the first exodus to Ireland, and the uncertainly regarding the construction date of these amphitheaters, I think there is enough slack within these uncertainties to allow them to meet at some point in the distant past. In which case, the present round-towers of Ireland may well have been influenced by the design of the Grianan, Cahergall and Staigue stadiums and their internal round-towers – with this religious symbolism being transported across the Mediterranean by the descendants of the various Hyksos-Israelite refugees, following their unfortunate but numerous forced evacuations from Egypt. See Appendix 1 for a flow-chart of these various migrations.

Navetas

The final piece of synergy between Ireland and the Balearic Islands is perhaps the most convincing of all, and it virtually proves beyond doubt that there were direct cultural links between the communities on these distant islands. As has already been mentioned, Minorca is also home to a Bronze Age monument known locally as a *naveta*. These large stone monuments resemble an upturned boat that has been cut in half, with a door placed in the opened section of the 'boat'. They appear to be tombs, but have been more accurately identified as ossuaries; or places where bodies are allowed to rot away and where the remaining bare bones can be stored (in these *navetas*, the bones may have been stored in the 'loft' or upper chamber). These *navetas* are thought to date from the fourteenth century BC, the same date as the *talayots*, and their shape indicates that the builders of these monuments were seafarers who came to the Balearics during the Bronze Age. Since the doorway of the Tudons Naveta measures exactly 52 cm across, and since this length equates to exactly one Thoth cubit (one Egyptian Royal cubit), it is highly likely that these seafarers had strong links with Egypt, as I have suspected.*

Further links to Egypt were found at the *talayotic* site of Torralba d'en Salord. There were several finds made at this site, which included some Amarna blue glassware, several scarabs and a small statue of Imhotep. The statue is seated and on its lap is a scroll that reads 'Imhotep, son of Ra-Ptah'. This type of statue is common in Egypt during the sixth century BC, which is much later than the construction of the site at Torralba, but it does indicate that this sacred precinct may still have been in use at this time and that its custodians or visitors had strong links to Egypt. Thus, the possibility exists that these people originally came from Egypt; but where may they have travelled to in future generations? Well, since these boat-shaped *naveta* monuments are more unique than the ubiquitous *talayots* or *nuraghi*, it is entirely possible that they can be used as a geographical marker, through which the migrations of this particular nation or culture can be traced. So are there any other locations in which these *navetas* and *talayots* can be found together? Surprisingly, there is.

I stumbled upon the Irish versions of a *naveta* while thumbing through a book on Irish archaeology in the Tralee library; a book that I very

---

* There is also a strong possibility of a 76 cm cubit being used in the *naveta* and *taule* monuments of Minorca, in addition to the Thoth cubit. These measurements are best explained by a 76 cm cubit that is divided by 5.5 smaller units measuring 13.8 cm each. The multiple of 5.5 may seem unlikely, but the Imperial rod was likewise composed of 5.5 yards. See the book *Thoth* for further details.

nearly dropped in surprise. For there, on the pages in front of me, were a pair of Minorcan *navetas* that were situated in southwest Ireland. It was a site that I had to see as soon as possible. The journey out to the end of the Dingle peninsular was made with great anticipation, and I was not to be disappointed. There, in a small enclosure, was the Gallarus Oratory, a perfect copy of a Minorcan *naveta* (see the colour section for a comparison).

The literature indicates that this structure is actually a boat-shaped Christian church, which dates from the sixth century AD. However, once more we find that there is nothing within this structure that can be dated, and so this presumed Christian identity and sixth century date is simply based upon a Romanesque arch to the rear window. However, even this observation creates its own chronological problems because the Roman arch did not arrive in Ireland until the twelfth century AD, and yet the

Fig 50. The statue of Imhotep discovered on Minorca.

construction techniques used on the Gallarus Oratory show it to be much older than this. The answer to these inconsistencies, in my estimation, is that this window has been re-carved into a Roman arch in a later era: for the keystones that form the arch are dangerously thin and are unlikely to have been designed in this fashion; while the arch itself displays evidence of post-installation cutting. In fact, the rear window may have originally mimicked the inverted boat-shape of the building itself.

Having taken the rear window out of the equation, the date and function of this structure becomes entirely fluid. It could be Iron Age, it could be Bronze Age. It could be a church, it could be a tomb or an ossuary. Indeed, since the *naveta* ossuaries on Minorca are said to date from 1400 BC, it is entirely reasonable to suppose that the identical Irish *navetas* date from the same kind of era. Thus the Gallarus Oratory would actually be some 2,000 years older than is currently thought.

While it is true that the Gallarus Oratory looks better constructed and substantially younger than the Minorcan equivalents, that may simply be due to the fact that the Dingle peninsular is made from a tough gritstone that has been naturally fractured. This means that very hard but roughly flat and angular stones were available to the architects in the west of Ireland, for very little cost in labour. In contrast, the Minorcan *navetas* are made of limestone, a rock which has to be labouriously shaped by hand and yet weathers easily. In addition, the Minorcan masons have used surface limestone instead of deep-quarry limestone, and so the blocks they selected had already been naturally weathered over the preceding millennia – just as the limestone pavements of Yorkshire are similarly weathered today. Thus, although they may superficially look to be of differing ages, the Irish and Minorcan *navetas* may share a common construction era and thus a common heritage. So, the Gallarus Oratory was probably designed as the Gallarus Ossuary, a boat-shaped chamber to contain the bones of the dead.

Once again we see a dramatic similarity between the cultures of the Balearic Islands and Ireland, and once again we need to find a cultural conduit that would allow for this fusion in beliefs, technology and architecture between these two widely separated islands. Once again we already have literary evidence for that conduit, provided for us by the accounts of the Irish and Scottish chronicles. But these chronicles attach certain dates to these migrations between Egypt, the Balearic Islands, and Ireland. Thus we can say with some confidence that the Balearic *navetas* were actually constructed in about 1300 BC, while the later migration to Ireland occurred a few generations later (say within two hundred years), and so the Irish *navetas* (and amphitheaters) would have been constructed in about 1150 BC.

The design of these *navetas* may also give us some further information about the design of the boats used by Aye-Gaythelos and Scota during their various migrations. These monuments were obviously modelled upon the form of an upturned boat, as the literature readily acknowledges, and the reason for this symbolism is fairly obvious. Having arrived in a new land, these people would have needed shelter fairly quickly. The plebeians would have to fend for themselves, but the easiest method for constructing a reasonably palatial abode for the aristocracy or a temple for the priesthood would be to select the worst of the boats in the fleet, cut them in half, and turn them upside down. Within a day or so, each boat could provide two houses or temples for the leaders and priests of the exiled population. These prefabricated constructions could have lasted for at least a generation, and so the society would have been very used to associating religion and privilege with a boat-shaped building. It would not take much of a leap in imagination to transfer this same shape to a house, temple or tomb constructed in more durable corbelled stonework.

The Tudons Naveta in Minorca measures about 5.7 m in width, while in a similar fashion the Gallarus 'Naveta' measures 5.75 m across. Since the doorway of the Tudons Naveta measures exactly 1 Thoth cubit (tc) in width, it is likely that the intended width of both these monuments was 11 tc (5.76 m).* This may sound like an odd figure to engineer, but it is actually a simple multiple of the standard 5.5-tc rod-length (tr) that was used extensively at Giza. While a unit of 5.5 tc may again seem to be an odd, fractional unit to use, it is exactly the same as the 5.5-yard rod that was incorporated into the British Imperial Measurements. The reason for this odd unit of length is that these Giza and Imperial rod units were actually a part of two very similar Pi-based metrological systems (see the books *Thoth* and *K2* for further details).

If these *naveta* monuments had been designed to mimic the original boats that comprised the Scotian's fleet in every detail, then we might speculate they their boats also measured about 5.75 m (11 tc or 2 tr) in breadth. If we were to apply the standard 7 : 1 length-to-breadth ratio that was discussed in Chapter V, then these same vessels would have measured some 40 m (77 tc or 14 tr) in length – dimensions that are similar to the reconstructed Athenian vessel called Olympias. Note here that we end up with a Pi based boat design, for the width of the boat is 11 tc and its length ratio is 7. The ratio of 7 : 11 is exactly $^1/_2$ the fractional approximation of Pi. Since the Egyptians were fascinated by mathematics and metrology, and fundamental units of maths were demonstrably incorporated into the design of the Giza and Dahshur pyramids, it would not be so surprising that an Egyptian-inspired boat would be constructed to the same sacred measurements and ratios.

Finally, it is probably worth mentioning that it was this direct association between Minorcan theological architecture and the sea that convinced archaeologists in Spain that the Minorcan people came from across the seas, presumably from the east. It is this same direct association between Celtic theological architecture and the sea that should likewise convince historians in Ireland that these early Celtic leaders (and many of their people) also came from across the seas. Since *Scotichronicon* clearly states that these people came from Spain and Egypt, an assertion that the design and metrology of these *navetas* positively confirms, it is highly likely that the Scottish and Irish chronicles are based upon historical facts rather than unreliable mythology.

---

*   The Gallarus Oratory measures 5.75 x 6.86 m externally and 3.15 x 4.65 m internally. The intended dimensions may therefore have been 11 x 13 tc external and 6 x 9 tc internal. Accurate measurements were not possible at the similar, but ruined, boat-shaped oratory that lies nearby at Kilmalkedar.

Scota's Tomb

According to local legends, the final piece of evidence that Queen Scota came to Ireland is the presence of her tomb, which lies in a valley just south of Tralee in Co Kerry. Of course, in my slightly revised version of this same mythology, this tomb would have been for a descendant of Queen Scota-Ankhesenamun, and not the queen herself. Nevertheless, it is entirely probable that Queen Scota's great-great-granddaughter carried the same name and rank as the founding monarch, and so it is entirely possible that a new Queen Scota migrated to Ireland around the tenth century BC.

Unfortunately, the local tourist office in Tralee was not sure where Scota's tomb was, and so I was directed towards the library. Eamon, the very helpful librarian, was a mine of information, and I soon had a pile of maps and old history books that showed exactly where her tomb lay. The data looked promising as the tomb was located up a steep-sided gorge to the south of town and this kind of topography was remarkably similar to the tombs in the Valley of the Kings and the royal tombs at Amarna. With the descendants of Scota having been denied their rightful resting place in the royal valley at Amarna, what better than to find an identical burial site in this foreign land?

The mythology indicated that the Scotian people landed along the Dingle and Iveragh peninsulars, which are located in Co Kerry in the southwest of Ireland. This did seem to be an unlikely location for the Scotians to make landfall as mariners in this early era preferred to hug the coastline. This kind of navigational technique may well have resulted in a colony being located near Wexford or Dublin, which lie to the southeast and east of Ireland respectively, but not in Kerry. However, in mitigation the myths do say that Scota's fleet was scattered during a storm, and so perhaps only a few lost ships found the rugged inlets of Kerry. The majority of the fleet may well have sailed on to Dublin, and thus we now see similar legends that emanate from opposite sides of the country.

But the landing in Kerry was not unopposed and a battle is reputed to have ensued with the local tribes, during which Queen Scota and Princess Uin were killed. In may be worth recalling at this point that the throne name of Pharaoh Akhenaton was Uin-Ra (see fig 2 for a larger version of this cartouche). According to legend, Queen Scota was laid in a tomb in the small valley that runs up to Mount Knockawaddra, where it lies to this day. It is also said that there was originally an Ogham inscription on the grave; Ogham being an old Celtic script of uncertain age and provenance. The inscription read 'Leacht Scoihin', or 'Tomb of Scothin'. However, upon translation it was decided that this inscription was a recent addition to the tomb.

| L | EA | C | H | T | S | C | OI | H | I | N |

Fig 51. The Ogham inscription on the Tomb of Scota.

I set off the next day, following the path of the stream up into the hill-country above the town. The path wound its way through a 'magical' forest of gnarled beech and holly trees covered with hanging moss, a scene that would have befitted many a fanciful Disney cartoon. Finally, there by the stream, I recognised the stone slab that marked Scota's tomb.

Unfortunately, this was not a tomb. This rough and misshapen slab of stone that lay beside the stream was merely an outcrop of natural rock, which thrust its way out of the vegetation that grew all around it. This location had never been the tomb of anyone, let alone an Egypto-Celtic queen named Scota. In addition, there was so much graffiti carved upon the surface of the slab that any Ogham inscription – had there ever been such a thing – had been completely obliterated. It was a disappointing end to a promising avenue of research.

All one can say is that there is a strong association, which has been passed down though the ages in local folklore, between a Queen Scota (a later Queen Scota) and this particular valley. But the underlying rocks in this valley are of a hard gritstone, and so a deep burial or an elaborate tomb is highly unlikely here. Perhaps there may still be a small cairn lying undiscovered in this fairly remote and undisturbed valley, which might contain a burial of some description, but any more than this is extremely unlikely.

This disappointing result does question the whole association between Scota and this region of Ireland. However, the Cahergall and Staigue amphitheaters and the Gallarus Ossuary are all located upon the Kerry peninsulas, so there is a definite historical link between the Balearic Islands and the southwest of Ireland. To trace the extent of the Roman Empire, one only needs to plot the locations of their ubiquitous triumphal arches on a map.* Likewise, in order to trace the migrations of the Scotian people, we only need to follow the trail of their boat-shaped *naveta* tombs.

Thus it is highly likely that some enterprising individuals from the Balearic Islands must have travelled up the Atlantic coastline and landed in Kerry, and some may even have settled and been buried there. Whether this cultural link also includes the location of a tomb for a queen called Scota is anyone's guess. Perhaps, in this case, the last words in this short chapter should be left to a seventeenth century Kerry poet:

> In yon cool glen, beside the mount, close by the wave, fell Scotia while pursuing the enemy across the hills.

---

* The Roman triumphal arch in Britain is located at Richborough in Kent. Unfortunately, only the concrete foundations of this huge structure remain.

Pharaoh Plunket

Within later explanations of *Scotichronicon*, and indeed within the chronicle itself, there is an amount of confusion about the era in which this exodus to Ireland actually occurred, and the geographical area that it originated from. It seems likely that this confusion has arisen because there were actually two immigration events that have, in some of these accounts, been telescoped together.

It would appear to be more than likely that the first wave of immigrants to Ireland came from Brigantia and Mallorca, and they set sail only four or so generations after Aye-Gaythelos and Ankhesenamun-Scota landed in Spain. This was the major exodus event that the chronicle relates. However, there was a further, and smaller, wave of immigrants that came from another location in a later era. Geoffrey of Monmouth, in his *History of the Britons*, says of this later wave of immigrants:

> Gurgant Bartrud, king of the Britons, was sailing back home through the Orkney Islands he came upon thirty ships full of men and women and when he enquired the reasons for their arrival, their leader ... said that he had been driven out of a region of Spain ... He asked for a small portion of Britain to settle in ... So when Gurgant learned that they had come from Spain and were called Basques and understood what their request was, he sent them to the island of Ireland. [SC1]

This passage is initially being presented as yet another story about Aye-

Gaythelos. But even as Bower quotes this passage in *Scotichronicon*, he also points out its discrepancies. The leader of these wandering tribes was called Partholomus, the great-great-grandson of Aye-Gaythelos; and yet the British king called Gurgant lived in the sixth century BC, which is many centuries after the voyages of Aye-Gaythelos and Scota. So how does this story fit into the saga of Aye-Gaythelos and his peoples? The answer may lie in the history of those people who chose to stay behind in Brigantia, instead of sailing off to Ireland in about the eleventh century BC:

> For about 240 years they stayed, poorly fed and meanly clad, among the Spaniards who attacked them ceaselessly. The desolate wastes and forest of the Pyrenees were entirely handed over to them by the Spaniards, so that they were scarcely able to survive, supporting life on goat's milk and wild honey. SC2

Had Brigantia been located on the river Ebro, and had the people there either been driven out or voluntarily migrated to new lands, an obvious choice would have been to retrace the flow of the river Ebro. This river was reliable and fertile, and no doubt its headwaters would be equally so; as are the upper reaches of the Nile. However, had these people been driven onwards and northwards, past the city of Zaragoza, rather further than they had intended, then they would indeed have found themselves up in the high Pyrenees – a land which becomes increasing cooler and less fertile. In fact, they would have found themselves exiled to the source of the Ebro at Naverra, which is the Basque homeland.

Although it is possible that the Brigantians (Scotians) had influenced and infiltrated the Basques, it is not really possible for them to be the Basques themselves. The Basque nation appears to be a separate culture from much or all of Europe, be that genetically, culturally or linguistically. Little, if anything, within Basque culture can be traced back to Aye-Gaythelos and the wider Egypto-Hyksos-Israelite nations around the Mediterranean; and so if there were Brigantian influences upon the Basques, they must have been quite subtle.

The only element that was readily visible, during my research, was their national emblem which is composed of four teardrops and known as a *lauburu*. In essence, this is a variation on the traditional four-legged swastika, which is known to be a Sun-symbol of great antiquity. However, the curved design of the Basque symbol is very similar to the legendary Irish four-leafed shamrock or clover, which is a symbol of luck (and not too dissimilar from the three-legged emblem for the Isle of Man). It is possible, therefore, that the Basques (or the Brigantians before them) brought this symbol to Ireland.

Fig 52.   *Basque lauburu*   *Irish four-leafed shamrock.*

The *lauburu* is said to be a Sun symbol, like the swastika; however, since this emblem has a distinctive curved design, there is another possibility for its design. The original symbol for Osiris in Egypt was the piece of flesh glyph ℚ , which spelt out the name Asar ⌇⌇⌇ (Osiris), as we have already seen. But on occasions, the flesh glyph can be displayed as a line of three 'teardrop' glyphs ⌇ , which is yet closer to the *lauburu* symbol. Only in the nineteenth dynasty, probably after Akhenaton's iconoclastic reforms, was this flesh glyph changed to the egg glyph ◌ , which was also the symbol of Osiris' sister-wife, Est (Isis).

Back in Eustar Dinau, the local name for the Basque country, the god-name that is given to the four-lobed *lauburu* is Ostri, which sounds a great deal like a combination of Asar and Ast (Osiris and Isis):

> **Ostri:**   The Sky in Basque mythology, he later became an equivalent of Heaven. This god is often represented by the *lauburu* (literally, 'four heads', like a swastika). [3]

It would seem that here, deep in the Basque country, we have a symbol of Osiris being venerated, and perhaps we can also speculate that this belief system was brought to this region by the bands of impoverished Brigantians who were migrating up the Ebro river system into the high Pyrenees. In a similar fashion, some versions of the *Scotichronicon* epic named the primary hero as Gaythelos Glas, or Gaythelos the Green. The *Labor Gabala* works this odd colouration into the tradition of there being no snakes in Ireland; however, a simpler explanation is that Osiris was the green god of Egypt and Aye-Gaythelos was being identified with Osiris. Since Aye-Gaythelos was no longer a devout Atonist, it would be natural for him to be depicted as Osiris upon his death, as all pharaohs were, and this is probably the origin of the title 'Glas'. This Osirian image survived through to mediaeval times, where it manifested itself in churches and cathedrals all over Europe as the ubiquitous Green Man.

Thus, according to Geoffrey of Monmouth and others, it would appear that in the sixth century BC some of these people in the Basque region set off for Ireland. Perhaps they had heard how well the Scotians were doing there, and sought to ape their success. Having sailed to Ireland and been given lands to settle in Scotland instead (as we shall see shortly), these people became known as the Picts. This is perhaps confirmed by another chronicle that says:

> After a long time had passed in which the Scots (the Irish) had lived in peaceful and quiet prosperity (in Ireland), a certain unknown people, later called the Picts, appeared from the lands of Aquitania and landed on the Irish shores. (Author's brackets.) [SC4]

As mentioned in Chapter I, the southern lands of Aquitaine lie against the Pyrenees, deep in Basque country; and so there was a long tradition that the Scottish Picts arrived from this region on the borders of Spain and France – the Basque country. The full title for the region just to the north of the western Pyrenees was originally Aquitania Novempopulana, or 'Aquitaine of the Nine People'. Since Osiris has already been identified in Basque culture, there is an outside possibility that the 'nine' may refer to the Egyptian Paut, the company of the nine great gods (or laws) *.

It is because of these many connections and traditions that it is thought by some researchers that the Pictish language may have been related to Basque; although because Pictish culture and language died out completely, this is far from certain:

> Of the non-Celtic element in Pictish, the best conclusion is that it is a remnant of one of the languages prevalent in Europe before the spread of the Indo-European language family. Basque is the only remnant of this type surviving today ... For this reason, some writers relate Pictish to Basque directly. [5]

Whilst not mentioning the Basques, the venerable Bede says of this same event:

> ... it happened that the people of the Picts ... reached Ireland and landed on its northern shores. There they found the race of the Scots (the Irish) and asked

---

* The Paut of Hermopolis (City of Thoth) were:
  Atum, Kek and Keket, Heh and Hehet, Nun and Nunit, Amen and Amenet.

  The Paut of Heliopolis were:
  Shu and Tefnut, Geb and Nut, Usar (Osiris) and Est (Isis), Seth and Neb-het (Nepthys), and Heru (Horus).

for places to settle in ... The Scots replied that the island was not big enough for both peoples (and advised they should go to Scotland) ... The Scots agreed to give them some wives on condition that (they should choose the royal secession) from the female line. [SC6] (Author's brackets.)

It should be noted that the royal succession through the female line is an Egypto-Israelite tradition, and so this agreement is exactly what one might expect if the Scotians had an Egyptian ancestry. This new Pictish settlement on the west coast of what is now Scotland became quite successful, and so wave after wave of Scotians from Ireland voluntarily decided to follow their Pictish partners to this new land. The Picts were unimpressed by this sudden influx of Scotians from Ireland, as an oracle had prophesied their extinction at the hands of the Scotians – and so it eventually proved to be.

It was through this later wave of migration, from Scotia (Ireland) to the northern half of Britain, that this land inherited the title that had originally been bestowed upon Ireland. The Scotians called their new land Scotland, and as the new colony grew and prospered, the usage of this same name declined in Ireland. They also called this new land Hibernia, after Heber, the son of Aye-Gaythelos, and it is through this process that Spain and Scotland now share a common name.

Language

One of the biggest problems in the whole of this revisionist history of Ireland and Scotland is the fact that no Egyptian hieroglyphs have been discovered in all the diverse places that these Egyptian refugees were supposed to have landed. How could a nation have forgotten such a fundamental aspect of their culture so quickly?

To be more accurate, there are virtually no inscriptions on these monuments whatsoever, which might tend to suggest that these Bronze Age cultures were in a pre-literate phase of their development. But this is not necessarily so, as we might say much the same of the early Irish monasteries. The Rattoo Abbey, for instance, was founded in the highly literate thirteenth century AD, and yet not one letter of script or one idolatrous image remains within the present-day ruins of the abbey. I imagine that any imagery was inscribed onto plasterwork, which has long since fallen away, but the result is a ruin that is completely devoid of inscriptions.

Another reason for the lack of Egyptian hieroglyphics in western Europe may lie in the notion that the Hyksos-Israelites, who were the ancestors of the Amarna regime, were originally supposed to have been immigrants to Egypt. I am not so sure if this is precisely so; however, it does appear that although the Hyksos adopted the vast majority of Egyptian customs, they were also regarded as being distinctly separate from Upper Egyptian culture. It is possible, therefore, that the Hyksos were not quite so wedded to the writing system employed in Thebes; and through their many contacts with neighboring countries to the north and east, they would often come into contact with alternative alphabets and languages that were substantially easier to learn and use.

As it happens, *Scotichronicon* makes this very same point about Aye-Gaythelos. The chronicle states that at the time of Jacob there was contact between King Phoroneus of Greece and the Egyptians, and a prince of Greece sailed to Egypt and was worshipped as a 'god'. This is interesting as it conforms to the biblical history that I outlined in the book *Jesus*. There, I stated that the (first) great exodus occurred during the time of the biblical Jacob, and that this incident was one and the same as the great Hyksos exodus from Egypt. So, Jacob may well have been the Hyksos monarch who is known to history as Pharaoh Jacoba (⟨𝕴⟩), and many of the Hyksos-Israelites may well have been scattered all over the Mediterranean at this time (c. 1600 BC). King Phoroneus' name is likely to have been a corruption of the Egyptian term *per-aa* ⟨𝕴⟩, meaning 'pharaoh'.

The chronicle then mentions that a prince of King Phoroneus sailed back to Egypt and was worshipped as a 'god'. This is quite possibly a simple retelling of the biblical story of Joseph. One of the twelve sons of Jacob was called Joseph, the favourite son who had a coat of many colours. Joseph is said to have gone down [back] to Egypt, and there he is said to have become vizier or prime minister of Egypt, and founded a highly successful dynasty. This is what I believe the chronicle is trying to describe, but it is using historical data rather than biblical data, and the chronicler has either not seen or did not want to see the obvious comparison between the two accounts.

The outcome of this similarity is that it is likely that during the first biblical Hyksos-Israelite exodus, some of these refugees from Lower Egypt ended up in Greece instead of Jerusalem. There, they became influential in the region and set up their own royal dynasty, but perhaps more importantly, they also adopted the local script and some components of the local language. Thus when Joseph came [back] to Egypt and became vizier, he already knew of and perhaps taught this new, simpler script to his immediate followers. It is possibly due to this cross-fertilisation that *Scotichronicon* claims that the Greeks and the Egyptian followed the same laws and language at this time. The chronicle says of this:

> Gaythelos, bearing in mind ... the laws which King Phoroneus had entrusted
> to the Greeks and which were still used by the Egyptians in Gaythelos' time,

imbued the people who followed him in these same laws ... Hence it is the proud boast of our nation, the Scots, that they still use these same laws up to the present day. [SC7]

The claim here is that the laws (and the script?) that Aye-Gaythelos took with him on the exodus to Brigantia were not pure Egyptian; rather, they were Hyksos-Egyptian-Israelite laws that had been incubated in Minoan Crete and Mycenaean Greece for more than two centuries, before being brought back to Egypt [by Joseph and Aye-Gaythelos] and then transported on the exodus to Brigantia. Had Aye-Gaythelos spent a number of years in a forced exile in Greece, as seems likely, it would have been readily apparent to him that their early Paleo-Phoenician script, which was spreading its way across the Mediterranean, was far easier to use. The chronicle alludes to this when it says:

> Gaythelos ... became highly skilled in a variety of languages. Because of his skill the pharaoh [posthumously Akhenaton] gave him his daughter and heir Scota as his wife. So since the Hibernians are descended from Gaythelos and Scota they are named Gaitheli (Gaels) and Scoti (Scots). Gaythelos, so they say, invented the Hibernian language which is also called Gaelic. (Author's brackets.) [SC8]

In fact, it is said that Aye-Gaythelos knew 72 languages, but this specific and rather implausible number is simply another of the coded messages that are frequently woven into biblical-type stories. A reference to the number 72, which occurs in many ancient texts and may have also influenced the name for the Septuagint Bible itself, simply means that the individual in question has been initiated into the cult of the 'Watchers' or 'Guardians'. The Watchers were the astronomer-priests of Egypt, and one of their primary tasks was counting off the astrological millennia. (The purpose for this laborious task is given in *Eden in Egypt.)* The Earth, in its orbit, precesses through all of the constellations of the zodiac in about 25,750 years. Thus one degree of precession (or one precessional 'day') equates to 72 Earth years. Therefore, the period of 72 years was an important element of the Watcher's ritual calendar, and hence this number has been implausibly forced into many odd locations to indicate the arcane knowledge of certain individuals. That this number should have been associated with Aye-Gaythelos again demonstrates that he must have been allied in some manner to the Egyptian priesthood.

Notwithstanding this, it may well be that Aye-Gaythelos was also an accomplished linguist, and so he would have been in a position to teach his people a variety of scripts and languages. Since the main allies of the exiled

Aye-Gaythelos were now in Greece, Crete and Israel, rather than in Upper Egypt, a move towards their language(s) and script(s) would not be so surprising.

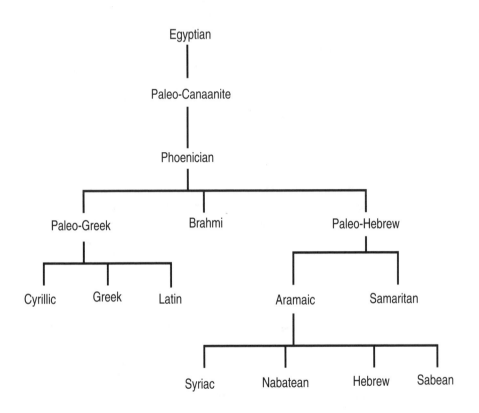

Fig 53. Chronology of Mediterranean scripts,
Linear-A and -B are completely separate from this chronology.

The early Minoan language, known as Eteocretan, used the Linear-A script, and both this language and its script have never been deciphered. Professor Cyrus Gordon has argued that Eteocretan was a Semitic language related to Phoenician, but this has never been proven – although it has to be said that such a heritage would make a great deal of sense. However, as was indicated in Chapter V, it is likely that this Minoan language did spread to Mycenaean Greece during the early part of the second millennium BC. This is a distinct possibility because the later Mycenaean (and Greek) language used the Minoan Linear-B script, which was a derivative of the Minoan Linear-A script and was not related to the later Phoenicio-Greek script.

This chronology means that the Greeks must have swapped scripts from Linear-B to the Phoenician alphabet around the ninth century BC, presumably because the latter was either easier to use or because it had a wider usage around the Mediterranean. This change in national script is similar to the wide-ranging reforms of Kemal Ataturk who, in 1928, changed the alphabet of Turkey from Arabic to Latin almost overnight. The Arabic language of Turkey is still unintelligible to most Europeans, but the change in alphabet signalled a significant political leaning towards the West. The only real advantage of this change, to visiting Westerners, is that Turkish signposts and shop prices are now much easier to read.

Aye-Gaythelos was also related to the Hyksos-Israelites, and so an alternative language and script that may have influenced him is Hebrew itself. This language was most certainly based upon the Egyptian language, as has been demonstrated in the book *Eden*, so it is more than likely that Aye-Gaythelos spoke a Paleo-Hebrew language as well as pure Egyptian itself. Just as with the later Greek script, the alphabet that the early Israelites used was and is demonstrably based upon the Phoenician script, and not the Minoan Linear-A or -B alphabets. Yet the Phoenician script is thought to have been strongly influenced by Egyptian hieroglyphs, and may have been a derivative of the cursive Egyptian demotic script. Whatever its source, the adoption of the Phoenician alphabet by both the Israelites and the Greeks in the eleventh and ninth centuries BC is certain.

In the following table, take a look at the Phoenician and Hebrew letters denoting the Latin z, k, l, m, p, ts and sh, and a direct comparison will be immediately apparent between the two scripts. Likewise, take a look at the Phoenician and Greek letters for a, b, g, d, e, u, th, k, m, o, q, p and sh, and the similarities will again be obvious.

Further evidence for the common ancestry of the Greek and Hebrew scripts can be seen in the common name for their alphabets. The Hebrew word for this list of letters is the *alef-bet* אלף-בית, which was derived from the first two letters of the Hebrew alphabet: the aleph א and the bet ב. Similarly, the Greek name for their alphabet is the *alpha-beta* αλπηα-βετα, which was again derived from the first two letters of their alphabet: the alpha α and beta β. This common heritage demonstrates that the Phoenicians were very influential throughout the Mediterranean, and the many nations and city states saw the potential of using this new, simplified alphabet.

*   *   *

Phoenician alphabet	Phoenician meaning	Latin	Hebrew	Greek	Cryillic
𐤀	ox	a	א	Αα	А
𐤁	house	b	ב	Ββ	Б
𐤂	throw-stick	g	ג	Γγ	Г
𐤃	door	d	ד	Δδ	Д
𐤄	window	he	ה	Εε	Е
𐤅	hook	w, u	ו	Υυ	У
𐤆	weapon	z	ז	Ζζ	З
𐤇	fence	h	ה	Ηη	Ч
𐤈	wheel	th	ט	Θθ	Ф(f)
𐤉	arm	y	י	Ιι	И
𐤊	palm	k	כ	Κκ	К
𐤋	goad	l	ל	Λλ	Л
𐤌	water	m	מ	Μμ	М
𐤍	fish	n	נ	Νν	Н
𐤏	eye	o	ע	Οο	О
𐤐	mouth	p	פ	Ππ	П
𐤑	papyrus	ts, z	צ	Σσ	Ц
𐤒	monkey	q	ק	Ψψ	
𐤓	head	r	ר	Ρρ	Р
𐤔	tooth	sh	ש	Σσ	С,Ш
𐤕	mark	t	ת	Ττ	Т

Fig 54. Evolution of the Phoenician alphabet. In chronological order, the Phoenician script evolved into the Hebrew, Greek and Latin scripts.

Although the Phoenician script is not thought to have been created until about the twelfth century BC, had an earlier Paleo-Phoenician script been in use at the time of the Aye-Gaythelos' exodus from Egypt (in the 1320s BC), it is highly likely that Aye-Gaythelos would have been familiar with it and used it in preference to the cumbersome hieroglyphic script. It is known that the Hyksos-Israelites did indeed get expelled from Egypt on at least two major exoduses, which spread far and wide across the Mediterranean and the Arabias, and nowhere do we see a concerted effort to retain the hieroglyphic script. It was obviously not a well-liked system of writing and preference was given to simpler 'foreign' scripts.

Thus, the most likely script that Aye-Gaythelos might have used is an early Paleo-Phoenician alphabet – an alphabet that may have had its origins in Egyptian hieroglyphics anyway – which may have been in use among the Minoan-Phoenician city states, combined with a Paleo-Hebrew-Egyptian language that had long been in use in the Nile Delta among the Hyksos-Israelites. Thus, it may well be that the exodus of Aye-Gaythelos and Ankhesenamun-Scota did not spread the usage of the cumbersome Egyptian hieroglyphic script around Europe, but an early version of the simpler Phoenician alphabet instead.

Beliefs

Another potential stumbling-block in this new history of Western Europe, is the apparent lack of commonality between the theology of Egypt and the theology of Spain and Ireland. But, as with my analysis of early Judaism in the book *Cleopatra*, it rather depends on what 'Egyptian' religion we are expecting to find. A cursory glance at Egyptian theology might convince us that we should be looking for pyramids, uterine temples, megalithic architecture and the standard pantheon of Egyptian gods.

However, these emigrés to the western fringes of Europe would have been impoverished, and unable to perform great feats of architecture. In addition, the bulk of these exiles to Spain and Ireland would have been from Lower Egypt (descendants of the Hyksos), and in the north of Egypt they had their own, idiosyncratic forms of belief. A typical example of this was arboreal veneration, a cult that was well established in Avaris in the Nile Delta and became a central component of early Judaism. In this arboreal creed we can see great similarities between Egypt, Crete, the Balearic Islands and Ireland; as was demonstrated in the chapters that referred to truncated round-towers.

Even today in Ireland, isolated *sceach* trees, as they are known, are deemed to be sacred: as they are said to be the portal into other worlds for the leprechauns, or little people. Indeed as recently as 1999 the Latoon *sceach* held up the construction of a new road to Shannon airport, as its potential destruction was declared to be unlucky. (The image of a windblown *sceach* was also adopted as a symbol of the Irish famine.)

Another similarity between Egyptian and Irish theology may be bull-worship. The Minoans were great followers of the original Apis-bull cult of Egypt, and if a large number of the sailors on this voyage were Minoan, this alternative cult may also have established itself along the western fringes of Europe. That a bull-cult was established in Spain needs no further explanation, but the evidence for a bull-cult in Ireland is perhaps more subtle. To uncover the Irish bull-cult we again need to look at the early manuscripts, and there we find the *Lebor na Huidre* (the *Book of the Dun Cow*). This is a twelfth century manuscript that was copied from much older texts and in part it relates a mythical tale known as the *Tain bo Cuailnge* (the *Cattle Raid of Cooley*). This is a semi-mythological tale about a battle to possess the most perfect cow in all of Ireland. There were two contenders for this title: the White-cow and the Dun- (or dark-) cow, and the two animals finish the story in a great mythological fight to the death, which was won by the Dun-cow.

There is an amount of synergy between this Irish story and the cult of the Apis-bull. Unusually for Egyptian theology, the Apis was a real animal; the most perfect black bull in all Egypt, with a white star on its forehead (a motif that was to be repeated in Anna Sewell's novel, *Black Beauty*). Like the Irish Dun-cow, the Egyptian Apis-bull was to be coveted and venerated as a symbol of power, and so it is not unreasonable to see a tentative cultural and theological link within these ancient tales.

More importantly, perhaps, this exodus was the exile of Aye-Gaythelos and Ankhesenamun-Scota of the Amarna regime, and so it is likely that the religion they would have taken with them was substantially Atonist – the original monotheistic belief system. Since I have already demonstrated that Atonism was an early form of Judaism, much of the theology of these first settlers in Ireland may have been largely indistinguishable from the Christianity that arrived many centuries later. Indeed, this could be one reason why Christianity was accepted so readily in Ireland, as it was simply a variation on an already established creed.

Lost pharaoh

While the golden torqs, faience beads, red hands, boat-tombs, round-towers and the epigraphic evidence from Ireland strongly hint at ancient cultural links with Bronze Age Iberian and Egyptian cultures, none of these items can be seen as being derived unambiguously from the Egyptian Amarna era. Nevertheless, having followed the trail of the descendants of Pharaoh Aye-Gaythelos and Queen Ankhesenamun-Scota all the way from Amarna, through Brigantia in Iberia and on to the 'Emerald Isle' of Hibernia or Scotia

(Ireland), it would have been nice to have discovered an artifact that came directly from Egypt. One might have hoped that the descendants of Aye-Gaythelos had followed the Egyptian custom of elaborate funerary rituals and ancestor veneration, which have provided such rich archaeological treasures in Egypt. Were it not for the funerary rituals of the Egyptian royalty, we would have very little information on the true history of Egypt.

While it is true that a forced colony like Brigantia would have been relatively poor, and unable to afford great tombs; nevertheless, such an ingrained, ancient tradition should still have resulted in small tombs containing a few hand-me-down items of jewellery taken from Egypt. The evidence from Thebes and Tanis even hints at the possibility that these burials would not necessarily have been left in Brigantia when the move to Ireland was made. In Tanis, some of the earlier royal burials in this region were moved into the tomb of Psusennes II. Their original burial location is not known, but it appears that they were exhumed and moved to Tanis when this new city was constructed. Likewise in Thebes, when the systematic looting of the tombs in the Valley of the Kings was in progress, nearly all the royal mummies were salvaged and relocated in a secret location behind the temple of Hatchepsut.

Thus, the tradition seems to be that the burials of ancestors would, if possible, be moved with the people rather than leaving them to be pillaged by strangers. So it would have been nice to have ended this investigation with the remains of a mummy, which may be linked in some way to the Amarna era: a discovery something like the burial at Tara with its necklace of Egyptian faience beads, the Tara Prince, but with a mummified body too.

Strange as it may seem, in actual fact the head of a mummy can be found in this very same part of Ireland, and it resides in the Catholic cathedral of St Peter's at Drogheda, which lies just a few kilometers from Newgrange. I was introduced to this odd feature of Irish history by Andrew Power, the author of *Ireland, Land of the Pharaohs*, and bearing in mind the title of this book, his obvious but controversial contention was that this head had to be linked to Egypt in some manner. This mummified head is supposed to be that of Oliver Plunket, the seventeenth century archbishop of Armagh who was executed in London in 1681 – but the reason for this head's strange state of preservation remains a complete mystery. Frank Donnelly, the author of a booklet on the mummified head, says:

> Although some of the features of the preservation of St Oliver's remains are strange and difficult to explain in scientific terms, it is not at all claimed here that there has been any miraculous intervention. [9]

'Difficult to explain' is an understatement. The unfortunate Oliver Plunket was said to have been hung, drawn and quartered at Tyburn, London, for the crime of being an agent of the Pope and plotting rebellion in Ireland. His severed head is said to have been placed in a tin and kept at the church of St Giles. However, the dark, dank recesses of a London church are hardly conducive to any form of natural mummification. Let's put this claim into its proper perspective; of the millions of people who have died and been buried in northwest Europe, absolutely none of these corpses have spontaneously embalmed themselves. Each and every one of them has rotted and decayed within a very short period of time, and left very little in the archaeological record. Miracles aside, which is a possibility that I dismiss out of hand, no corpse is going to mummify itself in the northern European climate (unless it is dropped into a peat-bog). It is impossible, therefore, for this to be the true history of the head that lies in Drogheda cathedral. Either Oliver Plunket had had a remarkably effective form of preservation and storage applied to his corpse, or this is not the head of Archbishop Plunket.

Even if we allow the former possibility to be true, I still wonder about the state of preservation that has been achieved here. Britain was not exactly at the forefront of the world's embalming industry, especially in the seventeenth century AD. If the head of Oliver Plunket really has been embalmed by an undertaker in London, then this is a remarkable and absolutely unique example of their work. Unlike Egyptian embalming, 'modern' techniques have revolved around pumping preservative fluids through the blood system, a technique which was discovered by William Harvey in 1628. The far more superior formaldehyde preservation was not discovered until 1868, by the German chemist William Hoffman. But even with these advanced techniques, the British Institute of Embalmers only admits to:

> The treatment of a dead human body in order to achieve an aseptic condition, temporary preservation and a pre-mortem appearance. [10]

Note the word 'temporary' in this quotation. But the embalming of Plunket's head is far from temporary, having already lasted for over 300 years. In fact, the very look of this head, in both colour and texture, is wholly reminiscent of the mummies that still lie in the Cairo museum, and which have remained in that state for 3,000 years or more. Like the Egyptian mummies, Plunket's head is on the small side, with a light blonde-ginger stubble to both scalp and chin.* The skin appears to have been desiccated and treated with resins, while the flattened ears and rucked skin show that the head has been wrapped with cloth at some point in time. But perhaps the most telling similarity to the Egyptian equivalents, is the mention of the head being 'sweet smelling'.

As far as the head of an Egyptian mummy is concerned, the full mummification process involved the removal of the brain through the nose, the drying out of the external tissues with natron (a natural salt), and then the filling of the brain cavity with resins. The resins used in this process differed, with some mummies having bitumen applied; but for royal burials, the resins were often frankincense and myrrh – the expensive and aromatic resins that were said to have been brought by the Magi to the infant Jesus. It is entirely possible that a skull full of frankincense and myrrh would still emit a faintly sweet aroma after 3,000 or so years. There is no natural reason for this aroma emanating from the head at Drogheda, but had the head been mummified in the Egyptian fashion, then perhaps some of the perfumes and resins applied to it still issue their sweet aroma.

It would seem likely that the head of Oliver Plunket may have an alternative history to the one advertised. Orthodox history claims that his head led a charmed life, as it was sent from London to Rome where it spent some forty years. Then, resplendent in a new casket, the head made its way back to Drogheda, where it spent some 200 years in the care of the Dominican nuns at the Siena Convent. In 1921 it was then transferred to the Catholic St Peter's Church in Drogheda, which was built as the Oliver Plunket Memorial Church.

Could this 'new' church, and the head it contains, be a central component in a much greater historical mystery? Well, despite the Catholic church of St Peter's being highly orthodox, this edifice is not without an element of covert symbolism. Like many Catholic churches around the globe, St Peter's contains a scene of the Last Supper; which was beautifully carved in milky white marble by the late Victorian sculptor, Edmund Sharp. However, as in Leonardo da Vinci's version of the Last Supper in the refectory of Santa Maria delle Grazie in Milan, the disciple on the right of Jesus is clearly a woman (who looks remarkably like the late Diana, Princess of Wales; see fig 55). Now this in itself is not so unusual, as at least half the Last Supper scenes I have investigated do indeed depict a woman on the right-hand side of Jesus. But these female 'St Johns' generally reside in the great stately homes of Britain, and not in the Catholic churches

---

*   Many of the Egyptian aristocracy, priesthood and royalty had shaven heads, presumably for health reasons, and so their mummies only sport a light stubble. Many of the Amarna royalty appear to have had reddish hair, while the mummy of Ramesses the Great has blonde hair. There is some uncertainty as to how much influence the mummification process has had in this colouration.

Fig 55. The Last Supper carving in St Peter's (Catholic) Church, Drogheda. The disciple to the right of Jesus is clearly a woman and so this is an overt portrayal of Mary Magdalene, the sister-wife of Jesus.

of Ireland. That this overt representation of Mary Magdalene, the sister-wife of Jesus, should reside in the midst of a Catholic church in the devout heartland of southern Ireland is quite remarkable.

This controversial depiction of the Last Supper would suggest that the Catholic Church is not always as orthodox as one might imagine, and there may be characters behind the scenes who know rather more than they would ever admit to. So could there be another mystery concealed under the soaring vaults of St Peter's in Drogheda? Could this head be a central component in the story of Aye-Gaythelos and Scota?

Well, without an examination of the condition of this mummified head's nasal bone and the content of the skull cavity, to see if the head was really mummified in the Egyptian fashion, this proposal will no doubt remain a intriguing mystery. While some readers might scoff at the proposition that this head was mummified in the Egyptian fashion by immigrants who came to Ireland from Egypt, this suggestion is no more fanciful than the present claim that Oliver Plunket's head managed to mummify itself through some unspecified but semi-miraculous process.

Given a straight choice between the two possible histories that have been outlined here, I myself would definitely opt for the Egyptian heritage.

Coda

Unfortunately, this is the end of the trail for research into Gaythelos and Scota. While much of the information presented in this book may be considered to be circumstantial, there is a growing body of evidence that points towards a historical basis for the various chronicles of the Irish and Scots. But if this is so, then this would mean that both Ireland and Scotland were seeded with much of the high culture and civilisation of Egypt during the Bronze Age.

Fig 56. The mummified head claimed to be that of Oliver Plunket.

That this implantation did not immediately result in a flourishing advanced culture in greater Britain, as was the result of similar contacts in Greece, may be due to the harsher climatic conditions in northwest Europe; which demanded a greater expenditure of energy just to survive.

Nevertheless, an echo of that advanced culture may well have rippled down through the millennia, for it was Britain that eventually shrugged off the oppression of the Catholic Church and ushered in the Enlightenment Era; and it was this Age of Reason that formed the foundations upon which the mighty edifice of the Industrial Revolution was based. It would be pleasing to think that our modern technological world was, in some small part, a by-product of Gaythelos and Scota's arduous journey to the Emerald Isle many millennia ago.

 End

Appendix

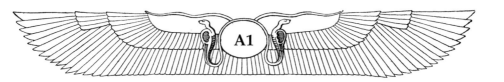

Exodus Timeline

This revised history of the Egypto-Israelite nation has highlighted a number of exoduses to and from Egypt. The complexity of this history has probably generated an amount of confusion, and so the diagram overleaf attempts to portray these migrations graphically, in order to clarify the situation as much as is possible. The top of the chart gives the names of the pharaohs of Egypt for each significant era, while the lower register gives the equivalent Old Testament patriarch who lived in that same era.

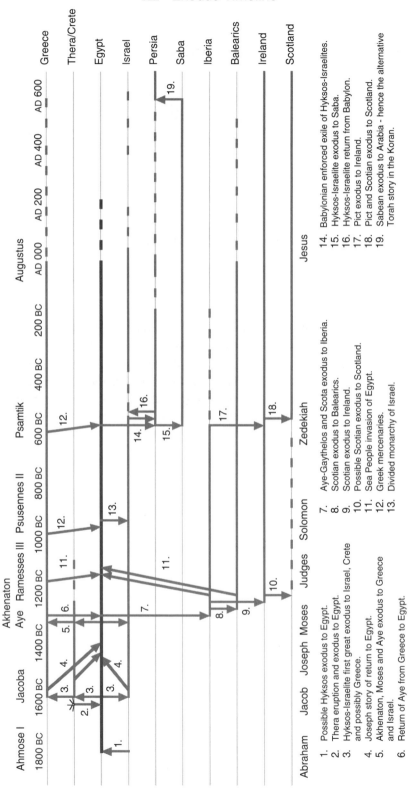

A1 Exodus Timeline

1. Possible Hyksos exodus to Egypt.
2. Thera eruption and exodus to Egypt.
3. Hyksos-Israelite first great exodus to Israel, Crete and possibly Greece.
4. Joseph story of return to Egypt.
5. Akhenaton, Moses and Aye exodus to Greece and Israel.
6. Return of Aye from Greece to Egypt.
7. Aye-Gaythelos and Scota exodus to Iberia.
8. Scotian exodus to Balearics.
9. Scotian exodus to Ireland.
10. Possible Scotian exodus to Scotland.
11. Sea People invasion of Egypt.
12. Greek mercenaries.
13. Divided monarchy of Israel.
14. Babylonian enforced exile of Hyksos-Israelites.
15. Hyksos-Israelite exodus to Saba.
16. Hyksos-Israelite return from Babylon.
17. Pict exodus to Ireland.
18. Pict and Scotian exodus to Scotland.
19. Sabean exodus to Arabia - hence the alternative Torah story in the Koran.

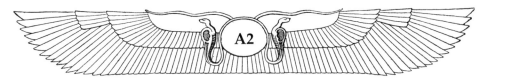

A2

Four-room House

In my previous books I have made a reasoned case for the Israelite exiles in Judaea being the Hyksos people from Lower Egypt. This idea has, of course, been vigorously denied by the academic establishment. One of the arguments devised to prove that I was wrong, was the 'fact' that the thirteenth century Israelite housing in Judaea is unique to the Israelites. So why would the Hyksos people, upon being exiled to Judaea, suddenly begin building a completely new type of domestic housing? Ergo, the Israelites cannot have been the Hyksos.

However, this supposed 'demolition' of my thesis does not stand up to closer scrutiny. The Israelite houses in Judaea are frequently designed around a standard 'four-room' layout. It has often been said that there is no antecedent for this design within Egypt; but in actual fact this confident assertion is wrong, for there *is* an Egyptian predecessor to the four-room layout. In fact, the design came from the standard layout for a Hyksos mortuary chapel, which had exactly the same layout as the Israelite house design. But it is the Hyksos mortuary chapel that predates the Israelite house by a considerable margin, and so it is likely that Israelites inherited this design from Hyksos at Avaris   because they were one and the same people.

The eminent Egyptologist, Manfred Bietak, also discovered the four-room house on the west bank at Karnak. He says of this discovery:

> Huts more than 3,000 years old belonging to workers – perhaps slaves –□ and with the same floor plan as ancient Israelite four-room houses have been identified at Medinet Habu, opposite Luxor in Egypt. These reed huts may represent extra-Biblical evidence of Israel in Egypt.

If true, Israelite or proto-Israelite workers were in Egypt in the second half of the 12th century BC, more than half a century later than has previously been thought. This evidence, in turn, would have important implications for the historicity of the Biblical narrative. [1]

Interestingly, these huts were found inside the temple of Pharaoh Aye on the west bank at Karnak. Professor Bietak dates them to the post-Amarna era, but whatever their exact age it is certain that they were in use at a date that is very close to the emergence of the four-room house design in Israel. Bietak is excited because this provides evidence that the Israelites were resident in Egypt at a similar time to the biblical exodus; but he then manages to reverse the exodus, using a logic that completely escapes me, by indicating that the Israelites were exiled from Canaan to Egypt and not *vice versa!*

In short, Bietak's arguments do not use all the evidence available and are therefore incorrect. The Avaris (Hyksos) chapels are much earlier than the Karnak houses, as they date from the seventeenth dynasty and it was not for several centuries that these same designs subsequently appeared in Israel and Karnak as domestic dwellings. Contrary to Bietak's theory, what these four-room house layouts really indicate is that this design was an ancient and well-established component of Hyksos culture long before the Israelites inherited it, and so it is highly likely that the Israelites were indeed the descendants of the Hyksos.

Strangely enough, although Bietak was keen to highlight his four-room house discovery in Karnak – which he instantly linked with itinerant Israelite workers slaving for the pharaoh in an appropriately biblical fashion – he makes no mention of the strikingly similar design of the Hyksos chapels in Avaris. This is doubly strange when one realizes that the excavation of the chapels at Avaris were performed by one Manfred Bietak. [2] It's amazing how far a (religious) preconception will go to maintain the status quo.

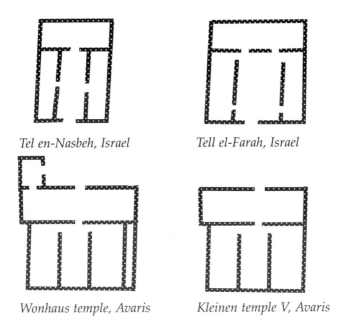

Tel en-Nasbeh, Israel   *Tell el-Farah, Israel*

Wonhaus temple, Avaris   *Kleinen temple V, Avaris*

Fig 60.   Four-room houses of Israel and four-room temples of Avaris.

185

List of diagrams

Photo credits

Plate 1.   View from the El Maestrat mountains in Catalonia - Ralph Ellis.
Plate 2.   Satellite image of the Ebro Delta, Earth Data Analysis Center.
Plate 3.   A reconstruction of the Dover boat - Ralph Ellis.
Plate 4.   The Dover boat - Ralph Ellis.
Plate 5.   Model of the Ferriby boat - Ralph Ellis.
Plate 6.   Bronze Age cartwheel from Dublin - Ralph Ellis.
Plate 7.   Solid gold cape, discovered at Mold, Flintshire - Ralph Ellis.
Plate 8.   The Ring of Minos, from Minoan Crete - Ralph Ellis.
Plate 9-10. Two golden torqs from the Dublin museum - Ralph Ellis.
Plate 11.   Ornate spiral torq from the Iron Age Snettisham hoard - Ralph Ellis.
Plate 12.   Partial reconstructions of Minoan Knossos in Crete - Ralph Ellis.
Plate 13.   Helen of Troy, by Evelyn De Morgan.
Plate 14.   Mary Magdalene, by Carlo Crivelli, Rijksmuseum, Amsterdam.
Plate 15.   Bull-leaping fresco, of Minoan inspiration, from Avaris, Vivian Davies.
Plate 16.   Bull-leaping fresco from Minoan Knossos, Crete - Ralph Ellis.
Plate 17-18. Truncated round-tower near Santanyi, Mallorca - Ralph Ellis.
Plate 19.   Truncated round-tower at Torello, Mallorca - Ralph Ellis.
Plate 20.   Pillar room, Santanyi, Mallorca - Ralph Ellis.
Plate 21.   Pillar room, Phaestos, Crete - Ralph Ellis.
Plate 22.   The Mount of Hostages, at Tara in the Boyne valley - Ralph Ellis.
Plate 23.   Truncated round-tower inside the Cahergall amphitheater - Ralph Ellis.
Plate 24.   The Gallarus Ossuary near Dingle, Co Kerry, Ireland - Ralph Ellis.
Plate 25.   The Tudons Naveta, near Ciutadella, Minorca - Ralph Ellis.
Plate 26.   Rattoo round-tower, near Ballyduff, Co Kerry - Ralph Ellis.
Plate 27.   Scota's grave, near Tralee, Co Kerry - Ralph Ellis.
Plate 28.   Last Supper carving in St Peter's Cathedral, Drogheda - Ralph Ellis.
Plate 29.   North Molton necklace, photo - Exeter Museum.

Notes & references

Bible: All references taken from the King James edition, although the text is often modernised for clarity.

Josephus: AA = Against Apion, Ant = Antiquities, JW = Jewish war, L = Life.
Page references are to the Loeb Classical Library system.
Quotes taken from William Whiston's translation, which was first published in 1736; some references are from the Penguin Classics edition by G. Williamson, first published 1959.

Manetho   All page numbers are taken from the LCL edition, editor G. Goold.

Within the referencing system in this book, some of the reference numbers are prefixed with letters. This is to give the reader an idea of the source of the reference, without having to look up that particular reference. This only applies to the more popular reference works, and the following have been prefixed:

B = Bible, M = Manetho, J = Josephus, H = Herodotus,
T = Talmud, KN = Kebra Nagast, K = Koran, S = Strabo
SC = Scotichronicon.

All references to Egyptian words are taken from:

An Egyptian Hieroglyphic Dictionary, E A Wallis Budge, Dover Publications. The entries in the dictionary are substantially in alphabetical (glyph) order, and so the references are easy to find and have not been listed in the references by their page number.

Abbreviations:
ECIiAT	= Egypt, Canaan and Israel in Ancient Times, Donald Redford.
TTIPiE	The Third Intermediate Period in Egypt Kenneth Kitchen,
EotP	= Egypt of the Pharaohs, Alan Gardiner.
ARoE	= Ancient Records of Egypt, James Breasted.
Kebra Nagast	= Translation taken from 'Queen of Sheba', W Budge.

Notes & References

Introduction

1. http://albanach.org/kilt.html

Chapter I

1. A history book for Scots (A selection from Scotichronicon) Donald Watt; Scotichronicon, Donald Watt, vol 1 pxv.
2. Veue of the present state of Irelande [1596].
3. Scotichronicon, W Bower bk 1 ch 10.

Chapter II

1. Ian Shaw, Oxford History of Ancient Egypt.
2. Scotichronicon, Walter Bower bk 1 ch12.
3. http://www.saxakali.com/suzar/madonna.htm
4. Scotichronicon, Walter Bower bk 1 ch 9.
5. Ibid bk 1 ch 9.
6. Manetho, Aegyptica Fr 50, Fr 53.
7. Hughes, Dictionary of Islam.
8. Bible Est 1:19.
9. James Pritchard, Ancient Near-Eastern Texts. Hieroglyphic Dictionary, W Budge.
10. Scotichronicon, Walter Bower.
11. Scotichronicon, Walter Bower bk 1 ch 9.
12. Bible I Maccabee 12:20-21.
13. The Greek Myths, Robert Graves bk 60.
14. The Greek Myths, Robert Graves bk 60.
15. Scotichronicon, Walter Bower bk 1 ch12.
16. She was the Amity Brig, Les Johnson.
17. Lebor Gabala Erein, The Book of Invasions.

Chapter III

1. Bible Ex 3:14.
2. Bible Ex 3:11-14.
3. Bible Ex 24:12.
4. Strabo 5.2.40, quoting Euripides.
5. Rock tombs of Amarna, N Davies vol 6.
6. Akhenaton, C Aldred.
7. Akhenaton, C Aldred p289.
8. Scotichronicon, Walter Bower bk 1 ch 9.
9. Bible Num 12:1.
10. Josephus Ant 2:238-253.
11. Scotichronicon, Walter Bower bk 1 ch 11.

Notes & References

Chapter IV

1. Scotichronicon, Walter Bower bk 1 ch 13.
2. Ibid   bk 1 ch 15.
3. Ibid   bk 1 ch 17.
4. Ibid   bk 1 ch 16.
5. Ibid   bk 1 ch 18.
6. Scotichronicon, notes by Prof D Watt, p121.
7. The Classical Gazetteer, William Hazlit (1851).
8. The Classical Gazetteer, William Hazlit (1851).
9. Scotichronicon, Walter Bower bk 1 ch 16.
12. Ibid   bk 1 ch 18.
13. Ibid   bk 1 ch 22.

Chapter V

1. http://touregypt.net/featurestories/tt56.htm
2. Helen of Troy, Bettany Hughes p59.
3. Connections between Egypt and the Minoan world, Manfred Bietak.
4. Minoan Painting and Egypt, Lyvia Morgan Quoted in: Egypt, the Aegean and the Levant, Vivian Davies.
5. Ibid.
6. Peter Warren, Minoan Crete and Pharaonic Egypt.
7. Minoan Painting and Egypt, Lyvia Morgan Quoted in: Egypt, the Aegean and the Levant, Vivian Davies.
8. The Decipherment of Linear B, J Chadwick.
9. The Decipherment of Linear B, J Chadwick
10. Kebra Negast Wallis Budge xii.
11. www.phoenicians.org
12. Biblical Concordance.
13. The World of the Phoenicians, Sabatino Moscati.
14. The World of the Phoenicians, Sabatino Moscati.
15. Aegeanet, Maria C. Shaw, ('Murex', May 13, 1999).
16. Palmer, Leonard R. (1963), The Interpretation of Mycenaean Greek Texts.
17. Bible Zech 5:1.
18. Bible 2 Ki 23:13.
19. Minoan Painting and Egypt. Lyvia Morgan Quoted in: Egypt, the Aegean and the Levant, Vivian Davies.
22. www.phoenician.org.
23. http://www.ekathimerini.com/4dcgi/_w_articles_politics_598535_03/10/ 2003_34767
24. Odyssey, Homer 5:227-261.
25. Coventry Boat-builders and Chandlery.
    Gloucester Street, Spon End, Coventry CV1 3BZ, U K.

26. The Athenian Trireme, J Morrison.
27. http://www.ferribyboats.co.uk
28. Murano Magic, the history of Murano glass, Carl Gable.
29. The Greek Myths, Robert Graves bk1-60.
30. Model Ships and Boats, G Reisner.
32. Gallic War, Julius Caesar 3:13.
33. Geography, Strabo 4:4:1.

Chapter VI

1. Scotichronicon, W Bower, bk 1 Ch 13.
2. A burial with faience beads at Tara, Prof Sean O'Riordain.
3. Ibid.
4. Ibid.
5. Letter from the Assistant Keeper of Irish Antiquities, National Museum of Ireland.
6. http://www.ucd.ie/news/mar06/030306_mound_of_the_hostages.htm
7. Sacred Mythological Centers of Ireland, J Roberts.
   Aye's mother's name can be pronounced as Tuyu or Tiyu.
8. Bible Gen 38:28.
9. Rock tombs of Amarna, N Davies vol VI.
10. Tutankhamen, Christine Desroches-Noblecourt, p144.
12. Bible, Exodus 4:6-7.
13. Sacred Mythological Centers of Ireland, Jack Roberts.

Chapter VIII

1. Scotichronicon, W Bower, bk 1 ch 23.
2. Scotichronicon, W Bower, bk 1 ch 21.
3. Basque Mythology, Olga Gomez http://www.pantheon.org/areas/mythology/
   europe/basque/article
4. Scotichronicon, W Bower bk 1 ch 30.
5. Pict resources. http://www.tylwythteg.com
6. Scotichronicon, W Bower, bk 1 ch 31.
7. Scotichronicon, W Bower, bk 1 ch 20.
8. Scotichronicon, W Bower, bk 1 ch 20.
9. Until the Storm Passes, Frank Donnelly.
10. http://www.bioe.co.uk/history.asp

Appendix 2

1. http://www.institutoestudiosantiguoegipto.com/bietak_I.htm
2. Biblical Archaeological Review.
   Avaris, the Capital of the Hyksos, by Manfred Bietak. British Museum Press.
   Research by Robert Giles, Arizona.

Index

Index

Index

Index

Index